WILF AND TRISH MBANGA

SERETSE & RUTH

TAFELBERG

Tafelberg Publishers Limited
40 Heerengracht, Cape Town, 8000
© 2005 Wilf & Trish Mbanga

Cover photograph by Time Life Pictures/Getty Images
Cover design by Doret Ferreira
Book design by Nazli Jacobs
Set in Caslon

Printed and bound by Paarl Print, Oosterland Street, Paarl, South Africa
First edition, first printing 2005

ISBN 0 624 04322 3

Contents

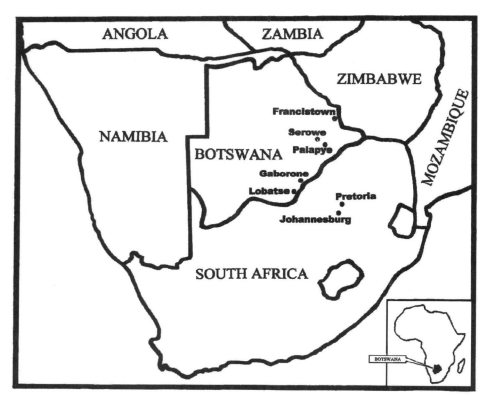

Formerly the British protectorate of Bechuanaland, Botswana adopted its new name upon independence in 1966.

Foreword

IN 1966 A NEW COUNTRY CAME INTO EXISTENCE. The Republic of Botswana was born into a troubled region and there must have been those who were quietly pessimistic as to the prospects of this new country ever being much more than a satellite of its more powerful neighbour. How wrong such predictions were! Under the guidance of its first President, Sir Seretse Khama, the new state showed that not only would it be a truly independent member of the world community but that it would be an example to the rest of the world of what could be achieved in a country dedicated to honesty and decency in government. In the years that followed, Botswana became a beacon in Africa, with a record of achievement in every sphere, notably in health and education.

Behind this success story there is the story of one family which was called by its historical position to play a central role in the development of the new state. This is the Khama family, and in particular Seretse Khama, statesman, paramount chief, husband and father. This book dwells on the last two aspects of this important figure, and tells, in the process, a story which I think is one of the great love stories of our times. In the face of great difficulties and opposition, Sereste and Ruth were united in a fruitful marriage which showed the world how people from different traditions might live in harmony and happiness. In many respects, their personal story, so movingly recounted in this book, is the story of the country itself, for Botswana as a state has always stressed the importance of social harmony.

Great love stories usually reveal the nobility of the human spirit. This tale does exactly that and we who read this account have reason to be grateful to Wilf and Trish Mbanga for sharing their own particular insight into a moving and memorable story.

ALEXANDER MCCALL SMITH

Preface

THIS IS A TRUE STORY. A love story. A story about a love that transcended the barriers of distance, race, creed and culture; that triumphed over injustice, treachery, exile, illness, loneliness and rejection. That was tested in the fires of adversity and emerged true and enduring as few loves of the hasty and selfish 20th century have been.

The story began when a young African prince from the vast and thirsty plains of Bechuanaland was sent to England by his royal uncles in search of education and fell in love with an English girl. Together they transformed his country from a poverty-stricken tribal society into the modern nation of Botswana. This book traces their remarkable journey.

Together Ruth and Seretse Khama faced and overcame enormous challenges, including international intrigue, family disapproval, tribal upheaval and racial bigotry. Strengthened by their devotion to each other and their dedication to the Bamangwato, they triumphed – and remained free from bitterness and deeply in love until they were parted by death.

Ruth and Seretse were pawns in an international game of political expediency and duplicity. They fell in love at the wrong time, in the wrong place. Inter-racial marriage was unusual and labelled 'miscegenation'. Their union stirred all sorts of basic emotions in family, politicians and church leaders at the highest level. The racial politics of South Africa, combined with its own avarice and political manoeuvring, played an important role in persuading the British government first of all to forbid the marriage, thereafter to condemn the couple to exile in Britain for five years, and eventually to force Seretse to renounce his birthright as Chief of the Bamangwato.

All the characters, places and events are real, as are all the quotations from official documents, speeches and newspaper articles – preserved by the British authorities both in Botswana and England. The dialogue has been created from archival material, personal interviews with those still living, and published biographies. Place names in usage at the time have been retained.

We have interspersed the narrative with vignettes depicting imagined meetings, events and conversations. But even these are based on the above research. They are intended to give the reader a deeper and richer insight into the story than would be possible from a mere re-stating of the historical records.

We are grateful to all those who assisted us in researching this story. We travelled widely in Botswana, visiting the village of Serowe where it all began, as well as Gaborone, Francistown and Lobatse. We interviewed many friends and relatives, who were all most helpful. The National Archives of Botswana provided a wealth of information as did the Library of Parliament.

In England we traced the couple's steps to many of their favourite haunts – including Nutford House, Oxford and the Embankment of the River Thames. We also visited the Inner Temple and spent many absorbing hours in the British Library, the British Newspaper Library and the School of Oriental and African Studies.

We take full responsibility for any errors in interpretation or judgment of the information made available to us. But memories do fade and for this reason we do not claim that this is an authoritative work.

We would like to thank, in particular, Linda Christmas for her hospitality and friendship during the time we spent in London; Tony Benn and Muriel Sanderson for their time, memories and encouragement; the Khama children for their permission to pursue our dream in writing this book; and the Stichting Tilburg Vrijplaats for a wonderful year in Holland during which we wrote it.

We wrote this book because we felt a special affinity with Ruth and Seretse. On a lesser scale, their journey has been our own. We too married when it was frowned upon – in a racially-divided Rhodesia in 1978. We too faced the pain of family rejection and the subsequent joys of reconciliation. Like Ruth and Seretse we learned to steel ourselves against public disapproval, and suffered as we watched our golden children struggling to fit in and find their identity. Like Ruth, Trish lost her job, and we battled to find accommodation.

Above all, like Ruth and Seretse, we know what it is like to be caught up in a love so powerful that the normal boundaries of colour, class, creed and public opinion cease to matter. We know that – buoyed and strengthened by such a love – criticism, ostracism and racism do nothing but fuel the determination to be together.

This book is a celebration of cross-cultural marriage, which thankfully is now so much more acceptable in many parts of the world. In a sense, Ruth and Seretse were pioneers, and we who follow in their footsteps salute them.

WILF AND TRISH MBANGA,
Southampton, 9 March 2005

I

The Meeting

SERETSE KHAMA LOOKED FORWARD TO THE HOSPITALITY EVENING – A SHERRY
in the warden's flat followed by dinner and dancing. He joined the group of
students clattering down the stairs. To a man they were smartly dressed in
dark suits and white, collared shirts – their individuality only showing through
in a fancy silk handkerchief here and a natty bow tie there. A gregarious
bunch, sunny-natured from sunny places around the globe, they had been
transplanted into war-time Britain in search of education. This was the Holy
Grail that would liberate them – and help them to liberate their countries –
from poverty, ignorance, fear of the unknown and colonial domination. They
chattered loudly in anticipation of the evening to come.

Although they were rather formal affairs, with staff members keeping a close
watch to ensure suitable behaviour, these evenings were welcomed by the young
men from the distant corners of the empire, for they were lonely in London.
Such occasions provided an opportunity to meet British contemporaries and
to have a few drinks at the warden's expense. There would also be music –
the lifeblood of the young. Seretse hoped there would be some decent jazz.
He was crazy about the newly-emerging bebop, forerunner of rock 'n' roll.

It was 1947, and Britain was sweltering in an unusually hot June. Seretse
found the high levels of humidity most unpleasant. Running his finger around
inside his collar – already damp although he had changed just half an hour
previously – he thought longingly of the dry heat of his motherland, the
Bechuanaland Protectorate, a barren place on the rim of the Kalahari Desert
in southern Africa. Raised in those great arid plains, the heir apparent of the
royal line of Khamas – whose lineage stretched back over 200 years as Chiefs
of the Bamangwato Tribe – Seretse had been sent to England by his royal

uncles to complete his tertiary education. His year at Oxford, where his uncle Tshekedi's reputation as an enlightened ruler had opened doors into the homes of the leading academics and leftist politicians of the day, had left him polished in the social graces of the British upper class. But although born to be king and possessed of a certain nobility of presence if one cared to notice it, Seretse in London, aged 26, was just another black student.

At the entrance to the warden's flat he stood aloof for a moment, his wide-set brown eyes surveying the gathering – an unusual one in Britain in the 1940s, for most of the men were black and all the women were white. Against the dark suits and complexions of the men, the pale women with their silky, shoulder-length hair looked like hothouse lilies. His heart, as it often did, went back to a scene from his homeland – the honey, mahogany, chocolate-skinned women in their bright cotton dresses, tight curls covered by gay *doeks*, gossiping around the well, or gathered outside the church after a Sunday service.

He accepted a glass of sherry, and after greeting the warden and his wife, squeezed himself into a corner beside his best friend Charles Njonjo – a cheerful fellow from Kenya who was also studying law. The buzz of conversation enveloped him like the sound of the noonday cicadas in the *makala* trees of Serowe – the musical West African intonation blending harmoniously with the Southern and Eastern African accents, while the clipped British vowels provided a staccato counter-point.

He and Charles were soon deep in conversation about their studies and the eccentricity of the British legal system, which required them to eat a specified number of dinners at the Inner Temple in order to be admitted to the Bar. Forbes Burnham, a fellow student, joined them and the discussion turned to his favourite subject – the shortcomings of British colonial rule. Seretse, not himself a firebrand nationalist at all, was well acquainted with Burnham's rather radical views, and his attention wandered. Glancing around, he noticed an attractive young woman with reddish-gold hair and blue, or were they green? eyes.

During supper she was placed at the farthest end of the table from him and seemed to be the centre of a lively group. The conversation around her was frequently punctuated by bursts of laughter. Seretse was engaged in a serious discussion with Charles about the relative merits of small group versus big band jazz. The big band sound had recently become extremely popular in Britain, particularly under the American band-leader Glen Miller. Seretse, however, did not care for it, considering it to be a divergence from 'true' jazz.

The main course was served, and he looked sadly at the small helping of stew on his plate accompanied by the usual wrinkled peas and mushy potatoes. Almost two years after the war, shortages of many basic commodities persisted. Beef was scarce, and this was a great trial to Seretse as he was of robust build, over six feet tall and accustomed to eating large quantities of meat. Bechuanaland was beef country. As the King's son, Seretse had always had as much as he could eat – except, of course, when he was away at boarding school, during which time he wrote plaintive letters to his uncle saying how much he longed for the holidays when he would be able to return home and eat beef and game to his heart's content.

When the gathering moved into the lounge to begin the dancing, he found an easy chair on the periphery and settled down to enjoy the music. He was a good dancer, but with the weather so oppressive that night, he preferred to watch the others. Going across to refill his glass during a break in the music, he chatted to Braim Nkhondo, one of the two Northern Rhodesian students resident at Nutford House. Braim was an irrepressible character, tonight sporting a polka-dot bow tie.

Taking Seretse's arm, he said: 'Seretse, my friend, you must meet Ruth – Muriel's sister. She's here for the first time and wants to meet us all.'

Braim steered him across the dance floor to a table where he recognised an acquaintance, Muriel Williams, who had often come to these social evenings. Sitting next to her, fanning her face which was flushed from dancing, was the girl with the red-gold hair.

'Hello, Seretse, how nice to see you!' said Muriel.

He leaned over to shake her hand. 'Good to see you, too. Hot, isn't it?'

'My goodness, it is. By the way – this is my sister, Ruth. Ruth, meet Seretse.'

'How do you do?' murmured Seretse. The girl smiled at him briefly, and let her eyes wander away over the room.

'He's a fellow southern African,' boomed Braim. 'He's the chap we told you about at tea, who likes your type of music.'

'So what kind of music is that?' she said, coolly.

'Count Basie, Louis Armstrong and the Ink Spots,' he said.

'Well, I agree with you there. The Ink Spots are the best, in my opinion,' she said.

One of the young men in her orbit left in search of a drink and Seretse took his seat. Her hair glowed in the light of a nearby lamp and he caught himself thinking of sunrise across the plains around Serowe, when the sandy expanse turned just that shade of reddish-gold.

'Whereabouts in Africa are you from?' she asked.

'The Bechuanaland Protectorate,' he replied. 'I don't think you would have heard of it – it's a small country next to South Africa. Actually, most of it is desert – the Kalahari Desert.'

'So this heat doesn't bother you then,' she said, fanning her face with a paper napkin.

'On the contrary,' he replied, mopping his neck with a handkerchief, 'the humidity here is something I have never experienced before. Our heat may be hotter, but it's a dry heat, which is much more bearable.'

'You do realise you're speaking to royalty, don't you? I hope you are going to be suitably polite,' interrupted the ebullient Braim.

'Royalty?' said Ruth, raising one eyebrow.

'Oh yes,' chipped in Charles. 'This boyo is our revered Chief Khama, don't you know?'

Ruth turned questioning eyes upon Seretse, who shrugged his shoulders and then said with mock pomposity: 'Yes, I'm the Paramount Chief designate of the Bamangwato nation. Any objections?' The group dissolved into laughter, and the music started up again.

'Actually,' said Ruth to Seretse, 'I have heard of your country. Isn't that the place the royal family visited recently? I seem to remember reading somewhere about them going to the Kalahari Desert. But I'm afraid I haven't a clue where it is.'

'Here, let me show you,' said Seretse. He took out his cigarette box and drew a rough map of Africa on the back of it. 'Bechuanaland is right here,' he said, marking the spot with an X as he spoke and handing the box to her. As she glanced at it, Harry Nkumbula, the other Northern Rhodesian student in residence, interrupted them.

'Come on Ruth, dance with me,' he said, pulling her on to the dance floor and proceeding to demonstrate his fancy footwork. Harry – witty, exuberant, hard-drinking and a student at the London School of Economics – was the unofficial leader of the African group of students at Nutford House.

Seretse lit up another cigarette and turned his attention to Muriel, who had taken Ruth's seat beside him. He had met her a few months previously and greatly admired her rather serious and sensible nature, as well as her sincere concern for him and his fellow African students. She was friendly and open, in contrast to many of her compatriots with their characteristic reserve, which often made the naturally extrovert Africans feel like fish out of water. She had been telling him for weeks that he must meet her sister Ruth, believing the two would have much in common.

'How did you become involved with the African students here?' he enquired.

'I went to a missionary conference and met a few of them. From Northern Rhodesia, actually. I had ideas about becoming a missionary at one stage. Anyway, they invited me to a couple of these evenings, and I enjoy them very much. I think it's so important to learn about how people from other countries live. What they think and feel.'

'And your sister? Does she care about how other people think and feel?'

Muriel laughed. 'To be honest, Ruth cares about having a good time and lots of friends. She's the glamour in the family. But she seems to be enjoying the evening.'

At a signal from the warden at 11.30 pm, the bandleader announced the last dance. As Ruth circled the floor in Harry's arms, Seretse experienced a pang of regret that he had not made an effort to dance. She and Harry ended with a flourish at the table, and Seretse and Muriel applauded.

'My goodness, I'm hot!' exclaimed Ruth, ineffectually fanning her hot face with a limp napkin. Seretse emptied his cigarette box, unfolded it into a makeshift fan and handed it to her with a smile.

'Oh, thanks!' she said in surprise, and then they all stood up to leave. The warden and his wife positioned themselves at the door to receive the formal farewells. Harry and Seretse accompanied Ruth and Muriel out onto the porch. They stood smoking companionably for a while, enjoying the slight breeze that was blowing up Brown Street, and then the girls set off to catch the last train back home to Lewisham.

'So, Seretse, you've met the beautiful Ruth. What did you think of her?' asked Harry as they went up the steps to the solid wooden double doors at the entrance to Nutford House.

'She's pretty, but rather frivolous, I should imagine,' Seretse replied with a small smile as he pushed the door open.

In the train on their way home Ruth and Muriel discussed the evening. It had been the first time Ruth had accompanied her sister to an event at Nutford House. She had not been particularly keen to go, but Muriel's enthusiasm about the excitement and novelty of socialising with the foreigners had been so infectious that she had agreed. Muriel was fascinated by the African students. She was later to recall: 'Our lives were so humdrum and ordinary at that time. Meeting the African students was the most exciting thing that had ever happened to us. It broadened our horizons most wonderfully.'

The presence of thousands of black American soldiers in Britain during the latter part of the war had given rise to a pronounced sociological phenomenon dubbed at the time 'Negro glamour'. One of the consequences was that jazz had become extremely popular. The Williams girls were part of the transitional generation during which England was transformed from being almost totally white by the influx of people of colour from the colonies. They stood on the brink of British urban society's awakening to racial consciousness. It affected them both profoundly, yet differently. Muriel was the more serious of the two, having become a fervent socialist during the war, when she had been evacuated from London to a coal-mining village in Wales. She had recently left the Anglican Church to join the Congregationalists, whose progressive social views she felt to be more in line with her own.

Ruth concerned herself more with having a good time than with public issues. But she told Muriel she had thoroughly enjoyed meeting the black students, and the music and dancing. 'Those Africans are very good dancers,' she said, 'none of the boys I've ever been out with can move like that. I'm worn out trying to keep up with them.'

'I told you you'd enjoy yourself,' said Muriel. 'They're also more intelligent than most of the boys we know around here – and much more interesting, and polite, if you ask me.'

A few days later, Muriel set out for Nutford House and one of her regular discussion groups. Ruth decided to accompany her. She had so enjoyed the social evening that she was keen to spend more time getting to know the black students. The girls agreed to keep their activities a secret from their father, George, who had served as a captain in the British army in India and was a typical product of his generation. Known as the Empire-Builders, they tended to regard all other races as being inferior. His attitude infuriated Muriel, who could not reconcile it with his otherwise kind, intelligent nature. Ruth was more pragmatic. He had been brought up that way, she knew, and would not change now, even though the times were changing. As long as George was not aware that they were socialising with black people, the girls decided, peace would reign in the Williams household.

'Let's have some music,' said Seretse, after the group session was over. 'George Webb's Dixielanders.' He went over to the gramophone and wound it up.

'That's a good sound,' said Ruth, going over to join him.

Seretse pulled chairs for them both closer to the gramophone. 'Have you heard the latest release from Jelly-Roll Morton?'

'No, I haven't.'

He jumped up, ran upstairs to his room and came down with an armful of records.

'My goodness, what a collection!' she said, riffling through them. 'Do you have this kind of music at home? In Bechu-a-n-a . . .'

He laughed. 'Bechu-a-na-land,' he enunciated each syllable slowly.

'Bechu-a-na-land,' she mimicked.

'That's it – you've got it. I suppose we do have a kind of jazz, but it's played on very different kinds of instruments. Wooden drums, penny whistles, home-made guitars. But I learned to appreciate American jazz when I was at Oxford.'

'When were you at Oxford?'

'I went up in September 1945 to read law. My uncle wanted me to study law over here so that I could guide the Tribe in future with some under-standing of the British way of doing things. I did a BA general degree at Fort Hare university in South Africa and then came over here straight after the war. I came down to the Inner Temple last year.'

'So are things very different for you here?' asked Ruth, finding herself more and more interested in this tall foreigner with the neatly-trimmed moustache and intelligent eyes.

'Couldn't be more different,' he said. 'The weather, the buildings, the roads, the cars, the people. At home there's only one mile of tarred road in the whole country. And we only have one railway line – but it goes all the way from South Africa to Southern Rhodesia along our eastern boundary. And there's only one train a day!'

'Hey, you two – are you going to sit in the corner and listen to music all night?' called Muriel. 'We've got a train to catch.'

'Why don't you come over tomorrow evening and listen to my new Dizzie Gillespie?' said Seretse.

'All right,' called Ruth over her shoulder, as she and Muriel hurried out of the door.

As they walked briskly down the Edgware Road to the tube station, Muriel said: 'You spent a long time chatting with Seretse. What do you think of him?'

'He knows an awful lot about jazz, and he's got really good taste,' said Ruth. 'He's the first person I've met who's not potty about Glen Miller.'

'He speaks well,' said Muriel. 'I like his accent – quite different from the West Africans.'

'Mmm,' said Ruth. 'Much easier to understand. And he has a nice, musical voice. I like listening to him talk.'

At 23, Ruth Williams was cheerful, outgoing and confident, with a pleasant warmth of manner and an engaging laugh. She was one of the new generation of British women whose lives had been changed forever by the hardships and upheavals of the Second World War. At the age of 17 she had been evacuated from her middle-class home in Blackheath to Surrey, but a bout of acute anaemia caused her father to bring her home to London and the blitz. As soon as she turned 18, she gave up her volunteer mobile canteen work and joined the Women's Auxiliary Air Force (WAAF) – as close as a woman could get to the war.

For the next four years, she fought house fires and drove ambulances, lorries and staff cars along the embattled south coast of England. Her postings included Eastbourne, Beachy Head and an emergency Royal Air Force landing field at Friston. It was a stimulating, exciting time, but it was exhausting and emotionally taxing too, as she was brought face to face with the realities of the bombing.

In appearance she was slender and fragile, but the years of war forged a core of toughness in her character, making her self-contained and self-reliant. After being demobbed in 1946 she had joined an underwriter for Lloyds Insurance Company in the City of London and begun to live civilian life as an office worker.

When Harry banged on the door of Seretse's room the next evening to tell him Ruth was asking for him downstairs, he dropped the book he had been reading and leapt up. He had thought she wouldn't come – they hadn't really made a proper arrangement. He hastily gathered up his precious collection of records and raced to the lounge, where he found Ruth and Muriel already ensconced in the armchairs, deep in discussion with some of the other students.

He stood on the edge of the group, and smiled a greeting at the girls. Although he was outwardly so urbane and popular, Seretse often battled with a sense of shyness. Ruth jumped up and greeted him warmly, taking his arm and dragging him across to the gramophone. He proudly placed his newest acquisition on to the turntable and they were immediately enveloped in the complex rhythms of Dizzy Gillespie.

'Tell me more about Bechuanaland,' she said, pronouncing the name fluently.

For a moment he was silent. How was he to communicate the vastness of the desert, with its thorn bushes and rangy, long-horned cattle, to this city creature who knew only green fields and flowered hedgerows and fat Jersey cows? How to explain the circular mud huts with their conical hats of thatch? The seminaked, barefoot children herding their flocks of goats, the incessant shrilling of the cicadas in the heat or the joyous high-pitched trilling of the women to mark special occasions? He closed his eyes as memories flooded in.

'Seretse?' Ruth prompted him.

'Sorry,' he said, leaning forward with his elbows on his knees to give her his full attention. 'It's actually rather difficult to explain to someone who's never been to Africa. You'll have to come and see for yourself!' They both laughed. Only adventurers, missionaries and colonial officials travelled to Africa.

'Well, you could at least try to give me some idea,' she said.

Seretse took a deep breath, 'Right, well for a start it is very sparsely populated and there are hardly any buildings. We have no cities and only one real town –

Lobatse. Then there are a few villages, like Francistown and Palapye. The royal residence is in Serowe – which is actually a village, but it is the largest settlement in the whole country with a population of more than 30 000 people.' He paused, glancing at her to see if she was still interested.

Chin in hand, she gazed back at him. 'Go on,' she murmured.

'Well, I suppose another big difference is that here you have a great deal of water – rivers and lakes everywhere, the sea and so on. Bamangwato country is desert. We are landlocked so there is no coast and while we do have rivers, they are mostly rivers of sand. You see, the rainfall is very erratic and the rainy season only lasts about three months. Some years it doesn't rain at all. So finding water is always a big problem.' She nodded sympathetically. 'But we do have the sky,' he went on. 'Our sky dominates everything – it is everywhere. You should see it at night. The stars are so bright, because of course we have no electricity. The night is just alive with stars, they seem much closer to the earth than they do over here. And the darkness is like velvet, it's so thick.'

'I can imagine that,' she said eagerly. 'During the war we had a total black-out here. Of course the skies are usually cloudy and we had all those air raids. But a few times, when I was on duty at night, it was all quiet and the sky was clear. The stars were breathtaking.'

'Well,' he said, 'imagine it being like that every night – but much brighter, without any buildings to block your view.'

'Tell me more,' she prompted him, the music forgotten.

'We have lions,' he said, making his fingers into claws and giving a muted imitation of a roar. 'They mostly keep away from the villages, but they can be a menace when they decide to attack our cattle. When they do, the local district official usually shoots them, because cattle are the most important commodity in Bechuanaland. They are our only real asset. A true Mongwato loves his cattle the way he loves his children.' Ruth laughed. 'I'm serious,' said Seretse. 'Cattle are terribly important to us. We have hundreds of thousands of them. We herd them using horses.'

'I thought they only had cowboys in America.'

'I could ride a horse before I could walk!' replied Seretse. 'I remember my grandfather lifting me up into the saddle from my nurse's lap and taking me to see his cattle herds. I couldn't have been more than two years old then. He was a great horseman.'

'I love horse-riding,' said Ruth.

Seretse's faint but fond memories of his tall, gracious, grandfather had been nourished by the constant telling and retelling of stories about him around the evening camp fires. He had often heard how he himself had been presented by his grandfather to the Bamangwato people as the new crown prince at the age of three or four months. According to the story, which he now related to Ruth, King Khama, a stooped but still regal figure in his late eighties, had moved slowly into the royal *kgotla* (tribal meeting place) in the autumn of 1921, with the baby prince carried tightly in his arms. He had held up the child to the assembled gathering of the Tribe, and in a strong voice proclaimed: 'Your king has been born!' The crowd roared its approval with the traditional cry of *Pula*! (rain or blessing). At this point the story was told that Khama playfully touched his royal staff of office on Seretse's tiny fingers, which opened to clutch it tightly. Again the assembly roared its approval. 'He shall reign,' added Khama, and then formally named him Seretse, which means 'wet earth' – a precious commodity in a barren land.

He felt as though he was back there again – the acrid smell of smouldering cow dung stinging his nostrils; the sand, fine as talcum powder, clinging to his skin, his hair, his tongue. He was out at the cattle post. It was night. The great beasts stamped and snorted behind the stockade as the boys huddled sleepily around the dancing flames of the campfire, their bellies full of tasty stew and thick porridge, listening to the stories. Stories as old as the Tribe itself, weaving the threads of each new generation into the fabric of the whole – creating a sense of belonging that was both exciting and comfortable. Stories of bravery and triumph, of hardship and tribulation, of good years and bad, failed harvests, drought and pestilence – the oral history of the Tribe, embellished and embroidered over the years with the individual memories of the storytellers.

A shout from Harry startled him: 'Seretse – what have you done to the music?' Seretse grimaced at Ruth and turned his attention to the gramophone, starting it up again with a flourish. Once again, he tried to put his homeland into words for the young woman who sat in rapt attention at his side.

'Serowe, my home, is a wonderful place,' he said, his voice deepening with emotion. 'It is most beautiful of all in summertime. That's when it rains, and the rainy season in the desert is an amazing experience. It rains incredibly fiercely – not at all like the rain here. The whole sky seems to heave and come alive with clouds and wind. It's a very harsh sort of beauty – completely different from what you see over here. Behind the village is a sort of escarpment, and the village lies in a shallow basin at its feet. Each family has its own cluster of houses and most people have a hedge around their homestead area. There is a kind of rubber plant that grows quite nicely as a hedge. In fact, it's the only thing that can form a hedge, because the goats don't eat it. They eat absolutely everything else. In the early mornings and evenings, the whole village is covered with a cloud of fragrant smoke from the thousands of cooking fires. And of course, there are goats, dogs and chickens roaming and scratching around all over the place.'

He came to an abrupt halt, thinking he was rambling on a bit too much, but she sat motionless, her eyes fixed on his face, totally absorbed. All too soon it was time for her to leave.

Like her sister, Ruth became a regular visitor to Nutford House. Together with Harry, Charles and Seretse, they formed a core group and spent many pleasant hours in the lounge chatting about a wide range of subjects – from politics to philosophy, food rationing and the weather, fashion and the future. There were some tensions between the main groups of students at Nutford House – mainly between the West Africans and the African-Caribbeans. But Seretse, as a southern African, moved easily between them. His ease of manner soon disarmed even the most unbending of characters, and his quick wit and ready smile could often defuse a heated political argument. And there were plenty of those. Pan-Africanism had caught fire among students of African descent in Britain after the 5th Pan-African Congress of delegates held at Manchester town hall in October 1945. Hours were spent arguing the relative merits and drawbacks of colonialism, imperialism, independence and self-determination.

Seretse looked up from his books and smiled as a familiar face appeared at his door one Saturday morning and greeted him. Dr Roger Pilkington, a director of the London Missionary Society and a Khama family friend, was a distinguished geneticist at London University, and Seretse's Uncle Tshekedi had asked him to keep an eye on the young student. The older man carried out this duty with tact and compassion, ensuring that Seretse lacked for nothing, and took a solicitous interest not only in his studies, but also in his social life, his health, his diet and his spiritual wellbeing. He invited the young man regularly to his house for home-cooked meals and godly conversation.

In turn, Seretse liked him and was grateful for his gentle ministrations, knowing that Roger was indeed a true friend of the Bamangwato. Seretse could trust him, and could converse with him easily and deeply as he could with no one else. Roger also had a clear understanding of Seretse's future obligations as the heir apparent. He considered him to be a most suitable candidate for Chief – trustworthy, honourable, intelligent and of high moral character.

'Hello there, Roger,' said Seretse, jumping up to shake hands.

'I don't want to disturb you, Seretse. I am sure your uncle will be happy to hear that you are studying so diligently,' said his visitor with a wink, 'but I hope you'll take a break from the books and visit us in Highgate for lunch tomorrow. If this weather holds, we could go for a ramble on the Heath afterwards.'

'Thanks, that sounds wonderful,' said Seretse. 'I need to get out of the city and into some space. I'll be there!'

In Bechuanaland there was nothing to stop the eyes from travelling unimpeded from horizon to horizon – across the shimmering expanse of veld to that distant, trembling line where earth and sky embraced. His grandfather's colonial-style house, built half-way up the craggy hill behind the *kgotla* ground to catch every passing breeze, looked out over a wide vista. He had always particularly loved the early mornings. In summer the sun was up by 5 am and even in mid-winter it rose only an hour or so later. His bedroom window faced eastwards and the first glance of the sun's rays never failed to wake him. The village woke early too – and the noises drifted up to the Chief's house: women chattering as they lit the breakfast fires, cocks crowing, children shouting and laughing. The terrors of the night fled and the huge, gnarled *makala* tree outside his window glowed with the growing light. He would inhale deeply the special smell of the new day – the scent of dew evaporating from dry, dry, ground.

Going to the clay pot of cool water, he would take a sip, and rub his eyes – conscious always, as all Bamangwato were, of the preciousness of water and the imperative need never to waste it. He would awaken his cousin, Lenyeletse, who was his constant companion, and the two would slip barefooted outside in their thin cotton shorts and shirts to enjoy the cool of the day before the sun became their enemy. He loved the feel of the earth: it was like silk – tan in some places, dark brown in others, pale pink and blood red in yet others – but always so soft, squishing between his toes. Sometimes, if they were not careful, the boys would step on the vicious devil thorns, and yelp and limp.

Often the early mornings were misty, which gave an ethereal beauty to the distant plains and low hills. On such mornings, dewdrops hung from the tips of leaves or caught among the strands of a spider's web, where they glistened like jewels, magnifying the whole world. Seretse loved to taste the mist on his tongue. Their favourite place at this time of day was up at the royal burial ground amid the rocks behind the *kgotla*. Clambering up, startling the fat rock rabbits who lived there, it seemed as though they were climbing a hill of gold nuggets. Gilded by the rising sun, this outcrop gave a magnificent 180 degree panoramic view of the village, the plains surrounding it and the low hills in the distance.

London was **so** different. Not only was it so grey and built up, tightly squashed and overcrowded, but there were bomb craters everywhere, making unsightly gaps in rows of soot-blackened Victorian and Edwardian terrace houses and blocks of industrial buildings. Massive warehouses lay open to the weather, their roofs torn off. Some of them were totally destroyed, basements gaping, exposed to the world. A profusion of weeds grew everywhere. Tons of rubble were being carted away to make room for reconstruction.

But he loved the River Thames with its many different bridges, and the way it reflected the lights of London in its steely waters. He would go out of his way to walk along the river bank whenever possible, and often went down to the Embankment to eat his lunchtime sandwich.

The next morning he was up bright and early, looking forward to a day out in the country. He was grateful to Pilkington and his wife for welcoming him so warmly into their family, and well aware that Mrs Pilkington, as a post-war housewife, was still hampered in her housekeeping by the straitjacket of austerity. She had done her best. She had made a stew with meat and some turnips grown in the back garden, and flavoured it with an onion. Little blobs of mock cream, made from margarine and corn flour, balanced atop mounds of wobbly pink blancmange. Seretse complimented her warmly and assured her that he had thoroughly enjoyed the meal. He and Pilkington insisted that she should put her feet up while they did the washing up. As he looked out of the kitchen window onto Hampstead Heath, stretching into a blue haze in the distance, up to his elbows in greasy water, Seretse laughed to himself at the thought of what his loyal subjects would think if they could see him now.

'What's the joke?' asked Pilkington.

Seretse felt comfortable enough with this man to share his thought. Pilkington laughed. 'There certainly are some advantages to being the *kgosi*,' he said, using the *ngwato* form of the title. The sound of his native tongue brought a lump to Seretse's throat. The language of his people was like music, very onomatopoeiac and with lots of soft guttural sounds formed by a *kg* or *kh*. He felt suddenly very homesick.

After a meal, the women would have taken the plates away, and brought water for the washing of hands. No man would ever have dreamed of washing up. That was strictly women's work. The men would have sat under trees or bushes, trying to find a scrap of foliage to shade them from the sun, discussing the latest disputes between members of the Tribe – over cattle, women, thieving, crops – and, of course, the possibilities of rain and the state of the cattle. Lunch would have consisted of a vegetable stew, with chunks of beef, scooped up with portions of the thick porridge made of local grain – *rapoko* or millet – rolled into a ball by nimble fingers.

Later that afternoon, striding with Pilkington across the Heath, Seretse was struck by how green it was compared with Bechuanaland. His land majored in shades of brown. The sky today was blue, glorious blue, almost as blue as it was every day at home. But there was always that different quality of the light – it was never the same here – the sun was too far away, he supposed. Its light always seemed so thin. At home, in Africa, the light was like an embrace, like a cloak falling in honey folds, caressing the skin. He suddenly found himself thinking of Ruth and wishing she was there. He could explain to her about the sky so much better out here than in the Edgware Road. He shook himself mentally. He turned his attention to what Pilkington was saying about the efforts of the London Missionary Society to educate the children of the Bamangwato and the problems he was experiencing in securing dedicated teachers for the task.

'I must say we do appreciate the efforts of the LMS,' he said.

'Well, we do our best,' replied Pilkington, who was proud of the extent and depth of the society's involvement in mission work in various parts of the British Empire. It was the LMS which had first taken practical steps to improve the plight of black students in London who experienced difficulty in finding accommodation, by turning Nutford House into a boarding hostel. In addition, the Society had demonstrated a sensitive concern for the young people in its care, endeavouring to alleviate their loneliness by organising social activities where they could meet young English people.

As Seretse entered the shabby but comfortable lounge at Nutford House that evening, refreshed by his day of rest, Harry slapped him heartily on the shoulder and said: 'I've arranged an outing for Wednesday night, my friend. I hope you're free – Muriel rang up and I had to answer for both of us in your absence. We're going down to the Leicester Square Theatre to see '*The Long Night*' with Henry Fonda. You owe me for the ticket.'

'That's splendid,' replied Seretse. 'The title sounds rather depressing though. What's it about?'

'Haven't a clue,' laughed Harry. 'But don't worry, you can always gaze at Ruth if you are not enjoying the show.'

'What on earth do you mean?' said Seretse.

'Well, you have rather monopolised her every time they've been here during the past few weeks, haven't you?' said Harry equably.

'I have not,' exclaimed Seretse. 'She keeps asking me to play my jazz records for her, that's all.'

'Calm down, old boy, calm down,' laughed Harry. 'She's a looker, I'll grant you that.' Seretse turned away and stalked upstairs to bed.

Ruth, Muriel and some other girls he didn't recognise were waiting for them in the cinema foyer. Seretse was alarmed at the surge of excitement which went through him at the sight of Ruth. She held out her hand, encased in a moss-green kid glove, and greeted them all warmly. Laughing and chattering, the group moved into the auditorium. Seretse followed them silently.

Despite its title, the film had quite a few thrilling moments. Afterwards, they all went to the nearby Lyon's Corner House for tea. Seretse found himself sitting beside Ruth.

30

'You've been very quiet this evening,' she said to him. 'Did you have a tough day at the office? What's it like at the Inner Temple?'

'Well, there are all these stuffy English lawyers in pinstriped suits and bowler hats beavering away behind huge piles of legal tomes,' he said.

'You look just like one of them yourself,' teased Ruth.

'Do I? Oh dear. I'll have to do something about that.'

It was getting late and the men escorted the girls to Charing Cross station. As they waited for the train, a group of youths, obviously having spent the whole evening in the pub, staggered onto the platform. Seeing the cluster of white girls and black men standing there, they started shouting obscenities.

'Don't say anything,' hissed Seretse urgently. But Ruth and Muriel were incensed. Their sense of justice had been offended and they felt compelled to stand up for themselves. They both started talking loudly about narrow-minded and uneducated Englishmen.

'We are supposed to be civilised,' said Muriel in a loud voice.

The group of young thugs moved threateningly closer.

'Please – the best thing is simply to ignore them,' insisted Seretse.

Thankfully, at that moment, the train arrived. However, the louts moved up quickly and entered the same carriage as the girls, from the other end. Alarm bells started ringing for Seretse. As the doors were closing, he leapt onto the train, to the great surprise of his friends. The train gathered speed. Despite the late hour, the carriage was quite full of respectable-looking English people, who were all staring at him. Feeling self-conscious, Seretse grinned at the girls and took a seat. The louts, still talking loudly, were gradually stared down by the other passengers – not so much because of their racial comments, but because they were obviously drunk and disorderly.

'That was a brave thing to do, Seretse,' said Ruth.

'You didn't need to do that,' added Muriel. 'This is the last train – how are you going to get back?'

'I didn't think of that. I'll have to catch a cab.'

'You'll be lucky to find one at this time of night, specially in our area,' said Ruth, alarmed at the thought of him stuck out in Lewisham all night.

'Well then, I'll just walk,' said Seretse, putting a good face on things. 'Actually, I need some decent exercise. Since coming down from Oxford I haven't done nearly enough. I miss it, you know.'

After a mercifully uneventful train ride, he did in fact have to walk some five miles back to the hostel. Although he was still reasonably fit, and had passed the time while walking with pleasant thoughts about Ruth, he was stiff when he awoke the next morning.

Regaling the other students with his midnight adventures at breakfast, Seretse was surprised at the intensity of the feelings many of them expressed. All the students had experienced racial discrimination while in England and many carried with them bitter memories from home.

'These people are racists, there are no two ways about it. They just can't bear to see a black man going out with a white girl,' said one.

'But they don't object when it's the other way round, do they,' chipped in Harry. 'These white bastards have their fun with our women whenever they feel like it.'

'But hold on a minute,' Seretse said, 'you can't tar everyone with the same brush like that. You've got to admit the racists are only a minority. And a lot of the prejudice is just due to ignorance. They're not used to having people of a different colour around.' The others grudgingly agreed.

'But that's not the case in South Africa,' said Harry. 'Now they're even talking about legalising racism.'

Seretse nodded gravely at this. 'The Southern Rhodesians are just as bad,' he said sombrely. 'If General Smuts does lose to Malan in the elections next year, we are going to be in a fix. And if the British are ever persuaded to give into South Africa's demands for incorporation of the Protectorates, millions of blacks in southern Africa are going to suffer.'

'What are we doing over here, anyway?' interjected another student. 'They don't want us here, so why did they allow us to come in?'

'Well, that just proves my point,' said Seretse. 'They're not all bad. Some of them, especially the missionary types, are keen to help us. They're willing to share their educational institutions with us and are genuinely interested in our welfare.'

'Well I don't know what you are up to,' chipped in Braim cheerfully, 'but I know what I'm doing – I'm making sure I learn the white man's ways. We've got to learn to beat these fellows at their own game. If Lobengula had been to Oxford, like our royal friend Seretse here, he wouldn't have been tricked into handing his country over to Cecil John Rhodes!' Glancing at his watch, his expression changed to one of alarm. 'Hey, look at the time! We can't sit here all day. Let's look lively and get learning!'

Seretse and Forbes lingered over a pot of tea.

'This extreme sensitivity over their women is a key issue,' mused Seretse. 'It demonstrates the extent of their double standards more than anything else. Our women are regarded as fair game – while their women are un-touchable. I remember when I was just a youngster there was the most terrible to-do about something my Uncle Tshekedi did concerning a young Scottish lad who had been making a nuisance of himself with some girls in Serowe.'

'Do tell,' said Forbes, leaning forward eagerly and replenishing his cup of tea.

'It really was most absurd, yet it placed Bechuanaland on the map and earned my uncle a degree of notoriety throughout Britain and southern Africa,' Seretse told him. 'The young man in question, Phinehas McIntosh, was recognised by everyone in the village, including the white traders, as a ne'er-do-well. But after my grandfather died the British decreed that whites could not be tried by the Chief. So when a case was brought against McIn-tosh for molesting a local girl and assaulting her father, my uncle referred it to the colonial authorities – but they did nothing. So eventually he ordered the obnoxious boy to be whipped.'

'Quite right too,' commented Forbes.

'I'm afraid that's not what the British thought,' said Seretse. 'You won't believe this but they called in the marines.'

'The marines?' exclaimed Forbes. 'Wherever from?'

'Two hundred of them in steel helmets with three howitzers came more than a thousand miles by train from the Cape,' said Seretse laughing at the mental image conjured up by his words. 'The Admiral summoned the prisoner, my uncle; proceeded to humiliate him in front of the whole Tribe and then banished him.'

'How appalling!' exclaimed Forbes. 'I trust the matter didn't end there?'

'Thankfully no,' said Seretse. 'The fair-minded British public came to his aid and the judgement was reversed in a matter of weeks.'

A few days later, Harry met Seretse in the entrance hall at Nutford House as he was coming in from work.

'I have a great idea,' he began enthusiastically. 'This glorious weather seems to be holding, so why don't we get a group together and go down to Oxford for a spot of punting at the weekend? I've spoken to some of the others already and, as you must know the place like the back of your hand, we've appointed you to be our official tour guide.' He slapped Seretse's shoulder. 'What do you say?'

'That's a great idea,' said Seretse. 'Who's coming along?'

'Well, now that you've agreed, I'll ask Muriel, and Ruth of course, and Charles and Forbes are keen already. Leave it to me. We leave first thing Saturday morning.'

Lying awake in bed that night, Seretse found his mind full of thoughts of Ruth. He wondered what she would think of Oxford. He closed his eyes, only to find his vision filled with honey-coloured hair and a pale, high forehead above widely spaced eyes. He turned over and willed his mind to become blank. He could not afford any distractions at this stage of the game. He should be working diligently to be called to the Bar so that he could get his law qualification and return home to govern his people. Uncle Tshekedi was doing a sterling job, but he couldn't be expected to continue as regent forever. The people wanted their Chief. He was 26 after all, and had been away from home for a long time. It was high time he went back and got on with the task he had been born for.

Dressed casually in slacks and blazers, the young men set out early on Saturday morning for the station where they were to meet Ruth, Muriel and Rose, a friend of theirs. Punctual as ever, Seretse looked at his watch. The girls had not yet arrived and the train for Oxford was due to leave in a few minutes. Anxiously scanning the platform, he suddenly saw them, laden with wicker baskets, running awkwardly towards him. He was totally unprepared for the surge of joy he felt at the sight of Ruth.

'Trust the trains to be running late today of all days,' she gasped, as she gave him her basket and took his hand to climb into the carriage. Once they were all settled, the girls surveyed their escorts with approving eyes.

'My, my, aren't we smart today,' teased Muriel. 'Oxford bags and all, I see! This makes a welcome change from those stuffy pin-striped suits, wouldn't you say? How do lawyers in your country dress?'

'Well, until I go back we don't really have any lawyers to speak of,' said Seretse.

Ruth was taken aback. 'No lawyers?'

'We don't have a secondary school in Bechuanaland, let alone a university,' he said. 'Actually the Bamangwato have dressed in western clothing for many years. My grandfather, King Khama, welcomed the missionaries almost a hundred years ago and one of the first things they did was to put a stop to loin-cloths, skins and seminakedness. We became almost British, you know. My grandfather even came to tea with your Queen Victoria!'

'Really!' exclaimed Ruth.

'Oh yes,' replied Seretse, grinning. 'It was in 1895, when he and the other chiefs in the area were worried that Cecil John Rhodes and the Boers would take over the whole Territory. They came to London by ship and begged the Queen to save them. She had tea with them and gave them each a British military uniform as a gift. In fact, many of the men back home have a British uniform of one description or another – a lot of them from the First World War! You should see my uncle. On formal occasions he puts on his full dress uniform, including leggings, metal pith helmet, plumes, the works – in spite of the heat! It's quite a sight.'

'You mean all those Tarzan pictures I've been watching where they dress in skins and loin cloths are not true?' Forbes interjected, drawing laughter from them all.

'Tarzan lives in Hollywood, in the jungles of California, don't you know?' quipped Braim. 'He's never been to Africa in his life!' As the rest of the group started to discuss the merits and demerits of the American film industry, Ruth and Seretse gazed out of the window at the passing countryside.

'Looks ugly, doesn't it?' commented Ruth, as they passed a mound of rusting barbed wire.

'Well, it's not long since you emerged from the war to end all wars,' said Seretse seriously. 'It's going to take some time to get over all that.' The jetsam of war was evident here and there: cornfields bore evidence of deserted anti-aircraft posts and pill-boxes, and the remains of concrete tank-traps could be seen lining some of the roads.

'Was it very bad for you, the war I mean?' he asked.

'Actually,' she said. 'it sounds odd, I expect, but there was such good feeling among everybody, such a feeling of all wanting to pull together and beat the Jerries – oh, I can't explain.' Giving him her straight, confident gaze, she went on: 'I joined the WAAFs as soon as I was old enough and drove ambulances and staff cars and so on.'

'Weren't you scared?'

'Now and then, of course. But there was usually too much to do. One forgot to be frightened, tearing around getting people to hospital or fixing up the vehicles when they broke down.'

'You're a mechanic?'

She laughed at his surprised face. 'Oh yes. All the WAAF drivers had to be able to deal with breakdowns. Give me a blocked fuel line or a blown gasket and I'm happy!'

'Good heavens! You'd be a godsend in the Kalahari!'

'But it wasn't all swanning around in the colonel's Landrover. We had some bad times, too.'

'Tell me?' His face was intent, compassionate.

'Some of the sights I saw in the blitz were too ghastly for words. People injured. And sometimes hunting through the rubble for their families. And I'll never forget the night some houses in our street were destroyed. We were sheltering in the cellar of the pub down the road. The noise was so loud I thought my eardrums would burst. Our house wasn't hit, but it was declared unsafe after that and we had to move. Oh well, we were luckier than some. But the good thing about it for me was the feeling that I was doing something worthwhile: that I was part of the whole effort.'

Reliving the memories, she stared out of the window. Anxious to fill the awkward silence that suddenly yawned between them, Seretse told her about the Bamangwato war effort.

'We are the smallest of all Britain's possessions, except the Falkland Islands, of course. But we were the most stalwart when it came to supporting our protectors during the First and Second World Wars,' he said proudly, recalling how zealous his uncle had been that their country should prove a loyal ally in order to secure British recognition and favour in the face of South African hostility. 'All in all we sent ten thousand troops to fight with the British, the highest number of troops per capita of population of all the allies.'

Suddenly Braim was shouting, 'Up you get everyone, we've arrived!' They collected their scattered belongings and alighted from the train.

'Lead on McDuff!' said Braim cheerfully to Seretse. 'You are hereby appointed our official tour guide for the day!'

'Right, I think a good starting point would be the martyrs' monument,' said Seretse, striding off at a brisk pace. Stopping at the unobtrusive spot in Broad Street, marked by a simple cross, where the three brave 16th century bishops, Hugh Latimer, Nicholas Ridley and Thomas Cranmer, had died, Seretse told them that they had been burnt at the stake by the Roman Catholic government of Mary Tudor because they had embraced Protestant doctrines and practices and had refused to renounce their beliefs even when faced with agonising death.

Adopting a theatrical stance, he quoted Latimer's well-known last words at the stake for his admiring friends: '*Be of good cheer, Master Ridley, and play the man, for we shall this day light such a candle in England as I trust by God's grace shall never be put out.*' They applauded him cheerfully and then made their way to the entrance to Balliol College.

Seretse remembered vividly his first sight of Balliol, founded in the 1200s and the oldest of Oxford's 39 colleges. It had been a memorable moment. It was old, so old! Incredible to think that the worn, stone steps at the entrance had been trod by the feet of scholars for nearly a thousand years! And so beautiful. He had been amazed at the huge size and age of the trees, gloriously attired in their autumn leaves. The dark woodwork with its intricate carving, the massive sandstone blocks forming the walls, the queer gargoyles adorning the gutters, the enormous vaulted ceiling of the dining hall, the massive organ with its pipes filling one entire wall, the pale wooden floors and gnarled oak doors – it was all amazing.

As he showed his friends around, memories came crowding in. He tried to describe to them the formal dinners he had so enjoyed: the long, wooden refectory tables, polished to a high shine, set with starched white linen, white candles in silver candelabra, fine crystal glasses, silver cutlery and white china crockery. They looked about them at the dark portraits of distinguished long-dead dons staring sombrely from the panelled walls and imagined a hundred candle flames flickering like fireflies, reflected in the stained glass windows. The formality of such occasions had sometimes amused the irreverent imp within Seretse, but his soul had responded to the awesome weight of history inherent in them. Glancing at Ruth, he was pleased by the rapt expression on her face as she gazed around the chapel and ran her fingers delicately over the carved panelling.

He took them next to the Bodleian, where he had experienced an almost religious sense of awe on his first visit. He felt it again that day. The Bodleian – the world's largest, oldest, library – has a similar effect on most visitors. There is something awe-inspiring about knowing that one is in the presence of tons and tons of books, manuscripts and documents containing all the world's knowledge and learning, information and ideas, all the poetry, all the hopes, all the inspirations of so many generations of venerable scholars.

Leading his little flock along the path bordering the glorious summer gardens of Christ Church and its adjacent meadow, Seretse recalled how, as riotously russet autumn had marched chillingly into his first European winter, his initial fascination with Oxford had been dampened by the rigors of cold, darkness and loneliness. He had found his fellow students at Oxford a dull lot, and counted them among the most unfriendly people he had ever met. He became miserable as the nights grew longer and the skies greyer. He had never known such cold and such damp. It permeated his bones until he thought he would never be warm again. The college rooms were Spartan and national coal shortages, persisting long after the war, made heating a luxury beyond the means of most people and institutions. 1946 was a difficult year at Oxford – the war had disrupted everything and devoured a generation of the nation's young men. Many of the students were older men, whose experiences in the war set them apart from the others. The new crop of undergraduates were school leavers, all younger than Seretse, and he was excluded from their camaraderie, despite his friendly nature and willingness to participate. He had finally become friendly with a Jewish student, John Zimmerman, who evidently shared his sense of isolation.

Passing the sports fields on their jaunt, he told the group about the growth of his love of rugby. 'That's when I began to enjoy Oxford,' he said. 'At first, I thought it was a crazy game and I much preferred soccer. I had played a bit at school, in the eastern Cape, but I really got into it for the first time over here. Fortunately, I was quite good at it and that, more than anything else, gained me some friends.'

A discussion ensued about the relative merits, rules and skills of the two different ball games – soccer and rugby. Seretse told them about the South African who had been captain of the team during his time at Oxford.

'What!' exclaimed Braim in amazement. 'You played rugby with a South African?'

'It is rather incredible, I agree,' said Seretse. 'It's strange to think that if we had been back home we probably wouldn't have even spoken to each other, let alone played on the same team. And yet, over here, we sweated together; we even showered together. And although I could see he felt a bit awkward, he was always decent to me.'

'Well, that's the answer to our problems then,' said Braim. 'We simply all have to become rugby pros and then we'll be able to get along together in southern Africa!'

Worn out by their long walk, and also hungry and thirsty by this time, the little group headed down past Magdalen College towards the river. Under some shady trees the girls spread out their picnic and they all sat down in the dappled shade to enjoy it.

'What's on the programme for this afternoon, Seretse?' asked Ruth.

'Punting, of course. This is Oxford, after all!' he replied, and after lunch they set off to hire two of the flat-bottomed boats. Seretse and Braim seized the long punting poles, and the two boats made their way rather erratically along the shallow Cherwell River, bordered by overhanging trees, lush undergrowth and summer flowers.

'Oh, this is heavenly,' exclaimed Ruth, lounging back against the cushions and lifting her face to the sunshine.

'Not bad for someone who comes from a desert, hey?' joked Seretse, propelling the punt along quite smoothly and with quickening pace.

'Wait for us,' shouted Braim, wobbling dangerously as he dug too deep with his pole. 'We didn't all come to Oxford and study punting you know!' Gliding under one of the many bridges, they espied a little pub settled comfortably in its colourful summer garden.

'Pull over to the edge here and I'll show you what else I learnt at Oxford,' said Seretse. They sat at a rough-hewn log table in the garden and ordered pints of beer from a buxom waitress.

On the way home in the train the others soon fell asleep, tired out from their long walk, their exertions on the river and the heat. But Ruth and Seretse sat in a corner together and talked quietly. This was the first time they'd spent such a long while in each other's company – a whole day together – and they were secretly loath for it to come to an end. Each felt entirely comfortable in the other's presence. He quoted Matthew Arnold's famous lines about Oxford to her:

'And that sweet city with her dreaming spires,
'She needs not June for beauty's heightening.
'Lovely all times she lies, lovely to-night!'

'That's beautiful,' she murmured. 'Describes it exactly. Dreaming spires . . .'

When they arrived back in London, he managed to hold her hand in a long farewell clasp. As the train pulled out of the station, bearing the girls on to Lewisham, she waved from the window.

Returning to the hostel, he didn't want to go to sleep because that would bring this day to an end and he didn't want it to end. He wanted to stay awake and savour every moment of it. Lying in bed, images of her face filling his head, he could no longer deny or fight his feelings. Something amazing was happening, and it was too all-consuming to hide from any more. His rational mind, conditioned by the racial consciousness of southern Africa in which he had grown up, shied away from the huge complications inherent in a relationship across the colour-line. But he could not continue to push it away into his subconscious. The emotions she aroused in him were too strong – they broke through into his every waking moment. Admitting his feelings to himself at last brought a measure of peace, and finally he slept.

2
The Courtship

THE NEXT DAY, SERETSE WAS FULL OF IMPATIENCE TO SEE RUTH. HE COULD hardly wait until a decent hour before ringing her up. He tried to sound casual.

'Would you like to go to the pictures tomorrow evening?'

'Why not?' she replied cheerfully. 'The usual group?'

'Well, I haven't actually mentioned it to the others.'

'Oh.'

Seretse's heart hammered in his chest. After a little pause she said: 'Well, that's fine. What time? Where shall I meet you?'

'Let's meet after work at the Wig and Pen at about six o'clock,' said Seretse, rather breathlessly. 'We can go on to the Odeon from there.'

'All right. The Wig and Pen tomorrow at six. I'll see you then. Bye.'

As soon as she put down the phone after Seretse's call, Ruth lit a cigarette with hands that were not quite steady. Did this mean there was a change in their relationship, or was she reading too much into it? 'Don't be silly,' she chided herself. 'You know he loves going to the pictures. He just wants to see a film, and he can't be bothered to organise the whole group to come along.'

The working day dragged, and her mind was a muddle of thoughts about love, race, society and prejudice. Eventually, unable to continue the pretence of doing anything useful, she pleaded a headache and left early. She walked briskly towards St James's Park, glad of the exercise and the coolness of the late afternoon, to which a hint of autumn had given a refreshing bite.

Once in the park she walked until she was tired, the thoughts continuing to rampage through her mind. She had been getting along so well, putting the war and all that behind her, enjoying herself – going out to parties, dancing, having fun. It was all such a lark – so light and easy. And now this had happened. This little leap of the heart whenever she thought about Seretse; this quiver of excitement whenever he looked at her.

She sat down on a bench and watched the ducks paddling in the murky water, racing towards a child who was throwing scraps of bread to them. A couple walked by, arm in arm. Nobody else paid any attention to them. But what would happen if one of them were black? People would stare and nudge each other. They would mutter. Some might even comment aloud. Would she ever dare to walk through the park arm in arm with Seretse? Did she care? Did he care? Why did she not mind that he was black? Everyone else seemed to, but it didn't bother her. In fact, most of the time she didn't even notice that he was black. He was courteous, kind, intelligent, funny – those were the things that mattered. Why couldn't everyone else see it that way too? But did he even care for her? Did she want him to? What was going to happen tomorrow when they went out to the pictures together?

She sighed, and made her way to the station to catch the train home. Would she go alone tomorrow night? Or should she ask Muriel to accompany her?

Seretse found it very difficult to concentrate on anything the next day. At last, the hands of his watch crept past five o'clock. By ten to six he had secured a seat at the bar counter of the old pub in Fleet Street, with a good view of the doorway, towards which he glanced anxiously every few seconds. Would she come? What had he done? Had he wrecked everything? She was probably only happy to be seen in public in a group. He must have been crazy to force the issue like this. What a fool, he berated himself. Of course she would be uncomfortable being seen out with him as a couple. 'Decent' white girls simply did not do that in Britain. It was socially unacceptable and he could no more change that than make the dry sands of

Serowe sprout daffodils in springtime. Of course she wouldn't come and he wouldn't think anything less of her for not coming.

Suddenly, there she was. He stood up to greet her.

'Hello,' she said, and at once he felt warm and happy. He ordered gin and lime for them both and she chattered on about her day at the underwriters, where she worked as a clerk. He sat smiling foolishly in his relief that she had come, happy just to have her there beside him.

'Shouldn't we be going now?' she asked at last, glancing at her watch.

'Oh yes, of course,' he jumped up, annoyed at himself – he normally made a point of being extremely punctual. They went out into the street and walked briskly along to the cinema.

He saw very little of the film as he could not help glancing surreptitiously sideways at her profile in the dark theatre every few minutes. Not many people had come to see the film and they had most of the row to themselves. It was deliciously agonising to have her so close to him and to be alone with her for the first time. Their eyes met and he quickly looked back at the screen. Did he dare touch her hand? How would she respond? His body urged him to make the move, his hand inching, almost of its own accord, towards her. He noticed that her hands were clasped loosely in her lap. He looked at her again. She turned her head to meet his gaze and smiled faintly in the darkness.

Their hands moved and before he knew it he felt the softness of her palm in his grasp. Softer than his grandmother's leopard-skin *kaross*. Softer than the fur of a new-born kid. They both glanced down at their clasped hands – his was almost invisible in the dark, while hers glowed dimly pale. The rest of the film passed in a blur as the nerve endings of their palms and fingers spoke to each other. As people started walking out, they sat motionless, watching the credits to the very end. Only when the lights came on and the cinema was empty, did he reluctantly release her hand. She turned to smile at him, and the radiance in her eyes filled him with a surging, hopeful joy.

They made their way out into the street, where they found the sky above them awash with rosy light. Delicate banners of gold cloud swirled across it.

'Oh, look at that – isn't it lovely!' she exclaimed. They both stood still and gazed up at the glorious sky.

'Beautiful,' he said. 'You know, at home we get the most amazing sunsets, particularly in summer, or when there's been a wind and the dust is thick. The whole sky goes crimson and the earth glows with the reflected colour. It's much more spectacular over there, because you can see the whole thing all at once. There are no buildings to get in the way. You can see from one horizon to the other.'

'Must be wonderful,' she said.

It was getting late and they headed towards the tube station, neither of them wanting the evening to end. He travelled with her all the way to Lewisham. For once they didn't have much to say to each other. It seemed as though in holding hands in the cinema, they had both crossed a certain boundary. They didn't notice whether there were any stares or mutterings from their fellow passengers. They had both had romantic relationships with other people before, but never anything like this. Seretse leaned out of the window of the last train back into town and said urgently: 'When do I see you again?'

The train began moving. 'Soon . . .' her voice floated up to him, and she stood waving until he was out of sight.

Ruth seldom ate breakfast, but the next morning she joined Muriel and her parents for a cup of coffee before setting out. 'So where did you go last night, Pud?' her father greeted her.

'Oh, just out,' she replied.

'And where is out?'

'To a film,' she said with a quick smile, glancing across at Muriel, who pulled a face.

'Well, who were you with?' he asked.

'A few friends,' replied Ruth.

George Williams gave up on getting any further details.

'Well, my dears, I'm off to the grindstone,' he said, and patted them both briefly on the top of their heads. 'Bye, Pud. Bye, Mid.'

'I wish he wouldn't still call me Pud,' complained Ruth. 'Makes me feel fat.'

Dorothy Williams' motherly antennae had been quivering throughout this exchange. When the front door banged shut, she pounced: 'What's going on, Ruth? You look like the cat who swallowed the cream.'

'Oh, Mother, don't fuss,' said Ruth. 'I'll tell you when there's something to tell, all right?' With that, she jumped up and gathered her things.

'Well I would like to meet him, whoever he may be,' her mother called out after her before turning her enquiring gaze upon Muriel.

'You won't get anything out of me, Mother,' said Muriel. Mrs Williams sighed and began to clear the table.

They met outside the Casino Theatre in London's West End on a very hot and humid evening – September 1st, 1947. It was only 7 pm and already exuberant crowds thronged the streets around the theatres from Shaftsbury Avenue to the Haymarket. Sticky and uncomfortable amid the jostling mob, Seretse, wearing a sports jacket and grey flannels, gazed enviously at Ruth, who seemed cool and composed in her trim navy blue and white costume. As he wiped his forehead for the hundredth time, Ruth laughed up at him.

'Come on, desert cowboy,' she said. 'Why are you wilting? It's not that hot.'

He groaned. 'How on earth do you manage to stay so cool? I bet you'd even manage to keep cool in Serowe!'

They had both been delighted to learn that their favourite American jazz group, the Ink Spots, was to tour Britain, and had been determined to get seats on the opening night. The all-black quartet, whose hit numbers had travelled across the Atlantic with lightning speed, were widely acclaimed as the best jazz band of that time. They had their roots in jazz and blues and were part of a developing trend – the precursor of rock 'n' roll, which, in the 1950s, would change the rhythms of popular music forever.

The Ink Spots was a highly professional group and delighted the British audience with a lively and polished performance. As they left the theatre after 11 pm, Ruth and Seretse agreed that the long wait in the sweltering heat had been well worth it. Arm-in-arm they hurried to meet Muriel, who was waiting for them under the clock at Charing Cross station.

As they waited for the train, a young man came over and tried to chat up the girls. 'Wot you doing wiv 'im then love?' he asked, jerking his head towards Seretse. 'Can't find a decent Londoner to go out wiv, then?'

'Oh, go away,' snapped Ruth.

'Is me mate not good enough for you then?' growled his stocky companion, coming closer. The heckling persisted, growing louder, and quite a crowd formed.

Seretse looked about him in consternation. This would not be the first time he had used his fists to confound a group of racists, and he was more than willing to risk a bloody nose in order to do so. But he knew the girls would be upset at any display of violence and so he was enormously relieved to hear a reassuring voice of authority behind him saying: 'Now then, what's going on here? Disturbing the peace, are we?' He swung round to see a burly bobby strolling along the platform, swinging his truncheon. 'That's enough of that, thank you very much,' said the policeman, 'or you'll be coming along with me for a night as a guest of His Majesty.' The thugs dispersed without a murmur.

Ruth and Muriel smiled their thanks at the policeman as the train steamed into the station.

'What a miserable bunch of clods,' said Ruth, as she turned to board the train. 'But they're not going to spoil our wonderful evening.'

Seretse watched to make sure the trouble-makers did not follow the girls into the train, and then left the station. Thrusting his hands deep into his pockets, he hummed the Ink Spots' latest hit, *Whispering Grass*, softly to himself and made his way back to Nutford House.

Although he had not made any conscious effort to do so, Seretse had been friendly with many Coloured and Indian students at the various schools he had attended in South Africa. His best friend at secondary school had been a weedy boy of Malay origin – Ralph Ontong. He and Seretse had been dubbed 'the ant and the elephant' by fellow pupils because of the marked difference in their builds. When Ralph had fallen in love with a Xhosa girl – and been ridiculed by the others – Seretse had been his champion, declaring that race and tribe were irrelevant. He was prepared to defend Ralph with his fists and such was his size and his reputation as a skilful boxer that not many students challenged him on this one. He often teased his friends about their cultural differences – but always with an irreverence that was at odds with the tense racial and tribal undercurrents of the time.

Back home for the holidays, Seretse had regularly been at the centre of efforts to defuse tribal and ethnic tensions among the Bakalanga and Bamangwato youths in Serowe. These disputes usually focused on girls and football, and the young Chief-to-be had demonstrated a wit and tact beyond his years in dealing with them.

From then on, Ruth and Seretse spent all their leisure time together. Determinedly impervious to any racial hostility that onlookers might display, they watched soccer and rugby games, went horse-riding and rambled for hours through the countryside. Ruth adored ice-skating. Seretse loved the way her face lit up whenever she spoke about it, and decided that he had to try skating in order to share her pleasure. Being fit and athletic, he was convinced that he would soon get the knack of it, as he had done with rugby and cricket. Ruth belonged to the Queen's Ice Skating Club in Queensway, Bayswater, and one night she took Seretse along with her. However, try as he might, he just couldn't get the hang of it. 'I guess you have to start when you are three or four years old,' he said, reluctantly admitting defeat after several painful falls.

He had experienced snow for the first time during the winter of 1945/46. Frost was quite a common occurrence in the desert, but nothing could have prepared him for the winters of the northern hemisphere. He had been fascinated by the slow, floating feather-fall, the all-encompassing whiteness, the Christmas-card transformation of the world around him. Its blanketing beauty fascinated him, but it chilled him like no desert night wind had ever done.

The more time they spent in each other's company, the more they realised how very similar their views were on so many things, from politics and humour to family values, music, sport, books, theatre and films. Ruth loved Seretse's intelligence, his calm, rational way of looking at things and his delightful sense of humour. As she watched him in his role as facilitator and peacemaker among his contemporaries, her respect for him grew. His generosity of spirit, even temper and complete lack of malice made him popular with the other students as well as with his colleagues at the Inner Temple.

Seretse, for his part, was attracted by Ruth's warm friendliness, her cheerful, practical outlook on life and her self-assured confidence. In drab, postwar London they moved in a bright bubble of laughter and happiness. Seretse no longer spent his spare time writing long letters to his uncle. He also spent less and less time with the Pilkington family. Finding himself loath to share this tender new relationship with anyone else, he increasingly declined Roger's invitations.

The couple experienced racist incidents on many of their outings. They were constantly surprised and dismayed at how many people so obviously resented the sight of them – two young people simply enjoying each other's company and out to have a good time together. There were also, however, heartening occasions when they would be on the receiving end of some bigot's ugly tirade and Ruth's fellow Britons would come to their defence.

Often, when they went out to dinner, the maitre d' would try to find them a place behind a pillar so as not offend the other patrons. They were never actually turned away, as they would have been in South Africa or Southern Rhodesia, but many evenings out were marred by these subtle displays of prejudice. Although they became hardened to such incidents, and Seretse, in particular, just laughed them off, refusing to allow them to spoil things, Ruth was unable to shrug them off so easily. She was both ashamed and appalled at the intolerant behaviour of her countrymen.

'We don't interfere with them, why on earth do they think they have a right to interfere with us?' she would demand. 'Why can't they just leave us alone?'

She had always believed prejudice was like a disease, and it was only right to point this out to people when they were suffering from it. In the past, she had spoken out boldly whenever she had come across it, particularly as a young WAAF when officers in her presence spoke disparagingly about the Jamaican ground crews or told anti-Jewish jokes in the mess room. How, she reasoned, could a country which had just fought a war against a racist enemy and which had welcomed friends of all colours to fight at its side, resent her being with Seretse? What had the war taught them? Had it all been a waste? She could not understand how a British pilot could risk his life to fight the Nazis and at the same time hold anti-Semitic views similar to those of the enemy. Did they genuinely feel racially superior, she wondered, or were they merely thoughtlessly mirroring the attitudes and opinions of their time?

Before she had met Seretse, her compassionate nature had made her sensitive to the hurt suffered by those on the receiving end of racist remarks. She had often gone out of her way to try and undo the harm done by her war-time colleagues. Although not at all what one would describe as 'a crusading type', Ruth found she just could not keep quiet when such racist slights happened in her presence. Speaking out in this way had made her unpopular with some of those on the base, but plenty of others had admired her courage, and she didn't lack for friends or admirers.

During one of their many discussions, Seretse told her that since coming to Europe he had changed his attitude toward the white races. 'I had based my opinions solely on the behaviour of the whites in southern Africa,' he explained. 'As a result, I had developed a personal distaste for white people. But since coming here and mixing with English people my attitude has changed, and I no longer see them merely as rulers and oppressors of Africa. I suppose, mixing with so many different people over here, most of them white, I have learnt to relate to them as individuals, rather than as a homogeneous group. And this has made it clear to me that they all have different attitudes and different shades of political opinion. One has to be very careful about generalising, you know.'

This depth of perception and wisdom beyond his years set Seretse apart from his peers and was to stand him in good stead for his eventful future as an avowed nonracialist and a national and international peacemaker.

What made this even more remarkable was that, like most southern Africans, he had already been subjected to humiliating racial discrimination. Travelling back and forth to school through South Africa, he was forced to use the cramped and uncomfortable third-class carriages, as first and second class were reserved for 'Whites Only'. Attending Wits University, he had to stay in segregated accommodation, carry an identity pass at all times and generally live as a second-class citizen. Before he could board the Union Castle Line ship that would carry him to England, he had been forced to sign a letter undertaking that he would eat the European food supplied. Little did the purser realise that Seretse had been happily eating 'European' cuisine since the age of nine when his uncle had paid extra for him to sit at the special Table 14, where such food was served, at Lovedale – the Church of Scotland's highly-respected boarding college for Africans in the northern Cape. His stomach was quite comfortable moving between the two types of diet – and he enjoyed the black beans, pumpkin and traditional spinach of the village no more nor less than the bangers and mash or fish and chips of Table 14.

George and Dorothy Williams had decided to go away to Brighton for a few days before the cold weather set in. Taking advantage of their absence to have an enjoyable evening in private, Ruth and Muriel decided to throw a dinner party for their Nutford House friends.

Ruth was a good cook, having done a domestic science course and worked briefly for a caterer before joining the WAAF. She planned the menu with great care and much pleasure, Seretse uppermost in her mind. The men complimented her extravagantly on the meal – which was indeed delicious. Muriel, totally undomesticated, was happy for her sister to receive all the praise – just as long as she, Muriel, didn't have to do anything but enjoy the dinner.

The foreigners described the varying cuisines of their own countries for the girls' benefit. Seretse was particularly eloquent when talking about the grilling of beefsteaks over the open fire, the rich stews bubbling in the three-legged, cast-iron cooking pots and his own favourite dish, *seswaa*, which was produced by boiling the meat, removing it from the bone with sticks and then grinding it up into a delicious mash. 'Our beef is the best in the world,' he boasted, amid good-natured teasing about his size and his appetite.

Afterwards, Ruth slipped away to do the washing up, knowing full well not to expect any help from Muriel.

'Oh, is this where you are? Let me give you a hand,' said Seretse, joining her a few minutes later; rolling up his sleeves and tucking his tie into his shirtfront. They were chatting companionably when Braim bounced into the room in his cheerful way. Seeing Seretse at the sink, elbow deep in dishes, he stopped stock still, his eyebrows raised.

'My, my, my,' he exclaimed. 'Hey everybody, come in here and take a look at this. How the mighty have fallen!'

'What are you talking about?' said Ruth.

'He's the Chief, woman! What's he doing washing dishes?' said Braim. Forbes and Harry crowded into the kitchen and began jeering at Seretse, who simply continued, unperturbed, to wash and stack the dishes neatly.

'Now I've seen everything,' exclaimed Harry. 'When some whites come to Africa, they go native. But our Seretse comes to Europe and goes European!' Raucous laughter filled the kitchen, but Ruth looked uncomfortable.

Seretse smiled at her gently. 'Get out, you rabble,' he commanded, brandishing his dishcloth, 'unless you're prepared to take up a cloth and do your fair share.'

The others retreated with alacrity and he and Ruth were alone once more. 'What was all that about?' she asked. 'Do African men never help with the washing up?'

'Well,' he began patiently, 'the short answer to that is no, they don't. Men in Africa never help with any domestic chores. In fact, they never even go anywhere near the kitchen. That is regarded as the woman's domain, and the women guard it jealously. They don't want men anywhere near their kitchens. Cooking, and everything that goes with it – including fetching water and finding firewood – is women's work and both men and women accept that unquestioningly. That's the way it has always been.' He went on to tell her that not only were men in Africa waited on by women hand and foot, but that often the women would serve from a kneeling position, actually crawling into the presence of men down on their knees in the dust.

'But that's because you are the Chief, I suppose,' she said thoughtfully.

'I'm afraid not, my dear,' Seretse said. 'That's the way all men behave in Africa. You see, every one of them is in reality a little chief in his own home. But you're right in a sense. My own situation is rather different because I am the Paramount Chief. For example, when we were at boarding school in South Africa, I never even did my own laundry. The other Bamangwato boys used to do it for me as a mark of respect for my birthright.'

Ruth appeared to be giving her full attention to drying the plates, but her mind was whirring with these new revelations. She was beginning to appreciate, for the first time, something of the enormity of the cultural chasm separating her from Seretse. The knowledge distressed her, because in so many other ways she felt she knew him well and had much in common with him. But right now he seemed very distant, and she despaired that she would ever be able to get close to him again. And she wanted to. She wanted very much to be close to him.

The incident caused Seretse to confront, once again, his own ambivalence on the issue of traditional practices in Africa – in the light of his education and exposure to other cultures and norms of behaviour. In particular, he had always instinctively felt that the age-old system of *bogosi* or chieftainship was coming to the end of its time. He remembered how, as a young idealist, he had fought with the other boys at school for calling him 'Chief' – insisting that they were all equal and that rule by one man, which he learnt in history classes to call 'dictatorship', was unacceptable.

But by the time he went to Fort Hare University he had accepted that he was born to be Chief and had reconciled himself to spending his life in the service of his people, but he had determined to be a 'modern' chief. He would rule through a process of consultation with all the people and would devote himself to improving their standard of living. The gender question had not yet taxed him, but the exchange with Ruth had opened his eyes to this delicate subject and given him food for thought.

Ruth and Muriel were careful to keep their activities with the Africans well hidden from their parents, especially their father. As the months passed, however, her motherly intuition told Dorothy that Ruth was seriously involved with a man. The girls knew that Dorothy was far more tolerant than their father. She was the one who had brought George to the point of accepting Muriel's move to the Congregationalists and her work among the foreign students. She had even gone so far as to tell her daughters that she had married whom she wanted to and, as far as she was concerned, they were therefore free to marry whomever they might choose.

Encouraged by this, Ruth finally arranged for her mother to meet Seretse. They went to Nutford House for tea one afternoon. Seretse met them at the bus stop. Always the perfect gentleman, he was his usual charming self throughout the encounter. Dorothy was warm in her praise of him as 'a delightful young man'. However, on their way home she cautioned Ruth not to take the relationship any further 'because society is not ready for this'.

Looking earnestly at her daughter, Dorothy said: 'Nobody will accept you, my darling. Certainly, your father would never accept him.' She hoped fervently that this relationship was just a passing fad and that one of the pleasant young boys who were always trying to date Ruth would come along and sweep her off her feet. 'I personally have no objection whatsoever to you having a black man as a friend,' she went on, 'but I know how much you'll suffer if you take it any further. There are so many bigots out there, you are going to be hurt. That's the only thing that bothers me. He's a very nice person, he really is. But you have to consider other people's opinions. You can't live on a desert island. You have to continue to live among society.'

She racked her brains for further arguments that would persuade her daughter. 'People think that white girls who go out with black boys are sluts. And you are not a slut. You're beautiful, you're intelligent, you have everything going for you. You've got a wonderful job. You wouldn't want to throw all that away, would you?'

'But I don't care what everyone else thinks,' said Ruth. 'I think he's wonderful and I love being with him. Nothing else matters.'

'Stop thinking only about yourself,' said Dorothy firmly. 'Think about your father and me. Think of how difficult and painful it would be for us, how ashamed and embarrassed we would be, hearing people say all kinds of dreadful things about you. Things that we know aren't true. Of course you can continue to be friendly with him – just promise me one thing: that you won't do anything foolish, like falling in love with him.'

Satisfied that she had filled Ruth's head with sufficient practical reasons why it would be foolhardy to take the relationship any further, Dorothy patted her daughter's hand and said: 'Now then, there's no need to mention any of this to your father. He would just get angry. We'll keep it between ourselves, shall we?'

<u>3</u>

The Proposal

WHEN RUTH'S VISITS INCREASED TO THREE AND FOUR TIMES A WEEK, AND the young couple were often spotted sitting very close together on the garden bench or in a secluded corner of the lounge, the staff at Nutford House nodded knowingly and exchanged approving glances. This was the kind of girl their royal charge deserved.

Mrs Jones, the matronly secretary, and her fellow staff members liked Ruth Williams immensely. She always took the trouble to pop her head around the office door to say hello and chat for a few moments – not like some of the thoughtless young women who hung around the hostel, eager for a bit of excitement and a good time at the expense of the lonely African and Caribbean students. Ruth behaved with decorum but she was no snob. Her warm friendliness enveloped everyone, and the effect she had on Seretse had not gone unnoticed. Since their meeting on that summer night in June 1947 he had undergone something of a transformation. His shyness and reserve had melted. Gone were the solitary visits to the cinema, the lonely hours spent reading cheap thrillers. A new Seretse had gradually emerged, expansive, urbane, self-assured.

Meeting in their favourite pub in the City after work one day, almost a year after their first acquaintance, Ruth and Seretse had a quick gin and lime and then Seretse suggested that they leave, as it was rather crowded and stuffy. They walked out into Fleet Street, down the Strand and left towards the bank of the Thames. They watched the sluggish flow of the grey river in companionable silence for a few minutes. Suddenly, Seretse turned and grasped Ruth's waist, lifting her up to sit on the parapet so that her eyes were on a level with his. She laughed in surprise and looked at him questioningly.

'Ruth,' he began, 'I have something very important to ask you. Please hear me out before you say anything. In fact, I don't want you to answer me today. Just listen to me and promise you'll think seriously about what I say.' Ruth nodded, her eyes widening. 'You mean more to me than anyone else in this world ever has or ever will. For months now I have thought about you constantly. I've not been able to concentrate on anything else. I feel that nobody understands me the way you do. I never feel at home with anyone else the way I do with you. I feel like a different person when I am with you. I know I love you, and I want you to marry me.'

Ruth gasped and he placed a finger to her lips and continued: 'I don't want an answer immediately. I know that what I am asking you will change your life forever, if you agree. You'd have to leave your home and live in Africa.'

For a time they remained motionless as the river drifted past. 'You must understand, my darling,' he said urgently. 'It is not going to be easy. The world does not want to see us together. Particularly that part of the world where we will live. I could never deny my birthright as Paramount Chief of the Bamangwato. I have to return to Bechuanaland to be king of my people as soon as I have finished my education. We will be living out our lives in Serowe – a simple, tribal village on the edge of the desert.' He stared into her still, intent face. 'There'll be no seaside, no ice-skating, no library, no fish and chips, no Ink Spots concerts . . . only me,' he said in genuine humility. 'That's all you'll have, only me, your whole life long, until you are a little wrinkled old lady, burnt brown by the African sun.'

Ruth looked at him lovingly, opening her mouth to tell him that he was all she would ever want or need. But he pressed his fingers to her lips again. 'Sssh,' he said. 'Don't say anything yet. I have to go back there; it is what I was born for and I know I could never be happy anywhere else in the world. But I also know my life would be meaningless without you to share it. I know I am asking you to give up your family, your home, your friends, your work, your whole way of life – for me. Please don't think I am asking you this lightly. I have thought about it for months, not wanting to ask you to make such a sacrifice. But I love you so much, I just want to be with you always.'

The pain that would be caused to their family members was uppermost in his mind. There was no mistaking what her father's attitude would be – total outrage. As for his family – he was well aware that as Chief he was not supposed to marry without the permission of the whole Tribe, so he knew his royal uncles would disapprove. But he was pretty sure that his uncle Tshekedi and aunt Ella, who had always loved him like their own child, would be supportive, if disapproving. He was prepared for the Tribe to stop him from becoming Chief.

'But even if that happened,' he told Ruth, 'I'd still want to go back there and serve them one way or another – they are my people. And I know that once we are there and they have a chance to get to know you, they will realise what a wonderful person you are, and they will be happy for me. But Ruth – once you decide, there will be no going back. If we do get married, I want it to be forever. There can be no divorce. Once you say "I do" I'll never let you go.'

Unspoken between them lay the knowledge that if they did marry in the face of all the opposition, it had to work. Failure would give a powerful weapon to all those who opposed mixed marriages.

'Seretse,' said Ruth, 'I love you too. I will think very seriously about your proposal.'

His heart, like a biplane, looped giddily as though it would soar right out of his body. He encircled her in his arms and she laid her head on his, feeling the prickle of his crisp, coarse curls against her temple.

They spent the rest of the evening wandering hand-in-hand beside the river, lost in each other's presence. The waters of the Thames sparkled, the dusty summer trees were more verdant than ever, the colours of the flowers had never been so brilliant. They watched the flaming sunset with a mixture of awe and reverence, and finally he took her home.

Waving from the platform as his train drew away, Ruth sighed deeply. Her mind could focus on one thing only – Seretse loved her and wanted to marry her. All the difficulties, the problems, the obstacles, the trials that would surely lie ahead were eclipsed by this single fact.

They continued to see each other several times a week, but no further mention was made of the proposal. The problems outlined by Seretse were so enormous that Ruth couldn't face thinking about them. So she blocked them from her consciousness, determined not to raise the subject again until he did.

Seretse, on the other hand, thought of nothing else. He waited anxiously for her to indicate that she was ready to give him her reply. He was well aware that the problems facing her seemed insurmountable. How could she possibly be expected to make the transition from her comfortable middle-class existence in England to that of the wife of a chief in the middle of Africa where there were not even the most basic conveniences? He loved his country dearly but he was under no illusion about the true nature of its underdevelopment, its poverty and the lack of such comforts as were taken for granted in Europe. It would all be so strange to her. Despite his despera-tion for her to say yes, he had tried to paint a clear picture of the hardships that lay ahead, even exaggerating these in some cases, to make absolutely sure that she could make her decision with her eyes wide open.

The days dragged by and yet Ruth made no mention of his proposal.

Seretse spent the time alternating between hope and despair. Sometimes, con-vinced that he was asking too much of her, he would plunge into depres-sion. Then they would meet and he would see her unusual eyes smiling at him with a hidden secret message that sent his hopes soaring. On such days, he managed to persuade himself that she would agree – and then he wrestled with the problem of how to break the news to his uncle and the Tribe. He rehearsed a thousand explanations in his head, drawing comfort from the fact that there were several precedents for disobedient royal sons marrying without formal permission. His own father, Sekgoma, had married without the permission of King Khama and the Tribe. But as a result, his son by that marriage was not in line for the chieftaincy. Only when Sekgoma had married a woman of whom the King approved was their issue, Seretse himself, eligible to be Chief. Tshekedi, too, had married Ella without the approval of the Tribe – but no-one had suggested this made him unfit to rule. Late in life, even his grandfather had married a woman – Tshekedi's mother – without the express permission of the Tribe. As he had explained to Ruth, the marriage of the Chief was of great significance to the Bamangwato. The Chief belonged to the Tribe and everyone had the right to have a say about whom he should marry. Even marriage between commoners was seen as a contract between whole families, not just between two individuals. And, as everywhere else in the world, royal marriages were often used to secure allies and to create strategic power bases.

Of course, the colour issue was a different matter altogether. Never had a chief taken a wife of a different race. He knew the succession issue would cause great concern among the Bamangwato. But they would cross that bridge when they came to it. Colour-blinded by the depth of his love for Ruth, he was convinced that she would win the hearts of his people just as she had won his.

After two weeks, he could bear it no longer. He telephoned her at work and asked her to meet him at their special spot on the Embankment at lunchtime. Today there could be no pretence of casual conversation. He took her hand.

'Have you thought seriously about what I said the other day?' he said.

'Yes,' she replied.

The silence lengthened.

'And what is your answer?'

'Yes,' she said again, simply.

'You mean, you do want to marry me, in spite of all the problems?'

'Yes,' said Ruth a third time, her heart overflowing with joy as she realised she had indeed made up her mind and she would gladly run the gauntlet of whatever hardships lay ahead, as long as they could be together. This was the man for her, no matter what.

Seretse scooped her up in his arms and held her close to his broad chest. 'I'm so happy,' he whispered into her ear, his voice almost drowned by the victorious drum beats of his heart. 'So happy. I'll love you and treasure you forever.'

She touched her forehead gently to his and quoted softly her biblical name-sake: '*Whither thou goest, I will go, thy people shall be my people . . .*'

After a while, Seretse said: 'What about your parents? Have you said anything to them yet?'

'No,' answered Ruth. 'To tell you the truth, I only made up my mind this very minute. I'll tell them tonight.'

Too elated to eat, they wandered along the Embankment with eyes for no one but each other. 'Even if they make me give up the chieftainship, I won't mind,' declared Seretse. 'I'd sacrifice anything to be able to spend the rest of my life with you.'

With great reluctance, they parted and returned to work. That evening, Ruth went directly home, determined to get the confrontation with her parents over with as soon as possible. She had phoned Muriel during the afternoon, asking her to meet her at the station so that she could break the news to her first and enlist her support for the forthcoming ordeal at home. Muriel was thrilled at her news and hugged her in an unaccustomed display of sisterly affection. 'He's the most wonderful person, Ruth, I'm so happy for you,' she said.

Finding her parents in the living room, Ruth wasted no time in beating about the bush. 'Mother, Father – Seretse has asked me to marry him, and I've accepted his proposal,' she announced.

Dorothy buried her face in her hands as Ruth went on to explain to her father that the man she had agreed to marry was Seretse Khama, a kind, gentle, loving man – and an African chief. He would be returning to Africa to rule his Tribe after completing his studies, and she would be going there to live with him. 'I am sorry for the hurt I know I'm causing you, but I love this man and I can't live without him,' she finished.

George erupted. His wife and daughters sat silently as he raged. He was utterly convinced that a mixed marriage would be an unmitigated disaster. His experience in India had given him ample evidence of the disastrous effects of racial mixing, he said. Furthermore, the children of any such union would suffer appallingly. They would be outcasts. They would be unacceptable to either race. They would belong nowhere. The neighbours would be appalled – she, his precious daughter, would be rejected, shunned by her own people. And once she arrived in Africa, they wouldn't want her either.

Turning to Muriel, he said, 'I should have stopped you getting involved with those damn darkies right at the beginning. That was the start of all this trouble. Look where it's got to. If she'd never met them in the first place, this wouldn't have happened, would it?'

There was a silence, and then he sat down heavily beside his younger daughter and took her hand in his. 'Pud,' he said, 'don't do this to us, don't do this to yourself. Don't throw away your life like this. You don't have to marry this man.'

'Yes I do, Father. I love him. I have never loved anyone like this,' said Ruth, crying now. Her father's gentle appeal hurt her more than his rage ever could. But faced with her continuing defiance, he hardened his heart.

'If you are determined to go through with it, I can't stop you,' he said. 'But you must know that what you're doing is wrong and shameful. You can stay here until you get married – this is your home. But if you marry that black man you will never be welcome here again.' He got up and strode over to the window, with his back to them.

At this point, Dorothy came to Ruth and put her hands gently over her daughter's, which were clasped so tightly in her lap that the fingernails were white with tension.

'My darling,' she said softly, 'please think about what Father has said. He does love you very much, and he's concerned about the hardships you will be bringing upon us all if you go through with this. No good can possibly come of it. What do you know of Africa? You'd have a terribly tough life out there. Please be sensible. I know you love him now, but there are plenty of other men in the world whom you could also grow to love.'

'Come on, Dorothy,' said George abruptly, 'let's go out for a drive and give her time to come to her senses.' Turning to Ruth, he said: 'I expect you to have changed your mind by the time we get back. If you haven't – don't speak to me again.'

Muriel tried to comfort her bitter tears. 'Don't worry,' she said. 'He'll come round eventually. He's just shocked, that's all.' They looked at each other, both knowing it was a vain hope. They went up to bed early, in order to avoid another painful confrontation when their parents returned.

For the next few weeks, Ruth avoided her father, leaving home early in the morning and returning late at night. They did not speak at all. The tension in the house was palpable. Her mother, torn between loyalty to her husband and compassion for her daughter, had to content herself with offering a few words of sympathy and concern during snatched moments in the kitchen or on the stairs. She begged Ruth to forgive her father for his harshness. 'He belongs to a different generation,' she pleaded. 'The world has changed so much in the past few years, he can't comprehend it all. And of course he's terribly worried about what the neighbours will think. It's very difficult for him. You must try to understand.'

No sooner had she arrived at work the morning after her confrontation with her father, than Seretse was on the phone. 'How did it go?' he asked anxiously, deeply regretful that he had been unable to be at her side.

'Oh, Seretse, it was awful,' she said. 'He won't speak to me at all and he says I must get out of the house as soon as we are married.'

'Oh, my dearest, I'm so sorry,' said Seretse. 'Do you want to reconsider?' His heart was in his mouth.

'No!' she said fiercely. 'I've decided. Don't ask me that again.'

'When can I see you?' he asked urgently.

'I have to go now, there's a bit of a flap going on here. And the boss is taking us out for a drink this evening. I'll come to the Wig and Pen as soon as I can get away, probably between 7 and 7.30.'

'I'll be waiting.'

As she put the phone down, one of Ruth's colleagues, Jane, looked at her quizzically. A friendly girl, she had sometimes accompanied Ruth and Muriel on their outings with the black students.

'Did I hear the word married?' she asked.

'You've got sharp ears,' retorted Ruth. 'But as a matter of fact, yes you did. Seretse has asked me to marry him and I have said yes.'

'Seretse!' gasped the other girl, clapping her hand to her mouth. 'Ruth, that's wonderful, you're so lucky, he's such an amazing man!'

That evening the head of their department took several of the girls out for a drink after work, as he did from time to time in the interests of improving staff morale. Once they were all seated in the pub with drinks and cigarettes in their hands, Jane could not contain her excitement at Ruth's news and before Ruth could stop her she announced to all and sundry in a loud voice: 'Let's all drink a toast to Ruth. She's just got engaged to a tall, dark, handsome man. In fact he's an African prince and Ruth will be going out to Africa to be his queen!'

A stunned silence greeted this incredible announcement. Even the barman paused in his polishing of glasses and glanced over at them to see the girl who had done such a thing. Then all at once everyone started talking. The girls gushed over Ruth, each trying to outdo the other as they offered their congratulations, sounding so false that she felt sick. As soon as she possibly could, she excused herself and almost ran to meet Seretse. Hadn't she told her mother she didn't care what other people thought? She would show the lot of them!

She stopped outside the Wig and Pen to compose herself. Then she sailed into the pub with her head held high, her mouth set in a defiant line. Walking straight up to Seretse, she kissed him.

'Hello,' he said, surprised. 'What's all this about?'

'I've had it with all the bigots around,' she said fiercely. 'I'm in love with you, and I don't care who knows it. I'm going to marry you and if anyone doesn't like it, they can lump it. I refuse to let them spoil my happiness for another minute.'

'That's my girl!' said Seretse.

The next day, Ruth's boss called her into his office. She had been half-expecting some sort of response to last night's announcement, but when the summons came she felt a tremor of anxiety. One look at his face confirmed her fears. Initially he took the benevolent angle, warning her of all the problems that lay ahead, appealing to her sense of self-preservation and encouraging her to think carefully about the future that would be in store for her if she went ahead with the marriage. He even tried flattery – telling her she was an asset to the business and if it would help her to get away from Seretse and take a clear view of things, he would arrange for her to be transferred to New York for a year.

She refused his offer and told him she believed Seretse was the right man for her and that she had made up her mind and would not be swayed. He then became very cold and formal. 'In that case, I'm very sorry but we no longer have a position here for you,' he said. 'Kindly clear your desk as soon as possible. I would like you to be gone by the end of the week.'

Ruth was shocked. She stormed out of his office and immediately called Seretse.

'Come down and meet me now at the Lyons Tearoom,' he said.

They sat down opposite each other, and she burst out at once: 'They can't do this to me! Can't you sue them or something? You're almost a lawyer now, aren't you?'

Seretse gripped her hands under the tablecloth. 'It's not worth it, love. The odds are stacked against us. We'd never win.'

She pulled her hands away. 'But we can't just let them get away with it!'

'Just calm down, sweetheart,' said Seretse quietly. 'You wouldn't want to go on working for people like that anyway, would you?'

'No,' she said thoughtfully. 'But it's the principle of the thing. They shouldn't be allowed to get away with it. They should be exposed for the racists they are.'

'Ruth,' said Seretse, taking hold of her face and forcing her to look at him. 'Listen to me. We can't fight all the time. If we do, we'll have no life for ourselves. Let it go.'

She gazed at him, perceiving the wisdom in what he said, loving his conciliatory nature and yet reluctant to give up without a fight.

'We'll show them,' said Seretse. 'We'll get married and live happily ever after and then they'll know how stupid they were to try and stop us. Now, come on, cheer up!' The strength of her love for him flooded back into her, and she smiled at him. In the past forty-eight hours she had lost her home and her job, and still she smiled at him.

'I'll start looking for a flat for us today,' declared Seretse cheerfully. 'Now, do you feel strong enough to go back, clear out your desk and walk out of there without a backward glance?'

'I think so,' she said, grasping his hand once again as if to draw strength from it.

Up to this point, Ruth had not thought much further than the disapproval of her family and the neighbours. She had not even considered that her relationship with Seretse could possibly jeopardise her career. But this was just a foretaste of what was to come. As she was beginning to see, the stakes were high, very high.

After work they went back to Nutford House together, as it was one of the few places where they could relax. They sat in the lounge drinking tea, Ruth still in a state of shock. The confrontation with her parents and subsequent loss of her home and the job she thoroughly enjoyed had all happened so quickly. She hadn't realised her whole world would collapse so quickly after saying yes to Seretse's proposal. Trying to bolster her with the strength of his love, Seretse sat beside her, stroking her hand.

'Hey, what is going on here?' said Braim, erupting into the room with his usual cheerful energy, and stopping abruptly as he saw Ruth wiping her eyes. 'Seretse, what have you done to make this beautiful girl cry?'

'Nothing,' sniffed Ruth, smiling weakly. 'He's only trying to make me feel better.'

Seretse grimaced fiercely and gestured to Braim to push off and leave them in peace.

'What's wrong, Ruth?' Braim persisted.

'I've just lost my job,' said Ruth.

'What? I thought you were the most efficient clerk they have. What's happened?'

'My boss found out that I was engaged to marry Seretse.'

Braim stared at her in shocked disbelief, his mouth open. 'You what?'

'You heard her,' intervened Seretse. 'We're engaged. Ruth accepted my proposal two days ago. I was going to break the news to you guys this evening – but you've stolen my thunder.'

Braim gave a loud whoop, which brought several of the other students into the lounge to see what was going on. 'Seretse and Ruth are engaged to be married!' Braim shouted, and began to hum the wedding march loudly.

'Shut up, you idiot,' said Seretse, as his friends began to crowd around, asking questions, slapping him on the back, shaking hands, kissing Ruth and generally exclaiming over the momentous news.

'So when's the wedding?' asked Charles, when he could make himself heard above the din.

'Soon,' said Seretse, beaming. 'Probably early October by the time the banns are called.'

'Come on everyone,' called Charles, 'let's celebrate! Let's take the happy couple for a drink down the road.'

They swept Ruth and Seretse off down to the local. Charles ordered champagne all round and once they were all ensconced at a corner table with their glasses charged, he stood up to propose a formal toast.

'To the happy couple, Chief Seretse and his Queen,' he said, raising his glass. 'May they confound all racists everywhere and live happily ever after!' Everyone roared their approval at this and there was much back-slapping and jubilation.

Ruth was exhausted after the emotional upheaval of the past few days, and by ten o'clock she was ready to collapse, so Seretse and Harry walked her to the station to catch her train home to bed.

Walking back to the pub, Harry put a hand on Seretse's shoulder and drew him to a halt.

'Listen, my friend,' he said seriously. 'This is some bombshell you have dropped tonight. But are you out of your mind? Now don't get me wrong, Ruth is a wonderful girl and I am very happy for both of you. But have you honestly thought about what you are doing? I know how easy it is for one's emotions to overrule one's judgment in cases like this. She's very attractive and she obviously thinks the world of you. But that is not enough, my friend. Marriage is a serious commitment. I don't see how it can possibly work between two people from such hugely different back-grounds. I mean, think about it, Seretse. She knows nothing about our ways. Are you planning just to dump your culture and your customs and live like an Englishman from now on? Or do you think she's going to change and become Africanised? I'm sorry, but I just don't see that happening. It might be wonderful for a few years, but in the long run I can only see heart-ache and misery for you both.'

Seretse smiled at his friend. 'I'm grateful for your concern,' he said warm-ly. 'But I know myself, and I know Ruth. We can make this thing work. We don't have to make hard and fast rules about living a European lifestyle or an African lifestyle. We can develop our own special combination – a bit from here and bit from there, whatever suits us. We can make a life for ourselves, I know we can. Don't underestimate the power of love!'

Harry shrugged. 'Well, it's your funeral if it doesn't work out. But I'd hate to be around to pick up the pieces. What about her parents – I can't imagine they are thrilled about this? And your family? And the Tribe? Do you seri-ously think they'll accept a white Queen? And even if they can be persuaded to accept her, will they accept a Coloured heir to the throne? Remember, they haven't had the experiences that you have been privileged to have – education, living in Europe and all that. To them the white man is still the ruler, and a rather unpleasant one at that. White people represent the unacceptable face of colonialism – and now you expect them to accept a white woman as their Queen. Think again my friend!'

Seretse held up his hands. 'Harry, don't think I haven't spent sleepless nights wrestling with those very issues. I don't know the answers. Of course Ruth's parents are horrified. Her father has actually forbidden her to come home once we are married, and he won't speak to her unless she changes her mind. She lost her job today because of me. I haven't even told my uncle yet. The only thing I'm sure of is that I can't live without her. She feels the same. I'm determined to go through with it.' He slapped Harry on the back, and said: 'So let's go and drink to that, shall we?'

But Seretse's inquisition was not yet over. No sooner had the two returned to the group awaiting them in the pub, than he was inundated with questions about his and Ruth's future. This had been the sole topic of conversation during their absence, and his fellow African students were all aghast at the magnitude of the problems that lay ahead.

'There's no way you can take her to live in southern Africa, Seretse,' declared Braim. 'The Boers would never allow it, and how on earth is she going to cope in a mud hut in your village, with no running water and no electric stove, surrounded by roaring lions?'

'She won't have to live in a mud hut, you idiot! And I'll shoot the roaring lions,' Seretse said, laughing. 'I have never lived in a mud hut! And as for the water and electricity – haven't you heard of those modern technological inventions – the generator and the borehole? I'll build her a beautiful new house on the hill overlooking Serowe and she can have all the comforts she has in Lewisham – plus a much better view!'

Seretse's newfound happiness was infectious, and they all laughed with him. They were amazed that Ruth would even contemplate moving permanently to the Bechuanaland Protectorate. She must really love him, they said, if she was prepared to give up her comfortable life in England and live in primitive conditions on the edge of the desert.

'But what about the Boers?' Braim persisted. 'They rule South Africa now, don't forget. They can make your life an absolute misery. Your country is totally dependent on them for everything: they're your major trading partner, your closest neighbour and they're very pally with the British. What if the British decide to hand the Protectorate over to them? They could well do that, you know.'

'Yes, I know that, of course,' said Seretse. 'It's a constant source of anxiety. My grandfather and my uncle both spent huge amounts of time and energy over the years making sure that the British didn't hand us over to the South Africans – and even though they haven't done it yet I don't think it's safe to assume they won't. After all, we only have their word. And of course it doesn't only concern us. Basutoland and Swaziland are also Protectorates in that region.'

'Well perhaps Ruth is the answer to your problem,' suggested someone jestingly. 'If you marry a British girl, that makes you their son-in-law, doesn't it? Surely that will make them less likely to throw you to the wolves?'

Seretse laughed. 'Well, I hadn't thought about it like that,' he said. 'Maybe you have a point!'

'That's right,' Braim chipped in. 'After all, that's how it used to be. The British themselves used strategic royal marriages to cement international treaties. Why can't the same principle work if an African prince marries a British citizen? That would certainly put an end to the Boers trying to take over your country.'

'Never mind the Boers, what about the British?' said someone else. 'They're not ready for this either. Look at the racial discrimination we all suffer over here. Have you forgotten that incident just last week, Seretse, when you were nearly beaten up by a gang of hoodlums at the station?'

'But at least racial prejudice is not legislated here, the way it is in southern Africa,' said Harry. 'Even in the Rhodesias there is racial legislation – not as bad as the apartheid legislation that the Boers have in place, but similar and just as offensive. They're determined to enforce white supremacy in the whole region. I don't think a black man with a white wife is going to go down too well, even if he is a chief. Maybe, specially because he is the chief.'

The odds were stacked too high, seemed to be the general feeling. Why couldn't Seretse just marry a local girl when he went home to take up the chieftaincy, they reasoned? There must a thousand beautiful women in Bechuanaland who would give their right hand to be the Chief's wife; Ruth would be miserable sooner or later. She would have no friends, no family, nothing. She would have to be made of stone to endure such a harsh existence.

'With all due respect, Seretse, what have you got to offer her? Forget this infatuation,' said Braim. 'Go home. You've obviously been here too long. How long is it since you have been home? Three years? That's too long without kissing the earth of your motherland. We may have joked about it before, but it seems to me you are in danger of becoming Europeanised.'

Seretse stood up and leaned on the table, facing them all. He was suddenly very much the Chief, clothed with authority, strength and purpose. The full force of his personality hit them as he said slowly and deliberately: 'I love Ruth. She loves me. We're going to be married and we're going to have a good life together. We're not going to allow anyone or anything to come between us. You just watch and see.'

In spite of their doubts his friends applauded warmly, showing Seretse that they were solidly behind him and wished him well.

4
The Letter

GETTING A FLAT WAS TO PROVE EASIER SAID THAN DONE. SERETSE RESPOND-
ed to a number of newspaper advertisements for what he thought could be
suitable premises, but invariably they had always just been taken. He began
to get suspicious at this seeming ill-luck when one landlord told him a complicated story about the rental having been a misprint and that the actual
price was way out of his range. His suspicions were confirmed when Ruth
agreed to ring up several of the same landlords and found that indeed the
properties were still available. Somehow, this subtle form of racial prejudice
was more irksome than the overt heckling of drunken young thugs. They
finally managed to rent a small flat on the second floor at No 10 Campden
Hill Gardens, just off Notting Hill Gate.

Ruth and Seretse were elated at finding their first home. Seretse moved
in immediately, and they spent many happy hours hunting for bargains with
which to furnish it. It didn't matter to them that it was tiny, with hardly
room to swing a cat in the kitchen or the bathroom. Here they could shut
the world out and just be themselves, away from prying, disapproving eyes.

There was an Anglican Church, St George's, nearby and they decided it
would be perfect for the marriage ceremony. The vicar, Dr Leonard Patterson, behaved very decently towards them, and arranged for a special marriage licence, at the going rate of £2.10s. The couple was grateful that Dr
Patterson, with typical academic detachment, didn't even raise an eyebrow
at the fact that Seretse was black and Ruth white. He seemed to see them
simply as a young couple in love, wanting to be married. In order to facili-
tate the calling of the banns during the next three consecutive Sundays, the
wedding date was set for 2nd October 1948.

After their visit to the vicar they went to a nearby teashop. 'You know,' said Ruth, leaning her elbows on the small table, 'we've never spoken about religion. I think we should, don't you?'

'Well, I don't think it's particularly important, but we can if you want to,' said Seretse, who was himself rather passive about religion, despite the fervour of both his uncle and his grandfather. In fact, Tshekedi often worried about his nephew's lack of religious devotion. While Seretse was still at university in South Africa, Tshekedi had written to him advising him to adhere to God as *bogosi* was ordained by God: *'As Chief, when you are in difficulties, God is your only help and salvation. So, my brother's son, I advise you to put God first in your life'.*

Seretse was not an atheist and he knew Ruth was a practising Anglican, but he shunned institutionalised religion, put off by denominational divisions and wrangling over what he considered petty doctrinal matters. He quoted to Ruth what he felt was a rather clever statement by the late 18th century sceptical deist Thomas Paine: *'The world is my church, to do good my religion'.*

'That's all very well,' she retorted. 'But it's a bit vague, isn't it?'

'Well, technically I suppose I'm a Congregationalist,' he said. 'Of course, the whole of Bechuanaland is Congregationalist!'

He went on to tell her how King Khama had undergone a radical conversion to Christianity as a young man and had held strongly to the faith throughout his life, living out his beliefs in a practical manner that had won him international acclaim. Ruth was fascinated to hear that Seretse's grandfather, at the age of about 15, had actually met David Livingstone when he had visited the village to try to convert Chief Sekgoma, Seretse's great-grandfather. The Chief was not swayed by the missionary's words, but permission was given for mission schools to be established.

Young Khama had been an avid student, and before long he had wholeheartedly embraced the Christian teachings and been baptised into the LMS church. His long reign as a benign dictator was characterised by a faithful observance of these teachings that embraced every aspect of Bamangwato life. In the face of considerable opposition from other royal elders, as well as ordinary members of the Tribe, he had courageously abolished all traditional tribal practices that he regarded as being rooted in, and therefore perpetuating, heathenism. These included the brewing of traditional beer, rainmaking ceremonies, witchcraft, *bogadi* (the payment of a bride price), polygamy, rites of circumcision and other customs, as well as the wearing of loincloths and skins. When his father and brother had challenged his chieftainship, he had treated them with truly Christian patience and generosity. Most of his Christian beliefs, over time, were incorporated into the body of tribal law. Even *kgotla* meetings began with a prayer.

'Sorry,' said Seretse, realising he had run on a bit. 'You wanted to discuss religion, and I've given you a history lesson!'

'Not at all!' she exclaimed. 'I want to know more. I need to know all about it now that it's going to be my country too.'

'All right then. What set my grandfather apart was his fanatical teetotalism. He was heavily influenced, through the LMS of course, by the powerful British temperance movement of the late 1800s. To this day my uncle quotes him fulminating against strong drink – the constant enemy, a corrupting influence and the root of all evil.' He grinned at the memory of his puritan uncle's vociferous denunciations of alcohol in any form. 'Anyway, the movement was an extremely useful ally in Khama's battle to keep our country safe from the acquisitive grasp of the Boers, the Germans and Cecil John Rhodes. When he came to England to look for protection, the LMS took him on a high-profile, nationwide, temperance tour!'

Seretse's noble ancestor, with his gracious bearing and lean, ascetic face, had won the hearts of the British people. His widespread, popular appeal had caused the government to think twice about handing the Protectorate over to Rhodes' British South Africa Company. As he searched for words to convey the full extent of the significance of his grandfather's reign, Seretse remembered a little book written by one of the LMS missionaries at the turn of the century.

'The author put it beautifully,' he told her. 'He said that, before the time of King Khama, the people were locked into the ancient laws of the Tribe and the vagaries of the tribal gods. Nothing had changed for centuries. But when Khama came the people became conscious of the possibility of change. '*He stood in the midst of the stream with the waters of the old ways swirling about him, and pointed to a new road.*' He was a history-maker.'

'And that is what you are,' said Ruth, smiling at him. 'I think you're going to be a history-maker too – just like your grandfather!'

Seretse had been particularly encouraged by a comment from John Zimmerman, his closest friend at Oxford, whom he had asked to be his best man. Upon hearing Seretse's astounding news, John had initially voiced concerns similar to those expressed by the others. But then he had said warmly: 'Follow your heart, Seretse. You have a noble heart – follow it and it won't let you down.'

With these generous words strengthening his resolve, Seretse steeled himself to write to his uncle with news of the engagement. He dreaded doing so, and had, on several occasions, tried to draft the letter and failed. But time was marching on, and the letter had to be sent. Eventually, on 12 September, he summoned up sufficient courage to tackle the difficult task. He sat in his room, smoking, the wastepaper bin full of his discarded efforts. What Harry had said the other evening had all been true – apart from the few missionaries who treated them decently, his people knew the white man mainly as an oppressor: harsh, inflexible and cruel. In addition to this, and apart from the racial aspect, the marriage of the Chief was a serious matter and had always been subject to endless debate and conversation among the members of the Tribe. They would not take kindly to being presented with a *fait accompli* in this way.

He began the letter with news of his change of address, before plunging into the heart of the matter, telling his uncle that he was about to be married to a young Englishwoman called Ruth Williams. Confident of his uncle's support, if not approval, and hoping to elicit his sympathy, he told him that Ruth was having problems with her parents as a result of their impending marriage. '*But I know that she will be received by you in a friendly way*', he wrote trustingly. '*I have assured her that no matter how hostile everybody might be at home, nevertheless she will find you and mother most considerate and kind and you will do all you can to make us feel welcome.*'

He wrote frankly about his anxiety concerning the Tribe's reaction to the news, telling his uncle that no matter what their response, he would willingly return home to serve his people in any capacity. He apologised for not having asked permission from his uncle and the Tribe to marry, as was required by dutiful sons in general and members of royalty in particular. '*I realise that it was my duty to have asked your consent beforehand. But I knew you would refuse and it would be difficult for me to disregard your advice. That is why I notified you when it was all done. Please forgive me.*'

Seretse went on to ask his uncle to send him some money so that he could start married life without financial worries. He ended with this plea: '*Please don't try to stop me, Father, I want to go through with it. I hope you will appreciate the urgency of my request. I do need help. Your son, Seretse.*'

Relieved that it was done at last, Seretse sealed the letter and immediately went out and posted it by airmail.

The letter arrived on 23 September. Tshekedi was visiting his favourite project – the building site of a large new college at Moeng, the country's first secondary educational institution. This was his pride and joy and he was showing it off to the Resident Commissioner, Anthony Sillery. Seretse's letter came like a bolt of lightning. Such was the strength of Tshekedi's shocked reaction to the news that Sillery later recorded the incident in his journal, noting that the regent had been extremely distressed. The visit was immediately suspended as Tshekedi urged the Commissioner to action. They rushed to the post office in nearby Palapye, where Tshekedi cabled his nephew and his lawyer in Cape Town, Douglas Buchanan. Sillery telephoned the High Commissioner in Pretoria to alert him that a Bamangwato row was brewing.

Tshekedi had taken the news far worse than Seretse had imagined he would, and his cable to the young prince was blunt: '*Get ready to leave at a moment's notice. I can only discuss your proposal personally after your arrival here.*'

He was devastated and outraged by what he considered to be Seretse's careless and selfish behaviour, and his initial reaction was to do everything possible to stop the marriage from taking place.

Rushing back to Serowe, he vented his anger on the hapless chickens that happened to stray across his path as he stormed across the courtyard to the meeting ground. A group of elders had been hastily gathered for an emergency *kgotla* and, grim-faced, the regent announced the shattering news. His fellow royal uncles were equally outraged, and congratulated him for sending the telegram demanding Seretse's immediate return to explain his foolishness in person. As word of the young chief's astounding break with tradition spread through the village and out into the fields and distant cattle posts, faster than a summer's wildfire through the thorn scrub, a shock of alarm shivered through the entire Tribe.

The flurry of telegrams continued, with Tshekedi instructing his lawyer Buchanan to do all in his power to stop the wedding from taking place. The LMS was on full alert and Roger Pilkington was urged to contact Seretse immediately and knock some sense into him.

Alone with Ella at home that evening, Tshekedi sank his head into his hands, exhausted by the emotions he had experienced on receiving Seretse's bombshell and his frantic efforts throughout the day. 'I just can't believe he would be so selfish, and so stupid,' he said in a weary voice. 'Surely he knows what something like this will do to the Tribe? It will be the end of it. The people will never accept a *kgosi* who is not black. How could they?' He was particularly wounded that Seretse, with whom both he and Ella had always enjoyed such a close relationship, had hidden the development of his romance from him. That it should have come to this – marriage! And he was not even aware that Seretse was courting an English girl. Ella jumped as he thumped the table with his fist, clenched in rage. 'Why didn't he even tell us he was falling in love with someone?' he asked bitterly.

'He probably knew you wouldn't approve and he didn't want anyone to tell him he couldn't see her,' she said gently. 'Don't you remember what it is like to be a young man in love? You were just the same when we met – so impetuous and unable to think of anything rationally!'

'Don't make excuses for him, Ella! He's the Chief. He's not just an ordinary young man. He has to take responsibility for this Tribe. He's their hope for the future. That's why we sent him to be educated in England – you know that!'

Putting her arms around him, Ella tried to calm him. But he was beyond the reach of her tenderness, and he stomped out into the night to rage at the silent stars. What was to become of the Tribe, if Seretse persisted in this madness? His thoughts turned from his personal pain and disappointment to the wider implications of such a match. A mixed-race marriage in a black tribal society that existed cheek-by-jowl with South Africa and its racist policies and increasingly repressive legislation against blacks would, he knew, be catastrophic. He sank down on to a rocky outcrop and shook his head in disbelief at the enormity of it all. Unless he could stop it, this would mean the destruction of the Tribe. Of all men, perhaps only Ruth's father, who had experienced similar devastating emotions a few weeks before, could have empathised with him fully that night.

Back in England, Seretse read his uncle's brusque telegram with consternation. He telephoned Ruth and told her his uncle was insisting that he return home immediately to discuss things. She rushed round to the little apartment at once.

'But why has he reacted like this? You told me he would be supportive,' she said, when Seretse had shown her the telegram.

'I don't understand it at all,' he replied, his brow furrowed with distress. 'I was convinced he would stand by me. He has been such a wonderful father to me all these years. We've always been very close. I certainly didn't expect this harsh response.' He rubbed a hand across his eyes. 'I can't imagine what has got into him. Perhaps the other uncles are pressuring him. I just don't know what to do.'

Ruth had never seen him like this. She was distraught. Was her love for

Seretse going to prove to be a destructive force that would ruin his future? Would he live to regret having proposed to her? As she voiced these anguished doubts, he put his arms around her and told her that his life, without her, would not be worth living; that he would rather have her than anything else in this world.

They clung together and drew strength from each other, as yet unaware of the momentous chain of events they had set in motion, and of the storm of cables burning up the wires from Serowe to Cape Town, Pretoria, London and back again.

Pressure on Seretse to come home immediately mounted with each passing day. The censorious telegrams continued to arrive. '*Your proposal . . . surest way of disrupting Bamangwato Tribe.*' And: '*On no condition can we agree to your marrying an English girl. Your proposal more serious and difficult than you realise. You seem to have forgotten that your home is in southern Africa, not in England. Have made arrangements for your immediate return. Get ready to leave at a moment's notice. I shall only discuss your proposal personally after you arrival here. I repeat, your proposal more serious and difficult than you realise.*'

Seretse read them with dismay as it became clear that his uncle personally was utterly opposed to the idea of his marriage. He was shocked and saddened by what he saw as his betrayal by the man who was his closest living relative, who had always addressed him as *ngwanaka* – a term of endearment meaning 'my son'. But he made no move to return to Serowe. He was adamant that he would go through with his marriage. With each day his resolve hardened, especially when he discovered that his uncle had cut off his allowance with immediate effect. Later, the newspapers were to make much of the similarity between Seretse and the Duke of Windsor, who, a decade previously, had made the agonising choice between true love and royal responsibility. By a strange coincidence, the Duke had in 1935, as King Edward VIII, unveiled the Bamangwato memorial to King Khama in Serowe.

Ruth was Seretse's constant companion, strengthening him with her love and her own resolve, despite the fact that her relatives, too, continued to bombard her with opposition to the marriage and dire warnings of the ostracism, misery and loneliness that lay ahead. The more their respective families tried to discourage them, the more resolute they became. Their love was like a fortress into which they withdrew to escape the barrage of opposition.

The British administration entered the fray at Tshekedi's invitation. The regent convinced them that the marriage would be disastrous for the Tribe and, such was his standing with the authorities, they were eager to help. Despite the irritation caused by his forceful determination and constant badgering for more development, Tshekedi had proved himself over the years to be an able, willing and energetic administrator who had made their job in Bechuanaland much easier than it might otherwise have been. Under his effective, if authoritarian, leadership, taxes were paid on time and things ran smoothly. Therefore, at his bidding, the District Commissioner in Serowe, the Resident Commissioner in Mafeking, the High Commissioner in Pretoria and officials at the Commonwealth Relations Office in London all sprang into action. Cables flew back and forth. Tshekedi's lawyer Buchanan cabled his brother John, a London notary: '*Chief authorises me to urge you to take every step, possible and impossible, to prevent Seretse, 10 Campden Hill Gardens, Notting Hill Gate, marrying English girl on 2 October. Consult Dominions Office re immediate priority air transport for Seretse to Africa. Suggest caution parson who called banns. If Congregational, contact London Missionary Society, if Church of England contact Archbishop. Consider extraditing Seretse . . . inform girl's parents of ostracism and misery awaiting her. Such marriage possible cause Seretse's deposition.*'

He cabled a similar message to the London headquarters of the LMS, addressed to Ronald Orchard, the Africa secretary, urging him to do all he could to prevent the marriage, and warning of the disastrous consequences for Seretse's prospects of becoming Chief if he went through with it. Next on the receiving end of the same message was Sir Reginald Copeland of

All Soul's College, Oxford. He was asked to help, as he had taken Seretse under his wing when the young prince was at Balliol. Buchanan then was so bold as to telephone the British High Commissioner, Sir Evelyn Baring himself, requesting an appointment to see him about a matter of great urgency. He also telegraphed Tshekedi, suggesting that he should prepare to fly to London to talk to Seretse personally. Tshekedi's doctor, however, advised against such a trip as the regent was, by now, at the point of nervous collapse.

Meanwhile, back in South Africa, Baring had acceded to the attorney's request for a meeting. The High Commissioner listened attentively as Buchanan, with legal precision, related the progress made so far. The two men discussed the consequences of Seretse's proposed marriage and Baring took serious note of Buchanan's warnings concerning the future and wellbeing of the Tribe. He then summed all the information up in a telegram to the Permanent Secretary of State at the Commonwealth Relations Office in Whitehall, describing the possible dangers and ending: '*Most grateful for any help you can give since marriage would be disastrous for Bamangwato Tribe and Seretse personally.*' The wheels of Whitehall began to turn. Aided and abetted by John Buchanan and the officers of the LMS, John Keith of the Colonial Office even went so far as to approach the Commonwealth Secretary, Arthur Bottomley, for his assistance in stopping the marriage.

True to Buchanan's word, the royal village of Serowe was in uproar. The villagers spent every waking minute discussing the calamity. Tshekedi and the senior members of the Khama royal family discussed the crisis for hours on end, often staying up most of the night in endless conjecture and recrimination over the young heir's unthinkable behaviour. It was decided a message should be sent to all the outlying villages and isolated cattle posts telling the men to come in to Serowe for an emergency *kgotla* as soon as possible.

As outside pressures to separate them intensified, Ruth and Seretse withdrew further into their fortress, spending every possible moment together.

Unable to concentrate on his work, Seretse stopped going to the Inner Temple. He called the Reverend Patterson about advancing the wedding date and was delighted when the obliging clergyman agreed to marry them that coming Saturday afternoon, 25 September. They sought escape in private, peaceful places – such as Kew Gardens on a weekday morning, when they shared its colourful, autumnal splendour only with the occasional pottering gardener. Wandering hand-in-hand along the neatly clipped walkways among the flowerbeds, still resplendent with late summer blooms, they found a bench half hidden beneath a prolific, fragrant climbing rose. Seretse guided Ruth towards it. 'Let's sit here and eat our sandwiches,' he suggested. Leaning back, Ruth removed her hat and pillowed her head on his shoulder with a sigh. The only sound was the humming of bees – drunk on the abundant golden pollen.

'Are you glad or sad, sweetheart?' Seretse asked.

'Both,' replied Ruth, sighing again as the beauty of the gardens soothed her spirit. 'I'm glad because we've managed to bring the wedding forward to Saturday, but I'm sad because my father won't be there to walk me down the aisle.' Seretse stroked her hair, but before he could think of something comforting to say, she sat up straight beside him. 'But I'm **not** going to allow that to spoil the day,' she said. Turning to face him, she smiled dazzlingly. 'Seretse - I've made a decision.'

'What?'

'It would be silly for me to get all dressed up in yards of satin and lace and pretend we're having a traditional white wedding when the father of the bride is nowhere to be seen. Why don't we abandon the whole traditional thing and go for something completely different?'

'Sounds good to me,' he said, thinking to himself that she could wear sackcloth for all he cared, just as long as he could get that ring onto her finger and make her legally his wife before anything happened to separate them.

'I'll wear a tailored costume,' she said, 'and a pillbox hat – they're all the rage now. And, of course, matching gloves. What colour would you like me to wear, Seretse?'

'Well,' he mused, gazing at a bed of delphiniums, 'what about blue? You know I love blue – and it does suit you.'

'All right, blue,' said Ruth, 'but what shade of blue?'

'Bechuanaland sky blue.'

'What blue is that?'

'Well, it rather depends.'

'Depends on what?'

'Oh, the time of the day, the time of year, how windy it has been, whether there's rain coming . . .'

'You're impossible,' Ruth said through her laughter.

Although the hail of protests from the Bamangwato seemed almost overwhelming to Ruth and Seretse, it was the mere murmuring of a breeze in the treetops compared with the storms that lay ahead. Little did they realise their love affair would have such a profound impact on the course of history – shifting the balance of power between nations and affecting intergovernmental relations at the highest levels. The repercussions of their decision to marry continued for almost a decade, and revealed carefully concealed prejudice and bigotry at top echelons of government, the church and the civil service. They were, of course, victims of the age in which they happened to live. The world was at a crossroads, grappling to come to terms with the aftermath of World War Two and the brave new world that had arisen from its ashes. Nationalism was on the rise, particularly in Asia and Africa, where powerful movements in the colonies were making increasing demands on Britain for political and economic independence. In addition, Britain was on the brink of the influx of African-Caribbean immigrants, which was to have such significant and far-reaching consequences. British Imperialism was on the wane. The rising star was the Commonwealth, of which the Union of South Africa was a significant member. Britain's close ally, General Smuts, and his fairly liberal United Party had only just lost the election to the racist Nationalist Party under DF Malan. Ruth and Seretse stood at this crossroads, their union a vivid testimony to the burgeoning new ideals of nonracism, tolerance, cooperation and self-determination.

5

The Marriage

RUTH SAT ON HER BED AMID PILES OF CLOTHING. HATS, SHOES, COAT HANG-ers, scarves, clothes were strewn all over the room. The dressing table was covered with bottles and pots of shampoo, lotions and make-up. Two large, empty suitcases lay open on the centre of the carpet. Muriel stood in the doorway, arms folded. She would happily keep Ruth company while she packed, as long as she didn't have to help. She was not good at folding and tidying.

'So he said he was giving me a present and would know it when he saw it,' Ruth rattled on, sorting clothes as she spoke. 'And it was amazing. We were walking down Kensington High Street and he stopped dead and pointed at a shop window. "That's it," he said.' Turning, she reached into the large cream-coloured box behind her, and drew out a tailored, linen suit of turquoise blue – her wedding outfit. 'He said this is the colour of the sky over Serowe in midsummer.'

'It's lovely,' said Muriel, stroking the material. 'Just your colour – you're going to look terrific in it.'

'Wait,' said Ruth. 'There's more. The model in the window was even wearing a pillbox – which was just what I'd had in mind. Look!' Opening another box she pulled out a hat with a little veil in the exact matching shade of blue. Lastly, she produced a small tissue-wrapped parcel. Pulling off the tissue, Muriel found a pair of satin-soft turquoise gloves.

They had spent days talking about the wedding, saddened that neither of their parents would attend. And now it was upon them already. First thing the following morning Ruth would move out of her parents' home forever – and into the flat in Campden Hill Gardens as Mrs Seretse Khama.

'It's all going to go fine,' Muriel said confidently.

Just then, Dorothy put her head around the door. 'Are you girls ready for a cup of tea?' she asked, determined to be cheerful. Her husband's attitude made her feel she was being pulled in two, but she clung secretly to the hope that one day she would be able to talk George around to accepting Seretse as his son-in-law. To be forced to miss her daughter's wedding was terrible.

'Thanks, Mother,' replied Ruth, busily folding, unable to look at the sadness in her mother's eyes.

'I'll just fetch the tray then.' She returned with the tea things and sat in the chair Muriel had hastily cleared of a pile of sweaters, balancing the tray on her knees.

'I've got something for you, Ruth,' she said, sounding almost embarrassed, 'I'd be so pleased if you'd wear it tomorrow – it will make me feel as though I'm part of it all.'

She handed Ruth a small parcel wrapped in faded pink tissue paper, embossed with cream floral sprigs. Ruth dropped the skirt she was folding and sank down on to the bed, holding the package in her lap as she undid the wrappings. She drew out a garter, made of lace and silk, embroidered with tiny cream seed pearls and forget-me-nots in a shade of blue identical to her sky wedding outfit. It was obviously very old – such fabrics had not been around in England for years.

'Did you wear this when you married Father?' she asked, tears in her eyes.

Dorothy nodded, unable to speak.

'I can't believe you've kept it all these years,' exclaimed Muriel.

'Something old, something new, something borrowed and something blue!' said Dorothy. 'Now you've got everything you need.'

Leaning gingerly across the tea tray, Ruth hugged her mother tightly, inhaling the comforting smells of lavender water and home-baked bread that had been her mother's own particular perfume for as long as she could remember.

Unbeknown to Ruth and Seretse, the battle lines were being drawn. A formidable group had assembled to map out a strategy for the wedding day. Seretse had made the mistake of inviting Roger Pilkington to the ceremony. When the date was changed, he rang Pilkington to notify him, not realising that his old friend was part of Tshekedi's team of opponents.

'Seretse, please listen to me,' Pilkington begged him over the phone. 'Don't be hasty about this. The Tribe is in an uproar – how can you even consider going through with your marriage when there are so many unresolved issues? What's your hurry? Why don't you go home and discuss everything with your family and the Tribe? If Ruth is the right woman for you, I'm sure she'll wait for you.'

'She'll wait for me, that's certain,' Seretse responded, rather aggressively for him. 'But we don't want to wait, Roger. Why should we? It's my life, even though I am the Chief. It's 1948, for heaven's sake, not 1920! Arranged marriages are things of the past. I'll still be a perfectly competent chief, and I am absolutely convinced that she'll be a wonderful chief's wife. She is an incredible woman.'

'But Seretse,' said Roger, 'just a few more weeks wouldn't make that much difference surely? Your uncle has alerted the Foreign Office, you know, and they are very concerned about possible disturbances among the tribesmen.'

'No, Roger,' said Seretse, 'we've made up our minds and we're not going to wait any longer. And it's got nothing to do with the British authorities. The Tribe might argue and protest, but there won't be any riots or anything like that. So what are they worried about?'

Realising that he was not going to make any headway over the phone, Pilkington suggested that he should go round and talk to Seretse personally. In view of their long-standing friendship and the high esteem in which Seretse held him, he agreed to meet Pilkington that evening at his flat. But he was adamant that nothing would persuade him to postpone the marriage.

Pilkington then rang up Ruth's parents. Dorothy was a little reluctant to discuss the matter over the phone with an absolute stranger, but after a few moments George came on the line and told him in no uncertain terms that he and his wife were totally opposed to their daughter's marriage to this young African, but had no influence over her at all. 'She is a very head-strong young woman, I'm afraid,' he said. 'We're all very upset about it, but we haven't been able to persuade her to change her mind.'

'May I perhaps have a word with her?' suggested Pilkington.

'I'll see if she will speak to you,' replied George.

Pilkington waited.

'Good afternoon,' Ruth's calm, pleasantly pitched voice came on the line. He introduced himself as a friend of Seretse and the Bamangwato people, and explained to her as succinctly as he could that the Tribe was extremely upset about Seretse's decision to marry without their permission.

'The whole royal family is very unhappy about Seretse's decision. If he marries you without their permission, he could very well be prevented from becoming Chief. I am sure you would not want to be the cause of him losing his entire inheritance and alienating him from his family and his people?'

There was silence on the other end of the line.

'So I would like to appeal to you to persuade Seretse to postpone the mar-riage until he has had a chance to consult fully with his uncle and the elders of the Tribe,' he continued.

'I'm afraid that won't be possible,' said Ruth.

Again there was silence, as Pilkington tried to think of something to say. The girl obviously had no idea of the gravity of the situation.

'Well, perhaps,' he suggested eventually, 'you would agree to meet with me and my wife to discuss the matter in greater depth. There are many complex issues at stake here, and we can't discuss them properly over the telephone.'

'I am well aware of the issues at stake,' Ruth replied. 'Seretse and I have discussed the matter at length. There's nothing more to say. I think it would just be a waste of your time.'

'It's no trouble at all,' said Pilkington, trying at all costs to keep his foot in the door.

'No,' said Ruth bluntly, 'I'm afraid I don't have the time. I'm busy packing up my things.'

'Well, why don't I write everything down in a letter to you,' said Pilkington, grasping at the only straw he could think of. 'I could have it hand-delivered to your house. Then you could read it at your leisure.'

'All right,' said Ruth, wanting only to be rid of him.

Pilkington put the phone down and stared out across the Heath, glorious in its autumnal colours, recalling the many happy hours he had spent striding across it with Seretse, deep in earnest conversation about the future development and education of the Bamangwato. Seretse had such great plans for his chieftainship. He was so level-headed, so determined to use his position and his education to liberate his people from their bondage to poverty and the vagaries of the weather. The Seretse he had spoken to on the phone seemed a total stranger. What on earth had got into him? What had turned him into a selfish and uncaring young man, obdurate almost to the point of rudeness, prepared to throw away his birthright without a second thought? A woman of course. Seretse had kept emphasising how much he loved Ruth. Could love be so destructive? What did Ruth and Seretse know of true love, un-selfish love?

Shaking his head to clear it of these thoughts, Pilkington set about summoning his fellow opposition team members, who now included the Rev A J Haile, LMS Regional Director for Southern Africa, who was in London on leave, as well as the Rev Orchard, Africa secretary of the LMS. These men of the cloth knew Africa and loved the Bamangwato, in their own way. They were earnest, dedicated, honourable – and utterly paternalistic – with a genuine concern for the primitive souls of the mission field. They agreed to meet that afternoon in Buchanan's legal offices. With hindsight their actions seem callous, cruel and uncaring, but if one looks deeper, to the heart, their motives were well-meaning.

'Well, this is a pretty pickle we've got ourselves into,' said Haile, after Pilkington had described his endeavours to reason with Ruth and Seretse. 'Now what are we going to do? You say Tshekedi is adamant the marriage must be stopped, eh, Buchanan?'

'Yes,' replied John Buchanan, smoothing his bushy moustache with forefinger and thumb and leaning forward to consult, yet again, the pile of cables, files and memoranda on the desk in front of him. 'I've been authorised to take every possible step to stop them going through with it.'

'Well, I suppose our next move has got to be to persuade the vicar to refuse to perform the ceremony,' said Orchard, drawing on his pipe. 'That's the only way forward that I can see.'

'Good idea,' said Haile. 'I'm sure he'll see sense, once he's in possession of all the facts.'

'And in the unlikely event of refusing to cooperate,' said Orchard, 'we can tell him we'll simply attend the ceremony and object formally at that point during the service when he is required to ask whether there are any objections to the marriage.'

'Brilliant, my dear fellow,' said Pilkington admiringly.

They all agreed to stay in close contact with the Colonial Office and the Commonwealth Relations Office, in the hope that one of these bodies would come up with something substantial in the statute books that could be used to prevent the marriage legally. Officials had already begun an urgent search through mountains of official records and files, which went on throughout Friday night. But they found nothing relevant and concluded that marriages between people of different races could only be stopped under Scottish law. John Buchanan should, the group decided, stay close to the telephone in his office throughout the day. They agreed to meet at St George's Church at 9 am the following morning, and dispersed.

Pilkington went home to draft his letter to Ruth, which would be delivered early the next morning.

It read: '*I have a cable stating that the Tribe is strongly opposed to Seretse's marriage to a European. In view of this and of Seretse's position of responsibility amongst his people, I strongly urge that you should take no action until Seretse has consulted his people about the matter. I would be glad to put you in touch with a man who knows the Bechuana* (sic) *well and could explain their views to you. Please let me know when you could meet him and others with recent messages from the Tribe.'*

The messenger, a junior LMS officer, was to return to him, having delivered the letter, with the distressing news that Ruth, smartly attired in turquoise and surrounded by suitcases, had put the letter aside unopened and told him there would be no reply.

Later that same evening, Pilkington set off for Notting Hill Gate and what he feared would be an extremely difficult encounter with Seretse.

The argument swung back and forth between the two men for several hours. Pilkington did not mince his words. He told Seretse that he was behaving disgracefully and would have to give Ruth up. He urged him to remember his birthright and to take seriously the obligations of his chieftaincy. Round and round the argument went, with Pilkington raising all the same issues that had been raging in Seretse's head for months.

'You were born to be Chief, Seretse,' he said earnestly. Seretse heard him out, and remained polite throughout the evening, although the harangue went on until 4 am, with Pilkington saying much the same thing, Seretse knew, that his uncle would have said had he been there. 'You can't have your cake and eat it too, my boy. Life's not like that. You have been privileged to receive an excellent education, the best in the world. You have so many advantages, you could do so much for your country and your people – why do you want to spoil everything now? Think of your people; you know their traditions and their culture. You've been away for a long time at their expense, try and consider their feelings. You have to put other people first – you can't think only of yourself. You are their king. Just imagine the upheaval you have caused in their simple lives . . .'

The monologue went on and on. Eventually Pilkington left, under the mistaken impression he had made an impact and Seretse would at least postpone the wedding and give himself more time to think about the consequences. He believed that Seretse was being pressured into a hasty marriage by Ruth.

This erroneous view of Ruth's influence over Seretse and her dominance in the relationship was to be echoed by much of the opposition. While she was indeed a young woman with a strong character and a determined will, how little they knew Seretse! They all, including his uncle, believed that if they could just get him on his own, away from Ruth, they could appeal to his rational, lawyer's mind and convince him of the impossibility of what he proposed to do.

Seretse's quiet, diplomatic manner and his skilled concealing of his emotions were extremely useful gifts in this situation. His legal studies had enhanced these natural gifts and made him a difficult man to read, and an even more difficult one to thwart. He kept the fact that he was determined to marry Ruth to himself, allowing his opponents to draw their own conclusions from his taciturn and passive manner. He also understood, and used to great advantage, the skill of tactical withdrawal. The barrage of opposition, the war of words, had done nothing to weaken his resolve to marry Ruth. If anything, they had strengthened it. But the mental and emotional strain of it all was taking its toll. He fell into an exhausted sleep, only to be up again four hours later to prepare for Ruth's arrival with all her things from Lewisham.

Pilkington, too, had only four hours' sleep before it was time to meet his fellow conspirators and implement their strategy for that fateful day. Having sacrificed their only free day of the week to do their duty by their fellow-Christian, Tshekedi, and the souls of the Bamangwato, the three men stood uncomfortably in Patterson's small hallway. Mrs Patterson fussed over their hats, coats and umbrellas – wondering anxiously whether she had enough biscuits left to offer these imposing gentlemen for tea. Pilkington took the role of spokesman for the group, explaining the complex situation to Patterson.

'So you see,' he concluded, 'it really is a rather ticklish situation and we'd be grateful if you could play ball, if you see what I mean.'

Patterson, as discomfited by the unexpected visitors as his wife, shifted uncomfortably on the edge of his chair and cleared his throat. 'Well,' he began, 'it's rather odd, isn't it – telling a man one can't perform his marriage service because his uncle doesn't like it!'

'No, no, that's not it at all!' Pilkington hastened to explain. Had the man not heard a word he had said? 'This young fellow is the Crown Prince. There is a whole tribe of people – about a hundred thousand of them – depending upon him. He has broken with their custom and tradition and his marriage could cause terrible problems and hardships.'

'But if he knows all this and still wants to marry the woman, then I am duty-bound to marry them,' persisted Patterson.

The argument continued in this vein for some time, as increasing frustration, confusion and ecclesiastical fervour eddied and swirled like an irritable tide against the confining walls of the small sitting room. In the face of Patterson's continuing reluctance to call off the ceremony, Pilkington finally lost patience.

'Look,' he said forcefully, 'there is going to be serious trouble with the Foreign Office if you insist on going ahead with this.'

Patterson wrung his hands in distress. This Congregational interference was most uncalled for, and it was not in his nature to cope with such confrontations. As he looked mutely and miserably at his tormenters, Orchard delivered the *coup de grace* by threatening to disrupt the ceremony with an objection to the marriage. The visitors finally convinced the wilting vicar to ring up Seretse and suggest to him that, in view of this threat, he should agree to postpone the ceremony, which had been scheduled for 1.30 pm.

Meanwhile, Ruth and Muriel had arrived at Seretse's flat, their taxi piled high with Ruth's belongings – three hat boxes, two suitcases, a hold-all and a number of cardboard cartons. The girls were still distressed by Ruth's parting from her parents. Seretse tried to calm them down with a cup of tea. He had tried to cheer Ruth by telling her how lovely she looked in her sky-blue outfit. He himself was conservatively dressed in a dark suit with a striped white and navy tie and a navy silk handkerchief tucked into his breast pocket. A white carnation for his buttonhole and a posy of cream roses tied with a satin ribbon lay on the hall table, having just been delivered by the florist.

'The roses are lovely,' said Ruth, trying to focus on the adventure that lay ahead.

'You haven't even noticed my new shoes!' exclaimed Seretse, extending one foot and striking a heroic pose. Ruth managed a laugh. 'I am walking into our future in a brand-new pair of shoes,' he sang foolishly, trying to lighten the mood. At that point, the telephone rang.

'What?' shouted Seretse into the receiver, and then, as the colour drained from Ruth's face, 'Please, Vicar, don't do anything. We're on our way to see you right now.'

Grabbing his hat and coat, he told Ruth he would explain on the way and the two of them rushed out of the flat and down to St George's Church. Muriel waited at the flat for John Zimmerman, the best man, who was scheduled to arrive at 12.45 pm.

'Am I to understand that you are refusing to marry us?' Seretse asked the vicar, as soon as they arrived.

'This is a free country and we are free people,' interrupted Ruth. 'What right do you have to refuse to marry us?'

'I am most awfully sorry,' he told them. 'It is all very distressing, I know. But in view of all that has happened, and particularly in view of the involvement of the Foreign Office, I must tell you that I am obliged to refer the matter to the Bishop of London before we can go ahead with the ceremony. If you can get permission from him, I will tie the knot with the greatest of pleasure. Just as long as you get back here any time before 6 pm this evening.'

Seretse and Ruth looked at each other in dismay. 'In fact,' the vicar offered helpfully, 'I happen to know the Bishop is due to conduct an ordination ceremony at St Mary's Abbott in Kensington this afternoon. If you hurry, you could catch him there, explain the situation to him, and get his permission for me to go ahead.'

'I know where St Mary's is,' said Ruth. 'Let's go!'

Hardly pausing to say goodbye, the couple grabbed their coats from Mrs Patterson, who was still fussing about putting them neatly on the rack in the hallway, and flew out of the vicarage. 'We'd better go back to the flat and let Muriel and John know what's happening,' gasped Ruth, struggling to keep up, in her smart high-heeled shoes, with Seretse's long stride.

'We'll come with you, of course,' said John decisively as Seretse rapidly paraphrased the gist of the vicar's bombshell, and all four of them set off briskly for St Mary's Abbott.

'It's just a few blocks away,' Ruth said. 'Let's walk – we can't spare the time to wait for a taxi.' They arrived just as the service was about to start and slipped in, taking seats near the back. Muriel was later to regret bitterly that she hadn't thought twice when she caught a glimpse of the Rev Orchard outside the church. She knew him from the LMS, but never suspected that he was there as part of the great conspiracy to scuttle the marriage plans. She berated herself for not raising the alarm, especially since Orchard, a Congregationalist, had no reason to be at an Anglican service.

Shortly after Ruth and Seretse's departure from Patterson's office, the three conspirators had arrived at St George's to carry out their plan to disrupt the ceremony. They were extremely annoyed that Patterson, who in their view was proving to be totally unreliable, had told Ruth and Seretse to see the Bishop of London, the Right Reverend William Wand. This meant they now had to get to him before the couple did. Leaping into a taxi, they sped round to St Mary's Abbott, arriving just before the Bishop. They went bold-ly into the cloister entrance, accosting him as soon as he arrived.

The Bishop was quickly convinced by the sincerity of his ecclesiastical colleagues. He quite concurred with their reasonable assessment that such an irresponsible marriage would have dire consequences, that the Tribe's refusal to give its consent could prove to be a legal barrier and that it should not be allowed to take place until consultations with the Foreign Office had been held.

Ruth and Seretse sat patiently in the congregation, their nerves shredded by the ponderous liturgy of the lengthy service, their fingers surreptitiously intertwined on the hard wooden pew between them.

They looked at each other and smiled every few minutes – each determined to be strong for the other. The phrases of his uncle's torrent of cables, furious and demanding, swirled through Seretse's mind like a summer whirlwind – arising from nowhere, sweeping dust, leaves and twigs into a spinning spiral and dropping them, scattered, as it died. Ruth's private torment centred on Pilkington's harsh words – destroying his future, estranging him from his family, dividing the Tribe, lonely and unwanted. And the children – never belonging, outcast, unacceptable. Dear God! Yes, pray! Here you are in the house of God, pray to Him! And as she did so, a measure of peace came. *Love is patient, love is kind, never rude, never self-seeking, always protects, always trusts, always hopes, always perseveres.* She squeezed Seretse's fingers and answered his questioning gaze with a radiant smile that sent the blood coursing through his veins like spring rain through a thirsty, sandy streambed.

At last, they were face-to-face with the Bishop. But to their amazement, he cut Seretse's carefully rehearsed speech off after only a few moments. 'Yes, yes, I know all about it,' he said brusquely in his well-modulated Oxbridge accent. 'I understand you have caused quite a spot of bother for the Foreign Office. We can't have that, can we? I've instructed Patterson not to conduct the ceremony until he gets the go-ahead from me.'

Ruth was speechless.

'But, Sir,' said Seretse, 'there is no legal impediment whatsoever to our marriage.'

Unable to keep quiet, Muriel stepped forward and said in her forthright way: 'This is simply outrageous!'

The Bishop fixed them all with a stern gaze. He was an imposing man, tall and fleshy, clean-shaven, with heavy jowls and pouches under his eyes. 'My position is quite clear. You get permission from the Foreign Office and I'll give Patterson the go-ahead. Until then, no wedding. I've made my decision and I'm not prepared to argue with you.'

Putting on his gloves, he looked beyond them to his waiting car. 'But, surely,' began Ruth, her voice quavering with unshed tears, 'this has nothing to do . . .'

'I've told you my decision, young lady. It's final.'

'But I've nowhere to go! My parents have turned me out. Am I to go and live in sin?'

'That's a matter for your own conscience, Madam.' The bishop cleared his throat and turned away, striding towards his car. The little group stared after him, stunned.

They walked disconsolately back up the hill to St George's, hoping against hope that they might yet persuade Patterson to do the right thing. Their hopes were dashed when he came to the door, obviously distressed.

'I've just had a telephone call from the Bishop's secretary,' he said, before they could even greet him. 'He has given strict instructions that I'm not to conduct the service until the British government has given its permission.' Mrs Patterson hovered anxiously behind her husband in the hallway. What a dreadfully upsetting day it had been! She clucked sympathetically at the sight of Ruth's woebegone face. The poor girl! Pushing past her husband, she reached out to touch Ruth's arm in a gesture of compassion.

'My dear, why don't you stay here for the night. We can gladly find a bed for you. You look exhausted,' she said warmly, while her husband nodded in agreement.

'Yes, yes, that's the least we can do,' he agreed. But Ruth shook her head wearily. She couldn't stay there – the Pattersons' well-meaning pity would be unbearable. She couldn't go home and face her parents again, that was out of the question. She couldn't stay at the flat. Where was she to go? Swaying slightly on her feet from exhaustion, emotion and lack of nourishment, she felt Seretse's solid bulk just behind her.

'Come, Ruth,' he said gently. 'Let's go and get something to eat, and then we can decide what to do next.' Shaking hands with the vicar, he said:

'Thank you very much, sir, Mrs Patterson. You've been very kind. Good evening.'

In an attempt to cheer them all up, John insisted they all go for a drink. But after a short time it was evident that the day's sorrows refused to be drowned. Ruth was inconsolable, and Seretse had endured the long ordeal with Pilkington the night before and was worn out. So they decided to book Ruth into the Bayswater Hotel for the night, go to bed early and try to get a good night's sleep before deciding what to do next. Although none of them had an appetite, Muriel encouraged them to have something to eat. Seretse then took Ruth back to the flat to pack an overnight bag. White-faced with strain, she flung the turquoise pillbox hat into a corner of the living room. 'I will never wear that hat again,' she announced. The carnation buttonhole and the posy of roses drooped on the hall table.

Ruth and Seretse's opponents had managed to buy some time, but no-one knew what the couple would do next. Buchanan received a call from John Keith in the Colonial Office, who had come up with a scheme he hoped would scuttle any future plans they might make to marry hastily. He proposed to circulate a rumour to all registry offices that Seretse was already married. However, such a step would require the backing of the Commonwealth Relations Office and the Home Office. Fortunately for the couple, administrative red tape and slow-moving bureaucracy prevented this course of action from ever being carried out. The tireless Keith had also sent a message to Seretse, making an appointment to see him on the following Monday, in the hope that the extent of the opposition, revealed by the sequence of events on Saturday, might have convinced him to reconsider his decision to marry Ruth. Seretse agreed to the meeting but did not keep the appointment.

The resilience of youth overcame her feelings and Ruth slept well in her pretty rose chintz room at the Bayswater Hotel. Before going to bed she had carefully rewrapped her mother's garter in its flowered tissue paper and held it to her cheek for a moment. She had kept it a secret from Seretse, planning to let him discover it for himself after the wedding. Inhaling its lavender perfume, she summoned all her inner reserves of strength. She **would** marry Seretse, someday, somehow. He **would** find the garter, and he would make her laugh about all this – one day. She laid aside her wedding nightdress of fine cambric, delicate ribbons and frothy lace, and put on her old flannel nightie instead.

Back at the flat, Seretse sat smoking, and drinking a final nightcap to ensure sleep would come quickly. In his hand he held the plain gold band that John Zimmerman had given back to him earlier that evening. Putting a comforting arm around his shoulders, his old friend had urged him not to despair. 'They've certainly upped the stakes,' he had said, 'but it's only round one. They might have won this battle – but I'm confident you'll win the war. She's worth fighting for.'

Turning the ring between his fingers, Seretse watched it glinting in the lamp-light. He made a fist around it and slammed it into his open palm. Everyone had deserted him. Even Pilkington – whom he had thought to be so enlightened, so reasonable. Even he, it would appear, could not stomach the thought of a black man marrying a white girl.

His family and the Tribe had objections to the match – but what had that to do with the British government, or the church? Their interference in his private affairs was intolerable! He had certainly underestimated his uncle's influence with the LMS, and was amazed at the cosy relationship between church and government, both in Britain and Bechuanaland, that the day's events had starkly revealed. Tshekedi had only to crook his little finger and the entire hierarchy of the LMS leapt into action, while at the mere mention of the Foreign Office, the Bishop of London had obediently toed the line.

The memory of Ruth's bitter comment about being forced to live in sin brought a wry smile to his lips. So much for the church, and its double-sided morality! 'Bunch of damned Pharisees, the whole lot of them,' he muttered angrily. Their false piety made him sick! He and Ruth would show them. They'd get married in a registry office! That was the answer! Holding grimly to this hopeful solution, he went up to bed.

He fetched Ruth from the hotel early the next morning and they returned to the flat for breakfast. Seretse brewed a pot of tea while Ruth made toast and scrambled eggs.

'Smells good,' said Seretse, encircling her waist from behind as she stood before the tiny stove.

'Got your appetite back?"

'Absolutely. I'm not going to let those obnoxious men of the cloth rob me of my food!'

Over breakfast Seretse told Ruth about his idea of a civil ceremony. 'I know it's not what you would have wanted, love, but its obvious that the church is now working hand-in-glove with our enemies. I don't see any other way.'

Ruth reassured him that all she had ever wanted was to be married to him. 'The church has refused to grant us its blessing, so as far as I'm concerned they can all go and jump in the lake,' she said, tossing back her hair. 'The registry office will do just as well.'

'Right. I'll go down to Kensington and organise a licence first thing in the morning.'

'What if they won't allow you to do that?'

'There is absolutely no way anyone can legally stop us from getting married in a civil ceremony,' Seretse said. 'I am convinced of that – and John agrees with me.'

'Well, if you're sure . . .' said Ruth uncertainly.

'I am sure,' said Seretse, desperately hoping that his faith in the incorrupt-ibility of the British legal system was justified and that the Foreign Office did not have any more tricks up its collective sleeve.

'Well, you're the lawyer,' said Ruth, still rather dubious.

'That's right, I am. So you just leave the worrying up to me. I'll send you my bill in due course.'

They spent a quiet day together at Campden Hill Gardens, reading the Sunday papers, happy simply to be in each other's company. By the time Muriel came over for tea in the afternoon, they had partially recovered from the dreadful experience of the previous day. She was delighted with the news that they intended to go ahead with a civil ceremony as soon as possible.

'I wonder how long we'll have to wait to get an appointment?' mused Ruth.

'I shouldn't think more than a few days,' replied Seretse, licking his fingers appreciatively. Muriel had brought over a batch of her mother's special Sunday scones and some home-made strawberry jam – together with a loving message from Dorothy. She had been anxiously awaiting Muriel's return the previous evening, dying to hear every last detail about her younger daughter's wedding. Horrified at Muriel's tale of woe about the abortive marriage, she had immediately sat down and penned a note to Ruth and Seretse telling them how sorry she was to hear that the day had ended in such disaster. Touched by his future mother-in-law's sensitivity and grateful that her note had brought a welcome pink to Ruth's wan cheeks, he allowed himself a ray of hope that, one day, family reconciliation might be possible after all.

The next morning he was waiting at the local registry office when they opened for business and with no problem whatsoever secured a marriage licence and an appointment for 9 am on Wednesday, 29 September 1948. Hurrying around to the hotel he broke the good news to Ruth.

'But what am I going to wear?' Ruth cried, as soon as she had finished hugging Seretse for his glad tidings.

'What's wrong with your wedding outfit?' said Seretse, masculinely matter-of-fact.

'I can't wear that again! How could you even suggest it? Look what happened the first time I wore it!' Seretse shrugged. 'I know, I'll wear black!'

'Black? Black for your wedding?'

'Yes,' said Ruth, her jaw set in such a way that he decided not to argue. He had said it once and he'd say it again: he'd marry her even if she chose to wear sackcloth. Wearing black would be her own personal, dramatic, statement to anyone who cared to notice that she had been forced to have a registry-office ceremony when she was quite entitled to a church wedding. It would make her feel better.

Having done all he could think of to assist his friend Tshekedi and the people he genuinely loved, Pilkington sat down to summarise the situation as he saw it: '*She* (Ruth) *does not care at all either for the Tribe or for Seretse as far as his position with the Tribe is concerned. Actually, this surprises me because I believe that she is not altogether a bad kind of girl but that she started this business off as a kind of emotional reaction to the colour bar in Africa . . . she and her sister were in the habit of visiting the colonial students' hostel out of a genuine interest in coloured people and their affairs. I can well understand her falling in love with Seretse, particularly if she had some kind of resistance in her home environment. I think it quite likely that she felt she would overcome the Tribe's resistance by her own personality and that she would help him to lead his country onwards. But at the same time, her unwillingness to listen to representations from his country seemed to indicate the kind of selfishness which, however, is not at all unusual in young people on the verge of marriage.*' He was later to admit, with not inconsiderable embarrassment, that his opinion of Ruth had been way off the mark.

'I wish I could just close my eyes for a moment and it would be Wednesday,' moaned Ruth. 'I know it's only the day after tomorrow, but I feel as though I'm stuck in treacle.'

'Why don't we go away for the day tomorrow then?' suggested Seretse. 'The time would go faster.'

'Brilliant! And we shan't have to answer the phone or see anyone or sign for any more furious cables from your uncle. Where shall we go?'

'Seaside?'

Ruth laughed. 'I might have guessed,' she said. Coming from a land-locked, semidesert country, the sea held unending fascination for Seretse, and she loved his small-boy delight in it. 'Don't forget to bring your bucket and spade!'

'Right, Brighton, here we come!' said Seretse, with something of his usual enthusiasm.

Early the next morning they were on their way to Victoria Station to catch the train. They had a lovely day together, walking along the pebbled beach and climbing the hill for an exhilarating stride across the top of the South Downs in a brisk wind. The sea frothed angrily as it sought to ravage the shore below them, its ferocity matching that of the forces arrayed against their marriage.

Sharp at 9 the next morning they arrived at the Kensington Registry Office, nervous but outwardly calm, to find John and Muriel already waiting for them. True to her word, Ruth was dressed severely in black. They sat in the waiting room, all preoccupied with the unspoken question: Would they succeed in 'tying the knot'? Or would the Foreign Office manage to thwart them once again?

'So who's coming to the party tonight?' Muriel asked, determinedly gay.

'We've invited all the old Nutford House gang, of course,' replied Seretse, 'and a few other friends of mine.' After a few minutes of trying to keep a light-hearted conversation going, John and Muriel gave up and the four of them lapsed into uncomfortable silence. Ruth found that staying angry was the best way to keep calm, but all the same her handkerchief was in shreds and the ashtrays in the waiting room almost full to overflowing with cigarette stubs by the time the ceremony finally took place. As the clock ticked towards 9.30 they exchanged worried glances through the cigarette smoke that wreathed about them in the stuffy little room. By 9.40 they were frantic, convinced that somebody had managed to persuade the local officials to refuse to conduct the ceremony. Other couples had started to arrive by this time. They cast surprised glances at Ruth's smart black outfit as they took their places on the hard benches, tittering and quivering in anticipation.

At 10 am, when they had endured a wait of more than an hour, a junior official, looking rather embarrassed and ill at ease, came over to Seretse and asked him to come into the office – alone. Ruth felt sick. Seeing her face go white, Muriel hastened to her side, dispatching John in search of a glass of water.

'I can't bear it,' Ruth muttered. 'I simply cannot bear it. They've got to them, I just know it. What on earth are we going to do?' Muriel squeezed her hand, not knowing what to say. John arrived with some water and Ruth took a sip. Two minutes later the office door opened and Seretse marched out, a broad grin on his face. Ruth almost dropped her glass.

'Come along then,' he said cheerily, taking her arm to help her up. 'In we go.' His smile was infectious and the other occupants of the waiting room smiled too and murmured good wishes.

'What's going on?' hissed Ruth, her rage flaring again as the anguish of waiting diminished. 'We're getting married,' said Seretse, unable to stop grinning.

'Why the delay, for God's sake?'

'An administrative error. I'll tell you all about it later. Nothing to worry about.'

From then on, things moved quickly. They were ushered into a small room with drab curtains. A arrangement of paper flowers in a vase stood on the table. Seretse was oblivious to these details, but Ruth noticed them. A jaded government official rattled through the precious and beautiful words of the marriage ceremony: '*Love and cherish, honour and obey, until death us do part.*' John fumbled for the ring and put it into Seretse's outstretched hand. He placed it on Ruth's finger and the official pronounced them man and wife. They signed the register and in no time at all were out on the street again, laughing hysterically with relief, as Muriel and John threw rice and Seretse swung Ruth around in jubilation.

They went back to the flat for drinks, and collapsed – exhausted by the past few hours. They had done it! They had actually managed to outwit the formidable forces ranged against them, including several departments of the British government and the energetic Mr Keith! Not to mention those worthy gentlemen from the LMS, the Buchanan brothers and – by remote control – Seretse's uncle. Later that day, Seretse cabled him with the news that he had married Ruth and requested two air tickets to enable him to come home and introduce his new bride to the Tribe.

While Muriel made tea and John opened the champagne, Seretse gave them the inside story about the agonising delay. There had apparently been some confusion on the part of the officials.

'On the application form it asks for your father's occupation,' he explained, leaning back on the sofa and still grinning like a big Cheshire cat. 'So I'd put down 'Native Chief'. And those poor blokes were having a terrible time because they didn't know what it meant. *"Native Chief, good heavens no, old chap, not a clue." "Well, I mean, what do they do all day, old boy? Must do something, what?" "Let's ring up old Carstairs, I do believe he went to Africa once, as a youngster you know."* I quickly put them out of their misery by explaining that he was a public administrator, and then they were happy again.'

Once they had recovered somewhat from the tension, they began preparing for the party that evening. They had invited all their friends from Nutford House, and soon the tiny flat was packed with representatives from Africa, Asia and the Caribbean, all anxious to congratulate the popular pair. The flat resounded with laughter and music, cheers, toasts and hilarious speeches. Ruth and Seretse were considerably uplifted by the strength of the approval, support and encouragement from these young people, who all regarded their marriage as a triumph and willed it to succeed.

This helped to ameliorate the distress they had experienced when a telegram from Serowe arrived, obviously having crossed with the one sent that afternoon by Seretse. Tshekedi's anger burned through the words and Seretse sighed deeply as he read it, aware that the battle was by no means over. In fact, it had hardly begun.

The message read: '*You are apparently taking no notice of my strong objec-*

tions to your marrying an English girl. I ask you to pay attention to what Commonwealth Office advises you. Your obstinacy can only result in serious consequences for yourself. Have asked CO to arrange your immediate return. On no condition can we agree to your marrying an English girl.'

Crumpling it with one fierce clench of his hand, he thrust it into a desk drawer. This was his wedding day, and he was going to enjoy it. The carpet was rolled back and everyone applauded as he and Ruth did a soft-shoe shuffle to their favourite Ink Spots number *Can you look me in the eyes?*

At the end of the evening Ruth flopped down into an armchair and surveyed her little nest with dismay. It was littered with dirty glasses, empty bottles, overflowing ashtrays and dropped peanuts. But she was happy. She thought briefly, and with sadness, about her parents. She had not seen or spoken to them since leaving home the previous Saturday, but Muriel had kept them informed of all the developments. Both girls refused to give up hope of a reconciliation.

Seretse sat down beside her and took her hand. 'Penny for your thoughts, my darling wife?'

She smiled and leaned against him, a strong tingle running through her at the word 'wife'. 'I was just thinking how sad it is that we didn't get a chance to enjoy the words of the ceremony, or to say them properly to each other. That horrid little man rattled off the sacred vows like a grocery list. I can hardly even remember saying *I do*!'

He leapt to his feet, pulling her up with him. Lifting her chin, he looked her full in the face and, holding both her hands tightly in his, said with great deliberation, his voice husky with emotion: 'Do you, Mrs Ruth Khama, take me, Seretse Khama, as your lawful wedded husband, to have and to hold, to love and to cherish, for richer, for poorer, in sickness and in health, forsaking all others, until death us do part?'

Ruth's eyes filled. 'I do,' she said.

'Now it's your turn,' he prompted her.

She composed herself and faced him once again. 'Do you, Seretse Khama . . .' she began, her voice quavering. He nodded encouragement and squeezed her hands. She continued in a firm voice, savouring the meaning behind each word: '. . . take me, Ruth, to be your lawful wedded wife, to have and to hold, to love and to cherish, for richer, for poorer, in sickness and in health, forsaking all others, until death us do part?'

'I do, oh, yes I do, I most certainly do,' he said, swinging her off her feet and whirling her round, shouting 'I do, I do!'

'Stop! I'm getting dizzy,' she cried, shaking with laughter.

'You may now kiss the bride,' Seretse pronounced in a pompous voice, giving his best imitation of a plummy British accent. They collapsed in a heap on the sofa, and he proceeded to do just that. 'Oh, Seretse,' said Ruth joyously several minutes later, her arms still entwined around his neck, 'we're going to have such fun being married!'

On the previous Monday, Keith had told Buchanan that Seretse had failed to keep their appointment, and Buchanan had immediately written to Seretse requesting that he contact him urgently. Seretse only did so after the civil marriage ceremony had taken place – his irrepressible wit showing itself in his comment: *Have married Ruth, do you still want to see me?*

The news that they had wed spread with alacrity, and the telegraph wires between England and Africa were humming once again as cables flew to and fro. The energetic Buchanan brothers cabled everyone they could possibly think of. Doom and gloom greeted the news everywhere. The comments ranged from Sir Reginald Copeland's blunt opinion: '*It will be a miracle if the marriage turns out happily in the end for either of them or for their children. It is a real tragedy, or so it seems,*' to that of the LMS director Ronald Orchard, who said bleakly: '*In future, when the realities of life make themselves apparent to Seretse he will not say that he got where he is for lack of suitable advice. I see most troublous times ahead of me as far as the Tribe is concerned, and with regard to Seretse a very gloomy future indeed.*'

The postmaster in Serowe was for some time unable to find anyone brave enough to deliver the news of his nephew's marriage to Tshekedi. When he finally did receive the news, Tshekedi was aghast. His rage was directed primarily at the British, whom he regarded as being all-powerful. His disappointment in what he considered to be their lack of serious attention to this disaster knew no bounds. Seretse was right there, in England. Surely there must have been something they could have done to prevent him from marrying Ruth?

Despite the huge volume of telegraphic correspondence between himself and his team in England, he was not satisfied that no stone had been left unturned in the campaign against his recalcitrant nephew. He fumed with frustration at his powerlessness, and the great distance between England and Serowe. But even now, with the marriage a legal fact in Britain, he was undaunted in his rock-like determination to save the Tribe from disaster. He telegraphed Seretse: '*Formal signing of document in England does not constitute your marriage. As far as we are concerned no marriage exists. Apparently you took my advice for a threat. We accept nothing short of dissolution of that marriage. Our decision firm, welfare of Tribe paramount in this case.*'

The harsh, dismissive tone of this cable cut Seretse to the quick and finally severed any hope he may have been harbouring that his uncle would eventually come round to accepting his marriage. He realised, painfully, that his uncle was in this respect his archenemy. He replied coldly: '*Dissolution unacceptable.*' However, his diplomatic instincts and his genuine love for his people asserted themselves and he added: '*Tribe and you important to me. Suspension of allowance being felt. Suggest passage for two.*'

Seretse realised that he could no longer avoid going home to Serowe to face the Tribe himself, and he determined to use his persuasive talents to bring them around to his way of thinking. He was concerned, however, that if he went out to Serowe alone, the British might find some way of stopping him from returning to England, or prevent Ruth from coming out to join him. He was reluctant to risk being separated from her, and therefore delayed the trip as long as possible.

Tshekedi was thinking along exactly these lines – and had, in fact, already encouraged Buchanan to make every effort to persuade the British to deny Ruth a passport. He still had the full support of the Bamangwato, who were adamant that they wanted their Chief to return but that they did not want his white wife to accompany him. The British, however, meticulous as ever, were unable to find legal grounds on which to prevent Ruth from travelling to Bechuanaland. In the absence of any convenient legal instruments, they told Tshekedi their hands were tied. Once again, he felt the full weight of the burden falling on his shoulders and damned them for their insistence upon legal niceties. His only remaining hold over Seretse was money, and he used that to good effect, ensuring the couple could not afford two tickets to Africa. This squeeze of the purse strings was indeed an effective tool which forced Seretse to go and see John Keith. He told Keith he would not be reduced to living off Ruth's savings as it was a man's duty to support his wife, and threatened to sue his uncle for some of the huge value of his father's cattle herds.

Like many desperate fathers before him, Tshekedi then resorted to using money in an attempt to persuade Ruth to divorce Seretse and forget all about him. His unwilling accomplice in this plan was John Buchanan, who, to his credit, regarded these latest instructions with extreme distaste. To maintain open lines of communication with Seretse at all costs, he had invited the newlyweds to lunch.

When he opened the door to admit them to his home, he found Ruth laughing up into Seretse's face as they enjoyed a joke on his doorstep. He was struck by the chemistry that was so evident between them. They greeted him warmly, and it was plain that they bore no grudge against him personally for his role in attempting to prevent their marriage. This disarming attitude was to characterise much of Ruth and Seretse's behaviour towards those who tried to do them harm. Against it there was no defence.

As the luncheon progressed, Buchanan became convinced that it would be in the worst possible taste even to mention Tshekedi's proposal of 'buying her off'. Having made his decision, he relaxed and began to enjoy their company. They all skirted the main issue until Seretse took the bull by the horns and asked Buchanan if he thought there was any hope of his uncle being reconciled to the fact of their marriage.

Buchanan studied the tablecloth for a moment before looking directly at Seretse. 'I'm afraid not,' he said matter-of-factly. 'My brother tells me he has never seen your uncle so distressed in the more than 20 years he has known him. Not even when he was hauled before Admiral Evans and his 200 marines, with the navy's cannons pointed at him.'

'And what about my allowance?' asked Seretse. 'He has put me in a very embarrassing situation by withdrawing it, you know.'

'Yes, I quite understand that,' said Buchanan, 'but I'm afraid I don't have good news for you on that score either.'

Seretse reiterated what he had said to John Keith about suing his uncle, adding regretfully: 'I'm extremely loath to take this route, but it seems as though my uncle hasn't left me any other option.'

'It would certainly be a most regrettable course of action to follow,' agreed Buchanan.

They took their leave amicably, and Buchanan was left with an unhappy sense of remorse that he had become embroiled in this messy business. He sat down to write to Douglas in Cape Town, spending considerable time and effort in trying to communicate what he had learned about the young couple that day, in the vain hope that his brother might be able to deflect the regent's wrath in some way.

Douglas, however, was firmly in Tshekedi's camp, and the two men were determined that Seretse must return to Serowe as soon as possible. They agreed that the Tribe would never accept an heir to the throne who was not fully *Mongwato*. The prejudice against so-called 'Coloureds' was extremely strong among black and white peoples in southern Africa, and people of mixed blood were regarded as being inferior to both races.

Now that Seretse had gone ahead and married Ruth in outright defiance of the express will of his uncle and his Tribe, Buchanan could see no solution to the problem other than divorce. He, together with Tshekedi and the royal uncles, sincerely believed that the cleanest way to do this would be for Seretse to come out to Serowe, and then simply not return to England – thus making it possible to arrange a divorce on the grounds of desertion. He believed the cost of such an action, together with any costs of providing for Ruth's subsequent maintenance, would be willingly paid by the Tribe if they could thereby resolve the catastrophe. This strategy, however, failed to take into account either Ruth's true character nor the depth of her and Seretse's love for each other and their resolve not to be separated.

With his characteristic bull-headed approach, Tshekedi embarked on a series of urgent meetings with his fellow councillors and groups of tribesmen. They all agreed with him that Seretse had been extremely irresponsible in marrying Ruth, and Tshekedi was encouraged by the fact that the Tribe as a whole stood solidly behind him. From this perceived position of strength, he sent a telegram to Buchanan in Cape Town: '*From telegrams and a letter so far received I am convinced that Seretse is not alive to this situation. He appears to have convinced himself that, the marriage being accomplished, everybody will acquiesce, but in this he is wrong . . . you have known me long enough to believe that I could not easily let the welfare of the Tribe go and their status, which I have suffered so much to maintain, just be blown to pieces by a single thoughtless action of my nephew. You know too how I had built high hopes on this lad.*'

His position with the Tribe was further strengthened when he made the welcome announcement that, at last, Seretse would soon be on his way to Serowe to explain himself. Tshekedi was particularly gratified to be able to say that the white woman would be staying behind in London.

As with every other titbit of news about their young Chief since the eruption of the crisis, this information was immediately relayed throughout the village and further afield to the most remote cattle posts. Throughout October, concerned tribesmen had been travelling long distances in the extreme heat to the *kgotla* ground where they heard the latest developments. Women were customarily not admitted to the *kgotla* – but with age-old wifely skill they managed to keep themselves just as well-informed as the men. After all, the future of the Tribe was their future too.

Ruth and Seretse were having breakfast one morning when the telephone rang. A male voice, identifying itself as a reporter with the *Daily Mirror*, congratulated Seretse on his recent marriage and requested an interview. Seretse was extremely reluctant, but the reporter was sympathetic, seemed to know an awful lot about the situation, and persuaded him to say a few words.

Ruth was horrified. 'I don't want us in the papers,' she said, her innate British reserve coming to the fore.

'They've got most of the information already,' said Seretse. 'There's nothing we can do to stop them publishing their version, so we might as well co-operate and make sure they've got their facts right.'

Early the next morning, October 16th, they walked down to the corner newsagent, anxious to see what had been published. While they were still some distance away, Ruth stopped in her tracks and gasped. The banner headline on the billboard in front of the little shop was clearly visible: RULER-TO-BE WEDS OFFICE GIRL.

'Oh, no, Seretse,' she exclaimed. 'They've made a big thing out of it.' They quickened their steps.

'Good morning,' said the cheery man behind the counter, looking up. As soon as he saw them his expression changed to one of shock. 'Why, you're the two with your picture in the *Mirror* today!' he exclaimed, reaching for a copy of the newspaper. Unfolding it on the counter before them, he pointed a stubby finger at the centre of the front page. There they were – slightly fuzzy, but definitely identifiable. He reached over and patted Ruth's hand, 'Congratulations, luv,' he said.

Seretse grinned at him, and paid for the paper.

They walked quickly back to their flat to devour the contents. Under the headline: '*Ruler-to-be weds office girl, is called home to explain*' it was reported that the heir to the African kingdom of Bechuanaland had secretly married an English girl, and had been ordered by his uncle to return home for talks of grave importance.

'Well, they seem to have the facts right. We should be grateful for that,' said Seretse.

'Oh, how can you say that?' cried Ruth, 'I absolutely hate it! Having our personal lives dragged out in the open like this for every Tom, Dick and Harry to read about! It's simply awful. And look at this,' she slapped the paper with her hand, 'they say I'm a typist. I can't even type!'

The telephone started ringing. The newshounds of Fleet Street knew a good story when they saw one, and this was definitely a very good story. Dealing with the press was a new experience for Seretse. He tried to respond courteously to each new caller, answering the questions put to him briefly, but after the fifth or sixth call, even his considerable patience was wearing thin. Eventually, in desperation, he left the telephone off the hook.

This was just the beginning. The following morning's *Daily Mail* carried its own version of the story under the headline: '*White bride causes tribal crisis*'. And from then on the couple had no peace. As the story gained momentum, bringing to the fore the whole issue of people of colour and initiating serious public debate on cross-cultural marriage, the world's media climbed on the bandwagon. Headlines about the black and white couple, together with an increasing selection of photographs, were almost daily fare from New Delhi to New York, and from Edinburgh to Cape Town. In South Africa the press predictably vilified such a flagrant example of interracial togetherness.

'I can't stand it any more,' said Ruth, a few days later. The attention from the press had reached a stage where they were virtually prisoners in their flat. Journalists and photographers camped outside for days on end, vying with each other for the best photograph of the couple and constantly pestering them for more information.

'Don't worry. They'll get tired of us before long and leave us alone. Try to ignore them.'

'Ignore them! How can I ignore them when I can't even move from one room to another without flashlights popping outside the windows? And I don't dare go outside without you, because they pounce on me.' She huddled in an armchair as far from the window as possible.

'I know it's awful, darling. But honestly, the only thing we can do is ignore them. We can't let them make our life a misery.'

'They've already made our life a misery!' she snapped. 'Can't you do something about them? Get the police to chase them away!'

'I'm afraid I can't. It's a free country. As long as they're not actually trespassing, there's nothing we can do.'

It was a problem which was to dog their life together for years to come as their story dominated the headlines in newspapers across the board, from gutter tabloids to quality broadsheets. Despite numerous factual errors in the yards of words written and printed about them, the press, by and large, were sympathetic to the couple. As the battle grew fiercer, Ruth would come to appreciate that the reports published had a profound and positive effect on public opinion and, consequently, government policy. But she never lost her distaste for this invasion of her privacy, and considered it a very high price to pay for public support.

One afternoon in the middle of October Seretse returned home from a meeting with John Keith and told Ruth he had been assured the authorities could not stop him coming back to Britain whenever he wanted to. With his arms round her, he said: 'I'll have to go, darling, and I'm afraid I'll have to go alone.'

Ruth knew his uncle had only sent a single ticket for Seretse to fly from Heathrow to the airport in Johannesburg. The price was a staggering £50. They couldn't afford a ticket for her, and perhaps, at this stage, it was best he went alone. While her head accepted this, her heart cried out in dismay at the thought of being parted from him so soon. She clung to him for a few moments, and then squared her shoulders and said: 'Well, we'd better pack your bag then, hadn't we?'

'That's my girl,' said Seretse, amazed as always by her strength of character in the face of difficult circumstances.

'What shall I do about these reporters when you're gone?' asked Ruth anxiously the next morning.

'Don't worry,' said Seretse, gripping her shoulder. 'I'll speak to them before I leave and tell them exactly what's going on and then I'm sure they'll leave you alone.'

That afternoon he went out on to the front steps of the flat and spoke to the gathered press. He told them he would be leaving shortly for Serowe to discuss the whole matter of his marriage with his uncle, the regent, and the Tribe's councillors. 'They may think differently about wanting me as Chief now that I have a white wife. But whatever happens, I will either be coming back to London for Ruth or sending for her,' he said.

This story hit the papers the next day, October 16th, alerting the South African press to Seretse's imminent arrival. Ruth was appalled when she read the headlines: '*Tribal chief will fight for me – ex-office girl*' (*Daily Mirror*, 22 October 1948); '*Wedding to typist starts throne crisis*' (*Daily Express*, 25 October); '*English wife must go – Tribe*' (*The Star*, 29 October); '*Typist has caused constitutional crisis*' (Johannesburg *Sunday Times*, 31 October).

6
The Kgotla

WHEN THE GRUELLING, BUMPY, 23-HOUR FLIGHT IN THE SOUTH AFRICAN Airways DC4 Skymaster from Heathrow via Tripoli in Libya, Khartoum in Sudan and Nairobi in Kenya finally touched down in Johannesburg, Seretse once more faced a barrage of flashlights and questioning reporters. Pushing past them, he was astonished but delighted to see the small, dumpy figure of his beloved half-sister, Naledi, there to greet him.

'Naledi! Why aren't you at school? What are you doing, coming here to meet me like this?'

'I have been so worried about you,' she said tearfully. 'I just had to come and meet you. School can wait.'

The coaches on the train between Johannesburg and Palapye on the eastern border of Bechuanaland were segregated. Those furthest from the steam locomotive were reserved for whites only, and furnished with sleeper bunks, complete with sheets, blankets and pillows, and washing facilities. A well-appointed dining car served four-course meals en route. The remaining carriages, offering only hard seats and a few smelly toilets, were for 'non-whites'. Naledi and Seretse, despite their royal status in Bechuanaland, were simply non-white when in South Africa. They boarded the train at lunch-time in Johannesburg, having bought something to eat on the journey from a grimy kiosk at the station. By this time Seretse was so tired that despite the discomfort of the bench on which he sat he fell into a deep sleep, slumped against Naledi's generous shoulder.

Arriving in Palapye the following morning, 25 October 1948, they were met by an emissary from Tshekedi who drove them to Serowe along the 32 miles of rutted dirt road. As they progressed through the bone-dry scrub, Seretse smelled the familiar dusty earth and felt the hot wind on his face. Home! How he loved the sight, feel and smell of it. He had been away in England for three years and he realised just how much he had missed his homeland. October in Bechuanaland is drought-stricken. But he would far rather have this searing dry heat and this shimmering vista of sand and scrub, than the cold, wet – though verdant – pastures of England. Looking up at the sky, almost white with heat at this time of the day and year, he wished fervently that Ruth were beside him. How he longed to show it all to her, to share with her his joy in it and to see it afresh through her eyes. He had no doubt that she would grow to love it the way he did.

He dragged his thoughts back to the present. He had been pleased to hear from Naledi that the young men of his age were behind him, even though they had not been able to say or do anything positive to support him publicly, because Tshekedi and the older men were so enraged. Apparently, tensions were running extremely high. The Bamangwato custom of grouping together men of similar age into a 'regiment' was effective in that it created a sort of brotherhood in each generation, ensuring tribal bonding and loyalty.

Formerly military units, these regiments had, during King Khama's long, peaceful reign, been increasingly called upon to perform a variety of public works. The young men of Seretse's regiment were part of a new generation – the first fruits of long years of effort by dedicated missionaries.

Seretse was very close to his cousin, Goareng Mosinyi, who had been his constant companion in childhood and at school, and who now worked in Tshekedi's office. They had kept in touch and Mosinyi had been the first to whom Seretse had cabled news of his marriage, in a triumphant one-word telegram: '*Married*'. He looked forward to hearing his cousin's analysis of the situation.

His thoughts were interrupted by the honking of the car's horn as it swung around the circular drive, skirting the *kgotla* ground and leading up to the chief's large tin-roofed bungalow with its spacious, shady verandahs. He wiped his dusty face with a handkerchief and climbed out to face his uncle, who stood on the highly polished stoep, his hands in his pockets. In spite of the increasingly unpleasant tone of the telegrams flying between them, Seretse had been prepared to embrace him. But his hands fell to his sides when he saw the stony expression on Tshekedi's face. His uncle was behaving as though he was a total stranger.

'I greet you, uncle,' he finally managed to say formally in Setswana, his mother tongue.

'I greet you, nephew,' replied his uncle, and turned on his heel to enter the house, obviously expecting Seretse to follow him. With a grimace at Naledi, whose eyes had filled with tears at this open display of hostility, Seretse did so.

In the main living room, once his vision had adjusted from the brilliant sunshine to the cool gloom, Seretse saw the chiefs of the two other major tribes, both old friends of Tshekedi's, who together with the Bamangwato comprised the Bechuanaland Protectorate.

'I greet you, Chief Kgari of the Bakwena, Chief Bathoen of the Bangwaketse,' he said formally, bowing slightly to each in turn. These two men fully endorsed Tshekedi's uncompromising stance with regard to the marriage and their greeting was equally cold. The niceties demanded by tribal custom as well as common courtesy were dispensed with, and they immediately launched into a bitter attack on Seretse, which continued unabated for several hours. They bombarded him with arguments against his marriage to the white woman. They railed against him for his selfish disregard of tribal custom and the time-honoured traditions of his people. Much of the harangue was similar to Pilkington's – only this time in Setswana – and with more emphasis on his responsibilities as *kgosi*. They accused him of risking the destruction of the Tribe's identity.

What distressed Seretse more than anything was the way they all dismissed his marriage.

'A piece of paper from a British Registry Office is not a wedding as far as we are concerned,' they said. 'What do we know of this woman and her family? Who are her parents? And what does she know about the duties of a royal wife?' The questions were fired at him but he was never given an opportunity to reply. On and on it went, endless repetitions and accusations, until he thought his head would split.

Then his uncle started on the issue of South Africa, about how Seretse's foolish marriage had given the Boers a perfect excuse to march in and take over the country, as they had long wanted to do – thus destroying all that King Khama and Tshekedi himself had worked for over the past six decades. 'Do you think the British are going to defend us against the Boers?' he asked, throwing his hands into the air in despair. 'Of course not!'

Eventually, exhausted, Seretse fell into bed, hardly noticing the panoramic night sky with its millions of brilliant stars which had always enchanted him in the past, as he lay in bed waiting for sleep's embrace. He was overwhelmed by loneliness. He had been an orphan since his mother had died when he was nine. Since then Tshekedi had been the mainstay of his life – a close, loving, supportive parent. The force of Tshekedi's rage had been as violent as a physical assault, leaving him mentally and emotionally battered. Turning his face to the pillow, he wept as he had not done since his beloved grandmother had died when he was 13. Ruth was all he had now. He must fight for her with every ounce of his strength. Like a wounded buffalo, kicked out of the herd, he would fight – to the death if necessary.

At breakfast the next morning, taken just after dawn while the air retained a little of the night's coolness, the verbal attack on Seretse continued. It was obvious that his uncle was determined to beat him into submission through endless argument. By evening Seretse could take it no more. He excused himself politely, gathered his belongings and moved out of his uncle's house, which had been his home for as long as he could remember. He was determined to find somewhere else to stay. As he carried his bag down the road, he saw his uncle Serogola approaching.

'Come and stay with me, Seretse,' said Serogola. As they walked through the dusty paths to his house, he told Seretse that he disapproved of Tshekedi having presented his personal views to the British authorities as being those of the Tribe. Seretse almost wept with surprise and gratitude to have found an ally at last.

He settled into his new lodgings with profound relief – free at last from the oppressive atmosphere of his uncle's home. With the windows open to catch every possible breath of the cool night air, he began the first of many letters to Ruth. Her beloved face filled his mind as he struggled to set down in logical sequence the events of the day.

Ruth was not having an easy time of it either. The press continued to hound her for comments and photographs. She had become quite a recluse, afraid to go out in case they pounced on her, and deeply resentful of their persistent pursuit and invasion of her privacy. Muriel moved into the flat to keep her company, and always brought in the daily newspapers and other supplies. Several of the Nutford House students also called whenever they could. Shielding her from the press, they took her down to the local for a drink and a change of scenery. Letters from Seretse began to arrive daily, keeping her fully in the picture about all that was happening in Serowe and assuring her of his love. She spent many hours replying to them.

Unmoved by his nephew's anguish, and as yet unaware of the power of his love for his new wife, Tshekedi was intent upon implementing the strategy he had discussed with Buchanan – to keep Seretse away from Ruth until he came to his senses. For two weeks, he was kept waiting, in the hope that the familiar sights and sounds of Serowe would break him down.

Finally, on 13 November, the leading elders took their places at the royal *kgotla* ground in the heart of Serowe. Here Seretse was greeted by the Tribe's nobility – a gathering of elderly men, clothed in an assortment of British uniforms, suits, and other western style dress, complete with trilby hats, pith helmets and cloth caps. Most of them sat on small, hand-carved wooden stools or folding deckchairs. From time to time, the whole assembly moved – escaping from the relentless sun into the shifting shadows cast by the tall *makala* trees.

As Seretse sat facing the assembled crowd, he remembered how he had sat as a young man, home on school holidays, alongside his uncle, listening to him try the cases brought before him. And now he himself was the accused.

As Tshekedi got to his feet, the hubbub of conversation subsided. He welcomed them formally, and outlined the crisis facing the Tribe. One after another, the elders took their turn at condemning Seretse for having married without their permission. The same condemnatory phrases were repeated over and over again: he was the Chief; he should have known better; his behaviour was deplorable; he had risked the welfare of the Tribe for his own selfish interests; they could not accept a white Queen because that would mean the future *kgosi* would be Coloured – and that was totally unacceptable. He was the rightful heir to the throne of the Bamangwato, they told him yet again, and in him the royal line of Khama was to continue to rule over them. As such, he was bound by the age-old rules of their society.

Seretse felt he would go mad with frustration. As he scanned the crowd, his eyes hidden from the glare by a pair of dark glasses, he noticed the faces of a few members of his age regiment, who had assured him of their support. Although they had been initially shocked, they welcomed Seretse's marriage to a white woman as a statement of freedom – and were pleased at the opportunity to cock a snook at the South Africans. Education had opened their minds to new ideas and new ways. They were flexible, receptive to change and painfully aware of the vicious repression of blacks in South Africa. They were, however, vastly outnumbered by the older men, most of whom had never been to South Africa.

Tshekedi played what he considered to be a trump card when he told the gathering that if they did not agree with the decisions that he felt needed to be made he would leave them and go and live with another tribe. Seretse was surprised to hear his uncle make such a categorical statement. This was the first time mention had been made of such a possibility, and the threat alarmed him. When at last he was given permission to speak, he emphasised that he did not want to lose either his uncle or his wife.

For much of the time he was forced to sit in silence, but whenever there was an opportunity for him to speak he was unwavering in his response: 'I will not give up Ruth.'

As she read his letter describing that day which reached her more than a week later, Ruth closed her eyes, and from Seretse's vivid descriptions, could almost visualise the royal *kgotla* ground. It was the Tribe's principal meeting place and judicial court, where the *kgosi* sat in judgment. Its oval expanse of sandy floor, roughly half the size of a soccer field, was demarcated by large, white painted stones. Not a weed, not a blade of grass was allowed to grow there. It was regularly swept bare of every leaf by the women, bending low over their reed brooms, whose presence there was otherwise forbidden. Trampled by thousands of feet over the decades, the *kgotla* was where the men of the Bamangwato sought justice for wrongs done to them, met with the colonial authorities, and made momentous decisions concerning the welfare of the Tribe – such as how many cattle were to be sold and where the missionaries were to be allowed to build their schools.

The *kgotla* was the very soul of the Tribe – and had been so for as long as anyone could remember. It was the ancient, tribal equivalent of government for the people, of the people, by the people – the traditional forerunner of modern democracy on a village scale. Based on the fundamental premise of freedom of expression, the *kgotla* system provided an opportunity to every male member of the community to participate in the laws and government of the day. In a time when administration was conducted man-to-man, by means of verbal dialogue, reasoning and consultation, the *kgotla* system provided for every man in society to have his say. A shepherd boy could talk to a headman. School learning and academic qualifications were irrelevant. Each man was individually dignified by the human intelligence granted by God. The universe, creation and the community each had its own vague, vast and indefinable laws – and everyone knew the rules instinctively. King Khama had added to these laws the Ten Commandments of his beloved Bible, but they were very similar to those the Tribe had always known were right –

thou shalt not kill, thou shalt not covet thy neighbour's wife nor his cattle, honour thy father and mother, etc.

Above all, the world of the *kgotla* was a world of human dignity and wisdom. Good and evil were clearly defined and perceived, and lay at the heart of every man. Truth was clearly truth. It was always there somewhere – at the root of every matter. The chiefs, headmen and councillors who presided at the *kgotla* had but to unravel the twisted thread of truth in every case, and justice would result. It was a peaceful system of government.

Poring over the pages of Seretse's letters, Ruth read of the bitter exchanges that had taken place in this ancient, sacred place, and longed to be there to comfort and strengthen him. Her letters, filled as they were with love and encouragement, warmed him through the chilly desert nights when he sat alone with his thoughts, faithfully recording each day's proceedings for her to share.

He told her how the local LMS missionary, Rev Alan Seager, had been commandeered by Tshekedi to take notes. Ruth bit her lip as she read how their marriage was denounced by Chief Bathoen who accused Seretse of being a coward, saying: 'He says he loves his people as well as his wife but nobody can cast fire among people he loves.'

She felt full of pride as she read how, out of respect for his Tribe, he had stood up to speak like a commoner, instead of remaining seated in the tradition of royalty.

Seretse told the *kgotla* meeting that he was well aware of the Tribe's customs relating to marriage. Even commoners did not marry without their father's approval. He knew full well that, as their Chief, he should have secured the permission of the entire Tribe before marrying anybody. Humbly, he asked their forgiveness for not having followed these time-worn customs. He told them that, despite all that had happened, he still wanted to be their Chief. But they would have to accept him and his wife. He appealed to precedent, outlining what everyone knew very well – that his grandfather, Khama the

Great, and his father, Sekgoma, had both married without the Tribe's consent, yet this had not prevented them from ruling the Tribe. The uncles had agreed that indeed this had been so, but had reminded Seretse in turn that on both occasions this had resulted in disruption and bloodshed. Surely, this time, such trauma should be averted?

Through Seretse's letters, the saga taking place in Serowe unfolded day by day for Ruth like an exciting story – only this was her life, her future, that was being debated. She read with alarm how, on the third day of the *kgotla*, some of the tribesmen had advocated imprisoning Seretse in the village and preventing her from coming there. That, they reasoned, would put an end to this matter once and for all. To her relief, Seretse reported that at this point Tshekedi had said he had already assured the British that no move would be made to prevent Seretse from returning to England if he so wished. She laughed in spite of herself, when she read Seretse's extravagant comments that they could say what they liked but he would walk through the desert and swim across the Atlantic if necessary – but nothing was going to keep him from coming back to her.

She read on, about how Tshekedi had unfairly used his position as chairman to prevent some people speaking, when it was the fundamental law of the *kgotla* that everyone should be allowed to have his say. Whenever a younger man had stood to speak in defence of Seretse or to support him in any way, Tshekedi had intervened, dismissing them as being too young and inexperienced to be able to speak with any relevance on so weighty a matter.

Seretse had railed against this curtailing of freedom of speech, and had struck back with bitter accusations that Tshekedi was attempting to break down support for his marriage using intimidatory methods that bore a close resemblance to those of the Nazis. This insinuation bitterly wounded the regent, as Tshekedi prided himself on being an Empire patriot and had placed hundreds of the Bamangwato's finest young men at the disposal of the British to help fight the Nazi scourge.

The meeting seemed unable, or unwilling, to state with any finality that they did not want Seretse to be Chief. The discussion went round and round without approaching any sort of conclusion – they wanted him to be Chief, but not with his wife.

It was left to Tshekedi, as chairman, to summarise the deliberations. He gave a rambling monologue in which the findings of the meeting were entangled with his own emotions. A total of 85 men had spoken during the five-day meeting, all but seven of them stating that they wanted Seretse as *kgosi* but that they did not want his English wife. None of these men had been under 40 years of age. The *kgotla* resolved that all possible steps should be taken to prevent Seretse's wife from entering the land. Tshekedi thanked the other Chiefs for 'coming to put water on Bamangwato fire' and the British for 'bothering' to send the District Commissioner to observe the deliberations of the tribal parliament.

Ruth laughed at Seretse's wry account of how the District Commissioner, who had been asked to close the meeting formally, did so with an announcement that the heir to the British throne, Charles, had just been born in London. He had then turned to Seretse and said: 'You have heard your fathers speaking to you, do not disregard them.'

There was tension in the village that evening, as the families of the Tribe gathered about their cooking fires to discuss the proceedings of the past five days. Everything was so inconclusive. What had they actually decided? Called upon by their women to summarise and explain things, the men found themselves in a quandary. A vague consensus began to emerge that, maybe, the all-powerful Tshekedi was up to something. They had discussed *ad nauseum* the issue of Seretse's marriage – but what was actually at stake here? Was it the marriage, or was it the chieftainship? Was the marriage being used as an excuse to disinherit the rightful *kgosi*? And, if so, did they really want to be a part of that? Hadn't their blood been stirred when the young heir apparent had stood in their midst, the grandson of Khama himself, and spoken to them in such ringing tones? He was indeed the rightful Chief. And yet, was anyone brave enough to oppose Tshekedi, who, after his long years as regent, perhaps coveted the chieftainship for himself?

As they debated, their young prince was seated beside a fire with his cousins and other members of his age regiment. They were all furious at the way in which Tshekedi had outmanoeuvred them – effectively rendering them voiceless. They argued vigorously across the flames, thumping their fists on the bare ground for emphasis.

'We have to hold another *kgotla*,' declared Goareng. 'The matter can't be left like this. There are many who support you, Seretse, believe me. But we could not speak.'

Following their advice, Seretse decided he had to stay on in Serowe. He wrote to Ruth that he was miserable at being separated from her, but it would be foolish to leave now. They had already been apart for longer than they had been married and the separation was taking its toll, but the daily correspondence was a lifeline for both of them.

The weeks passed drearily for Ruth, living for the postman's daily delivery and Muriel's arrival with the newspapers. Together, the sisters would scan them for any mention of goings-on in Serowe. Often there were a few inches of copy sent through by one of the South African-based stringers or syndicated from papers within the Union. But the accounts were brief and often so at variance with Seretse's letters that Ruth wondered whether she was reading about the same event.

One afternoon she heard Muriel's coded tap at the front door and ran to let her sister in. To her surprise and delight her mother stood beside Muriel on the doorstep.

'Mother! Oh, Mother!' she exclaimed, 'I can't believe it!'

'But you're looking so pale, darling!' said Dorothy, holding her at arm's length and scanning her face. 'Come and sit down and tell me all about it.'

While Muriel made the tea, Dorothy told Ruth that George had gone away on a business trip.

'I asked him if he would mind if I visited you while he was away,' she said, 'and he said no! He left this morning – so here I am!'

Ruth sat holding her mother's hand. The weeks of anxious waiting and sleepless nights had sapped her strength and the comforting presence of her mother was just what she needed.

'It's all right,' said Dorothy, 'I'm here now. And your father won't part us again – I'm sure of it.'

In Serowe, the hours dragged for Seretse too, but the days brought increasing hope as his friends related how the Tribe's suspicion of Tshekedi's lust for the chieftainship was growing daily. Tshekedi inadvertently fuelled these suspicions by holding a number of private meetings with groups of Bamangwato at which he harangued them about the dangers of accepting a white queen. In his fervour to preserve the tribal customs and values of his people, the regent overdid it. His threats about the disintegration of the Tribe and the loss of its identity began to fall on deaf ears. He was, it seemed, out of tune with the people's real desires and gut feelings. Like so many rulers before him, in clinging to the past, he was in danger of losing the future. The two men stayed out of each other's way as much as possible, but whenever they met, acrimonious discussions erupted. It was finally agreed that another *kgotla* was necessary and this was scheduled for December 28th.

Ruth was devastated to receive Seretse's loving and apologetic letter informing her that it would not be possible for them to spend their first Christmas together. She had just finished reading it when Muriel arrived.

'Look, Muriel!' she said, holding out the letter. 'Look what he says! Our first Christmas – and we're going to be six thousand miles apart!'

'It's the most awful bad luck,' said Muriel, 'I can't believe it's taking them so long to decide. What on earth have they been doing all this time? He's been gone for weeks!'

'Eight weeks tomorrow,' said Ruth. She sat at the kitchen table while Muriel put the kettle on.

'I'm sure he's missing you terribly,'

'Of course he is. His letter is so sweet! He says . . .' she riffled through the pages of flimsy airmail paper covered with Seretse's firm writing, 'here it is . . . he says *"I'd rather be with you in the sleet, snow, wind and darkness than without you in this sunny paradise where the birds are singing and the grass whispers your name every time the breeze blows."'*

They giggled at Seretse's extravagant turn of phrase. 'He does write beautifully,' said Muriel, sipping her tea. 'Does he say when he hopes to be back?'

'Yes, thank heavens. He has promised to come back early in the New Year as soon as this other meeting is over. I can't wait.'

Muriel nodded in sympathy. Ruth had been having an awful time. Rumours that she was already pregnant when they got married had been doing the rounds, and various sections of the press had portrayed her as a shallow and flighty young creature jeopardising the welfare of a foreign people for the passing whim of being a queen, and it seemed to be rubbing off on the family. Just the previous week, Dorothy had reported that an old friend had crossed the street to avoid greeting her.

'Why don't you come home and spend the night?' Muriel suggested. 'Daddy's not due back until tomorrow evening. You don't want to be on your own tonight, and Mummy would be thrilled to have you.'

'What a super idea! I'll go and throw some things into a bag.'

The following morning, Dorothy and her daughters enjoyed a leisurely breakfast, having stayed up late the previous night talking and looking at old photographs. Then Muriel went off to work and Ruth and her mother went shopping and for a stroll in the park. They arrived home in the middle of the afternoon and Ruth went to the kitchen to put the kettle on.

'Is that you, Dot?' she heard her father's voice call from the living room. She looked round at her mother in alarm, and then began to tiptoe towards the front door.

'Dot?' came her father's voice again, accompanied by a rustling of the newspaper.

'Hello, George,' called Dorothy faintly. 'Just coming.'

Ruth had her hand on the front door knob when the door to the living room was opened and there stood her father.

'Well, who have we here?" he said.

'Hello, Father, I – I was just leaving.'

'Well there's no need to rush off like that. Why don't you stay for a cup of tea?'

He spread his arms wide and she stepped into his warm, familiar embrace.

'Now then,' he said, stroking her head as he had done when she was a little girl, 'why don't you put the kettle on, Dot, my dear?'

And thus it was that Muriel returned to find the three of them settled in the living room, her father reading the paper while her mother knitted and Ruth leafed through magazines. Knowing better than to risk commenting on his change of heart, she simply said: 'Hello, everyone.' One glance at Dorothy and Ruth's faces told her that the reconciliation they had hoped and prayed for so fervently had happened. 'Just in time for Christmas!' she thought to herself.

Later that evening, when the two girls were having a natter in Ruth's room before bed, Ruth told her George had not been able to bring himself to apologise and had made a point of saying he still disagreed with her decision to marry Seretse. But as long as she needed a bed and a family she was welcome in his house. He could not, however, bring himself to welcome her husband as well.

'But it's a start,' said Muriel. 'He'll come round in time, I know he will.'

At the next *kgotla* Seretse managed to swing the discussion from being focused on his marriage to what everyone suspected was the real issue at stake – his uncle's usurpation of the chieftainship. A number of young men spoke in support of him before being silenced by Tshekedi. The meeting continued for several days.

'*Most of the older tribesmen are more anxious about the succession than any-*

thing else,' Seretse wrote to Ruth. '*My uncle Phethu was most vociferous today, saying the Tribe could never be ruled by an offspring of mixed blood. I know his fears are a result of the racial intolerance that holds the whole of southern Africa in its grip.*' He went on to explain that the hundreds of thousands of people of mixed race in the region were considered to be the bastards of society, but they often regarded themselves as being superior to blacks. The whites never accepted them and the blacks resented their striving for superiority.

There were, therefore, murmurs of assent from around the *kgotla* ground when the old man stated: 'We cannot be ruled by a chief who looks low on the people, a chief who will probably call the black people *kaffirs.*'

'*At this point,*' Seretse wrote, '*I felt I had to say something. Loving you as I do has forced me to confront all racial prejudice, including my own! So I asked them to consider the fact that, if we judge people according to their skin colour instead of according to their character and ability, we are no better than the South Africans. I said we should make every effort not to fall into the Boers' trap of thinking along racial lines. I don't know whether I got through to them, but I did see quite a few heads nodding as I spoke.*'

In his summation, Tshekedi announced that more speakers had spoken against the marriage than for it. He infuriated the young men of the Tribe by continuing to dismiss their contributions as being of no consequence, oblivious to the fact that in so doing he was alienating them and sowing the seed of his later defeat. Disgusted by his uncle's partisan handling of the meeting, exhausted by the endless discussions and desperate to be reunited with Ruth after an absence of more than two months, Seretse made plans to return to England. He flew out on 31 December 1948.

Ruth decided to wear the black outfit in which she had been married to welcome Seretse home – it would be a happy omen.

She waved cheerfully to the pack of press hounds at her door, and set off for Heathrow in good time to meet the plane. As soon as Seretse appeared she ran to him, oblivious to the popping flashlights and the shouts of the reporters, and they clung together, aware only of the reality of each other's presence.

In view of the delicately balanced situation he had left behind him in Serowe and anxious not to do anything which could compromise negotiations, Seretse refused to make any press statements. However, he did find himself stung into responding when one of the journalists shouted: 'So the Tribe will only accept her if she digs potatoes, is that true?'

'We don't grow potatoes,' he retorted. 'She won't have to dig anything.'

Despite the paucity of response from their quarry, the press managed to come up with a considerable number of column inches with which to satisfy their readers – for whom Ruth and Seretse had become romantic heroes. The *Mail* and the *Mirror* both carried the story of their reunion, with pictures of them laughing, arm-in-arm at the airport.

'It looks as though we'll be staying in England for a while,' said Seretse, as they were tucking into the celebratory homecoming meal. 'So we'd better start looking for a more comfortable place to live, don't you think?' He looked around the small flat, which after the wide-open spaces of Serowe looked even smaller.

Ruth agreed with enthusiasm. That would give her something to do while Seretse went back to his legal studies. He told her that the issue of his allowance had been resolved and that he would be receiving £60 a month. 'Do you think you can make do with that?' he asked, conscious as ever of his desire to provide for her in the manner to which she was accustomed.

'Of course,' she said. 'That's a princely sum!'

The next day, a phalanx of pressmen were gathered outside the flat.

'Oh no!' said Ruth as she rushed to draw the blinds, 'I'm so sick of it!'

'We mustn't let them rattle us. I'll just tell them I'm not going to say anything, because I don't want to jeopardise the delicate situation back home.'

He went to the door and told the assembled press that he would not be giving any interviews.

'Please respect our wishes and privacy,' he said. Flashbulbs popped and the pack yelled questions, but he closed the door firmly.

The couple's reluctance to talk to the press, however, only served to fuel public interest in them. Frustrated by the couple's determined silence, some reporters resorted to writing articles filled with fabrications.

'Look at this!' exclaimed Ruth the next morning as they pored over the papers. 'I never said a word of it!' Seretse was incensed. It was not the first time this had happened. Ruth had shown him back copies of the newspapers she had saved for him, and he had been at first amused, but then angry, at the way the press had embroidered her monosyllabic answers to their questions.

'I've had enough of this,' he said, reaching for the telephone. 'I'm going to get the Commonwealth Relations Office to do something about it. If it goes on like this it could well jeopardise my chances of resolving the crisis.'

But he was soon to learn that freedom of the press was such a hallowed British tradition that not even the mighty CRO dared do anything that could be construed as interfering, or exerting any pressure whatsoever, on the journalists' right to inform the public.

'That's absolute nonsense,' Seretse declared as he hung up. 'What about facts being sacred and all that?'

He made a list of numbers and began to ring up the editors personally. Even this drastic step did not buy them any peace. The editors were prepared to publish his corrections – if he would give an interview addressing all the disputed points. Hanging up with a sigh, he told Ruth they would just be getting themselves deeper into the mess if they tried to correct everything. 'We're just going to have to leave it,' he told her. 'Cheer up. Remember, by tomorrow all these,' he slapped the pile of newspapers with his hand, 'are going to be just wrapping for fish and chips!'

Ruth grinned. He was such an optimist! His sunny outlook on life never failed to lighten her spirits when she felt depressed. His view was that nothing mattered so much that it was worth being miserable about.

While Seretse rather reluctantly returned to his law studies at the Inner Temple, Ruth embarked on a serious search for a bigger flat. At weekends she would take him to inspect the possible new homes she had identified. At last, they settled on a spacious ground-floor flat in Finsbury Park, North London – No 34 Adolphus Road – where the landlady's cheerful acceptance of them as 'That delightful couple I've read about in the papers' warmed their hearts. Thrilled that they could move in right away, the couple set about shopping for suitable furniture.

They soon settled into their new home, and Ruth set to work in the little garden, intent upon keeping Seretse well-nourished with fresh vegetables from her creative labours in the big kitchen. They found a convenient pub nearby, the Hornsey Wood Tavern, which soon became their favourite watering hole.

'Ruth, listen to this,' Seretse called one morning early in June, having just opened a letter from home. 'Goareng says he is convinced that the majority of people now support us. They are turning more and more against the tyrant Tshekedi and becoming convinced that he is trying to steal the chieftainship from me. If there were to be another *kgotla*, he says the Tribe would undoubtedly agree to install me as chief, even with you as my wife. It appears my uncle no longer has the support of anyone other than his councillors and a few of the conservative elders.'

Ruth wiped her hands on a dishcloth, her eyes shining, and snatched the letter away from him to read it for herself. 'Marvellous!' she exclaimed. 'So what do you have to do to arrange another *kgotla*?'

'Strike while the iron is hot.'

Things moved quickly after that. Seretse dashed out to the post office to cable Goareng that he would be returning shortly but that Tshekedi should not be told yet. He booked a flight for the following week, and went home to pack.

'Cheer up! You'll soon be joining me,' he told her as she folded his shirts slowly, caressing the folds as though they contained his body. 'We've won. I just know it. I can feel it in my bones!'

132

7
Pula

THE JOURNEY HOME SEEMED EVEN MORE INTERMINABLE THAN IT HAD DONE six months previously, but at last Seretse arrived in Mafeking.

Because of the territorial machinations that had taken place in southern Africa during the late 19th and early 20th centuries when borders had been frequently and arbitrarily redrawn, the capital of the Bechuanaland Protectorate was situated in a pocket of land that was now part of the northern Cape province – an anachronism that irked Seretse and was to have dire consequences in the future. Loath to invest any money in new construction projects, the British arranged that the town should be regarded as an enclave of the Protectorate while remaining on South African soil. All government business was conducted from the Resident Commissioner's office there.

Going directly to this office to announce his arrival, Seretse took the staff by surprise. He was not expected. Breaking the six-month silence between them, he cabled his uncle who, alarmed that Seretse might be seeking to influence the British authorities in Mafeking unilaterally, left immediately for the capital. Meanwhile the British received word that the Bakatla Reserve in the south was proposing to send a formal delegation of its young men to form a ceremonial escort that would bear Seretse triumphantly to Serowe. The Resident Commissioner's fears of a breakdown in law and order seemed about to be realised, and a District Officer was hastily dispatched to put an end to this grandiose plan.

The meeting between Seretse and Tshekedi in Mafeking the next day was ugly. The two men, once so close, could now barely stand the sight of each other. In a brisk exchange, Seretse accused his uncle again of trying to usurp his position as Chief, while Tshekedi reiterated his belief that Seretse's selfish marriage to a white woman would destroy the Tribe. Administration staff leaned out of their windows at the office compound, alarmed to see the two men raising their voices and gesticulating angrily.

'The Tribe has a right to make their views known,' Seretse was saying.

'They have already made their views known,' shouted the regent.

'You would not allow the younger men to speak in the previous *kgotla* meetings. You do not know their views at all. They never got the chance to speak!'

'All right then, we'll have another *kgotla* – but this will be the last,' bellowed Tshekedi. He turned on his heel and stormed off towards his truck. He roared out of the compound, leaving his nephew standing in the dust. Never before had his uncle failed to provide transport for him, whether it be train tickets to school and back over the years, a horse to visit the cattle posts or a truck to drive into Palapye for soccer games. He felt it was the end of an era.

Stepping down from the overnight train in Palapye the next day, 15 June 1949, Seretse found a smiling Phetu Sekgoma, one of his senior uncles, waiting with a lorry to take him to Serowe. Now the informal leader of the anti-Tshekedi camp, Phetu spent the dusty, bone-crunching journey regaling Seretse with triumphant tales of how public opinion had swung in his favour. Back and forth across the cooking pots, round the cattle post camp-fires, Bamangwato tongues had been wagging. Theirs was a culture of verbosity. As they talked, their mood began to shift. Seretse was born to be their King and they loved him. Khamas had been their kings for centuries. Tshekedi was a harsh and unforgiving man, not gentle and sweet-natured like their young prince. Had he not been uncommonly harsh in rounding up their straying cattle for himself? Had he not sent their young men across the seas to fight and die for the Great War of the British?

As the reliable old Bedford bounced along the rutted track, there was a sudden downpour. Seretse stuck his head out of the window and laughed. '*Pula!*' he shouted joyously. Every drop of rain to a person born and raised in a desert is a gift from heaven. Rainfall is prized above every other thing –

as it means life. For rain to fall upon any occasion is a positive omen. If it rains, all will be well. Blessings will follow – success, peace and joy. Opening his mouth wide to catch a few of the precious drops on his tongue, Seretse breathed deeply the exquisite scent of moisture on dust, the life-giving meeting of rain and dry earth – there was nothing like it in all the world.

Tshekedi, too, had felt his spirits lifted by the unexpected shower, and opened the *kgotla* meeting a few days later with the statement that rain was a symbol of peace and the Tribe should deal peacefully with the issue before them. A telegram from the High Commissioner echoed this desire, and wished the Tribe well in its deliberations. Tshekedi's dire warning of disruption had not fallen on deaf ears, and the British administrators had taken every precaution to ensure that they were well equipped to deal with any violence. The police force in Serowe had been augmented by extra men, and the District Commissioner, Richard Sullivan, reiterated the need for calm debate when he addressed the crowd. It was announced that the final, decisive *kgotla* would take place in five days' time.

During the next four days, the men of the Bamangwato arrived in the village in a constant stream and the talk on every street corner and beneath every shady tree was the same – was the regent, who had ruled them vigorously and sometimes cruelly for more than 20 years, now greedy to retain his power over them? Was he trying to rob their young prince of his rightful throne? They well knew the corrupting influence of power, and yet some of the older people remembered how lovingly Tshekedi had cared for Seretse over the years, treating him like his own son, going to extraordinary lengths to ensure that he had the best of everything. Would he really try to unseat him now? What a dilemma! Time had worked its healing magic upon their initial dismay at the news that they were to have a white queen. Their resentment at Seretse's failure to secure the Tribe's permission to marry had softened in the intervening months. They loved their young Chief and were proud of him. They had waited a long time for him to come and rule them. They did not want that pleasure snatched away from them.

His eyes once again shaded by dark glasses, Seretse stared out across the crowded ground. He had never seen it so full. The closely packed bodies of his people sat motionless in the winter sunshine. There must be 4 000 or more, he thought to himself, as he squared his shoulders and prepared to fight for his future with the only weapons permitted in the *kgotla* – words.

He noted with surprise and approval that, in recognition of the significance of this final *kgotla,* Sullivan was accompanied by the government secretary, Vivien Ellenberger, who had obviously undertaken the long journey from Mafeking to represent the High Commissioner. He had known Ellenberger all his life.

The Englishman was something of an institution in the Protectorate. Having lived there since he was a young man, he actually enjoyed the status of a Motswana elder. Believing that he knew the country and its people intimately, he had assured his superiors that this was just another Bamangwato row, which would soon blow over. In his estimation Ruth was a flighty young adventuress who would tire of her experiment in good time, resulting in a divorce and the restitution of normality. All that was needed was for the authorities to bide their time.

Aware of a bristling presence behind him, Seretse turned to see the smart ranks of the Serowe police, arrayed in full force behind the ground. Were those really teargas canisters? he wondered in alarm. The British must be taking this more seriously than he had thought. Next, his gaze alighted on the neighbouring chiefs, and he frowned at the distasteful memories of their unpleasant reception when he had arrived home the previous October. He nodded a greeting to Alan Seager, the faithful minute-taker, who was once again in attendance. His eyes wandered to a motley collection of white men seated at the edge of the ground, cowering in a small patch of shade from the onslaught of the sun. Here was a most remarkable new phenomenon, never before seen in Bechuanaland – a phalanx of international pressmen. The Seretse Affair, as it was now known, had captured popular imagination to such an extent that British newspaper proprietors felt the expense of sending a reporter all the way to Serowe, and keeping him there, was sufficiently justified.

This brought an altogether new dimension to the proceedings of the *kgotla*. It was something akin to the BBC's televised Prime Minister's question time – decades before its time. This was no longer a Bamangwato affair. Through the eyes, ears and pens of these pale intruders the *kgotla* was now a stage and all the world its audience. Both Seretse and Tshekedi grasped the significance of this fundamental shift and were encouraged by it – each believing that he could use it to elicit sympathy for his cause. It meant direct access to a public of millions. The British officials were wary of the spotlight. It would mean their every word and gesture would be closely observed. The newspapers' version of the events taking place would be read by their superiors in London long before the carefully-worded official documents had even been typed. Their avowed policy of neutrality in this domestic dispute would come under strict scrutiny.

A few of the pressmen doffed their hats to Seretse as they noticed him gazing in their direction. He recognised most of them, and nodded slightly in response. Some were obviously South African – he could tell by their casual dress, sensible headgear and suntanned skin. The British members of the press corps were easily identifiable. Several were evidently novices to Africa, already suffering from sunburn, their necks and forearms an ugly, painful-looking red. The old Africa hands were attired in comfortably cool safari suits and broad-brimmed hats, balanced on their shooting sticks, hip flasks at the ready.

Their hired cars, an assortment of modern Chevrolets, Humbers and Fords, were parked haphazardly alongside the perimeter road – ready for a quick getaway in the frantic chase to be the first to file their copy should anything dramatic happen. The little boys of Serowe were gathered about them, open-mouthed at these glorious machines with their chrome-finished headlights, white-walled tyres and shiny metal trims. They surreptitiously polished the dust from little portions of the bodywork with their ragged shirts, chattering delightedly to one another as the gleaming paintwork was revealed, reflecting their own images.

Seretse's musings stopped abruptly as Tshekedi rose to welcome everyone and invited Ellenberger to address the crowd. Seretse suppressed a smile as the government secretary proceeded pompously to address both the regent and himself in Setswana, as '*Kgosi*'. He glanced at his uncle and noted with satisfaction that his eyebrows beetled in annoyance at this breach of protocol. Grinning inwardly, Seretse thought: 'How very British!'

When at last he was permitted to speak, Seretse did not mince his words: 'I've come here to await the decision of the Bamangwato. If they refuse me, I will go; if they accept me, I will come with my wife. It has been suggested that I should keep my wife overseas or that I should leave her. I refuse to leave her. You must have us both or refuse us both.'

His clear young voice rang out uncompromisingly over the hushed *kgotla* ground.

On the second day, in keeping with African tradition where the aged are revered above all, the most ancient of the royal uncles, Photo Mphoeng, launched the first attack on Seretse. The ebony parchment of his face contoured by the passage of the years, his voice quavering with age, he said: 'The beginning of all the difficulties was the woman. We, the uncles, have already told Seretse that he has broken the law of the Tribe. I am amazed that discussions have begun again. Seretse is the heir, the son of Sekgoma, we all know that, but a chief's son should obey. He does not install himself. He is installed by the people so I still refuse to accept him. To do otherwise would be to change the Tribe.'

There was much more in this vein and Seretse sank his head into his hands, dismayed that nothing seemed to have changed after all. But the tide was about to turn. He heard the voice of one of his supporters, Gaoletse Tshukudu, relate how he had witnessed Tshekedi touring the cattle posts to claim *matemela* (stray) cattle and elephant tusks as his personal property. Everyone knew, of course, such cattle and ivory belonged to the Chief. But Tshekedi was not the Chief. He was simply the regent. His actions thus took on a malevolent significance, and a rumble of agreement greeted Gaoletse's bold declaration: 'It has never been the Tribe that has refused a chief. It has always been the relatives of the chief. It is Tshekedi and his friends who say Seretse cannot rule. The Tribe does not say so. I agree to the woman. Let the Tribe and the British install Seretse.'

After the ice had been broken in this way, allegations against Tshekedi followed thick and fast. Tempers flared as he was branded a thief and a cheat. Some even alleged that he had paid them with money meant for the building of the school. Alarmed at the force of emotion causing the *kgotla* to simmer and bubble like a cooking pot, Ellenberger interjected an appeal for calm, while Tshekedi arrogantly dismissed the allegations and once again used his authority to prevent people from speaking. Even his allies noted that he was becoming increasingly arbitrary and irrational in his handling of the meeting. He was still convinced that the people of substance in the crowd were firmly behind him. Seretse objected to his high-handedness and the crowd grew restive. Fortunately, the sun was low and the meeting was dispersed without any unpleasant incidents.

Seretse wrote exuberantly to Ruth that evening, telling her the end was in sight and he was confident of victory. He also wrote how pleased he was that the issue of divorce had been raised and successfully dismissed once and for all. One of the senior speakers had quoted his grandfather, whose word was still highly respected among the Bamangwato, saying: 'I hear men calling for Seretse to divorce her. Divorce is when two people fail to agree, people are not ordered to divorce. The throne is his and the woman is his. If he leaves her, where should she go? Khama said people should be allowed to marry whomever they want.'

In view of the strict enforcement of King Khama's no-alcohol edict in Serowe, many of the international press corps chose to trek the uncomfortable 32 miles to the watering hole in Palapye every evening. The tensions in the bar equalled those at the *kgotla*, where the British and American newsmen were appalled at the overt racism inherent in the attitudes, conversation and biased reporting of their South African counterparts, particularly those from the Afrikaans press. The manner in which they defended the indefensible principle of white supremacy and condemned the 'primitive' proceedings in Serowe was extremely distasteful to the foreigners. Some of the British rookie foreign correspondents were confronted with their own, hitherto unacknowledged, prejudices. They noted with amazement the complexity of the civil administration run by the Bamangwato themselves, and the fact that the people were not at all subservient, but intelligent, animated and dignified.

Wednesday began with Serogola rising to confront Tshekedi: 'I say, let the woman come and their child shall succeed.' Seretse was encouraged by the extensive murmurings of support that greeted this bold statement. As the day progressed, Tshekedi's chairmanship increasingly resembled that of a man trying to plug a breach in a dyke with his finger. For every speaker who spoke in favour of Seretse, he cast about desperately in search of someone who would speak on his own behalf. The tide had turned, there could be no doubt.

When Tshekedi rose to deliver yet another monologue the next morning, his words were greeted with murmurings of discontent from every quarter of the crowded *kgotla* ground. Recognising with dismay that he was making no headway with the people, he turned and spoke directly to Seretse: 'These people want to destroy the house of Khama by separating me from you. The house of Khama is Seretse's house, I want you to beget a black chief for me, not a white one. I had wanted to give you the chieftainship peacefully, properly without disturbance. I will call on those of his uncles who think as I do, who grieve as I do, to stand up.' Nine stood up. 'Seretse looks on us all as his enemies because we refuse to recognise this marriage. My last word is this: there are many senior men in the Tribe thinking as I do – shall we all be exiled?'

Seretse gauged the mood of the crowd superbly. He recognised his uncle's moment of weakness and effectively grasped the initiative from him. Leaping to his feet he declared: 'Now let my relatives who agree with me stand up for you all to see.' His steady gaze raked the crowd. As thirteen men rose to their feet, Seretse declared: 'I want it known that I also have uncles on my side.'

His next move was an unprecedented departure from hallowed custom that marked the beginning of the end of autocratic tribal rule in Bechuanaland. In firm tones that rang out across the hushed ground he threw the vote open to the ordinary Bamangwato tribesmen, who had never before been invited to vote in *kgotla*. He asked them all to stand if they did not want him to rule them with his white wife. At different points in the crowd 40 men stood up. Seretse paused dramatically, to allow the full significance of the moment to be felt by the thousands who thronged the meeting place. The Tribe held its collective breath. Then, with all the authority of his birthright ringing in his voice, Seretse called out: 'Now, I ask those who say let the woman come to stand up.'

It was as though a wind swept across the ground. The rustling of thousands of garments was the prelude to what erupted as a deafening roar, continuing for several minutes, as the entire gathering stood up and began pounding their feet and shouting the triumphant cry: '*Pula! Pula! Pula!*' over and over again - an exuberant chant of victory and joy.

Seretse stood motionless, the red dust swirling about him, choked with emotion. Hearing the din, the women, who had hovered as close to the ground as they dared throughout the momentous deliberations, came running, their voices raised in that unique, high-pitched trilling sound of celebration – the *moduetsa* – which defies translation.

A stickler for correct procedure even in this, his darkest hour, Tshekedi formally adjourned the meeting before turning on his heel and heading up the hill to seek solace from his beloved Ella. Seretse, surrounded by jubilant supporters, made his way home to his uncle Serogola's house. Naledi, tears of excitement streaming down her cheeks, ran to meet him. The strain of months was lifted from the village and the talk around the fires that night was happy and peaceful, the way it used to be.

But it was not over yet. The next morning, the indomitable Tshekedi gave the floor to Chief Bathoen yet again. These old men still believed in the invincibility of the tried and tested traditions and customs that had served their ancestors for hundreds of years. The momentous happenings of the previous day signalled the end of an era, but they could not accept it. They could not comprehend that history could march forward without their permission. They did not recognise it at the time, but they had just experienced the equivalent of a modern-day bloodless *coup d'état*.

So they closed ranks and prepared to make their last stand. But their defiance wilted in the face of constant heckling from the crowd, and eventually they sat down – silenced. The astute Ellenberger, determined to ensure there should be no loopholes left which might give rise to problems in the future, insisted on satisfying himself that the assembly was representative of whole Bamangwato nation. He therefore asked men from each subdistrict to stand and identify themselves. Once this had been done, he pronounced himself content and offered his good wishes to Seretse, explaining that he would report the result of the *kgotla* to his superiors. The Tribe's decision would, however, have to be ratified by the British government in London before Seretse could assume the chieftainship.

Aware of the tragic figure seated forlornly beside him, he felt compelled to say a word about the regent who had been so roundly defeated. He had, after all, worked closely and efficiently with the British administrators for more than 20 years. He therefore addressed the crowd once more: 'To Tshekedi I would express my esteem and regard. It was suggested at the meeting that Tshekedi had as his motive the wish to keep Seretse from the chieftainship. I wish to say to you that the government entertains no such suggestion or belief. On the contrary, Tshekedi's record of public service to the Tribe has always been of the highest order.'

Tshekedi looked out across the crowded ground for the last time, his eyes filled with pain. After all the projects, the hours of labour, the years of dedication and sacrifice – was this all the thanks he was to get? Anger rose up to choke him and, for once, words failed him. He growled the formal dismissal: '*Phatalalang*! (disperse)' and turned on his heel to make arrangements for his self-imposed exile. The *kgotla* erupted like a bunch of children let out of school. The crowd leapt to its feet, congratulating one another joyously, stomping and shouting, crowding round Seretse.

A number of factors combined to make the events that took place on Thursday 23 June 1949 in the unheard-of backwater of rural Serowe headline news across the world. Although somewhat tarnished at this stage, the British imperial sceptre still held sway over much of the world. Anything involving Britain, therefore, reverberated throughout a massive territory and touched the lives of millions. The news was generally dreary – the economy was in dire straits and the pound faced devaluation. Against this background, the drama of an English girl marrying an African prince and causing havoc among his Tribe in a faraway land was a bright bauble and it caught the public's attention. Starved of glamour and drama, the British public embraced the story of Ruth and Seretse with surprising fervour. Headline writers had a field day: '*Seretse's tribe accepts Ruth as queen*' (*Daily Graphic*); '*Tribesmen hail Ruth as next queen, 6000 cheer at rally*' (*Daily Mirror*); '*Marriage that rocks Africa*' (*Daily Mail*).

Watching from a distance as her future was decided by the Tribe was agonising for Ruth. It would be at least 10 days until Seretse's letters began to arrive and so, apart from a few brief cables, the newspapers were her only link with him until then. From the varying accounts she managed to piece together a picture of what was happening in Serowe, although some of the reports were overdramatised and sensationalised to the point of falsehood. Carefully cutting out everything published about them, she pasted the clippings into a scrapbook to show Seretse, complaining to Muriel at the way some newspapers still insisted on calling her a 'London typist'.

'This is quite good, though,' said Muriel, 'listen.' And she read out Noel Monks' latest dispatch published in the *Daily Mirror*: '*Cecil Rhodes may have changed the whole history of Africa, but the London typist, by marrying her*

African chief, has reversed the traditional black-versus-white situation, and threatens to disrupt social and political relations in all Southern Africa. The 'Seretse Affair' as the marriage of the young couple is officially, and unofficially, labelled, is the talk now of all the kraals, missions, trading posts, towns and cities south of the Line. Its impact on the hundreds of other tribes who no longer rely on drums to spread news is causing district and resident commissioners concern from the Congo across to the Zambezi and down to the Limpopo.'

'Well,' Ruth said, 'they make me sick, the whole lot of them. Do you know several of them have actually had the gall to offer me money?'

'No! Really?'

'Would I be interested in some financial inducement to give an exclusive interview – that was how they put it,' Ruth said.

'I just hung up without saying anything. But I did manage to outsmart them yesterday. You know Annie, from next door?' Muriel nodded. Annie was a friendly young woman, about the same age, height and build as Ruth. 'She offered to disguise herself with a headscarf and dark glasses so that I could get out without them following me as they usually do. It worked like a charm! She went out and they all followed her. And then, a few minutes later, I slipped out and there was no-one there.'

'Brilliant! You ought to do that every time you want to get out.'

But Ruth's pleasure at recounting this little victory was short-lived.

'I wish I could go there! I don't understand what the delay is, now that the Tribe has accepted Seretse as their Chief even though he is married to me. I'm desperate to go there!'

June turned into July – and still there was no summons from Seretse.

Ruth was surprised to receive a telephone call one morning from Gerald Nettleton, the deputy Resident Commissioner from Mafeking who was in London on leave. He requested a meeting, and now that the Tribe had accepted her, Ruth felt it would be politic to accept, even though she was reluctant to do so in Seretse's absence. She set out for the colonial office with some trepidation.

They discussed the hardships of life in England, the weather, and a little of Ruth's experiences during the war. She noticed that Nettleton's eyebrows rose as she described her revulsion at the racism demonstrated by some of the airmen. He asked her what she knew about Bechuanaland, and having thoroughly absorbed all Seretse's lectures about his homeland, she gave a creditable performance.

She was never really aware of the exact purpose of the meeting, and after a cordial cup of tea Nettleton ushered her out. His mission accomplished, he immediately sat down at his desk and wrote a confidential report for his superiors: '*Ruth Khama is a nice looking girl, much nicer than she appears to be from her photos, with pretty golden hair. She was nicely and simply dressed – and conversed freely and intelligently. She has an undisciplined and intolerant streak in her. In fact she's a tougher proposition than we had hoped she might be – and she will never be bought off.*'

A few days later, Ruth received another invitation to lunch – this time from John Keith. Unbeknown to her, he had been instructed to find out whether she was pregnant. Again, small talk masked the real intentions and Ruth naively believed the British administrators were keen to get to know her because the Tribe had now accepted Seretse as Chief 'with the woman'. Keith reported back to his superiors that she had been '*eager to cooperate, distressed by the press attention and desperate to join Seretse*'. Having eyed her slim waist surreptitiously, he could also confidently report that the rumours of her being pregnant were unfounded.

With little to entertain them in Serowe or Palapye, the foreign correspondents, when not propping up the bar in Palapye, harassed the local administrators for news. Competition was fierce for snippets of information and they were constantly bombarded with cables from their editors demanding copy to satisfy their readers. Worn out by their constant badgering, District Commissioner Sullivan and his staff found themselves forced to issue regular briefings in order to keep the hounds at bay. Sullivan tried to keep personal contact with the reporters to a minimum, often simply issuing a typewritten statement. However, in the interests of maintaining cordial relations with the reporters, most of whom after all were his fellow countrymen, he was persuaded to hold a press conference towards the end of June.

Chairs were set out beneath the sunny winter sky in the garden and white-clad waiters served tea and cucumber sandwiches to the assembled press corps. Clearing his throat formally, Sullivan made his announcement – the British authorities in the Bechuanaland Protectorate accepted as final the Tribe's decision to accept Seretse as Chief. He fielded the barrage of questions as best he could with the limited information available to him. Nobody knew when Seretse would be confirmed, whether Ruth was coming out to Serowe, what would happen to the ex-regent, etc. After 15 minutes he could endure it no more and, perspiring with the effort of it all, he mopped his face and retired to his office, leaving the junior staff to disperse the gathering.

Meanwhile, Ellenberger was reporting to Sillery in Mafeking that the *kgotla* had been properly constituted and appeared to reflect the overwhelming feeling of the Tribe. Leaning back in his chair, Ellenberger tapped the thick report he had placed on the Resident Commissioner's desk with the tip of his pencil. 'It's all in there, sir. I don't think there's any cause for alarm. The *kgotla* was pretty decisive. In fact it was quite a stirring sight, one for the memoirs you know, seeing that whole crowd stamping and yelling like that. And it's been quiet since then. Once old Tshekedi moves out there should be no reason for any further agitation.'

'Well, thank goodness that's over then,' said Sillery. 'What a storm in a teacup! All those dire warnings of Tshekedi's have given me a few sleepless nights, I can tell you. We haven't even got enough money to fix up the roads, never mind mounting a full-scale peacekeeping operation. All we needed was some bloody native uprising – when we've only got a handful of policemen and a few vehicles to cover the whole Territory.'

'I must say, though,' said Ellenberger, 'I feel rather sorry for the poor bloke. He's given his life to that lot and they've shown him scant regard in return. He was a broken man by the end. Pathetic really. Told them he was going into exile and they just ignored him.'

'Well, you can feel sorry for him if you want to,' said Sillery, 'but I've had enough of him and his antics. When I think of all that drama last year trying to get the marriage stopped. And now it turns out the Tribe is quite happy about it. What a waste of time and effort! He's like a damned bulldog. Once he sets his mind on something, he never lets go! And he's obviously been exaggerating things to force us to react. From what you tell me there's nothing like a serious split in the Tribe. And we've certainly seen no signs of rioting. I'm taking everything he says with a pinch of salt from now on.'

'Well, you can relax now. It's all over. I know H E is prepared to recommend Seretse's immediate confirmation to London. All we're waiting for is the official say-so from head office and he can go out to Serowe and do the installation and that will be that.'

H E (His Excellency) was inter-departmental slang for the High Commissioner. Fortunately for him, Sillery was unaware of what 'that damned bulldog' was planning. He would enjoy a few more nights of peaceful sleep before the next storm broke.

Looking out over the scene of his final humiliation from the deep verandah of the large brick house built for King Khama by one of the age regiments, Tshekedi reached for Ella's hand. She and the children were his only source of comfort during these bitter and painful times. A schoolteacher, trained by the LMS, Ella was one of the first of a new generation of educated Bamangwato women. She was a strong and practical Christian, and unlike most Motswana men of that time, Tshekedi regarded her almost as an equal and freely unburdened himself to her – sharing problems, ideas and emotions in a way that was totally unknown among his fellow tribesmen.

Plans for their move were well under way. 'My dear, we don't have to go, you know,' said Ella, squeezing his hand. She was worried by his highly emotional and frustrated state of mind, fearing this might cause him to do something foolish. 'Nobody is forcing you to leave.'

'They all hate me now,' Tshekedi growled. 'You know they do. I can almost taste it. How can we stay – surrounded by their hatred every day?'

She had no reply, for what he said was true. The Tribe had turned against him. When she thought of all the energy he had expended on their behalf for the past 20 years, she could weep. It was so unfair. He had sacrificed everything for the Tribe, and now here he sat beside her, a shadow of a man, shattered by their jealousies and libellous talk. She shook herself mentally. She could not afford to become embittered. She had to stay strong – for him.

As if reading her thoughts, her husband gripped her hand more tightly. 'All these years . . .' he muttered. But his sorrow turned to rage as he thought about the British. They had deserted him in his hour of need. He would not let them get away with it. He would show them what happened when the rabble was allowed to take control of the sacred *kgotla*. They must learn that they could not govern in this manner, by mob rule.

Turning to Ella, his energy fuelled by his rage, he almost shouted: 'They must make a ruling on the white woman's status. I will make sure that they do so. Before I leave this place, they will have to decide about that woman.'

He stomped off to his office to compose his final farewell speech to the Tribe. *'We have been compelled to take this drastic step not because we do not love the country of our birth,'* he wrote, *'but because we have great concern for the future of the Bechuanaland Protectorate if the manner in which Seretse contracted his marriage with Ruth Williams and the steps so far taken to proclaim him Chief of the Bamangwato are accepted as precedents to be followed in similar matters in future.'* Gnawing the tip of his pen, he cast his mind back to the discussions of recent days around the evening fires. The 40 men who had stood in the *kgotla* when Seretse had asked who was against the marriage had come to him in twos and threes by cover of night – fearful of the disapproval of the mob. To a man, they had pledged their support for him and their intention to follow him into exile. In a sense they were the cream of Bamangwato society – all senior men. Seven of them were *dikgosana*, members of the royal family, or *bakgosi,* while many served as senior administrators and tribal tax collectors. Their going would deal a severe blow to the administration. The avowals of loyalty and esteem by these men of standing in the Tribe had been balm to Tshekedi's wounded soul.

'If we stay here there will be bloodshed,' they told him. 'We must do what our fathers before us have always done. This is our tradition and we must follow it.'

Indeed it had always been thus. The close-knit community bred tensions from time to time. Whenever these reached an intolerable peak and the daily life of the Tribe was in danger of being disrupted, one of the persons at the centre of the dispute would move away from the main body and settle elsewhere. This was hallowed African tradition and had led to the peaceful migrations among the Bantu tribes for generations. But that non-confrontational age was coming to an end. The self-exile of Tshekedi and his followers to a remote and inhospitable spot in the land of Chief Kgari marked the last such migration.

Tshekedi now turned his attention to the British. Although the statement was addressed to his fellow tribesmen, it was an official document, and, as such, he knew would be read by the administrators.

'*We will not challenge the validity of Seretse as heir, but we question the legality of the steps he and his supporters have taken in their attempt to proclaim him chief and Ruth Williams queen,*' he wrote decisively, and then delivered his *coup de grace*: '*We therefore request a judicial inquiry to declare once and for all the position as regards the white woman and her children.*'

Despite being involved in the turmoil of uprooting his family and moving out of the territory, Tshekedi continued to pursue, with ruthless tenacity, this issue of a judicial inquiry. This idea had actually come from Buchanan. Eager to assist his long-time friend and honoured client, the lawyer had been digging around in the files and had come upon proclamation number 32/1943 of the Protectorate Statutes, which stated: '*Chiefs are chosen by the tribe in kgotla. Names must be submitted for the High Commissioner's recognition and the Secretary of State's confirmation. The High Commissioner may direct a judicial enquiry to be held where it is alleged that the chief is unacceptable, unworthy or not a fit and proper person.*'

'Ah ha!' he had exclaimed, when he read this. It was just what they needed to delay the installation of Seretse for long enough for the Tribe to come to its senses. He had immediately notified Tshekedi, who had planted the seed of the judicial enquiry in his farewell address. Not satisfied with this subtlety, his next move was to take the matter further by going to Pretoria, accompanied by Buchanan, to present a formal request for a judicial enquiry directly to the High Commissioner himself.

Meanwhile, Seretse had been invited to go and see Sir Evelyn Baring. His excitement at the prospect of being told that his installation was imminent was dampened only by the distaste with which he viewed travelling in the Union. Pretoria was the administrative capital of South Africa, where all the civil servants were headquartered, and the stronghold of Afrikanerdom. He found the very air there oppressive. Under the new government of Malan, egged on by the rabid right wing under Hans Strydom and driven by the Dutch Reformed Church, there had been a purge of all anglophile civil servants, including anglicised Afrikaners and the few blacks who had managed to secure positions in the public service. The new regime was busy drafting further legislation aimed at a permanent separation of the races in pursuance of its policy of apartheid (separate development).

As he climbed the stairs of the High Commission on 4 July in response to Baring's summons, Seretse was aware of tension lifting from him. At least the British were uncomfortable with overt racism, he thought. He had always been treated by the colonial authorities in Africa and Britain with scrupulous politeness and the deference due to his position as chief-designate. And he had a good feeling about this meeting. The *kgotla* had been decisive – and he was convinced the British could not deny him the chieftainship, despite his marriage to Ruth. His optimism was confirmed by the High Commissioner's warm and friendly greeting. Both men had walked the hallowed halls of Oxford, and their conversation flowed smoothly. In addition to the old-school-tie bond, there was a certain chemistry between them. Baring was both surprised and pleased by the articulate young man before him, while Seretse felt at ease in the presence of this sensitive and learned diplomat.

Although Seretse received the distinct impression that his recognition was imminent, Baring was not quite as definite as he would have liked. 'I must tell you that this is merely an informal discussion,' he said. 'No decision regarding your confirmation as chief has yet been taken by London.'

'Have you any idea how long it will take? I am most anxious for my wife to come out and join me as soon as possible.'

'I'd rather you didn't send for her just yet.'

'May I ask why not?'

'Well, I understand emotions in the Protectorate are running rather high at the moment, and we don't want to do anything to precipitate trouble of any sort. I think it would be advisable to wait until after the installation. It should only be a matter of three weeks or so.'

As Seretse left his office, Baring fell into a reverie about the fate of blacks in southern Africa. Revulsion rose up within him at the thought that a man like this would, under the apartheid system, automatically be labelled 'non-white' and therefore subjected to discrimination and considered inferior to some ill-educated white person simply on the basis of skin colour. He compared Seretse mentally with some of the Afrikaner civil servants whom he knew. By contrast, the young prince was sophisticated, perceptive and civil. He spoke impeccable English and was entertainingly versed in the art of small talk. Baring's heart sank when he contemplated the many complex implications of Malan's new policies.

He recalled a sentence from Alan Paton's novel, *Cry the Beloved Country*, which had been published to international acclaim a few months previously: '*And the conscience shall be thrust down, the light of life shall not be extinguished, but be put under a bushel to be preserved for a generation that will live by it again, in some day not yet come; and how it will come, and when it will come, we shall not think about at all – cry the beloved country, for the unborn child that is the inheritor of our fear.*'

Seretse went down the stairs with a little less bounce in his step. To cheer himself up, he popped into the first post office he could find, joining the '*nie-blankes*' (non-white) queue. Leaning awkwardly on his cigarette box, he scribbled a message telling Ruth to be ready to fly out within three weeks. Leaving the post office, he bought a copy of that afternoon's Johannesburg *Star* and was delighted to read a headline saying that the Tribe's acceptance of him was thought to be final.

Back at his lodgings, he cut out the article to post to Ruth. Then he sat down and wrote her a long letter all about his meeting with Sir Evelyn Baring, describing the High Commission, its furnishings and décor and the park-like acres of garden in great detail, knowing how she loved to read exactly what he was up to while they were apart. Baring, he wrote, seemed to be a man of his word and he was therefore confident that they would be together again within the month.

In the meantime, he was preparing for her coming by selling some of his grandfather's cattle to buy a car. '*It will have to be a good, solid, American make,*' he wrote, '*in order to survive the roads. The British makes just aren't up to the local conditions, I'm afraid.*'

Arriving at the High Commission on 7 July, intent on persuading the authorities that a judicial enquiry was essential, Tshekedi fully expected to be received by Baring as he had been in the past. However, he was now the deposed regent rather than the ruling regent. Accordingly, in one of those subtle demonstrations characteristic of scrupulous British attention to protocol, he was not accorded an audience with the High Commissioner himself, but with other, lesser, officials.

Knowing the British as he did, Tshekedi immediately discerned the truth and was cut to the quick. He and Buchanan were given a cup of tea but told in no uncertain terms that the High Commissioner would not entertain the idea of a judicial inquiry, and that Seretse's confirmation as chief would be a mere formality. Little did they know that the officials could speak with such conviction because Seretse had been there just three days previously and had been most cordially received by H E himself with tea and biscuits.

When Tshekedi pressed his point concerning Ruth's status, the officials were nonplussed. Why, naturally, she would be Seretse's queen! Heavy-hearted, the pair left the High Commission offices. Slapping his old friend on the shoulder, Buchanan tried to cheer him up, but couldn't think of anything very useful to say. He shook his client's hand, and left.

The following night he was called to the telephone to hear a jubilant Tshekedi on the other end of the line: 'Great news – Baring has changed his mind about the inquiry. He wants us to stay here in Pretoria so that we can be available at short notice.'

'Wonderful news, old boy,' replied Buchanan. 'I wonder what made him change his mind?'

8

Storm Clouds

SIR EVELYN BARING ARRIVED FOR WORK IN PRETORIA ON 7 JULY 1949, UN-
AWARE that the events of that day were to have a profound effect on him
personally and the government he represented, as well as on the likeable
young chief he had met a few days earlier and his English bride.

The day began innocently enough with a cup of his favourite Earl Grey
tea and the morning newspapers. Soft winter sunshine fell across the carpet
in his office, taking the edge off the chill of the highveld winter. He was 46
years old. Both he and his father before him had devoted their lives to imperial service, first in India and then in Africa. Now the doyen of the British
foreign service in Africa, he had been the Empire's youngest governor when
he was appointed to that position in Southern Rhodesia in 1942. He had an
unblemished record thus far and looked forward to an illustrious career over
the next 20 years or so. He did not relish the thought of meeting the deposed regent later that day to rehash yet again the interminable objections
to Seretse's assumption of the chieftaincy. He was satisfied that the people
had made their decision, and was perturbed that Tshekedi seemed doggedly
determined to keep flogging a dead horse.

Unbeknown to Baring, a train of events had been set in motion just a week
previously that was about to arrive, with disastrous and far-reaching consequences, on his own doorstep. On 30 June the South African High Commissioner to London, Leif Egeland, on instructions from Prime Minister Malan,
had visited the Secretary of State for Commonwealth Relations, Philip Noel-
Baker, to deliver personally a special message of protest from the South
African Cabinet.

Alarmed by the prospect of a split within his own party, Malan was reluctant to push the British into making any official policy statement on the Seretse affair. He therefore instructed Egeland simply to test the waters, and to make it clear that the meeting was by no means intended as official. In the strongest possible terms, the message conveyed the repugnance aroused in the government and people of South Africa by the mixed marriage on their borders, and asked the British to deny official recognition to Seretse for three reasons – he had married a white woman; his uncle was a most competent administrator and should be kept in power; and the marriage would not last, causing further disruption when it broke up.

While not spelling out exactly the likely repercussions should the British decide in favour of recognition, he stressed they would be dire.

Noel-Baker, a highly-respected, senior and experienced member of Her Majesty's government, with an illustrious Cambridge and Oxford background, received Egeland's message with distaste. He found the racist regime's reaction to Seretse's marriage entirely predictable but, at that stage, did not consider that it gave sufficient reason to override the express wishes of the Tribe. Always a stickler for detail, he diligently recorded the interview in his own handwriting and made a specific note that it had been 'unofficial'. He found the episode, and indeed all that followed, extremely offensive to his highly-developed sense of justice, and personally most distressing. When the matter was later raised in the House of Commons, and British Ministers were questioned concerning the involvement of South Africa in the decisions taken by Cabinet, they denied that any such communication on the matter had taken place.

Oblivious to all this, Baring was reaching for his telephone, having decided to relegate the meeting with the ex-regent to another member of staff, when it rang. His secretary advised him that Douglas Forsyth was on the line, wanting a word with him. 'Put him through, put him through,' said Baring at once. He made a point of ensuring he was always available to Forsyth, the Secretary for External Affairs and private secretary to former Prime Minister Jan Smuts, who had been kept on by Malan. He liked Forsyth personally –

the man had a good war record and was a thoroughly decent chap. More importantly, he was the only anglophile who had survived the recent Afrikaner purge, and he had intimate knowledge of the workings of the South African Cabinet. Forsyth had only survived, Baring knew, because Malan felt inadequate in the area of foreign affairs and needed the sophisticated Englishman. Forsyth remained on friendly terms with the British authorities, despite the new government's thinly-veiled hostility.

'Rather a delicate matter,' came Forsyth's voice down the line.

'Well come over straight away, then,' said Baring. 'I'll clear my diary.'

'I'll come straight to the point,' said Forsyth as soon as the two men had exchanged greetings. 'The PM is very concerned about the possibility of Britain recognising Seretse.' He went on to explain that the new Cabinet was very definitely split over how to deal with this issue. 'Two distinct camps seem to have emerged, one behind Malan and the other siding with Strydom. The Strydom faction, as you know, represents the extreme right wing of the Nationalist Party. They are pushing for a referendum. It's really quite serious. The issues at stake are annexation of the Protectorates and leaving the Commonwealth.'

'What?'

"Fraid so. They want to declare a republic and be rid of the British once and for all. Their position, therefore, is that nothing should be done about the Seretse affair. They want to keep quiet and let you go ahead with official recognition. That will be their signal to whip up white public opinion against the British among both English and Afrikaners, and call for a quick referendum while emotions are running high. Now Malan and his followers, in order to pre-empt this lot, want to make an official hue and cry about recognition, declaring it intolerable and provocative. The PM sent Egeland to see Noel-Baker in London last week to insist, unofficially of course, that Seretse is not confirmed. Or else. He didn't specify what the 'or else' would be, but I'm pretty sure Noel-Baker would have got the message.'

He sat back in his chair and sipped his tea, giving Baring time to digest the implications of his report. Both men knew full well the extent of racial animosity and intolerance in the country.

At the beginning of June the Mixed Marriages Act and the Immorality Act had passed through the South African parliament with virtually no opposition. Increasingly draconian apartheid legislation was being drafted daily. This included the Group Areas Act, which designated residential areas into black, white, Indian and Coloured. The government's aim was clear – total separation of the races from birth to the grave.

The Dutch Reformed Church had great influence on the majority of Afrikaners, who were very religious and regarded themselves as God's chosen people. Like the Israelites of the Old Testament, thousands of years before them, they believed this gave them the right to subjugate other tribes. Senior officials of the church had made formal representations to the Prime Minister just a week or so previously. They had urged him to take every possible step to stop the recognition of Seretse, as this would have serious repercussions on race relations in South Africa.

A general assembly was scheduled to take place a few weeks later, purportedly to discuss social evils, which was guaranteed to raise public awareness and whip up sentiment levels to boiling point. The following statement made by one delegate to that assembly encapsulates the extreme intolerance of their views: 'The whites are a spearhead of Christendom and civilisation in a land containing eight million natives, of whom at least half are semicivilised, unconverted or living in barbarism. Anything calculated to reduce the prestige and influence of the white man as the standard-bearer of civilisation will harm the best interests of all people living in South Africa today.'

Steepling his fingertips, Baring regarded Forsyth with dismay. 'What on earth are we going to do?' he asked. 'I've already recommended that Seretse's installation be approved. He's a delightful chap, probably the most educated black man in the whole of southern Africa at this point. How do you tell a fellow like that he can't rule his own people? Especially when they've just publicly acclaimed him in their own version of parliament?'

'I'm sorry to be the bearer of such bad news,' said Forsyth, 'but I thought I'd better let you know exactly what's brewing.'

'Of course,' said Baring quickly. 'I'm most grateful to you, most grateful indeed. Thank goodness its not too late.' He stood up to usher Forsyth out, anxious to be alone to think matters through.

Alone in his office, Baring sank his head into his hands. Annexation of the Protectorates. Departure from the Commonwealth. It could not possibly be worse. And all because a young black man had fallen in love with a white woman and had the temerity to marry her. Had the world gone mad? He forced himself to think logically. First – annexation. The three territories, Bechuanaland, Swaziland and Basutoland, had come formally under the administration of the High Commissioner in 1891. In the South Africa Act of 1909, the possibility of handing them over to South Africa was contemplated on the assumption that the Union would remain an integral part of the Empire. From 1913 onwards, the British were on the receiving end of almost continuous pressure from South Africa to incorporate the Territories into the Union.

In 1934, alarmed at the passing of racist legislation by the South African parliament, the British government had issued a white paper in which it stated: '*Britain is pledged that no transfer shall take place until the inhabitants of the Territories, native as well as European, have been consulted and the British Parliament has been given the opportunity of expressing its view.*' This had been augmented by the evolution of colonial policy during the 1940s to the point where '*colonial land is held in trust by the Crown until such time as the native inhabitants are strong and competent enough to handle their own affairs.*' Baring had taken his government's proclamation to heart and had spent his energies unstintingly in seeking to implement this enlightened colonial policy during his tenure as High Commissioner responsible for the Protectorates.

There existed a profound difference between the rights and advantages enjoyed by inhabitants of the territories, compared with those of the blacks in the Union. Politically and socially, the peoples of the territories were in a favourable position, but economically they were all at the mercy of their giant neighbour. Their most important export was manpower, largely for the mines, and in fact none of the Territories had any economy to speak of.

Impotent. Baring scribbled the word on his pad and underlined it several times. Had Britain the will and the wherewithal to win back the Territories once they were lost? This spot on the map was so very far from home. He doubted it. Annexation would go unopposed, and it would condemn the future of the Bamangwato just as surely as South Africa's own blacks were condemned. Everything in him cried out that in order to fulfil the sacred trust of civilisation, Britain had to safeguard the independence of the Protectorates.

He turned his attention to the second threat. The significance of South Africa leaving the Commonwealth could not be overemphasised. It would be a mortal blow to the substantial British interests in the Union, and might even result in the nationalisation of British capital holdings such as gold mines. South African gold, although valued in US dollars, was sold exclusively through the Bank of England. This was essential in providing much-needed dollars for the British economy, still reeling from the devastation wrought by the Second World War. The fragile economic situation made Britain even more dependent on its international investments – and those in this region were particularly lucrative, based as they were on mining and banking. Any action that might jeopardise them in any way was simply unthinkable. In addition, the Cape sea route was increasingly important, both militarily and commercially, as an alternative to the Suez Canal.

Baring wrote another word on his pad and underlined it: *Uranium.* This strategic commodity had been discovered in South Africa a few years previously. In 1945 British Prime Minister Clement Attlee and Smuts had begun negotiations for the purchase by Britain of South African uranium. Protracted and delicate negotiations had continued for years. Finally, a contract had been drawn up and was due to be signed at the end of 1948. However, in

June of that year the Malan government had come to power and the tenuous progress had been stalled yet again. By 1949 the Americans had joined the list of potential customers and Britain was desperate to gain the upper hand by signing an exclusive trade agreement. Everything relating to this delicate subject was classified Top Secret. Early in 1949 the South African government, which had embarked on a programme of rapid industrialisation, needed ready cash and Malan had indicated that he was ready to re-open discussions about selling uranium.

Each new thought added more implications to the situation. Forcing himself to remain calm and methodical, Baring captured his thoughts onto the pad. Recognition of Seretse would undoubtedly create a white backlash which would make it virtually impossible for the pro-British Smuts to be re-elected. What a frightful dilemma! To give in to the racist government of Malan was unthinkable. And yet there was so much at stake – the dignity of hundreds of thousands of people in the Protectorates, the wellbeing of the British economy, naval strategy, vital access to uranium. And what about the two innocents involved? What would this mean for their lives?

The day drew to a close and still he had come to no decision. His secretary, who had waited anxiously for some word from him throughout the day, finally plucked up the courage to tap on his door. Some urgent dispatches had arrived and it was long past time for her to leave the office. He raised his head and gave her a weary smile as she placed the papers before him.

It had been a bad day and it was not over yet. The papers before him brought news of more protests against the recognition of Seretse from both Southern and Northern Rhodesia. He read that the Southern Rhodesian parliament was in an uproar over the issue, and had described the decision of the *kgotla* to accept Seretse and his European wife as 'disastrous'. Prime Minister Godfrey Huggins had been applauded in parliament when he said he had already written to the High Commissioner to complain but would send another message to inform him of the strong opinion of the House against recognition. Baring shook his head in despair as he read of the politicians' denunciation of the Bamangwato decision as showing 'a disastrous lack of racial pride'. Similar sentiments were being expressed in the parliament of Northern Rhodesia.

The whole of the next day, Baring closeted himself in his office and wrestled alone with his dilemma. At its core was the attitude of white South Africa. As he considered its unreasoning prejudice, he thought of his personal friend and priest, the British-born Father Trevor Huddleston, whose highly developed sense of justice had made him something of a messiah to the 'non-white' races. He had become most unpopular with the administration by declaring publicly at every possible opportunity that the policy of apartheid was shameful, morally reprehensible and, above all, an abomination in the sight of God. A Nationalist Party Cabinet Minister had actually suggested that, in bygone times, Huddleston would have been burned at the stake for such heresies. When he had first come to South Africa, Baring had been shown around a bit by the priest. He still recalled his distress at seeing first-hand the conditions under which most blacks lived.

On impulse, he rang his secretary and asked her to get the priest on the line. 'Trevor, can you come and have a sandwich with me in my office at lunchtime?' Baring asked, knowing Huddleston's abstemious habits. 'There's something I need to talk to you about rather urgently.'

'I'll be there,' the priest replied, characteristically brief and to the point.

As soon as Huddleston arrived, wearing his customary black cassock, Baring outlined in concise terms the dilemma facing him. The priest remained silent for a long time, absorbing the full extent of the complexities inherent in the decision faced by his friend. The two of them then discussed the matter at length. Finally Huddleston rose, and placed a hand on the bowed shoulder of the High Commissioner.

'This is a tough one, Evelyn,' he said sadly. 'A very tough one. Solomon himself couldn't have solved this one. But as I see it, your main responsibility is to the peoples of the Territories. You can't condemn them to the life of inhuman degradation that will certainly be their lot if they are annexed by South Africa. The suffering of the non-European peoples of this land, who represent 90 percent of the population, is intolerable. Don't sacrifice the Protectorates if you can possibly help it.'

Baring mulled over these words after the priest had left. His options were becoming clearer at last. He must buy time. Time was what was needed. Perhaps Ruth would indeed be unable to take the pressure of her high-profile marriage and the demands made on her by her position as queen of a backward tribe in the middle of a desert. Of course, people should be entitled to marry whomever they wished. That went without saying. But perhaps Seretse had been a little hasty. Perhaps he had shown a selfish disregard for the political consequences of such a marriage, which would be so disastrous for his people. He could simply return to the UK if things went wrong, but a hundred thousand Bamangwato would suffer. In time, the Tribe might even reverse its decision. Seretse might tire of Ruth. Anything could happen – he must buy some time.

Looking no further than this, he realised that Tshekedi had provided him with the perfect instrument with which to do so. A judicial commission of inquiry. That was the answer! Feeling a weight lifting from his shoulders, he instructed his secretary to get the ex-regent on the line at once and set up a meeting with him for the following day.

Tshekedi and Buchanan sat speechless in Baring's office as the High Commissioner told them he had carefully considered their application for a judicial enquiry and had decided to recommend such a procedure to his superiors in London. Buchanan found his voice first and immediately requested that he and his client be given the opportunity to comment on the terms of reference of any such commission of inquiry before they were finalised.

Baring had not thought that far ahead yet, and gave him a non-committal reply before ushering the pair from his office and settling down to draft his dispatches to Sir Percivale Liesching, the newly-appointed Permanent Secretary of the Commonwealth Relations Office: '*My first reaction to the news of the tribe's decision was to recommend the recognition of Seretse. I thought we should face as soon as possible the inevitable storm of criticism in southern*

Africa. I have always felt, and I still feel, that where there is a straight and una-
voidable choice in our Territories between fostering the interests and preserving
the confidence of Africans on the one hand and the maintenance of good relations
with the Union on the other, it is our relations with the Union which must be
sacrificed. This is the advice I would offer if consulted on a request by any South
African government for transfer of the High Commission Territories against the
will of their inhabitants. I have however with great reluctance and after much
thought, decided that in this case I should not advise on these lines. The result of
the collision would, as I will endeavour to show, be disastrous.'

He went on to explain that official recognition of Seretse, who would then take up residence in Serowe as chief with his English wife as chieftainess, would set a match to the gunpowder of the racist powder keg. This in turn could result in the annexation, by force if necessary, of the Protectorates and the withdrawal of South Africa from the Commonwealth, not to mention further alienation of the pro-British Smuts. *'In these circumstances,'* he continued, *'I feel that we must play for time. I am well aware that if we do so we shall be accused of weakness . . . yet the political results of recognition would be so serious and the effect on the tribe of a quick decision, if wrong, would be so bad that I have no alternative. I therefore recommend the appointment of a judicial inquiry into the succession issue.'* The ill-feeling caused among Africans by the abandonment of the Territories would, he explained, be far greater than that caused by refusal to recognise Seretse. *'We are faced with choice of two evils. Refusal to recognise is, I think, the lesser evil – but it is still an evil,'* he concluded, determined that the authorities in London be forced to understand the complexity and importance of what he was advising them to do. Enclosing Ellenberger's report on the third *kgotla* and marking it all 'Top Secret and Personal', he sent it off to London.

Liesching was a neat and fastidious man with a reputation as a stern administrator who got things done. He had joined the Colonial Office in 1920, and felt he had special insight into southern Africa. He had been the political secretary at the High Commission in Pretoria in 1933, when the navy had marched in to sort out the Tshekedi vs. McIntosh affair. He was known to be receptive to South African remarks and opinions, and revealed his racist views in a hand-written note, which he added to Baring's report before forwarding it. Claiming to be 'doctrinally correct' on the question of the department's attitude to the colour bar, he admitted that he found the matter difficult to come to terms with on a personal basis. He would side with the many, he said, who were unable to view 'without revulsion' the prospect of their son or daughter marrying a member of the 'negro race'.

His note went on to warn of the probable racial reaction to recognition: '*South Africa might whip up feeling in Southern Rhodesia, in Kenya and in Tanganyika. I have little doubt that Southern Rhodesia will react violently and there has always been an unholy alliance between the South Africans and the Kenyan settlers over native policy and the colour bar. Tanganyika can be just as easily infected. In short, there may be a very bitter harvest here and account should be taken of that possibility.*'

Liesching was not alone in holding such racist views. In fact, if the truth be known, they were echoed by many British officials to a lesser or greater degree. The new Assistant Minister, Patrick Gordon-Walker, actually went so far as to make the outright suggestion that Seretse should be barred by means of a new administrative declaration that a 'native' chief could not have a white wife.

Amid the welter of documents on this issue that began to pile up on his desk, Noel-Baker was confused. His officials seemed to be losing their heads. In less than two weeks they had done a complete about-turn in their advice to him on the handling of the affair. What had appeared to be a simple matter had metamorphosed into a dilemma of enormous proportions – attended by the gravest implications.

The political analysis from Baring, in whose ability he had the utmost confidence, was positively frightening. Noel-Baker was well aware of the vulnerability of the Protectorates. He read Baring's warning of an armed incursion by South Africa with a sinking heart – coming immediately to the same conclusion the High Commissioner had reached: *Impotent*. From both a logistical and a financial standpoint, the defence of Bechuanaland from a South African invasion was a nonstarter.

It was the threat of withdrawal from the Commonwealth, however, that really shattered Noel-Baker. The Commonwealth had been formed in April 1949 from the ashes of the Empire. The ink was barely dry on its brave manifesto: *We remain united as free and equal members of the Commonwealth of Nations, freely cooperating in the pursuit of peace, liberty and progress,* before this challenge threatened to make a mockery of it. The toll taken on the British economy by the Second World War had left the stage free for the emergence of the United States of America and the Soviet Union as the world's two superpowers. Determined not to be relegated to third place, Britain had put a Herculean effort into establishing the Commonwealth. In addition, the benefits accruing from the club's various trade deals on raw and manufactured goods were vital to economic recovery. South Africa was one of the most important members. Her withdrawal would be a disaster.

To make matters even worse, Noel-Baker had just received a hand-written note from Egeland indicating that he understood it was doubtful whether his government would be ready to discuss the sale of uranium before November. No reasons were given for this postponement, but the timing was of momentous significance. The Seretse affair dominated every agenda. (When, six weeks later, the Russians stunned the world and entered the atomic age with their first nuclear explosion, the matter became imbued with almost frantic urgency.)

Leaning back in his chair, Noel-Baker pressed his fingertips to his aching temples. What a mess! Damn those Boers! Britain could not be seen to be giving in to pressure from them – and yet they seemed to hold all the aces. He was going to have to find a way to appease them without anyone ever finding out the truth of the matter. The first thing was to ensure that all official documents were kept clean of any reference to protests or pressure from either the South Africans or the Southern Rhodesians – who were proving to be almost as racist as their neighbour. The next thing would be to get

Cabinet to agree to Baring's very sound suggestion of a judicial inquiry to slow things down a bit and avoid a direct confrontation.

He began to draft his recommendation for the next Cabinet meeting. *We cannot exclude the possibility of an armed incursion into the Bechuanaland Protectorate from the Union if Seretse were to be recognised forthwith, while feeling on the subject is inflamed,* he wrote. *There are two possible courses of action. We can immediately declare that Seretse should not be recognised. This, however, would be difficult to justify on any grounds that could be made public. The alternative course would be to play for time by setting up a judicial inquiry to look into the whole affair.* He pointed out that he understood Ruth was preparing to leave shortly for Bechuanaland and urged the Cabinet to make a quick decision, thus maintaining the upper hand, before the press crowned her 'White Chieftainess' on her arrival. Cabinet quickly agreed to the judicial inquiry, stating that it *would afford time for reflection by all the parties concerned.* Great pains were taken to ensure that the issue was clearly seen not to be about the merits or demerits of mixed marriages. Express instructions were issued that the government should *vigorously rebut any suggestion that their attitude was in any way determined by purely racial considerations.*

The Cabinet minute went on to say: *The principal objective of the policy must be to safeguard the future well-being of the Bamangwato themselves and there could be no doubt that the recognition of a chief with a white wife might have consequences gravely prejudicial to good government and to the stability of the local native administration.*

Baring was delighted to receive the news that his proposal had been accepted, which arrived together with an effusive handwritten note from Liesching thanking him for his '*extraordinarily valuable reports over this terribly difficult Seretse problem*' and assuring him that '*your reputation here is exceedingly high as well it might be, and your judgment is trusted to an extent which has never been exceeded*'.

Meanwhile, Seretse had been counting the days since his meeting with Baring. As had happened the previous year, what he had hoped would be a brief separation from Ruth was stretching into months. He tried to fill his days with activity, visiting the cattle posts to inspect the royal herds and making plans for her arrival. He was determined that life in Serowe should be made as comfortable for her as possible. He took pride in his new car – a good, solid Chevrolet in Ruth's favourite shade of apple green, complete with the whitewalled tyres currently in vogue.

Almost to the day, three weeks after his meeting with Baring, he received a message telling him that the High Commissioner would like to meet him in Mafeking on 26 July. He left immediately, putting the new Chev through its paces on the long dusty road to the enclave. He was surprised and annoyed to see his uncle there. Having made such a performance about leaving the Tribe, what was he doing in the Protectorate's capital? The first quivers of alarm ran down Seretse's spine.

Baring had travelled personally to Mafeking to inform both Seretse and Tshekedi of the Cabinet decision. His news hit Seretse like a thunderbolt. He couldn't believe it. A judicial inquiry? Where on earth had that come from? Questions tumbled from him, one after another. Baring regarded him compassionately, distressed that he was the cause of the young man's anguish. Keeping hold on his anger, Seretse asked for details.

'What precisely will the inquiry be looking into? The Tribe has acclaimed me as Chief and you yourself told me their decision would be respected. It was just a matter of time before the official recognition was granted, you said. What has gone wrong?'

Baring replied vaguely that the exact terms of reference would be announced later, but that the inquiry would seek to establish whether Seretse was a 'suitable and fitting person' to be Chief.

Seretse stood up. 'It's South Africa, isn't it? Don't tell me the almighty British are afraid of the Boers?'

'Come now,' said Baring, alarmed that Seretse had immediately jumped to the correct conclusion. 'That's not the case at all. Let's be calm about this and wait for the commission's findings.' He wished he could take this angry young man into his confidence. But of course that was impossible.

'Is there nothing more you can tell me?' Seretse demanded, his voice tight. 'Am I just to wait?'

'I'm sorry,' said Baring, 'please remember, I am under orders. It's not my decision.'

A gentleman to the end, Seretse shook hands with the High Commissioner and took his leave, although he was almost speechless with rage and disappointment. Deciding that he was not going to play the waiting game on his own, he immediately went to the post office and cabled Ruth to fly out as soon as possible.

Baring proceeded to Cape Town, where the inquiry was officially announced on 30 July 1949. Sillery, meanwhile, had been dispatched from Mafeking to inform the Bamangwato in Serowe – a weary journey of 280 miles – while Noel-Baker wrote a personal note to Egeland. 'Buying time' was the administration's watchword, and this brief flurry was followed by a long period of 'carefully orchestrated inertia', during which the wheels of British bureaucracy ground exceedingly slowly towards the appointment of the commission of inquiry under Sir Walter Harragin, the Chief Justice for the High Commission Territories, and the formulation of its terms of reference.

Seretse fully accepted that the Tribe and his uncle had a right to be involved in the question of his marriage. It was also reasonable, he supposed, for the British government, as the ultimate administrative power in the Protectorate, to take an interest, particularly in view of Tshekedi's dire threats of the marriage leading to disruption of law and order. But he was not prepared for the momentous wave that was about to break over their lives, when it seemed as though the whole world was entitled to an opinion on whether or not he should have married Ruth.

The *Guardian*, on 27 June, was the first to perceive and highlight the dilemma confronting the British government – the approval of Seretse as Chief would scandalise most South African whites, both English and Afrikaans-speaking, while rejection would obviously offend blacks throughout Africa. *'In the history of Bechuanaland this is, on its lesser scale, a crisis comparable with the abdication of Edward VIII and its possible implications are almost un-limited,'* said the editorial. The *Mirror*, too, was absolutely correct in its analysis of the situation – warning of repercussions among blacks in the rest of Africa if Seretse was not recognised. *'What lies before the British government is a democratic decision of the tribe and it would be liable to give rise to harmful misunderstanding not to accept it. Whatever happens, the British government must not appear to take the least notice of impertinent intervention from South Africa or do anything to weaken the trust of Bechuanaland that Britain will shield her from South African racial policy. The Protectorate's greatest fear is en-gulfment by the Union. Better informed Africans throughout British Africa will watch this decision closely,'* read the editorial columns.

What neither paper foresaw, however, was that the international community outside Africa would also dive into the fray. Newly independent nations around the world were quick to condemn Britain. India and Pakistan, in particular, took a very hard line with the British and South Africans. The issue soon became the great racial divide, with nations taking sides predictably – white governments, with the notable exception of the USA, siding with the British, while all nations of colour were firmly for Seretse and Ruth. Almost before it had been formed, the Commonwealth was split along racial lines, as tension over the Seretse Affair threatened its very existence. On the positive side, however, the affair served to focus the world spotlight on developments in South Africa under the Nationalist Party. It gave a tangible example of the workings of apartheid legislation, and in the long run went against them.

The Johannesburg *Sunday Times* of 3 July had carried an ominous headline: *'Govt does not want Seretse Khama's white wife to land in Union.'* Ruth therefore decided not to risk any unpleasantness and booked a seat on the flying boat, which took five days to do the trip from Southampton to Johannesburg. She would leave the plane during its stop at Victoria Falls and go by small plane to Francistown. Determined to thwart the press, she booked her ticket under the name of Mrs Smith, and packed up the flat secretly. Friends agreed to send her trunks on to her after she had left. Carrying small and inconspicuous bags, she visited her parents daily – taking with her everything she would need for her trip to Africa.

The days sped past as she shopped and packed and dreamt of the land Seretse had so vividly described to her. Her scrapbook of press clippings grew by the day as the British press continued to keep the story alive. Noel Monks wrote colourfully in the *Daily Mail*: '*From the realm of the Rain Queen Modjadji, chieftainess of the Blaabadu tribe in the far Northern Transvaal, down to Cape Town, where the coloureds who used to be Hottentots live in tragic isolation called apartheid, the prospect of a white chieftainess is regarded with suspicion and wonder. In spite of the advance of civilisation, tribal laws, customs and taboos are still very strong and a white chieftainess will arouse deep human feelings.*'

His columns also carried dire warnings of the South African response: '*Politically, the marriage could not have come at a worse time. Rabid nationalists in South Africa's Malan government have long being crying: 'Basutoland, Swaziland, Bechuanaland' in much the same tones as Mussolini's 'Nice, Corsica, Tunis' patter. Southern Rhodesia has long had her eye on Northern Bechuanaland, where there is believed to be great mineral wealth. A split in Seretse's tribe, after the arrival of his white wife in Serowe, that might well lead to violence would be a heaven-sent opportunity for Southern Rhodesia and South Africa to press their claims to annex Bechuanaland under the old, old alibi, 'restoring order'. But the social and racial implications are even bigger and more serious than the political ones as far as southern Africa as a whole is concerned.*'

But Ruth was far too excited at the thought of being reunited with Seretse to consider these warnings seriously. On the day of her departure, 15 August, she caught a regular train rather than the boat train at Victoria Station to Southampton, to avoid the press. On arrival in Southampton, she kept her head lowered and walked quickly to the airline's hotel where she would spend the night before the flying-boat left at 9 am the following morning. In later years, people would comment about how brave she had been. But at the time she hadn't felt brave at all. She had simply been going to join Seretse. She felt incomplete without him – and she was going to be made whole.

9
Together Again

AFTER AN EARLY CUP OF COFFEE, SHE MADE HER WAY TO THE QUAYSIDE. A battery of pressmen and photographers crowded around the barrier, vying for vantage points as the passengers boarded the plane. Ruth immediately pulled her hat down over her eyes and tried to appear inconspicuous. Somebody must have leaked the story of her departure. They had probably been made a financial offer they couldn't refuse. Was there no-one she could trust?

With her head down she walked briskly towards the plane. To her relief, no one shouted her name, there was no popping of flash bulbs. As she reached the stairs, she glanced backwards and the press pack leapt into action. The focus of their attention, however, was not Ruth but another girl who was smiling widely at them and waving. Ruth gasped and then laughed. 'I mustn't be so paranoid,' she told herself. She later found out that the press's quarry had been a South African ballerina returning home after her successful London debut.

Settling into her seat, Ruth prepared to endure the four-day journey. She watched the landscape passing slowly underneath, some of it very beautiful. They spent the first night in Sicily, and the second in Luxor in Egypt. As the lumbering four-engined plane bounced over the camel-coloured Sahara desert towards Uganda and their overnight stop at Entebbe, Ruth gazed down at the expanse of sand beneath her. Was this what Bechuanaland would be like? Would she be able to cope with such heat? Such desolation? Of course you will, she told herself with characteristic determination, holding firmly to the armrests.

As the desert receded, the vegetation beneath her gave way to lush green savannah, interspersed with big bodies of water. The plane landed on Lake

Victoria and as the doors opened the heat hit the passengers like a furnace blast. But the hotel was dark and cool, and as night fell a pleasant breeze ruffled the surface of the lake. Dark waiters, spotless in starched white uniforms, attended to the visitors' every need. After dinner, Ruth wandered out onto the verandah and gazed up into the African sky, marvelling at the brilliance and abundance of the stars. Just as Seretse had said, they seemed much closer here than they ever had in England. She slept soundly for the first time in months.

Finally they were on the last leg. That evening the plane would touch down on the Zambezi River, just above Victoria Falls. Then one last night on her own, a short hop to Francistown, and they would be together again.

As the weary travellers disembarked at Victoria Falls late that afternoon, the press corps was there again, jostling one another for the best positions amid coarse tufts of buffalo grass and ivory palms on the sandy riverbank. They were joined by several local residents carrying little cine and box cameras. The ballerina waved and smiled charmingly, but the bulbs did not flash. The press had put two and two together when Ruth did not appear in London for a few days and were staking out all possible arrival points in southern Africa.

Despite her hat and dark glasses she was immediately recognised and the press began shouting 'Mrs Khama! Mrs Khama!' Ignoring them as best she could, she hurried on to the waiting bus. As it wound its way slowly into town, the bus was trailed by a long line of pressmen, locals and holidaymakers, all anxious to catch a glimpse of the 'White Queen'.

Ruth's distress quite marred her appreciation of the gracious Victoria Falls Hotel, set in its lush tropical gardens. She was relieved to find a British colonial official there to meet her. He assured her that a small plane had been booked for the following morning and accompanied her to dinner in the hotel's magnificent, high-ceilinged dining room, shielding her from further press and public attention. They planned to leave very early the next morning, well before breakfast, in order to give the press the slip.

Ruth was up with the dawn. It was only a 45-minute flight to Francistown. And Seretse would be waiting for her there.

As the light aircraft circled the bumpy grass airstrip to make sure there were no grazing animals to impede its landing, she looked out of the window, gripping her hands together. She saw a car waiting, the figure of a man standing beside it. The plane landed. Staring tensely through the window, she saw that the waiting figure was not Seretse. The man was white, and he was reaching for a camera. She shielded her face with her hat as the man approached the plane and tried to photograph her through the window. A few minutes later, the apple-green Chevrolet bounced across the airstrip and there was Seretse, laughing, shouting, waving. He drove right up to the plane. And then nothing else mattered. Their embrace was hidden by the open doors of the Chev.

Hustling her into it, he introduced his cousin Goareng Mosinyi, who greeted her from the back seat, and they drove off along the dirt track to Palapye. The man with the camera did not follow them.

Tearing her eyes from Seretse's beloved profile, Ruth looked around her at the unfamiliar countryside. The sparse, grey-green scrub vegetation was like nothing she'd ever seen before. It stretched in every direction. There were no signs of civilisation – not even a telegraph or electricity pole; no buildings, no other vehicles. Just the sky. Pale blue from horizon to horizon, unbesmirched by the slightest whiff of vapour. Even with Seretse's detailed descriptions she had not imagined anything like this. She breathed the dry, dusty air as a film of sand as fine as talcum powder settled in her hair and on her clothes. Seretse's hair was already covered with it and she brushed her hand across the kinky curls.

'Gone grey already, darling?' she teased him. 'I didn't know you'd missed me that much!'

'It's my cooking,' quipped Goareng from the back seat, having taken an immediate liking to Ruth.

As they drew closer to the little settlement of Palapye they began to see cattle and donkeys nibbling the few tufts of palatable grass that grew beside the rough track that passed for a road. There were several clusters of mud-daubed huts with their shaggy conical roofs of thatch.

Suddenly a group of people tilling a field through which they were passing started shouting and running towards the car, which was already well-known throughout the Protectorate as belonging to the new young Chief. Word had spread quickly among the Bamangwato that the British had decided not to install him officially until after the inquiry. But that made no difference to them. He was the son of Khama. And now he had come home to rule them.

Seretse braked and they crowded around the car, delighted to see at last the woman who had caused so many problems. They marvelled at her hair and the whiteness of her skin. Seretse had already taught her a few words of greeting. '*Dumela*!' she said carefully, causing a delighted outbreak of chattering, laughing and shrill ululating from the women. The car was stopped several times in this manner on the journey to Palapye, where Seretse had made arrangements for them to spend a few days in the home of a white trading family whom he knew well.

'There's a big brick house being built on the outskirts of Serowe,' said Seretse. 'It was going to be for a foreign agricultural expert recruited by my uncle. But he is going to be accommodated elsewhere. It's almost finished and the DC says we can move in as soon as the water supply is sorted out. There's a well in the garden and water will be pumped from there into the house.'

'Dear, oh dear!' said Ruth. 'You mean I can't go to the river with clay pots balanced on my head?'

'No. I plan to keep you in the manner to which you are accustomed. Anyway, you'll be far too busy attending to my slightest whim, like a good African wife.'

Palapye seemed to spring suddenly from the bare horizon. Painted signs bore testimony to human habitation, Coca-Cola, Shell, Anadin. The town seemed to Ruth a bit like a cardboard cut-out of a frontier town in an old western movie. This was the last stopping place before Serowe, where travellers could buy cigarettes or cold-drinks and send their last postcard, telegram or letter.

They went directly to the large bungalow that was home to Mrs Shaw – one of the earliest traders to settle there. She had known Seretse since he was a little boy, his pink palm held out for the sweets she always gave him and his eyes bright with intelligence. She was an enlightened woman, a successful trader and leader of the local temperance movement. She approved of the young Chief and was honoured to open her home to his new wife.

'A cup of tea is what you'll be needing,' she said, after greeting Ruth warmly.

'Yes, please," said Ruth, her throat parched by the unaccustomed dryness and dust. Ma Shaw (as she was affectionately known) introduced her son Tommy and his new bride, Barbara, who had also recently arrived from Britain.

'You two girls just sit down and make yourselves at home in here,' said Ma Shaw, 'while Tommy and Seretse bring in the luggage.' After tea she settled the couple comfortably into her circular spare room with its conical tin roof, which Ruth found charming.

Back in Victoria Falls, the press was in a ferment of activity, hiring planes and cars in a desperate attempt to find its quarry, which had flown the coop early that morning. It didn't take them long. Seretse's car was a dead giveaway, and by the time the guests at Ma Shaw's had eaten lunch, reporters and photographers were crowding around the house. Tommy went out and got rid of them by threatening to call the police if they dared trespass on his mother's property.

'Don't tell me they're here already!' exclaimed Ruth in dismay. 'They followed me everywhere in London, they were at Vic Falls, there was one at Francistown and now . . .'

'Now don't you worry about them,' said Ma Shaw. 'Tommy will keep them away from you. Don't let them spoil your day.'

'Perhaps we should talk to them. If we give them a story, maybe they'll go away and leave us alone,' Ruth suggested.

'No, I don't think we should do that,' said Seretse. 'It's better to ignore them. They'll only twist what we say. I don't want to give the British any ammunition to use against me at the commission of inquiry.'

'I suppose you're right,' said Ruth. 'We'll just pretend they're not there. Now, tell me all about this commission.'

'Not much to tell, actually,' said Seretse. 'The High Commissioner was very cagey. He didn't seem to know much himself, or if he did he wasn't going to let on.' He told Ruth in detail about his meeting with Baring.

The press corps had retreated to the local hotel – the only one in Palapye – which had been built to service the railway line from Bulawayo to South Africa. In deference to the thirst of the colonial travellers who frequented this route, alcohol was available, but only to whites. The journalists gathered around the bar to swap stories about their experiences. Many of them had expected to find nothing but a cluster of mud huts and a tribe of seminaked savages. Hot and dusty, some new arrivals trekked in, desperate for a drink. They had been on a wild goose chase to Serowe in the noonday heat, believing that Seretse would take Ruth directly to his village. Although hardened by years of reporting for Fleet Street from the four corners of the world, the frustration of this particular assignment was taking its toll. An ice-cold beer was a very welcome prospect.

Australian-born Noel Monks, the *Daily Mail*'s Africa correspondent, was undoubtedly the most flamboyant of the lot. He had earned his stripes, so to speak, as a war correspondent, and since then had been roaming around Africa, keeping the British public supplied with a steady stream of entertaining, forthright copy about the demise of the Empire. When the story about Ruth and Seretse broke he had been the first international reporter on the scene, apart from the South Africans. Leaning comfortably on the bar, he regaled the newcomers with yarns of his travels.

As the hours dragged by and there was no sign of activity from Ma Shaw's house, the journalists began to get edgy, knowing that their editors were depending on them for stories and pictures of Ruth's arrival in her new kingdom. As darkness fell, several of them, armed with flashlights, crept through the garden and up to the house, trying to see through the windows. Tommy Shaw, who had decided to move in with his mother in order to help Seretse deal with the press, was incensed. He rushed out through the screen door on the broad verandah, brandishing a pistol and shouting '*Voet-sek!*' – coarse but effective Afrikaans slang for 'Get lost!' The intrusion put a damper on the evening and, pleading exhaustion, Ruth and Seretse retired early. Ma Shaw went into the room ahead of them and firmly drew the curtains. 'There you are, my dears,' she said, patting Ruth's arm. 'Don't you worry about that lot. We'll make sure you aren't disturbed tonight.'

'Thank you, Ma,' said Ruth gratefully, but the experience of the flashlights probing through the thick darkness had unnerved her. As she lay clasped in Seretse's arms, Ruth shuddered at the thought of strangers trying to get into the house to take photographs of them in bed together.

'Don't let them get to you,' murmured Seretse. 'I'm sorry we can't go and look at the stars, though.'

'Oh, I saw them last night! It was incredible. We must look at the sky together tonight!'

'Well, let's wait until later, when everyone's gone to bed. The stars will look brighter once the moon has set anyway.'

In the darkest hours before dawn he woke her to see the night sky. They could not risk going outside but they opened the windows wide and leant out across the broad sill, craning to see the massive expanse of blackness above them. She leaned back against him as the chill of the night air touched her skin. They gazed at the glittering star-studded void above them, listening to the sounds of the night – a slight rustling of leaves, the chirp of a nightjar, the far-away bleat of a young goat, thirsty for morning.

Seretse tried to defuse the tension over the press attention by making it into a game. As they left Palapye for Serowe the next morning, the press chased them in their hired cars. Seretse revved the Chev hard, delighting in the ease with which the big American car chewed up the rough tracks. He laughed as the hounds were left far behind, choking in clouds of red dust, and sometimes getting bogged down in the thick desert sand. Determined to get a photograph, the indefatigable Monks even pursued them in a small hired plane. The evasive tactics of Seretse on the ground, the pilot trying to follow him and the photographer hanging out of the open door, turned the expedition into a circus, alarming the elderly tribesfolk but delighting the children who danced about and waved at the strange new bird.

Tshekedi had effectively moved out of Serowe by the time Ruth arrived. He had spent weeks separating his own cattle from those of the royal Khama inheritance, which he had husbanded over the years on behalf of Seretse. He had vowed he would not share Serowe with Ruth and as soon as he learnt of her imminent arrival he made his move. His followers numbered some 200, together with all their dependants. Their farewell statement was read out in the *kgotla* and the great trek began.

He had bought four bright-red Bedford trucks and these were loaded with household possessions. The residents of Serowe watched the move with malicious approval, referring to the vehicles as *kgaphamadi* – the colour of blood. Cattle were rounded up, supplies were bought and farewells said. With her youngest child, still only a year old, strapped to her back, Ella packed up her worldly goods and her four other children with cheerful determination. Her innate sense of humour was to stand her in good stead when they arrived at their new home.

It was a barren and deserted place. The new settlers had to build their homes from scratch. There was no school for the children. Lions would come right into the settlement at night to kill the cattle. Unlike many of the other women whose husbands had dragged them to Rametsana, she never uttered a word of complaint.

Although Seretse's house would not be ready for a few days yet, he was anxious to introduce Ruth to Serowe and to be among his people, so the couple accepted an invitation to spend a few days with the Rev Alan Seager and his wife at their western-style bungalow, which was near the large LMS church built during King Khama's time.

As they drove into Serowe, with the press trailing behind them, swallowing their dust, hundreds of people spotted the cavalcade from a long distance off. They came running, and crowded along either side of the main street to welcome their new young Chief and his English bride. As if in blessing, the sky opened and there was a sudden unseasonal downpour, which sent the crowds almost delirious with delight. They danced and shouted and ululated, stretching out their hands towards the car in gestures of welcome until all Ruth and Seretse could see was a forest of waving black fingers.

Ruth was overwhelmed by the effusive welcome. If she was dismayed by her first impressions of Serowe, with its haphazardly scattered huts, wandering goats and the obvious poverty of the people, she didn't show it. The car crawled slowly through the sea of people. Seretse, of course, was accustomed to receiving such homage, but he was particularly thrilled at this public demonstration of welcome for his bride. Beaming and nodding at the crowd, he drove with one hand and waved regally with the other.

Ruth's senses were assaulted by the sight, sound and smell of the crowd mobbing the car; hundreds of shiny black faces, mouths widely smiling, white teeth gleaming, voices calling in greeting, the high-pitched shrilling of the women, the smell of hot, sweaty, bodies, animal dung and dust. She could not help herself from shrinking back from the thousands of dirty hands stretching out to touch her. She felt as though she couldn't breathe.

She muttered at Seretse: 'There are too many of them. What must I do?'

'Just smile, darling. Smile and wave,' he said.

Turning back to the open window she did so, and the crowd roared with delight and pressed even closer. As she gazed at them, her initial alarm fading, Ruth began to see the individual faces – a gap-toothed child with two big dimples; a mother, her face worn and lined; an old man, his eyes barely visible in the mass of crinkles caused by looking long distances in the glaring sun. These were Seretse's people. How they loved him! These were her people now. She would love them, she would care for them. They needed her.

They were greeted cordially by the Seagers, but Ruth detected a slight lack of warmth on the part of both the missionary and his wife. They seemed to be putting on a good face for their visitors. Mrs Seager served tea and the four made awkward small talk. As soon as she finished her tea, Mrs Seager said she had to see to the preparation of lunch. Ruth immediately offered to help.

'But you are the Chief's wife, Mrs Khama. You mustn't be seen getting your hands dirty in my kitchen.'

When she and Seretse were alone in the simply furnished spare bedroom, Ruth whispered: 'I don't think they like me.'

'Well, they are colonials, after all. They just happen to be missionaries as well,' replied Seretse. 'They're very well intentioned but they find it quite difficult to see blacks as their equals. So they can't understand why you've married one. They like blacks, but they're only happy with the master-servant relationship. That's just how colonials are. Don't let it bother you; we'll only be here for a few days. Oh, and Seager is a close friend of Tshekedi's, so my uncle has no doubt filled him with stories about you being the devil in disguise!'

'Don't say that – not even as a joke.'

'Hey, what's wrong?'

She sank down onto the edge of the bed and covered her face with her hands. 'I'm all right,' she said, her voice muffled. 'I'm just hot, and tired and a bit overwhelmed by everything. And I can't relax with these people – I feel as though they are shooting daggers of disapproval at us the whole time. They hate me. Why did they even invite us to stay with them?'

'They're just doing their Christian duty,' replied Seretse. 'And who cares if they hate you, I love you! What more do you need?'

A loud gong sounded. Ruth started. 'What's that?

'Lunchtime, I suppose.'

'Well, I must have a wash. I'm so hot and dusty.'

'Me too,' agreed Seretse, taking off his shirt.

Ruth began to search through their luggage for her sponge bag. Twenty minutes later, feeling fresh again, the couple wandered into the living room.

'Oh there you are!' called Mrs Seager from the adjacent dining room. 'Didn't you hear the gong?'

'Yes, we did, thank you,' replied Seretse politely.

'I'm afraid the soup's gone cold,' said their hostess, and called for a Motswana serving girl from the kitchen to fetch their plates.

'Oh, don't worry,' protested Ruth. 'It's so hot, I could gladly eat cold soup.'

'Good heavens, my dear,' said Mrs Seager, 'not at my table, you won't!'

They waited while the soup was warmed up and served again. Seretse and Alan Seager did their best to keep the conversation going, talking mainly about the weather and the state of the cattle. Once the meal was over, Ruth rose and began to clear away.

'No, no, my dear, don't touch those. The servants will clear away. They'll just get confused if you try to help them.'

'Sorry,' murmured Ruth. Declining the offer of coffee on the verandah, she and Seretse escaped back to their room as soon as possible.

'Well, I'm sorry, but twenty minutes late for a meal is considered downright rude in my book,' Seager's wife declared, the minute they were out of earshot.

'Now, dear,' said her husband, 'they'd only just arrived. I suppose they needed to wash and change. We are bound to offer hospitality, you know.'

'I know. And I am trying – but they are just so . . .' she groped for the words to express herself.

'I know what you mean. It's very difficult. They just look so . . . wrong together.'

'Yes,' agreed his wife. 'That's exactly it – so wrong.'

'I've always tried to be unprejudiced about colour,' mused Seager, aloud.

His wife nodded. 'Of course. I mean, we've sacrificed our whole lives for these people. We're stuck out here in the back of beyond trying to make life better for them. We love them in our own way. So why do we find Ruth and Seretse so difficult to accept?'

'I don't know, my dear, I just don't know. I'm going to have to do a lot of soul searching on this one. They are obviously in love, but seeing them together offends me somehow, deeply. I don't feel good about it, it's so un-Christian. But I have to be honest.'

Mrs Seager knew how her husband felt – that guilty twinge when one knows that one's behaviour is out of line with one's professed beliefs. But she was not as deep a thinker as he was and soon tired of the mental exercise required to delve to the roots of her racial prejudices.

'I just hope they're on time for dinner, that's all,' she said briskly, and went off to supervise her afternoon women's Bible study.

Seager went into his study to wrestle with his conscience, but found no relief. He was bothered about Seretse's seeming disregard for the welfare of the Tribe. Did he simply not care? Somehow, too, he was uncomfortable with Seretse's impeccable English and his westernised manners and social graces. And then there was his wife. The way he looked at her, the way he touched her . . . Did God really intend the races to inter-marry? Of course, the way the South Africans were going about the whole race question was morally wrong – of that he was certain. And yet . . . Ruth and Seretse just seemed wrong together.

And what about their children? How would they possibly fit in? Where would they belong? Which school would they go to – the one for the village children or the one for the white traders' children? How would they make friends and who would be their role models? At last he decided to confess his misgivings in writing to his superior, Ronald Orchard. Perhaps a more seasoned, wiser Christian than he would have some light to shed on this difficult matter; some answers as to how to deal with this disagreeable worm that had suddenly reared its head in the depths of his soul.

When the sun had passed its blazing zenith and the shadows grew longer, making it bearable for Ruth to go out of doors, Seretse took her to visit their new house. Set well back from the dusty track leading to it, under a canopy of feathery-leafed acacia trees, the solid brick building was large by Serowe –

and British – standards. Along two sides ran a deep, shady verandah. It had a steeply-pitched corrugated iron roof and a shallow flight of steps going up to the front door. Its most striking feature was the large, curving bay window that looked out over the front garden and on down into the valley and then up to the hills beyond. Despite Seretse's enthusiastic descriptions, Ruth didn't know what she had been expecting, but it certainly wasn't anything as spacious or attractive as this.

'Welcome to your new home, Mrs Khama,' said Seretse, bowing low as he handed her up the front steps.

'It's enormous!' exclaimed Ruth, 'and I love that window.' She embraced him impulsively. 'It's wonderful!'

'For you, only the best!' With their arms entwined, they wandered through the house. It was still cluttered with workmen's tools and they had to duck under ladders and skirt around tins of paint and boxes of tiles and plumbing fittings. But by and large the building was complete. The airy bedrooms, with wooden floors and ample built-in cupboards, opened out onto the verandah. There was a modern bathroom with a white china bathtub, and a spacious kitchen, soon to be complete with hot and cold running water. The kitchen windows looked out on to the sun-baked red clay soil of the large yard surrounding the house. There was even a fireplace in the living room, for cold winter evenings. Ruth was thrilled with it all.

'Do you think the bedrooms are large enough?' asked Seretse, 'and what about the kitchen – do you like that tiling? How about the floor?'

'I like all of it – don't worry,' she assured him. 'When can we move in?'

'Well, now that we're on site I'll be able to put pressure on the workmen to finish the painting, tiling and plumbing as soon as possible, so a week or two at the most, I should think. And of course we'll have to organise the furnishings, but we can do all that here in Serowe. The traders will order whatever you want from Johannesburg. It doesn't take long for goods to come from there.'

'I can't wait to begin.'

Ruth walked through the rooms again, making a mental list of what would be needed. 'I'll need a tape measure,' she murmured to herself. 'And I think shades of cream and beige for the living room, and maybe blue in the master bedroom . . .'

'We'll come back first thing tomorrow and you can get started,' said Seretse. 'We'd better get going now, though. We don't want to be late for dinner, do we?'

Ruth's heart sank at the thought of the long, awkward evening ahead of them, and she turned reluctantly towards the front door. As they walked arm in arm down the steps the sun was bidding Serowe a glorious farewell just above the hills opposite the house. Smoke from the cooking fires swathed the horizon in a saffron robe, and the soft cooing of doves and distant bleating of goats were the only sounds. They stood silently watching until the light drained from the sky and the golden trees and hills became black with night.

When they arrived back at the Seagers', they found that, after all, they were late for dinner. Seretse apologised profusely while Ruth tried to capture the sunset in words for the benefit of their hosts. But Mrs Seager's peremptory summoning of the servants to warm up the soup, again, quelled the light in her eyes and her voice faltered '. . . it was just lovely,' she finished lamely. They struggled through the meal and retired as soon as possible afterwards, Ruth pleading a headache.

'I do hope you're going to be able to adjust to this heat,' said Mrs Seager. 'It's like this most of the year round, you know. You'll never cope if you're going to get a headache every five minutes.'

'Such a catty thing to say!' she protested to Seretse, brushing her hair with short, fierce strokes. 'And they're supposed to be people of God!'

'Have you forgotten the Bishop of London already?' he asked her. 'Racial prejudice has nothing to do with religious conviction, it goes much deeper than that. In fact, it seems to be a subconscious thing. One has to make the effort to overcome it on an intellectual level.'

'But I don't feel like that. Why don't I?'

'Thank goodness you don't,' Seretse replied, putting his arms around her. She pushed him away half-heartedly, wanting a more substantial answer. But he held her tighter. 'Don't let them bother you. You are right and they are wrong, simple as that.'

Decades of Christian influence and the example of King Khama had made Sundays in Serowe a sacred day of rest. No work was done at all. Everyone washed and dressed in their Sunday best and all paths led to the LMS church, fashioned in gothic style from large sandstone blocks.

Dressed in a pink floral frock, Ruth held Seretse's hand as they walked across the sloping, stony yard between the Seagers' house and the church on their first Sunday. From the western edge of the village hundreds of men, women and children, attired in clothes of every hue, wound up the rough track like a colourful ribbon, streaming towards the church. The wooden floorboards creaked under the weight of Serowe's feet – some shod but mostly bare, cracked, calloused and tough as leather from a lifetime of walking and exposure to the weather.

The uncomfortable, roughly-built wooden benches were packed to capacity – women on one side of the centre aisle, men on the other. Seretse led Ruth to the front, right-hand side bench which was reserved for members of the royal family. Naledi was already seated there and she smiled warmly in greeting when they arrived. As they walked up the aisle, Ruth was aware of all the eyes upon her, but she sensed only interest and curiosity, not disapproval or disgust. She began to relax. She was loved here. Seretse loved her and his people loved her too. She would be happy.

Since the demise of Seretse's grandfather, no one had sat in the massive throne-like chair that King Khama had had especially made for him. It stood at the front of the church, a monument to the man who had built God's house in Serowe. It was cool and dim in the church and at a signal from the choirmaster the entire congregation rustled to its feet. The leading soprano led into the first line of the first hymn. The voices swelled and rose, harmoniously blending in the melody of Africa – men's deep baritones finding the bass, several sopranos soaring to the high notes, while hundreds of others joined in like the different instruments of an orchestra until the whole building throbbed with sound and it seemed the tin roof would lift off, allowing their praises to rise directly to the very throne of God himself.

The mass of bodies swayed rhythmically in time with the beat, although there was no drum to guide them. The people sang in Setswana, and Seretse joined in, his eyes closed, his body swaying as he sang the well-worn phrases of his mother tongue. He had come home at last, and his childhood memories of Sundays in church swept over him like an incoming tide – his grandfather, his father, his mother and grandmother, his little brother – the memory of all these loved, lost ones was strong here in this place, embracing him, welcoming him.

Most of the men were dressed in suits. As the service progressed, the heat grew increasingly oppressive. The church's high roof and thick, stone walls helped, but the sun beat down on the tin roof. There was no ceiling. Ruth breathed deeply from the handkerchief she had soaked with lavender cologne, as the overpowering smell of the perspiring congregation wafted towards the open space at the front of the church. Alan Seager stood on the raised stone dais, flanked by a couple of Motswana deacons. The whole service was in Setswana. Ruth did not understand a word, but she loved the gentle sound of the phrases. For all his awkwardness with her and Seretse, Seager was obviously beloved by his flock and his preaching was greeted with many appreciative 'ahs' and 'amens' from the congregation.

As they left the building after the service, Ruth and Seretse were swamped by hundreds of people wanting to greet them. This exuberance would take weeks, if not months, to die down. Ruth smiled bravely and tried to touch as many of the outstretched hands as possible. Released from Sunday school, the children, their faces shining with Sunday Vaseline, their Sunday clothes spotless from scrubbing on the rocks by the stream, flew across the churchyard like a multicoloured flock of starlings. Ruth reached out to caress their heads, feeling the tight curls beneath her fingers. Seretse, at her side, was smiling and chatting easily. Finally they managed to get away to the Seagers', only a little late for Sunday lunch.

At last, the house was complete. With profound relief they packed their bags, thanked the Seagers for their hospitality, and moved in on 29 August 1949. Many visitors arrived throughout the day to welcome them into their new home, making it difficult for them to finish unpacking or to have any time alone together. But none could be turned away – many had walked up to 100 miles to come and greet the new Chief and his white wife. Ruth was touched by the gifts they brought. No-one arrived empty-handed – a few eggs, a scrawny chicken, beautifully woven baskets and mats, a bowl of *rapoko* (grain), a gourd of groundnuts, clay pots of different sizes, fashioned from the black earth found near the river banks after good rains.

At last the visitors were all gone.

Ruth and Seretse sat on their wide, shady verandah enjoying the cool that accompanied the dying of the sun. Sipping frosty gin and lime from their new glasses they toasted each other.

Ruth sighed deeply. She was content. They gazed out over the valley, where the departed sun had left a luminous green glow. The dusk comes quickly in Africa, and as they watched the sky darkened and soon it was alive with stars.

The stream of visitors continued for several days. Alan and Doris Bradshaw were among the few whites who came to welcome them. Doris had baked a sponge cake, which they all enjoyed. Alan was a recruiting officer, based in Palapye, for the South African gold mines.

Although they were of South African descent, he and his wife were without racial prejudice and Ruth and Seretse found them to be good company.

'How are you adjusting to the heat?' Doris enquired.

'Much better, thanks,' replied Ruth. 'This house helps, of course. And I don't go out at all between noon and about 3 o'clock.' The two women chatted about the best places to shop while Alan and Seretse discussed Seretse's development plans.

'It's so frustrating because until the Brits confirm me as Chief my hands are tied,' Seretse said. 'And there is so much to do.'

Alan nodded sympathetically. 'I wonder what they're up to? You can never trust them. They don't call a spade a spade – they beat around the bush. Give me the Afrikaners any time. At least you know exactly where you stand with them.'

'I suppose so. But personally I can't get on with them. If the truth be told, I prefer dealing with the British. There's something about their subtlety that I rather enjoy.'

'I can't tell you what a relief it is to be in our own home,' Ruth was saying to Doris. 'The atmosphere in the Seagers' house was dreadful. They just couldn't stand me. She was really quite frosty.'

'Extraordinary!' said Doris. 'We don't have much to do with them, I must say, but they're very well liked among the Bamangwato.'

'I always thought he was a cold fish,' interrupted Alan. 'There you are, Seretse, there's a perfect example of what I was just talking about. Here he is, a do-gooder white man ministering to the poor black people, and he can't stomach you being married to Ruth.'

'It's all so complicated, isn't it?' said Seretse. 'Something seems to happen to the British when they go overseas. The average Brit in the UK is a decent chap. I mean, people were perfectly decent to me most of the time. Once Ruth and I started going out, we had a bit of trouble, but the majority of people were not bothered at all.'

'And yet English-speaking South Africans are just as racist as the Afrikaners. How do you explain that?' said Alan.

'It's beyond me,' said Seretse.

The Bradshaws left, having invited Ruth and Seretse to dinner in Palapye the following Saturday. 'Come early and we'll go over to the hotel and watch the Saturday night bioscope,' said Doris.

The small, close-knit, white community in Serowe, about 80 people in all, was deeply divided by the Ruth and Seretse affair. They were a motley collection of pioneering people who loved the bush and the peace and quiet of their rural backwater. They lived quite a hard life, by no means in the lap of luxury, but it was a good life, simple and free. Many of them insular, some even eccentric, they discussed the marriage *ad nauseum*. It had been the hottest topic of conversation ever since the news of Tshekedi's letter from his nephew had first been received. They never tired of it. And now that Ruth was actually in their midst, there was so much more to talk about. What she looked like, what she wore, the length of her skirt, the colour of her hair, what she said and didn't say, where she went, what she bought; this was grist to the mill of gossip for the women of the community: 'Nothing but a little London typist, my dear, but such airs and graces!' 'She has simply no idea what her life will be like here – she won't last long.' 'African men are polygamous by nature. Seretse will soon have his bit of fluff on the side – I wonder how she'll like that!'

The talk among their menfolk around the bar was not very different: 'She's going to make things very difficult for us. Every Motswana man is going to want to have a white woman now.' 'There's going to be trouble. I just know it, man.' 'Seretse will soon tire of her. These blacks are never faithful to their women.'

Noel Monks' latest article had informed his readers that he had interviewed almost all the white traders in Serowe, and the majority of them had been against Ruth coming to Serowe. He had been forced to invent some choice quotes as none of his interviewees was willing to be quoted in the press. Early on, positions had been taken – for and against. Apart from the Bradshaws, who were not classified as trading families and therefore slightly excluded from the warmth of the fellowship anyway, only four families welcomed Ruth – the Watsons, the Blackbeards, the Woodfords and the McIntoshes. One by one, they called on the young couple in their new home. They were warm and friendly and made it clear that they could be counted on for loyalty and support. Ruth and Seretse were moved by their overtures of friendship.

The other families shunned them – but carefully. Since King Khama's time, the traders' presence in Serowe had been subject to the whim of the Chief – and they knew it. It simply would not do to antagonise the new Chief. But that did not mean one had to hobnob with him and his English fancy woman either. Their words and smiles cast but a thin veil of civility over their attitudes. Dislike was ill-concealed behind frivolous chit chat. Ruth hardened herself to their disapproval, and held herself aloof. To some this made her appear proud and distant, but those who took the trouble to get to know her recognised the self-protective mask for what it was.

Early one morning, Ruth rose before dawn. Shivering with excitement and the early morning chill, she dressed and went through to make a cup of tea. Seretse had decided it was time for her to broaden her knowledge of his country by visiting a cattle post. He whistled as she brought him his tea, a neat figure in her tailored jodhpurs.

'Hello, gorgeous,' he said. 'Do you come here often?'

'Hurry up, dear fool, they'll be here any minute!'

'Relax, dawn doesn't mean 5.30 am sharp. It can mean anytime between 5 and 6 am.'

Before he had even finished speaking, they heard the clip-clop of horses' hooves and the clank of the front gate being opened. Seretse leapt out of bed. A group of horses was led into the yard by one of his uncles and a young lad who would accompany them. Stamping and snorting, the horses were loaded up with bedrolls, foodstuffs, fresh water and other supplies. Ruth covered herself with insect repellent and skin cream before receiving a leg up into the saddle from Seretse. Leaning over the horse's head, she caressed the soft nose and whispered into its ear.

They set off through the early morning misty scrubland. Despite the dryness, droplets of moisture, miraculously distilled from the cold night air, clung to the shrubs around them. The sun peeped over the horizon and soon its voracious tentacles sucked the moisture upwards, covering the land with a soft, white blanket just a few feet high, from which trees and bushes emerged like flotsam on a beach. Within half an hour the mist was gone, and the gently undulating countryside spread around them as far as the eye could see. Seretse rode beside Ruth, pointing out various landmarks and naming the different trees and birds that they saw. Once they startled a young duiker from his hideout beneath a cluster of shrubs.

'There you are, Ruth, your first *phuti*!' exclaimed Seretse. The little deer was the Tribe's emblem and Ruth recalled the legend Seretse had told her in London of his ancestor, Ngwato, the founder of the Tribe, being protected by a *phuti* while hiding from his enemies in long grass.

Just as the sun was becoming unbearably hot, Seretse pointed out a cluster of makeshift huts in the distance. The smell of cattle dung reached Ruth on the slight breeze and she wrinkled her nose. As they drew near to the cattle post, the herd boys, who had been alerted to their visit, came running to meet them. Clad only in ragged cotton shorts, these youngsters were delighted at the prospect of company to relieve the hours of boredom, especially such exalted company as the new Chief and his bride. They gazed in awe at this woman who looked so different. She, meanwhile, was staring at the hundreds of cattle dotting the plain before them. She had never seen so many beasts in her life – calves jostling their slow-moving mothers; ponderous udders swinging; long-horned steers lowing and stamping. The stench of their dung was now overpowering. The cattle swished their tails and flicked their ears in a never-ending battle to keep away the flies, whose constant buzzing filled the air with a background hum throughout the day.

While the herdboys unloaded the horses, Seretse led Ruth into a small hut that had been made ready for them. It was freshly swept but the smell of dung and the flies pursued them inside. Ruth sank down gratefully in the shade and prepared tea from the basket she had packed. She fanned herself with a small grass fan and took frequent deep breaths from her handkerchief. This was going to take some getting used to. But Seretse was so obviously happy to be here that she tried to put aside the discomforts and see it through his eyes. The harsh beauty of the African bush had its own enchantment and she was its willing captive. Even when Seretse showed her the primitive 'long-drop' and ablution facilities, she was determined to adapt to this new environment.

Once it was cooler, they ventured out again and Seretse inspected his herds. As she watched him running his hands along their backs, stroking their noses and inspecting their ears for ticks, Ruth remembered what he had told her at Nutford House – a Motswana's cattle are like the members of his own family. The herdboys kept up a running commentary about the number and gender of calves born, steers sent for slaughter, cows suffering from mastitis and bulls traded.

That evening, they sat outside their little hut in folding chairs sipping their gin and lime and watching the fathomless sky fill with jewels. Darkness brought a welcome respite from the flies, but soon the air was full of moths, midges and mosquitoes. Seretse kindled a small fire to drive them away. A little distance away, their dinner was being prepared on the cooking fire. The chatter and occasional laughter of the herdboys and family retainers drifted towards them with the smoke. In the background, the stamping and snorting of the cattle provided a constant accompaniment.

A smiling retainer served their dinner in tin plates, with no cutlery. It was Ruth's first exposure to traditional cooking. She tentatively imitated Seretse rolling a ball of the stodgy maize porridge in his fingers and dipping it into the stew. It tasted wonderful. She had not realised how hungry she was. Seretse watched in amusement as she cleaned her plate. 'That's rude,' he commented.

'What's rude?'

'In Bamangwato custom we consider it rude for a guest to clean the plate because it means we haven't provided enough food,' Seretse explained.

'Oh dear. Now what shall I do? Quick, give me some of yours.' She hastily took a handful from Seretse's plate and placed it on her own, smiling at him triumphantly.

After washing their hands in a clay pot of tepid water, they moved their chairs closer to the larger fire where the storytelling had already begun. Seretse translated softly for Ruth as the older men in the group retold the history of the Tribe for the benefit of the youngsters. The semidesert landscape began to chill soon after the sun had hidden its face. In their hut the royal couple lay together beneath Seretse's grandmother's warm kaross, and slept soundly.

A few days later, back in Serowe, as Ruth stood up to clear away their plates after lunch she felt suddenly faint. Putting her hand to her head, she staggered a little. Seretse leapt up. 'What's the matter?'

'I feel . . .' murmured Ruth, and collapsed in a heap.

He caught her in his arms and carried her to the settee, murmuring: 'Ruth, darling girl, speak to me.' After a few moments her eyes fluttered open. 'Thank goodness,' breathed Seretse hoarsely. 'Don't do that again, my darling, you gave me the fright of my life.'

'I feel awful,' she murmured.

'Don't move. I'm going to get the doctor.'

On his arrival, the doctor conducted a thorough examination, and then diagnosed nervous exhaustion. 'I'm ordering complete bed rest. No visitors. No excitement and no anxiety.'

Seretse put Ruth to bed and nursed her tenderly. But it was to be a full six weeks before she was up and about again. The strain of all they had been through during the past year had taken its toll – the long separation so soon after they had married, the split with her family, moving to Africa, setting up house, the tension with the Seagers, harassment by the press. All these experiences, combined with the mental and emotional strain of being constantly in the limelight, had worn her out. In addition, she didn't know it yet, but she was pregnant. The house was kept quiet. Seretse read to her for hours and they listened to music and the radio together. The staff prepared simple meals which they ate in the bedroom.

Once word of her illness got out, hundreds of concerned Bamangwato came to the house. Visiting the sick was a hallowed element of their tradition. But once Seretse explained that Ruth was not sick, just worn out and in need of complete peace and quiet, they nodded their heads, said a prayer, left their gifts and went home.

In the gossip circles of Serowe, however, the response was not so compassionate. 'Maybe she's homesick?' 'Nonsense, my dear. She's suddenly come to her senses and realised what she's done. Now she's got to find some way to get out of it.' 'I wonder how much longer before we'll be rid of her?' 'I'll bet she'll pack her bags and scoot back to England before the end of the month.'

During the weeks of her convalescence, Ruth fell more and more in love with the country. The special smell of the air early in the mornings, the sound of the cicadas at noon, the swift springtime with nesting birds and tender new leaves budding on the trees, the thunderous build up of heavy clouds and the earth's thirsty longing for the rain – all these became precious and familiar to her. She loved the golden, winter veld grass, the light and the space and the sky.

Their wedding anniversary, September 29th, came and went. They celebrated it quietly with an ice-cold bottle of white wine. Each morning, she and Seretse awoke to a chorus of bird song. An extended family of yellow weavers had built their nests in the boughs of the *makala* trees outside their bedroom window. Sparrows and doves vied with each other for the crumbs from the table. Bees fussed in the butter yellow blossoms of the acacias. As spring became summer, the air became thicker with dust and smoke after long months without rain. Sometimes it seemed to her that the light was almost like honey. She learned from Seretse that the tribesmen read messages of rain in the wind, analysing its source and temperature. Some days the air was totally still, on others a hot wind blew, making the children restless and the women irritable.

Seretse tried to stay with her as much as possible, but she encouraged him to go to the *kgotla* often and to keep his lines of communication open with the Tribe and its administrators. One day he came home from such a trip and found her dressed in her favourite pink frock, sitting in a chair on the verandah with her feet up, reading a novel. He leapt up the steps and bent to kiss her.

'Hey, what are you doing out of bed?'

'I feel much better today.' She smiled up at him.

Settling down beside her with a cool drink in his hand, he stroked her arm. 'Are you sure you're okay to be up?'

'Quite sure. And I have decided that I am never again going to make myself sick with worry. It is not worth it. I'm going to stay strong for you.'

'Good. You've seen how the people love you – and you know how much I love you. Those are the things that matter. Not what the press writes or what those racist traders think of you or say about you behind your back. Just ignore them from now on.'

'I will,' she said, putting her hand to his cheek.

It was the beginning of a happy, happy time.

10
The Harragin Debacle

CABINET HAVING AGREED TO THE COMMISSION OF INQUIRY, IT NOW FELL TO the Commonwealth Relations Office to come up with the terms of reference for it, and appoint the commissioners. Noel-Baker informed his energetic parliamentary under-secretary, Patrick Gordon-Walker, in mid-August that he was putting him in charge of this delicate operation. Gordon-Walker was undaunted by the task. A challenge like this would give him a good opportunity to show what he was made of and, hopefully, advance his career a notch or two – but his superior had a grim foreboding that this was a conundrum nobody could solve. And it was not going to make any of them look good. Quite the reverse, in fact.

Gordon-Walker went to work at once. He set up a committee of senior men and outlined the key issues at stake. The inquiry had to give the government the result it needed – a good reason **not** to recognise Seretse as Chief of the Bamangwato. The real reason was, of course, extreme pressure from South Africa and the imperative need to keep that nation within the fold of the Commonwealth, while preventing an armed incursion and annexation of the Protectorate by Malan's government. And the reason the South Africans were taking such a strong line was that the would-be chief had married a white woman and proceeded to live with her in neighbouring Serowe under the very noses of the architects of apartheid. However, the real reason could not be stated. Therefore, the commission had to find some other excuse to enable the British government to withhold recognition – ensuring that the economic blackmail by the South Africans was kept a secret.

In addition, Cabinet was adamant that the specific issue of the marriage, and even general issues of interracial relationships must be completely excluded from the scope of the inquiry. For two months they pondered the matter and dug into reference documents, searching for precedents and new ideas, while Gordon-Walker continued to wrestle with the inherent risk of the commission coming to the wrong conclusions. He had to ensure that the final decision was retained by the CRO – it was simply too risky to allow the commission the freedom to make its own findings. He was hamstrung, however, by the terms of the legislation Buchanan had unearthed – Proclamation No 32 of 1943. This provided for a judicial inquiry to be held where it was alleged that the chief was 'incapable, unworthy or not a fit and proper person' to rule the Tribe.

Officials were set to work trying to dig up evidence in other parts of Africa that liberals of all races were opposed to the marriage. It was hoped that such evidence could be used to persuade the British public to change its mind. However, apart from a few friends of Tshekedi's in high places who predictably condemned Seretse, there was no evidence of general disapproval of the marriage to be found anywhere in Africa – outside of the racist south of course.

Then Baring came up with a suggestion that made Gordon-Walker rest a little easier. The High Commissioner had been consulting the Chief Justice for the Territories, Sir Walter Harragin. This amiable gentleman was well known to espouse good 'old fashioned' values and could be relied upon not to rock the administration boat. He would make the perfect chairman. In choosing the commissioners, the committee decided to strengthen its hand even further, appointing not Sillery, who was felt to be a little too sympathetic to Seretse, but his deputy Gerald Nettleton. The third member of the trio was to be R S Hudson, the head of the African Studies branch of the Colonial Office in London, who was known to be sceptical about the whole issue of tribal succession. With Harragin as chairman and these two carefully picked men as his commissioners, the committee felt the government's interests were in safe hands and finally agreed upon the terms of reference for the commission:

1. To report whether the *kgotla* held at Serowe between 20–25 June 1949, at which Seretse Khama was designated as Chief of the Bamangwato Tribe, was properly convened and assembled, and its proceedings conducted in accordance with native custom.

2. To report on the question whether, having particular regard to the interests and well-being of the Tribe, Seretse Khama is a fit and proper person to discharge the functions of Chief.

On 15 September 1949 Baring made the official announcement that the judicial inquiry, under the chairmanship of Harragin, would commence in Serowe on 1 November. Malan and Huggins were delighted with the news. It appeared their bullying tactics had worked.

However, the details of the terms of reference were received with dismay by both Tshekedi and Seretse, as well as by the Bamangwato. To have their revered *kgotla* called into question like this was an outrage, as was the suggestion that Seretse, who had been born to be Chief and educated well beyond the dreams of any tribesman, was unfit to take the throne. Worse than this, however, was the announcement by the District Commissioner that 'for the sake of convenience and clarity' the inquiry would consider Tshekedi to be the plaintiff and Seretse the defendant – and that both parties would have the usual rights of plaintiff and defendant in a civil action. In so doing, the authorities had ridden roughshod over the personal relationship and the feelings of the two men concerned in a fashion that would be condemned by human rights activists today.

Tshekedi stormed into his hastily-constructed home at Ramotsana, shaking a fistful of papers and shouting for Ella.

'Look at this!' he fumed. 'Just look at this!'

'What is it?' cried Ella, running to him.

'They have completely missed the point,' he said, stabbing his forefinger at the papers. 'And they have placed me in an intolerable position.'

'Calm down,' urged Ella, leading him to a chair. It was no good for his health, to get all worked up like this again. She had hoped the worst was over, but apparently it was not.

'They have not even mentioned the marriage at all,' Tshekedi told her, his voice shaking with rage. 'There's nothing about the woman in here. Nothing! And they have made me the plaintiff! Me – against Seretse as the defendant. They've made it into a personal battle between the two of us. Why can't they understand? It's not about me, it's about the Tribe. Their commission is going to be a waste of time unless they address the real issue. The problem is the woman. Not Seretse. He is perfectly fit to be Chief and everyone knows that. It's that white woman who has caused all this trouble.'

For once Ella had nothing comforting to say. It seemed the British would stop at nothing to destroy her husband. She knew he was not a racist at heart, in fact she knew his heart well – it was brave and self-sacrificing. He was the most considerate husband, the most loving father. God had blessed her by giving her this man. Surely He would not now stand idly by and watch him destroy himself with rage and frustration over his nephew's marriage? If the truth be told, but she dare not tell it, Ella could see no reason why Seretse shouldn't marry a white woman. Unless, of course, her husband was right and such a step would goad the South Africans into marching in and taking over the land. But why would they want such a desolate, barren place when they had so much land already, and all that gold, and diamonds? It was beyond her comprehension.

For the next four weeks, Tshekedi buried himself in preparing his case for the inquiry. No matter that the British had gone about it so badly, they had given him his judicial inquiry and he was determined to make the most of it. But first he must try to undo the harm they had done in making it appear as though he was battling Seretse for the chieftainship. In a rare demonstration of selflessness on the part of a ruler, he wrote immediately to Baring, formally renouncing all claims to the chieftainship, both for himself and his children. However, his noble gesture was ignored by the British. He never received a reply.

Seretse was deeply upset at what he perceived to be his uncle's treachery in engineering the judicial inquiry. Meanwhile, the inhabitants of Serowe watched in fascination as workers laboured in the hot sun to erect a huge tent in the centre of the village for the commission hearings. Truckloads of wooden benches and tables stood ready to be unloaded. 'Whew, it's going to be hellish sitting inside that thing all day,' commented Seretse.

The night before the inquiry was due to open, he and Ruth were shocked to hear an announcement on the BBC World Service that they had been declared prohibited immigrants in South Africa. They listened in alarm as the report gave some background to the inquiry, saying that the government of South Africa had welcomed the announcement by the British that a judicial commission of inquiry would be held to determine whether in fact Seretse Khama was a fit and proper person to discharge the functions of Chief in neighbouring Bechuanaland.

Seretse clearly understood that this was another manoeuvre by his enemies to frustrate his recognition. By banning him, the South Africans had made it impossible for him to travel to Mafeking – something the commission would surely use as an excuse for not recommending his approval as Chief. How could he fulfil his proper functions if he couldn't go to the capital of his own country? The Resident Commissioner and senior staff had their offices there, and it was where all the meetings on administrative matters took place.

The hearing was packed to capacity with a varied crowd, including the press, the British officials and the white traders. The 3 000 tribesmen who had gathered to witness the commission's activities squatted in patient silence around the entrance to the tent, unable to hear most of what was going on. But key phrases were passed back to them and spread quickly throughout the gathered throng. A growl of disapproval greeted the news that Tshekedi had requested the inquiry. The mutterings continued as he rose to address the commissioners.

First, the former regent addressed the issue of his having been named as the plaintiff. 'This places me in a position which is not of my making. I had and have no desire to be a party to any litigation,' he stated. 'It is only because I have been asked to do so, and not as a plaintiff or party to a suit, that I am placing what information I can before the commission.'

He was at pains to explain that he and his supporters had never intended, and did not now intend, to challenge the position of Seretse Khama as heir-apparent to the chieftainship. They only challenged the legality of the steps he and his supporters had taken in their attempt to proclaim him Chief and Ruth Williams queen – and therefore the rights of their children to the chieftainship. He reiterated his renunciation of the chieftainship for himself: 'If, in the interests of peace and good order, this commission decides that Seretse cannot be recognised, I, as the next in the line of succession of Khama's family, could not under any circumstances continue as Chief.' He emphasised that this personal position could in no way be affected by the outcome of the inquiry. Once again, his abdication fell on deaf ears. The Bamangwato were not in a mood to appreciate his point of view.

Seretse took up the story at dinner that evening, for the benefit of the Bradshaws who had been unable to attend the opening session. 'My uncle then insisted that he was no longer safe in Serowe and demanded that the entire inquiry move to Lobatse so that he could speak freely.'

'Why does he want to do that?' asked Alan.

'The feeling against him is pretty strong,' said Seretse. 'There's a rumour going around that I will never be Chief as long as my uncle is alive. He seems to think his life will be in danger if he stays in Serowe.'

'My goodness!' exclaimed Ruth. 'Do you really think somebody might kill him?'

'You never know. Feelings run very high. The chieftainship is an emotive issue and it has its roots deep in the past. People aren't always rational about it.'

'Things have been tense around here lately,' commented Alan. 'The people don't know who's in charge. According to the British, Tshekedi remains the titular head. But in effect you're the Chief.'

'The worst thing is that people are afraid – and that's why we're getting all these rumours and alarms,' said Seretse. 'The place is deserted by 9 pm.'

'I've never known Serowe like this,' said Doris.

'Well, everyone is terrified to go out in case Tshekedi's thugs are lurking in the bushes,' said Seretse. 'And nobody comes to the *kgotla* because there's no Chief to try their cases. I believe the DC is holding a court to deal with serious assaults and cattle thefts – but basically there is no law and order and no recourse to justice. It's not good. It's not good at all.'

Seretse objected to the decision to move the hearing to Lobatse on the grounds that it was of intimate concern to the Bamangwato and therefore should be heard in Serowe. The judge took his point and ruled that only Tshekedi's evidence would be heard in Lobatse and the commission would then return to Serowe.

Not many tribesmen were able to make the long trip to Lobatse, but a group of about 200 went to support Seretse, who endured the proceedings with regal detachment. His relaxed air was even more marked when compared with the state of extreme tension in which his uncle gave his evidence.

Tshekedi read haltingly from his copious notes, and was sadly ineffective in communicating his passion for the Tribe's welfare. His main argument was that Seretse's marriage would be harmful for the Tribe. However, he focused on precisely the point the British did not want brought under the spotlight – the fact that the circumstances prevailing in southern Africa at that time were such that this marriage was not in the best interests of the Tribe. He emphasised that it was Seretse's responsibility, as heir-apparent, to make the interests and well-being of his people his prime concern.

The officials did not take kindly to being told rather directly, and by an African, that their administration had failed to keep order and that the Tribe was disintegrating into chaos and anarchy while both he, the rightful regent, and Seretse, the rightful chief-to-be, were forced to stand by and watch it happen. If it had not been for the interference of the British administrators, Tshekedi told the commissioners bluntly, he would have acted decisively at the first *kgotla* when the Tribe made it patently clear that they could not accept a white woman as their queen.

Tshekedi then played his last card. Mindful of the McIntosh flogging episode, when he had firmly been put in his place as a 'native ruler', he explained carefully to the commissioners that 'native' law did not apply to Europeans. Therefore, the Chief's wife would be above the law of the people. And what was more, she was already flouting the laws of the Bamangwato by purchasing liquor and supplying it to Seretse and other 'natives' at her house.

When the inquiry moved back to Serowe, the commissioners, the public and the thousands of tribesmen who assembled to view the action were not disappointed. Attired in his lawyer's suit, calm and assured, Seretse was every inch the Chief. Even the commissioners were moved as he declared boldly that he was the rightful heir to the chieftainship and the Tribe wanted him as their king. He spoke with great dignity of his love for his wife, and made it clear that nothing could make him abandon her. He admitted freely that he had married her without the consent of the Tribe, but he had sought and obtained their forgiveness for this breach of custom.

'I could never accept from any tribe or nation a decision that I should divorce my wife. Husband and wife are one,' he said, and the commissioners found themselves nodding in approval.

Of course, he had the advantage of his Oxford education and his time at the Inner Temple. If it were not for his complexion, the commissioners would have thought he was one of themselves. Indeed, with eyes closed, one could well believe that it was an Englishman standing there, speaking so eloquently.

Under cross-examination he was lucid and concise and the weighty matters under discussion did not dent his natural urbanity and sense of humour. With regard to the accusation by Tshekedi that he was drinking illegal liquor, he admitted this openly but informed the commissioners that he was as able as any one of them to decide when he had had enough. Furthermore, as he did not drink to excess, he didn't see that his consumption of a gin and lime at the end of a hot, dusty day could be considered an obstacle to his becoming Chief. After all, he pointed out, no one had objected to him enjoying a pint or two while studying at Oxford, and he had been required to drink both claret and port during his dinners at the Inner Temple.

Rebutting his uncle's points one by one, Seretse told the commission that the last three rulers of the Tribe, including the regent Tshekedi, had all married without the consent of the Tribe and had been forgiven. The question of his wife, he told them boldly, had nothing to do with the British – it was purely a matter for the Tribe to consider. With regard to his banning by South Africa, he suggested a compromise, whereby meetings could be held on the Bechuanaland side of the border.

'It is hardly my fault that the Tribe is administered from a hostile foreign country,' he said, appealing reasonably to the commissioners – who could not help but agree with him.

Even the biased South African press were impressed. The Johannesburg *Star* of November 16th 1949 reported: '*During the deliberations he took notes and argued persuasively, and even humorously, on his feet like a born trial lawyer. He looked the commissioners full in the face and said he claimed the chieftainship because it was due to him and his Tribe wanted him: "My morals are as good as any chief or regent in the Bechuanaland Protectorate, my educational qualifications are probably better."*'

Tedious and uncomfortable though they might have been, the proceedings within the sweltering tent were not without a certain charm. On one occasion a grizzled headman rose to bear testimony to the issue of forgiveness, which Seretse so confidently claimed. Dressed in a stained greatcoat and shapeless shoes he addressed the commissioners with an elaborate courtesy that took his listeners back at least half a century to a more gracious time. His references were to truths even more ancient than his manner.

'Forgiveness is a great thing indeed,' he said reverently. 'In fact it is greater than all else. As we are all Christians I can mention Chief David who, as we read in the Bible, married in the wrong way but did not lose his kingdom. Seretse has been pardoned. He is a son of Khama's Tribe. I do not think that any woman can be pushed onto him or that he can be expected to love any woman besides the one he already loves. And if God blesses him, the son that he may get becomes the heir to the chieftainship.'

In marked contrast to this ancient sage was Walter Pela, representative of the new generation of Bamangwato, educated, polished, smartly attired in a shiny suit and tie, wearing city shoes that had never known the dusty trek from village to cattle post and back again. Despite his modern ways he spoke of the ancient paths – the sovereignty of the *kgotla*. He clothed the age-old truth in learned language – but truth it remained: 'However individuals or the Tribe may feel about a Chief's marriage, there is no precedent for barring his succession merely because he marries without consent. The *kgotla* can legalise illegalities. The Chief is subservient to its authority.'

At last it was over. The hearings ended on November 18th and the tribesmen dispersed – tramping into a red wall of dust, for the long-awaited *pula* had not yet come. Everything had been said. Their future was in the hands of the British.

Back in Pretoria, the commissioners laboured over their report for two weeks. They had been given an impossible task, and try as they might they could not twist the information they had been given, together with the evidence of their own eyes and ears, into a report that was going to give the British government the excuse it wanted to deny Seretse the chieftainship. Harragin was determined to make good his understanding with Baring that the commission would return findings favourable to the government. But that would require mental gymnastics of epic proportions. Confusion was the result.

The bulky package, containing 10 volumes of evidence and three files of submissions, was completed on December 1st and finally dispatched to

London on December 6th. It arrived on Noel-Baker's desk three days later, and plunged him into despair.

Seretse was frustrated by the delay. There was so much he wanted to do for his people, but his hands were tied. His only happiness was the news that Ruth was pregnant. The baby was expected in May. Ruth was in excellent health again and pregnancy suited her. She was also acclimatising well to her new environment and emotionally supported by Seretse's devotion. Contrary to what the critics prophesied, he had eyes for no other woman.

The postal delivery was something they both looked forward to. Friends in England wrote often. Muriel and Dorothy were faithful correspondents, keeping Ruth supplied with news from home and regularly sending newspaper clippings, new books and small gifts.

Two weeks before Christmas, Seretse returned from a trip to the post office with a parcel wrapped in brown paper. 'It's from Muriel,' he called, running up the steps to where Ruth was waiting on the verandah. 'Probably a Christmas present.' As Ruth tried to take it from him, he held it up beyond her reach. 'No! I'm going to put it away until Christmas Day.'

'Don't be so mean. It's nearly Christmas. Why can't I have it now?'

'No,' he said firmly. 'It's for Christmas Day. Self-control is good for you.' He took the parcel through to the kitchen and instructed one of the household staff to keep it well hidden until he asked for it.

'Well, I'm fed up,' said Ruth crossly, when he returned to the verandah with long, cool drinks for them both. 'It's so hot and there are no decorations anywhere. No holly, no Christmas trees, no mistletoe, no mince pies, no nothing.'

Seretse laughed at her long face. 'That's not like you! Come on, cheer up. Let's take a trip into Palapye and see if Ma Shaw has anything Christmassy in stock.'

Ma Shaw did indeed have something Christmassy in stock. Although the Bamangwato had embraced Christianity and Christmas was a hallowed event, they did not indulge in the festive trimmings that were so alien to their culture. But the traders always brought in a supply of Christmas decorations for the local white families and the British officials. Ma Shaw's little store was gaily decorated with streamers and tinsel.

Greeting Ruth and Seretse warmly, the genial old trader offered them a cup of tea and a homemade mince pie to celebrate the season. They spent a happy hour with her and Ruth picked out a selection of red, white and gold ribbons, baubles and lights and an artificial fir tree in a pot.

'Don't forget the mistletoe,' called Seretse from his chair in Ma Shaw's office.

'I know what you're going to get up to this Christmas!' she said.

'Well, I've got to make up for lost time,' said Seretse, laughing. 'I was stuck out here on my own last Christmas and didn't get any at all!'

Ma Shaw sent them on their way cheerfully with a dozen mince pies and her own special recipe so that Ruth could make some more.

The British authorities responsible for the administration of the Tribe waited anxiously for word from London. District Commissioner Sullivan complained bitterly about the difficulties he was experiencing in keeping a firm grip on things. As a result Sillery, the Resident Commissioner, decided to appoint Sullivan as 'native authority' in place of Tshekedi.

The long silence on the part of the administration merely served to confirm Seretse's supporters in their belief that the British government was bowing to pressure from the white governments of South Africa and Southern Rhodesia. There could be no other reason, they deduced, for such a lengthy delay in confirming Seretse as Chief or announcing the findings of the commission of inquiry. It could mean only one thing – they were preparing to bar him from the throne.

Meanwhile, in London, the CRO was humming with rumour and counter-rumour concerning the Harragin Report. Noel-Baker played his cards very close to his chest – but of course word soon got out that there had been a blunder. The commissioners had agreed with Seretse on every point. The truth of the matter was, except for his unfortunate marriage (which they could not cite as the reason), he would make an excellent chief. But his marriage had ruined relations with Southern Rhodesia and South Africa – and the impoverished and under-developed Bechuanaland Protectorate was almost entirely dependent upon the good offices of these neighbouring countries. Already South Africa's action in banning Seretse had made it virtually impossible for him to carry out his duties. The cost of moving Mafeking to Protectorate territory was estimated at a million pounds.

The inquiry was therefore left with no alternative but to find South Africa as the sole reason for rejecting Seretse as Chief. The report stated that the unfriendly policy in the Union and Southern Rhodesia would have devastating effects on the Protectorate. In addition, it was quite evident to the commission that Tshekedi was the most unpopular man in Bechuanaland and that his decision to remove himself had not disrupted the Tribe at all – quite the contrary in fact. But Harragin had given Baring his word. The commissioners therefore seized upon this straw – 'disruption of the Tribe' – as a key reason for recommending the rejection of Seretse. The report itself, however, contained no evidence of any such disruption. Their final point, as Seretse had feared, cited his banning by the South Africans as a major obstacle to his carrying out the duties of Chief. Noel-Baker was appalled.

To his horror, the commissioners had even gone so far as to insert a paragraph recommending that Seretse would indeed make a wonderful Chief 'if conditions change . . . as they well might in a variety of ways'. This obscure reference appears to have been to the still hoped-for possibility of Seretse divorcing Ruth. Noel-Baker responded by sending an urgent message to Baring, whose formerly sound judgment he was now beginning to doubt, demanding that he come to England on the first available flight to help sort out the mess.

Then he dashed off a top-secret memo to the Prime Minister. '*I very much regret . . . warning . . . imminent danger . . . major political scandal,*' the words flew from his pen, propelled by his exasperation. '*Strongly recommend . . . show no-one . . . conceal the report . . . inflammatory . . . contains explosive material.*' Attlee was duly alarmed on receipt of this almost hysterical missive from his normally unflappable Minister for Commonwealth Relations, and instantly agreed to his recommendations. The report was suppressed. Circulated copies were hastily recalled and disposed of.

As soon as Baring arrived in London, Noel-Baker summoned his senior team and they closeted themselves in his office. The Minister made no effort to hide his displeasure.

'This is a disaster,' he said angrily, slamming the single remaining copy of the report onto the table before them. 'It's a mishmash of convoluted reasoning which the Opposition and the press would rip to pieces in an instant. God forbid they should ever get their hands on it. The whole point of the inquiry was to come up with some reason other than South Africa. The whole exercise has been a waste of time. And now the press are clamouring to hear the results. What are we going to do about it?'

Several hours later, the room was thick with cigarette smoke, the table littered with empty tea cups and the men around it mentally and emotionally drained, but they had finally concocted some extra reasons that could be used to refuse recognition.

The reasons they came up with were as fallacious as they were imperialistic. First on the list was the fact that the Bamangwato, a primitive and unlearned people, could not make up their minds by themselves. At the first *kgotla* they had rejected Seretse and his white wife. Six months later they had acclaimed him. Clearly the *kgotla* as a form of government was unreliable and there was a need to evolve a more acceptable and representative system. The fact that this contradicted the express finding of the inquiry regarding the legitimacy of the *kgotla* was conveniently ignored.

Secondly, Seretse had demonstrated gross irresponsibility in marrying without the prior permission of the Tribe. The grizzled headman's eloquent phrases about King David and forgiveness obviously cut no ice in Whitehall. Thirdly, they were unable to get away from the 'White Queen' issue – but they couched their deception rather more subtly than poor old 'Pop' Harragin had been able to, referring obliquely to the 'unsuitability of Ruth Khama to be a traditional queen and of her children to be Seretse's successors'.

To his credit, commissioner R S Hudson objected strongly to all these additional arguments, declaring them invalid. His was the lone voice, however, and he was railroaded by the economic and military imperatives of securing uranium and keeping South Africa within the fold of the Commonwealth. Even Clement Attlee was embarrassed by the whole affair, stating privately that refusing to recognise Seretse was 'as if we had been obliged to agree to Edward VIII's abdication so as not to annoy the Irish Free State and the USA'.

Back in Serowe, Ruth and Seretse continued their happy lives, tranquilly awaiting the birth of their first child. Seretse had installed a ping-pong table at one end of the verandah and they played daily. Ruth laboured over her Setswana grammar book in an effort to improve her command of the language. They rode horses, went for walks, watched the local soccer matches, visited the cattle posts and drove into Palapye each weekend to enjoy the Saturday night bioscope and to visit the Bradshaws, who had become their dearest friends.

Sitting round one evening after dinner, they discussed with Alan and Doris the problem of the press, who were still persistent despite the couple's resolute refusal to say anything to them at all.

'What a way to earn a living,' Alan laughed. 'I can't even go to the bar without them trying to buy me free drinks and pestering me for details about my relationship with you two. The questions they ask are unbelievable!'

'He's actually stopped going to the pub,' said Doris, 'because they upset him so much.'

'I'm afraid of having one too many and saying something I'll regret,' admitted Alan. 'I have to be on my guard the whole time. It takes all the fun out of it!'

'Tell them about that woman photographer,' Doris urged her husband.

'Oh yes,' said Alan. 'She's an American. Just been to Russia of all places to take a photograph of that bloke Stalin.'

'Really?' said Ruth, leaning forward. 'Must be the same woman who has been trying to persuade us to let her take our photograph. Margaret some-body. Been to Russia, has she? That's amazing! Imagine Stalin agreeing to pose for an American woman photographer. How on earth did she manage that?'

'She's an astonishing woman,' said Alan. 'She's been all over the world. She brought some of her photos into the bar the other night. I must say I was really impressed. They were terrific. She's very talented. And she's quite a character, let me tell you!'

'Well,' said Ruth, 'perhaps we should meet her and hear all about her trav-els.'

'It might be a good idea to let her photograph you,' said Alan. 'Her name is Margaret Bourke-White. She's world famous.'

'Hang on a minute,' said Seretse. 'We don't want any publicity.'

'Don't be too hasty,' Alan counselled his friend. 'Think about your situ-ation for a moment. Stuck in no man's land, the Chief and yet not the Chief. The British are stalling like mad and I bet they're up to no good. It might work in your favour if you get your photograph splashed around the world a bit, especially in America. Don't underestimate the power of publicity!'

Seretse nodded slowly. 'You may very well be right,' he said.

Ruth had been listening to this exchange with growing alarm. Meeting Margaret Bourke-White would be a wonderful diversion in sleepy Serowe, but the thought of being photographed and having her face plastered across the international media was appalling.

'Maybe we should have a preliminary chat with her,' Seretse was saying thoughtfully.

'No!' exclaimed Ruth.

Seretse took her hand. 'I know how you feel about our privacy, but we really don't have any, do we? I mean, our faces and our story have already been published in newspapers just about everywhere. So what harm can it do? Tshekedi is talking to them, the British are talking to them. We're the only ones who aren't putting our side across. Most of the journalists have been very decent to us. I think we should start playing along with them. Especially, as Alan says, in view of the British dragging their heels.'

'Well,' said Ruth uncertainly, 'if you really think it's a good idea . . .'

Slapping his knee, Seretse exclaimed: 'I do, I think it would be good strategy. Good public relations is just what we need right now. It might even persuade the British to get a move on. I'm sick of sitting in limbo.'

'It's just that they always twist everything we say,' protested Ruth. 'Don't you remember how awful it was when we were still in London?'

Alan and Doris did their best to persuade her that Seretse was right and by the end of the evening she was reconciled to the idea. Before returning to Serowe they penned a note that Alan agreed to deliver to the hotel for them the next morning, inviting the lady photographer to tea that afternoon in Serowe.

Margaret Bourke-White was delighted when eventually the Khamas agreed to be photographed. She had sat around the bar in Palapye for days listening to the tales of frustration from the other photographers, none of whom had managed to get much more than a fuzzy long-distance image of the couple as they ran from house to car or sat well back in the shadows of their verandah. She had captured some marvellous images in and around Serowe, but without a few clear shots of Ruth and Seretse to tell the story, these would be meaningless. She therefore accepted the invitation with alacrity and duly presented herself at the bungalow.

She had a portfolio with her as well as some back issues of *Life* magazine containing her work. Ruth and Seretse pored over the photographs, fascinated by their content and impressed by the remarkable quality. Margaret proved to be most entertaining company, regaling them with amusing tales of her assignments to photograph Joseph Stalin and Gandhi. By the end of the afternoon, it had been agreed that she should spend the following day with them and take photographs as they went about their normal daily routine in Serowe.

She arrived the next morning in time for breakfast, strung about with an impressive array of cameras and lenses, carrying a bag full of rolls of film. With the professional skill and tact that had made her one of the world's top photographers, she soon set the young couple at ease.

'Try to pretend I'm not here. Just be your normal selves,' she encouraged them, snapping away.

The two photo features that appeared in *Life* as the result of this assignment propelled their love story to an enormous new audience in America, where the press had previously been fairly uninterested. American journalists now jumped on the bandwagon, and the ripples spread ever wider, touching lives and stimulating public debate and opinion across the United States and Canada.

Following their momentous decision to open up to the press, Seretse finally agreed to talk to the persistent Noel Monks. Monks was delighted that his patience had finally paid off. His pen flew across the notebook, covering page after page with his own brand of shorthand, as Seretse answered his questions in a wide-ranging interview. Monks made sure that he covered every possible subject, from Seretse's view on the tribal administration to his relationship with his uncle, his plans for the chieftainship and, finally, the attitudes of the local white community and the complex, touchy question of racial discrimination in neighbouring South Africa.

Monks shocked Seretse by revealing that all British men serving in the administration had to sign a pledge undertaking that they would not be a party to miscegenation.

'Don't you find it remarkable,' Monks probed, 'that whites in England don't have a problem with your marriage to Ruth – in fact, most of my readers think it's absolutely wonderful. And yet, out here, the two of you are ostracised by just about every white family in the country?'

Seretse nodded soberly. 'Yes,' he admitted. 'I must say it's something that does confound one. Ruth and I have often spoken about the change that seems to come over the British once they come out here to southern Africa. We've not found any satisfactory answers.'

'It seems to me that they are influenced by the Boers,' commented Monks. 'After all, the South Africans regard your country as their backyard. I must say I was surprised to find that racial segregation is just as much a fact of life here as it is in the Union.'

'Not at all,' said Seretse stiffly. 'We have no racist laws here. People are free to move about and live wherever they please. The black man still has dignity in Bechuanaland.'

'Really?' said Monks mockingly. 'The Palapye Hotel won't even serve a beer to a black man!'

'Ah, but that is different,' explained Seretse. 'The local law here, introduced by my grandfather, prohibits blacks from buying alcohol. King Khama was a great temperance supporter, as I'm sure you know. The traders have had their fingers burnt before – they will not serve liquor to a Mongwato.'

'But the hotel won't serve blacks at all,' Monks insisted. Seretse felt a prickle of unease at the direction the conversation was taking. Despite Monks' apparent sympathy for himself and Ruth, he still did not trust the journalist fully and was wary of being drawn into a discussion on the emotional subject of race lest he be misquoted.

'I'll tell you what,' Monks continued. 'Let's go over there right now and see what happens. See if they will serve you. After all, you have been proclaimed Chief in the *kgotla*.'

Seretse's rational mind knew that he should not rise to Monks' bait. Everyone knew the hotel was for whites only. There was no law. It was an accepted fact. Blacks simply did not go there. They did not need to. Most of them had probably never even thought of going there. What for? A cup of tea? They could have that at home, or with friends. Going to a hotel was simply not part of their culture. The whites were welcome to it. And yet . . . unwillingly he found himself rising to his feet and following Monks as the journalist, salivating at the thought of yet another glorious headline, strode across the road to the hotel.

As they entered, heads swivelled and the lunch-time chatter was cut off in mid-sentence. The customers, all white, stared in shocked disbelief. In the silence the floorboards creaked as Monks headed for the bar. Glancing up, the barman saw Seretse following in Monks' wake. His jaw dropped, his eyes widened. His hand shook as he carefully set down the glass he was wiping.

Monks leaned over the bar counter and said casually: 'A cold beer – and a lemonade, please, Jannie.'

The barman looked from Noel to Seretse and then at his customers. What was he to do? He knew the customers would back him. 'Sorry Noel, you know the rules. No blacks in the bar. I can serve you, but not Mr Khama.'

'I am a resident of the hotel,' said Monks firmly. 'And I'm ordering drinks – are you refusing to serve me?'

The barman was sweating by now, seething with anger that the journalist had engineered this situation. 'I can give you a room at the back and serve you there,' he said, anxious to prevent an ugly incident that might drive away his customers.

At last one of them, a burly farmer dressed in khaki shorts with hands like hams, came to his aid. 'You bloody *uitlanders* come here and want to cause trouble,' he said to Monks, in a thick Afrikaans accent, totally ignoring Seretse. 'We can't have blacks in here. That's the rule. You're a visitor here. Either stick by our rules or get out.'

'You stay out of this, I'm talking to the barman,' said Monks, turning his back. The burly farmer rose to his feet and the bar began to hum with anticipation.

A British official, enjoying his noonday gin and tonic, tapped Monks on the shoulder. 'I say, old man,' he began. 'No need for this sort of thing you know. Be a good chap and don't cause a scene. It's far too hot.'

Seretse stood silently, his arms at his sides, his eyes watching the gathering, feeling the waves of animosity. A deep-seated anger rose within him, tinged with sorrow. He realised the situation was only going to degenerate. The point had been made. 'Let's go, Noel, I'm not thirsty any more,' he said with a quiet dignity that silenced the angry murmurings. Turning on his heel he walked out of the bar.

Monks followed reluctantly. It would have made a better story if the farmer had punched Seretse, but this was good enough. It would bring home to the British public the reality of discrimination in southern Africa.

11
Treachery

BARING, THE WEIGHT OF NOEL-BAKER'S IRE HEAVY UPON HIM, HAD RETURNED from London to map out a strategy with the men on the ground. Summoning Harragin, Sillery and Nettleton to his office, he went straight to the point.

'I'm afraid there is considerable disquiet in London about the commission's report,' he said bluntly. 'The Minister is furious and doesn't want it published. It doesn't give him the ammunition he needs to deny Seretse recognition, and the South Africans are champing at the bit. I am sure you have all read Malan's statement in the press yesterday.' The South African Prime Minister had made a public announcement that he would soon present a formal demand to the British for the transfer of the Territories to South Africa.

'So . . .' the High Commissioner leaned back in his chair and let his gaze travel slowly around the table. 'It's up to us. Seretse will be refused recognition. We have to find a way of getting him and Ruth out of the Protectorate without any disturbances. And once they are out, we have to keep them out. Any ideas?'

Total silence greeted this statement. 'I know. It's a tough one,' said Baring. 'But it has to be done, and the sooner the better. All this shilly-shallying around is not doing us any good. If we simply announce that we are refusing to recognise him while he and Ruth are in Serowe there will be all hell to pay. The Tribe will go berserk. So we have to get them to leave willingly. Once they're out we can do whatever is needed to keep them out. Now, how are we going to get out of this mess without bringing down on our necks the wrath of the South Africans or the wrath of the Bamangwato?'

Once again, the group received his words in silence. Was the High Commissioner suggesting that Ruth and Seretse should be enticed out of the Protectorate under false pretences?

'Well,' began Sillery hesitantly.

'Yes, yes, speak up, man!' said Baring.

Sillery was another of the British officials, and there were to be many of them, who was uncomfortable with the role being imposed on him by virtue of his position in the government. He knew and loved Bechuanaland and her people, and this matter of disinheriting the rightful Chief was becoming more distasteful to him with every twist of the path. He said: 'If we are going to do it, it would be best to do so during the rainy season. Certainly before mid-February if possible. Because that would mean a large proportion of the people are away from Serowe, tending their crops. I believe this would go a long way towards minimising disturbances. As you know, sir, the police force is totally inadequate to cope with any large-scale rioting.'

'Absolutely,' agreed Baring. 'Good point.'

'It's most unfortunate that things have turned out the way they have,' Sillery went on, speaking almost to himself. 'The people really seem to like Ruth. And she seems quite at home in Serowe – it's amazing actually. Of course most whites won't have anything to do with her – but she doesn't seem to mind. Some of them are friendly . . .'

'Yes,' said Baring, 'but we mustn't allow ourselves to get sentimental about this. And we must find a way of getting them to go willingly, without upsetting the Tribe. Of course, we don't want to upset Seretse either. It's important we keep him on our side. Who knows, if Ruth doesn't last we'll be working with him as Chief before very long.'

Harragin cleared his throat and began pompously: 'Of course we can exclude him under Proclamation No. 15 of 1907.'

'Quite,' said Baring with ill-concealed irritation. 'But that would hardly meet our criteria of them leaving willingly and the Tribe being happy to let them go, would it?'

The judge subsided, hurt that his efforts on the commission of inquiry and the subsequent report had evidently been appreciated by nobody. He had been given an impossible task and now he was in trouble for having failed to perform it. He decided to take no more part in the discussion.

'Well,' ventured Sillery again, 'I do know they are a bit short of money. Because of this delay in confirming him as Chief he hasn't been able to sell any of his cattle. And then of course there's still the dispute with his uncle over King Khama's will. That's an added complication. So he doesn't have much ready cash.'

'That's useful,' said Baring, 'very useful indeed. We can certainly sweeten the pill. Sweeten it considerably, I dare say.'

At last Nettleton spoke up. Although he had not spent as much time in the Protectorate as the veteran Sillery, he had come to know the Bamangwato quite well, and much of the face-to-face dealing with Seretse had fallen to him. 'We'd have to be very careful about how we made the offer, sir,' he said cautiously. 'Seretse is a decent chap. I'm not sure he'd take kindly to a bribe.'

'We're not going to offer him a bribe, man,' Baring rounded on the younger fellow. 'Heavens above, don't go saying things like that! We are simply going to give him a decent allowance to enable him to live comfortably without having to earn his keep as Chief of the Bamangwato.'

At this point, Sillery felt obliged to support his junior. 'Sir, I do think you need to consider the fact that Seretse is a highly principled individual. He may be extremely offended by even the suggestion of some sort of payment. It would have to be done very carefully indeed.'

'Yes, yes, I understand,' said Baring. 'Point taken, thank you.'

But Sillery had not finished. 'If I may, sir,' he continued diffidently, 'the amount should be fairly substantial in order to make sure that he doesn't feel it's being offered to him as a sop. The figure needs to represent a correct estimation of his worth as a chief . . .' His voice tapered off uncertainly.

'Well, Sillery, what sum do you have in mind?' Baring challenged him.

Sillery looked at his shoes.

'Fifty pounds a month, sixty, seventy?' asked Baring.

'At least a hundred,' muttered Sillery, embarrassed at the High Commissioner's jockeying tone. 'A hundred pounds a month!' Baring almost shouted. 'You must be out of your mind! That's at the top end of the salary scale! For a young fellow like that? To sit in London doing damn-all?'

'He is the Chief, Sir,' Sillery said boldly. 'And I'm sure he would rather sit in the *kgotla* ruling his people than in London doing damn-all.'

Nettleton gazed at his superior in admiration, while Baring's brow furrowed at this uncharacteristic display of impertinence by the scholarly Resident Commissioner.

'Well,' he said, deciding to ignore it, 'that decision, of course, is not up to us. We will recommend to London that they take into account the fact that he is the chief-designate when fixing upon the exact sum to be offered. Now, are we all agreed?' He ticked off the points on his fingers as he spoke: 'One, Seretse and Ruth are to be invited to London before the end of the rainy season. Two, they must be persuaded to leave willingly in the belief that such a trip is in their best interests. Three, they must persuade the Tribe likewise. Four, once in London they must not be allowed to return. The Minister thinks Seretse can be prevailed upon to give up the chieftainship voluntarily, but I doubt that. I doubt it very much. My own feeling is that they'll have to refuse to recognise him and sweeten the pill by offering him an allowance.'

The group nodded collectively, dismally. The meeting had left a bitter taste. Without exception, they wished themselves elsewhere that day.

Meanwhile, Noel-Baker in London had been wrestling with the dilemma. An honourable man, he could see no honourable way out. The South Africans were implacable and powerful. Through long, dark winter evenings he sat deep in thought at his desk. The stress was beginning to take its toll, and his health was failing. Confirmation from officials in Serowe of Ruth's pregnancy, which had been maliciously rumoured ever since the couple had married 15 months previously, increased the urgency. Something had to be done.

In desperation, he grasped at the only straw to hand – a report from the High Commissioner's office in Pretoria which had come through a few weeks previously and which he had initially dismissed as unthinkably dishonourable. In a way, he rationalised to his protesting conscience, it was simply a modification of his original plan to take Seretse into the government's confidence. He had been disappointed when this had been ruled out as being too risky. But now Baring had unwittingly presented him with a chance to follow his initial instincts.

Once again, he summoned Baring to London for consultations. The High Commissioner was brutally frank. He could see no other way out. The strength of his personal conviction was vibrant in his words. Summarising his initial report, he told Noel-Baker firmly: 'I believe we have no option but to propose to Cabinet that we recommend Seretse and Ruth be invited to London on the pretext of further discussions regarding the chieftainship. Once they are here, we make them an offer they cannot afford to refuse. Then we prevent them from returning – for a reasonable period. I know it's a tough one, sir, but there is no other way. The furore will die down after a while. And it will be much better if they are in London before we announce that we are withholding recognition. The distance will create some sort of a barrier, and make it easier for our chaps on the ground out there.'

Noel-Baker was distraught. He berated himself for not following his instincts right at the beginning and inviting Seretse over to London for talks – man to man. After all, Seretse was an Oxford graduate, he must be a reasonable fellow. Surely they could have come to some agreement – anything would have been preferable to this complicated and far from honourable situation. Perhaps even now it would be possible to persuade him to do the right thing, to abdicate, voluntarily, for the good of the Tribe.

'With all due respect, sir, I don't believe that will work,' Baring replied. 'This is a no-win situation for all of us. The sooner we realise that the better.'

Anxious to get the unpleasant business out of way as soon as possible, and mindful of the looming general election – and of course Ruth's pregnancy – Noel-Baker summarised his proposals in a memorandum to Cabinet. He stressed that the commission of inquiry had found Seretse not a fitting and proper person to be Chief. At its meeting on 31st January 1950, he urged Cabinet to make a hasty decision. In the absence of any better ideas, they obliged. They also confirmed that the Harragin Report could not be published. The Cabinet Secretary was instructed to recall all copies of Noel-Baker's memo referring to the inquiry's unfortunate findings. A white paper would be published instead.

On 2 February Noel-Baker cabled Harragin (who was standing in for Baring in Pretoria) telling him to instruct Sillery to invite Ruth and Seretse to London for talks about their future.

Sillery's heart sank when he received the telegram containing these instructions. During the long silence from London he had allowed himself to dare to hope that his masters were devising a plan more in keeping with the nobler aspects of the British tradition of foreign rule. But it would appear London had swallowed Baring's plan hook, line and sinker. The cable emphasised that the couple should arrive in London before 16 February and that Sillery should do his best to persuade Ruth to come too. She was to be offered the best possible medical care during her pregnancy and confinement.

He was grateful to note that there was no mention of the issue of financial inducement. At least he would be spared that embarrassment. He was authorised merely to handle any queries regarding costs rather vaguely with the phrase 'they would not be out of pocket over the journey'. Like Baring, Sillery was convinced that it was the lesser of two evils when compared with the South Africans marching in and taking over the Protectorate, which he knew they were fully capable of. What dismayed him, however, was the apparent lack of backbone of the British in not being prepared to defend the Territory against such acquisitiveness.

As January had passed with no word from the British, the Bamangwato had waited restlessly. To be without a Chief was an unsettling business. They did not know how to deal with it. Of course, most of them regarded Seretse as their Chief. But until the British recognised this fact, he could not sit in the *kgotla* and listen to their problems as the Chief should, or tour their lands on horseback, giving encouragement and advice as the energetic King Khama had done. They tried to carry on with life as usual. The brief rainy season was upon them and there was no time to be lost if a crop was to planted in time to yield a harvest that would see them through the dry months.

Ruth was bloomingly pregnant. Her feet swelled in the midday heat, but Seretse insisted she lie down every afternoon and by evening the swelling had gone down. They would stroll through the sandy paths at dusk, watching the colourful dying of the day, responding to the greetings of the women busy at their cooking fires and joking with the children who waved shyly from the shadows. Serowe was now home for Ruth. She knew her way about and was content with Seretse's constant company and the budding life within her. They enjoyed the friendship of the few whites who offered it and ignored the others. They both tried to live for the moment, resolutely pushing away thoughts of the future.

The ringing of a bicycle bell heralded the arrival of a khaki-uniformed messenger from the DC's office, bearing Sillery's telegram. Seretse bounded down the steps to seize it from him. 'News at last!' he shouted.

Ruth caught her breath. Dear God, please let it be good news, she prayed silently. 'It's from the Resident Commissioner,' Seretse told her as his eyes scanned the brief message, 'he wants to meet us urgently in Lobatse. To-morrow!'

'Well, well,' said Goareng, 'it looks as though the wheels of bureaucracy are turning at last. I wonder what they are up to now?'

'Yes, I wonder,' agreed Seretse. 'But at least there's some action. They want to talk to me. That's better than playing the waiting game day after day.'

Ruth nodded in agreement. 'But aren't you a bit surprised that they have invited me too?' she asked. 'This is the first time they've acknowledged that I even exist!'

'Maybe it's because you are now carrying the future heir to the throne of the Bamangwato,' said Seretse, patting the bulge of her pregnancy, which was now clearly evident. 'But are you sure you feel up to the trip to Lobatse? We don't want to harm the future heir.'

'Of course I am. I'm as fit as a fiddle. And I'm not letting you go all that way on your own. I want to know what they're up to!'

Early the next morning they set off. Ruth by now was well-established in her picnic basket tradition – which was to last all her life. She never set out on a trip without her basket. Seretse teased her about it, but was always grateful at some point in the journey when she produced a cool drink, a crunchy apple or a refreshing face-wipe.

In Lobatse, Sillery welcomed them warmly. True to British civil service tradition throughout the Empire, a cup of tea was produced for them. After some small talk about the state of the crops and the possibility of sufficient rain, which Ruth endured with ill-concealed impatience, he finally broached the subject of the meeting. The Secretary of State for Commonwealth Relations, Philip Noel-Baker, had invited them both to a meeting in Whitehall to discuss the future of the Bamangwato. As there was a general election scheduled in Britain at the end of February, they were wanted in London before mid-February. He had therefore taken the liberty of booking two tickets on the flying boat leaving Victoria Falls on 10 February. He trusted that would give them sufficient time to prepare for the journey.

Ruth and Seretse's eyes met – hers full of excitement and hope, his masking the furious activity of his brain in trying to fathom the purpose behind the proposal. Squeezing her hand beneath the table, Seretse turned his gaze on Sillery, whose furrowed brow betrayed his anxiety lest he fail in this crucial assignment.

'What has happened to the report on the Harragin inquiry, if I may ask?' said Seretse mildly.

Sillery played dumb. 'London has not yet decided yet what action to take on the Harragin Report,' he replied.

'There has been considerable speculation in the press that I am not to be confirmed after all,' Seretse probed further.

'I am informed that the government hasn't taken any final decision yet,' Sillery was quick to assure him. 'That's why they want to discuss the matter with you further.'

'Well, of course, I'll have to consult the Tribe,' said Seretse. 'I couldn't possibly make such a decision on my own. You do understand?'

'Yes, yes, I quite understand,' Sillery replied. 'But please bear in mind the time constraints.' Seretse nodded and the couple rose to take their leave.

No sooner had they driven off than Sillery cabled Liesching: '*They were neither very communicative nor could I form a clear estimate of their attitude.*'

Seretse did not know what to make of the invitation, but he felt instinctively that they should accept it. It seemed the only way to move the impasse forward. But he was determined to make no decision without consulting the Tribe. He dispatched a messenger that evening to inform his uncles, councillors and age regiment members that an urgent *kgotla* meeting would be convened the following morning.

Seretse told the assembled tribesmen of the invitation to London. Grizzled heads nodded sagely. Yes, this was good. King Khama had gone to London for a meeting with the Great White Queen and good things had been the result. On the other hand, their young Chief had travelled to London before, and look what had happened! He had returned with this woman, with skin like milk and hair like the sun on a field of corn, who could not speak their language. But she was a good woman. They had grown accustomed to her now. Yes, it would seem going to London was a good thing.

The younger men, the new generation of western-educated Bamangwato, frowned in puzzlement at this new twist in the saga. The trust that their elders still had in the British, their protectors against the Boers, had been severely dented by the Harragin inquiry and the long delay in confirming Seretse as Chief.

They also perceived disturbing contradictions between what they had been taught by the missionaries, and the behaviour of most of the government officials. What was more, many of them had travelled in the Union and had experienced racial discrimination at the hands of British whites as well as Boers. Education and experience had given birth to suspicion. The discussion went round and round for hours.

Ruth had awoken that morning with a sense of disquiet. The more she thought about the invitation, the more she had become convinced, despite Seretse's assurances, that it was strange she had been invited too. Seretse conveyed her misgiving to the meeting. It was seized upon by the young men. They argued forcefully, believing that it was a very real possibility that the British would find some way of keeping Ruth in London if she left the safety of Serowe. And then that would mean Seretse would have to stay in London, too. His oft-stated devotion to her left no doubt in their minds about that. Finally, agreement was reached. Seretse would ask the Resident Commissioner for a written assurance that both the Chief and his queen would be allowed to return whenever they wanted to. Then the Tribe would agree to them going to London for the meeting. Not before.

Sillery had arrived in the middle of the morning to monitor the process of the *kgotla*. Tempers were obviously running high in Whitehall and Liesching pestered him ceaselessly for news from Serowe. Anxious to placate his seniors, but unable to participate formally in the *kgotla*, he invited Ruth and Seretse to lunch at the DC's residence the following day. When they arrived, Seretse immediately broached the Tribe's demand for a written guarantee that they would be able to return freely. Sillery responded vaguely that it would not be necessary, while he mentally cursed Malan, Baring, Liesching and the entire CRO for putting him into a position where he was forced to betray his own principles in the line of duty.

Seretse tried to press him, insisting that the Tribe required a guarantee.

'I couldn't possibly give such a guarantee,' stalled Sillery. 'It would have to come from Pretoria. We don't have time for that, I'm afraid. And I don't think you should worry about it. Why would London want to stop you from returning?'

'Well, it's mainly for Ruth, actually. They are worried that the British might try to keep her in London,' explained Seretse.

'Nonsense!'

'But you won't give us a guarantee,' Seretse persisted.

'It's beyond the limit of my authority. I'm sorry, but you'll simply have to take our word for it,'

Ruth spoke up for the first time. 'I'm afraid that might not be acceptable,' she said. 'Unfortunately, the Tribe doesn't seem to have much regard for the word of the British authorities any more.' She met Sillery's surprised glance with a steady gaze.

They ate lunch in an awkward atmosphere. Seretse was subdued and did not have much of an appetite. Ruth tried to cover for him by chattering gaily, giving Sillery the mistaken impression that she was quite keen on a shopping trip to London. He kept trying to steer the conversation towards their decision regarding their response to Noel-Baker's invitation, but neither would be drawn.

'We are subject to the Tribe. They feel we might not be allowed to return. I have to respect that,' was all Seretse would say. Having burnt his fingers once over not securing the permission of the Tribe, he was determined never again to make a similar mistake. He told Sillery they would go back to the *kgotla* and tell them that no letter of guarantee was possible. Their response would be conveyed to him by nightfall. For good measure, Sillery assured him that no British official would address a *kgotla* while he was away.

After they had left, Sillery summarised the discussions in another lengthy cable to Liesching. The morsel about Ruth talking gaily of shopping in London was seized upon to indicate that the couple would accept the invitation. Noel-Baker threw his last reserves of energy into ensuring that the Seretse affair would not damage Labour's chances in the general election. Top-secret meetings at the highest levels were held, with great emphasis on the 'sensitivity' and 'delicate nature' of the 'Bamangwato succession problem'.

Sillery was wrong. Ruth had no intention of returning to London. His bluster about the guarantee at lunch had not fooled her for a moment. 'They'll never let me back if I go, I just know it,' she said. 'Seretse – don't go! Please! I can't face being separated from you again. Think of the baby.'

Through his thin shirt he could feel that her face was wet. 'Ruth, my dear love, don't cry. You'll upset the baby. Shush now, shush.'

'Sorry,' she said, scrubbing at her face with his handkerchief. 'I'll be all right. It's just the thought of being separated again . . .'

'I know. I feel the same. But I have to go.'

'I know you do. But damn them for putting us in this position! I know it's all because of South Africa. Why are they kowtowing to those racists?'

'It won't be for long, I promise you. I'll be back in a few weeks.'

'Are you sure they can't stop you from coming back?'

'It's my country, how can they stop me? Besides, I trust old Sillery. I know you don't like him, but . . .'

'It's not a question of not liking him,' Ruth interjected. 'I just don't trust him – I don't trust any of them any more. After all they've done to us I don't know how you can trust them either.'

'An Englishman's word is his bond, my dear. That's what they are taught at school and college. That's how they are brought up. It's part of their culture. I learnt that at Oxford. Sillery is an honourable chap. He wouldn't lie to me. If he says they'll let us back, then I believe him.'

'But he also said it wasn't up to him, remember? He said it was outside his authority.'

'He was talking about the letter of guarantee. It's just red tape, that's all.'

Together with millions throughout the former Empire, Seretse believed the many public pronouncements of the Labour government's commitment to the principles of equality and freedom for all races. What he didn't realise was that under Proclamation no 15 of 1907 he could indeed be kept out of the Bechuanaland Protectorate. This was the secret weapon in the British armoury, if all else failed.

That afternoon's *kgotla* meeting had been as heated as the previous sessions.

'Tell them to give me Ruth's ticket. I will go in her place and explain that the marriage of our *kgosi* is none of their business. Why do they want to take him far away from us now?' shouted one young hothead. Many nodded in agreement.

Then one of Seretse's uncles stated the argument in a way they could all understand, according to the male supremacy of the time: 'Why must the woman go? This is no business for women! Women do not attend the *kgotla*. Government is the business of men. Women stay at home and care for the household.'

Enthusiastic applause greeted this statement and the argument was clinched. The Chief would go. His wife would remain at home.

It was unremarked at the time, but this *kgotla* represented the end of an era. It was a sad day. A crack had appeared in the bridge of trust that had been established between the Bamangwato and the British by the missionaries a century before, and sustained through decades of diligent British administration. It soon became a gaping wound. The bridge was to fall down completely.

On 10 February 1950, Seretse left Serowe alone. Goareng drove him to Francistown to catch the small plane to Victoria Falls. After attempting cheerful conversation for several miles with no response from his stony-faced cousin, Goareng gave up and the journey was completed in silence.

Seretse carried with him a letter to Noel-Baker from the Bamangwato, confirming that they had decided Ruth should not accompany 'our Chief' because the administration 'refused to make a promise' that she should be safely returned to them. The letter went on to raise the issue of South African and Southern Rhodesian objections to the marriage. '*Throughout our history both these countries have sought to dispossess us of our land and our rights and it was on account of this very apprehension that we originally sought the protection of Great Britain. We submit that our apprehension at present is not unfounded. We as a free people deny that they have any right to try even to influence the eventual decision which rests solely with ourselves and your government.'*

They did not receive a reply.

On 15 February 1950, Seretse's flying boat landed at Southampton. There to meet him was John Keith of the colonial office, accompanied by a burly bodyguard from Scotland Yard, who said smartly: 'Evening, sir,' and took Seretse's briefcase from him.

'What's this?' Seretse asked Keith, in surprise. 'Does the Minister think I need a minder?'

'No, not at all,' Keith was quick to reassure him. 'We thought he might be useful to you, that's all.'

The man did indeed prove useful in shielding him from the press who besieged him as soon as he came ashore, but Seretse made it clear that he did not want him as a constant companion.

Once they were settled in the car en route for London, he turned to Keith and said: 'Can't you tell me what's going on, John? I mean what is really going on? Why am I here?'

Keith was another of the British officials involved in the Seretse affair for whom his duties brought a crisis of conscience. He respected the young man enormously, admired him and was sympathetic to the ordeal he had endured so far. But he was a British civil servant. He couldn't let the side down. At this juncture, he hoped against hope that Noel-Baker would succeed in persuading Seretse of the wisdom of standing down voluntarily. His task was to inform the Minister of Seretse's state of mind and mood, in order to arm him with every possible tool to make the meeting a success. He was determined to do whatever he could to contribute to this, and parried Seretse's questioning as best he could. Later that evening he wrote the first of what would become almost daily reports on Seretse's mental, emotional and physical state for his superiors in Whitehall. *His mood is firm and he has a shrewd appreciation of the issues at stake,* he wrote. *He is obviously not going to give in here and now. This is not a personal matter. He would have to go back and consult his tribe on any proposals made to him. He is a gentleman and has a lot of moral courage.* Reading this report later that night, Noel-Baker pencilled in the margin '*I agree.*'

They arrived in Whitehall on a grey, damp evening. Black clouds, soggy and threatening, hung low over the city. Seretse immediately felt his spirits lowered by the February weather he remembered so well. He was taken directly to the Permanent Secretary's office, where he met Percivale Liesching for the first time. Although at pains to appear courteous, Liesching's manner was brusque. He repelled Seretse – who was by now in such a state of heightened tension that his emotional antennae were extra receptive to every nuance and shadow of meaning.

Although tired by his trip, Seretse managed to appear both relaxed and alert. The Permanent Secretary's first comment, although couched in a roundabout fashion, was: where was Ruth? Seretse chose not to answer, whereupon Liesching obscurely advised him 'to reflect upon this in the interval between now and your meeting with the Secretary of State tomorrow morning'.

12

Dishonour

At 11.30 am on 16 February 1950, Seretse presented himself once again at Whitehall. He was joined by an elderly solicitor, Lord Rathcreedan, whose services had been procured for him by his South African lawyer Percy Fraenkel. The two were escorted along the sombre corridors to the Minister's suite of offices. Noel-Baker, flanked by Liesching and the Lord Privy Seal, Viscount Addison, shook Seretse's hand warmly.

'How good of you to come, Mr Khama. May I introduce Viscount Addison? Sir Percivale, of course, you have already met. And this is Sir Sidney Abrahams, our legal adviser.' Seretse shook hands with them all and introduced Rathcreedan.

Thanks to the blood of his royal forebears and the social polish he had acquired in the stately homes of his uncle's friends while he was at Oxford, 27-year-old Seretse was not overawed by this gathering of distinguished, powerful gentlemen. His body was tensed, as an athlete before a race, and his mind was honed razor-sharp by anxiety and an overwhelming desire to have this thing resolved once and for all. He clasped his hands together beneath the table and breathed deeply. Whatever they were about to throw at him, he was ready.

He regarded the men opposite him with a clear gaze. Noel-Baker looked back at him, a deep sadness within him, a useless frustration burning in his tired mind.

'I trust you had a good trip, Mr Khama?' he enquired courteously.

Seretse nodded. 'Yes, thank you.'

'We're very grateful,' the Minister continued, 'that you have so resolutely refused to speak to the press. They can be quite ruthless in their pursuit of a story.' Again, Seretse acknowledged the courtesy with a polite inclination of his head. 'I understand there is quite a gathering of the press corps out in Bechuanaland too?' Noel-Baker continued.

'Indeed there is, sir,' said Seretse, acutely aware of Liesching's cold stare.

'Well now,' Noel-Baker steeled himself to proceed to the crux of the matter. 'I extended an invitation to Mrs Khama to attend this meeting as well as yourself. Is there any particular reason why she has not accompanied you?'

'May I enquire why you invited her? We were rather surprised as she has never been consulted before,' replied Seretse. As Noel-Baker cleared his throat and glanced at Liesching, Seretse seized the initiative and pressed his point. 'Actually, if I may speak quite frankly, the Tribe believes this is a trick on the part of the British government and that they would have difficulty in getting her back. We asked for a guarantee about her return but this was refused. This confirmed the Tribe's suspicions and, I must confess, I have come to share them myself.'

His gaze was fixed on Noel-Baker who, aware of Liesching's steely presence beside him, forced himself to follow the agreed game-plan for the meeting. 'Don't you think her presence would be helpful now?' he asked.

'That depends on the outcome of this conversation,' replied Seretse. 'Can't a guarantee be given now?'

As the men facing him maintained their silence, Seretse's heart sank. Ruth's instincts had obviously been correct. He almost smiled as he imagined her satisfaction.

Noel-Baker eventually spoke. 'Don't you think it would be in the interests of the Tribe if you gave up the chieftainship voluntarily?'

Seretse exhaled deeply, unaware that he had been holding his breath. At last they'd come out into the open. This was what it was about. They wanted him to abdicate. Like Edward VIII. But Ruth wasn't divorced – she was only white.

The Minister hurried on: 'If you did, we would advance you £1,100 a year as an allowance, and help you find some suitable employment. We would exclude your uncle from the Bamangwato Reserve and do everything possible to obtain the best medical attention and accommodation for Mrs Khama during her approaching confinement. The whole affair would be kept under review.' Unable to meet Seretse's eyes, the Minister stuck rigidly to the agreed text: 'We regard this as a friendly proposal on behalf of the British government to diffuse a potentially explosive situation which threatens the best interests of the Bamangwato Tribe.'

Later, the men of the government were to comment among themselves on the young African's amazing calm and courtesy. Not once did his tone or manner betray his inner turmoil. He looked them straight in the eyes and said firmly: 'The Tribe and I believe the government is refusing to confirm me as Chief of the Bamangwato because you are frightened of annoying Dr Malan and the rest of the South African government. You are also frightened of offending the whites in Southern Rhodesia who, like the South Africans, believe in persecuting African people. It has been very difficult for me to believe that the government would act like this, particularly towards the people of one of its own Protectorates. Nevertheless it looks as though you would rather hurt the Tribe than annoy Dr Malan.'

Now that the issue of South Africa had been raised, the Minister took the bull by the horns and allowed himself to deviate from the script. The young man before him was obviously far too intelligent and astute to be fooled, and he for one was sick of demeaning himself by trying to pull the wool over his eyes. 'I will tell you in strict confidence,' he said, ignoring Liesching's restless shifting at his side, 'on the understanding that you will not quote me on it, that we differ greatly on many areas of policy from the governments of both South Africa and Southern Rhodesia. Anybody who follows our colonial policy at all closely would realise that it has always been the intention of the British government to do what they thought was right regardless of the views of these two countries.'

Seretse could only shake his head at the duplicity of this statement. If Noel-Baker believed that, then why was he asking him to abdicate? Why not demonstrate this 'difference of policy' by letting him reign with his white wife? He looked questioningly at Rathcreedan beside him. The old lawyer had

235

not said a word so far. Surely he could say something to refute the obvious anomalies in Noel-Baker's little speech? But Rathcreedan merely shuffled the papers before him, and remained silent.

'I am in no position to take any decisions myself,' stated Seretse. 'The Tribe must decide everything in *kgotla*. That is the way we do things in Bechuanaland. I would not like the people to think I have sold the chieftainship for money.'

He tried to explain to them that Africa, too, had a noble history of democratic government. The people, through the *kgotla*, made the Chief. The Chief could not make himself. Once again, silence. They did not want to understand.

'It would help,' Seretse continued, 'if we could see a copy of the report of the judicial inquiry into my suitability as Chief. May I?'

Again, Noel-Baker could not meet the young man's eyes. 'I fear I cannot show it to you,' he said.

'You refer to disturbances within the Tribe,' said Seretse. 'I can assure you that there will be no disturbances if I am confirmed as Chief. Might I not be allowed to rule for a probationary period?'

'I'm afraid not,' replied the Minister.

Seretse shrugged helplessly and looked again at his lawyer. Rathcreedan shook his head slightly.

At last Liesching interposed: 'Perhaps we should all adjourn at this point – and give you time for reflection. You might then see the wisdom of our proposal.'

Seretse agreed to the postponement as it would allow him time to send for Fraenkel. He could not face them single-handedly again. Rathcreedan had turned out to be more of a liability than a help. He wanted his own lawyer. Liesching proposed that they meet again on 25 February. They all nodded and rose from the conference table.

Seretse was stunned by the calm and unemotional manner in which Her Majesty's officers had suggested that he forego his birthright. His hand trembled as he lit a cigarette. Inhaling deeply, he struggled to get a grip on himself. His rage was foul as bile within him. He must remain calm. He would fight them to the end. But he must not allow his rage to make him mad, or careless.

He sent a brief telegram to Ruth: *Govt requests abdication in return for annual allowance. Am sending for Fraenkel. Another meeting next week. Love Seretse.* He also cabled Fraenkel to come to London immediately.

Thrusting his hands deeply into the pockets of his overcoat, the brim of his hat pulled well down to hide his features from passersby, Seretse walked aimlessly along the Haymarket. Of their own accord, his feet carried him towards the river – his favourite haunt. It was full of memories of Ruth. Realising where he was, he made his way along the Embankment to the spot where he had proposed to her, and stood there for a long time.

Rumblings from his empty stomach eventually reminded him that he had not eaten since the previous day, and he set off for a Lyons teashop.

He closed his eyes while sitting waiting for his tea, and saw again Ruth's fresh young face coming towards him in the Wig and Pen for their first date – her expression daring anyone to criticise her for meeting a black man alone for a drink. What a woman she was! Opening his eyes, he thanked the waitress who had arrived with his tea, and turned his attention to the mound of buttered toast. He was ravenous.

Returning to the flat, he sat down to write Ruth a long letter about the meeting. '*I couldn't believe it,*' he wrote, '*when he asked me to give up the chieftainship just like that. "Don't you think it would be in the interests of the Tribe?" he said. I can't believe the lengths to which these people seem prepared to go to appease the South Africans. And imagine offering me a thousand pounds a year to abdicate! That's what the Chief earns as a salary. And has done for years. What a nerve! What an insult!*' The incredulous phrases raced from his pen. '*What kind of Judas do they think I am? That I'd sell my birthright like that! I am totally sickened by the whole thing. And now I have to wait a whole week before anything else can be done. And as for that bumbling old idiot Fraenkel organised to represent me at the meeting, he never opened his mouth! He was absolutely no help whatsoever. I've cabled Fraenkel to get over here as soon as possible.*'

And now I've just got to wait – for a whole week. What on earth am I going to do with myself? I wish you were here! But I'm glad you are not because they still wouldn't give me a guarantee about your return to Serowe. They obviously have something up their sleeve. You were right, my darling. As you always are! And I daren't contact any of my old friends. Negotiations are at such a delicate stage. I simply cannot risk saying something out of turn, or speaking to anyone who could possibly be persuaded to speak to the press. Noel-Baker was most insistent that I should "keep quiet until after the general election". And of course, that's understandable. They don't need the boat to be rocked at this stage of the game . . .'

On and on he went, pouring out his heart to his wife, page after page, finding release in sharing it all with her – just as he had done during the *kgotlas*. He laughed wryly as he thought how upset he had been during that time. It seemed like a picnic compared to his current situation. At least there he had been surrounded by his family and his people. Now he was utterly isolated – more alone than ever before, because now he knew what life with Ruth was like. The fulfilment he had found in her in the early stages of their relationship had swelled like ripening fruit. She was, indeed, the other part of him. She might be 'the white woman' to everyone else but to him she was simply his Ruth. And now she bore his child within her. He imagined the soft swelling of her belly beneath his hands. He had no stomach for this dirty fight the British had forced on him. He was no longer sure of the rules, or even if there were any. But he would fight for Ruth, and for their baby, with everything in him.

The week dragged. Every evening, Muriel and a group of his friends gathered for drinks and discussion of the situation Seretse smoked and drank and didn't eat properly. A few cables came from Ruth and Goareng, assuring him of the Tribe's full support and wishing him well. He, in turn, cabled Ruth telling her to stay in Serowe, no matter what. When they had first learnt of her pregnancy they had agreed that the baby must be born in the village, as Seretse himself had been. Ruth had the utmost confidence in Dr Don Moikangoa, a senior doctor at the local hospital.

Fraenkel could not get there before 2 March because of the period required for yellow fever inoculation. So Seretse told Keith, who called in from time to time to see how he was getting on, that the meeting would have to be postponed until 3 March. Noel-Baker was relieved to receive this news. By then the general election would be behind them and he would be able to give the matter his undivided attention. Perhaps he could yet find a way to resolve the crisis by honest persuasion instead of underhand dealing and deception. But it was not to be. Labour was returned to power with a majority of just seven seats. Alarmed by the deterioration in his Commonwealth Secretary's health and the lack of progress on the Seretse affair, Prime Minister Attlee decided that he should be given a less onerous position, and promoted the energetic Gordon-Walker.

Like his predecessor, Gordon-Walker saw clearly that there was much at stake to warrant the government's policy of appeasement towards South Africa. However, unlike Noel-Baker, he was of a more modern generation of politician – with fewer scruples when it came to telling the lies necessary to carry the policy through.

Unmoved by Keith's regular reports which informed them that Seretse was depressed, worried, homesick and determined to return to Serowe as soon as possible, Liesching kept in touch with Baring. Both men were determined to see the matter through to its conclusion, no matter what it cost the young Chief, his wife or his Tribe.

The Permanent Secretary was delighted to find that his new Minister agreed with him regarding Seretse and the Bamangwato. This encouraged him to be even harsher in his recommendations – cabling Baring that Seretse should not be allowed to return to the Protectorate at all, not even to settle his affairs. He told the Minister Seretse would never relinquish the chieftainship voluntarily and they would be doing him a favour by imposing exile upon him. He proposed a five-year suspension of recognition, with payment of an allowance on condition both Seretse and his wife remained abroad.

Gordon-Walker took this proposal to the first working session of the new Cabinet on 3 March. Remarkably, in view of the desperate state of the British economy and the election set-back, the first subject on the agenda was 'Bechuanaland Protectorate: Chieftainship of the Bamangwato Tribe'.

Cabinet urged a few superficial changes to soften the blow – perhaps five years could be rephrased as 'a substantial period', while Seretse should be told recognition was not being 'refused' but 'postponed'. Such window-dressing made little difference to what was to go down in history as 'a very disreputable transaction'. The Minister was also instructed to make one more last-ditch attempt to get Seretse to resign.

Meanwhile Fraenkel had arrived in London and requested the minutes of the previous meeting in order to prepare himself. On Liesching's instructions, the minutes had been amended to exclude Noel-Baker's personal comments to Seretse about South Africa. Officials assured Fraenkel that the account they gave him was a full record of the meeting.

At 3 pm on March 3rd, Seretse and Fraenkel faced Gordon-Walker and his team across the table. The new Minister apologised for the delay occasioned by the general election – evidently unaware that it had been Seretse himself who had requested the postponement. The atmosphere was tense.

The Minister came straight to the point. 'Have you come to a decision yet?'

'As I told your predecessor,' Seretse replied cordially, 'it is not my decision to make. I must consult the Tribe before I can give you any answer.'

Fraenkel, keyed up by the long waiting period and anxious to redeem himself before his client, jumped in quickly. He told the meeting that the government had failed to give his client any reason why he would not be installed as Chief, and questioned their motive in asking him to give up his birthright on the vague grounds that to do so would be in the best interests of the Tribe. 'My client is eminently suited to be Chief and he has the support of the whole Tribe,' he declared. 'There is no danger at all of internal troubles if he is installed. I can't say what repercussions there might be if he is not.'

The Minister insisted he had inside information about dissension within the Tribe. He reiterated the government's offer of an allowance and assistance in finding suitable employment. At this point Seretse lost patience. 'The government's objections are ridiculous! I know of no previous occasion when a Chief was asked to give up his chieftainship because of dissension within the Tribe. In my case, it is obvious to everyone that I have done more to unify the Tribe than to divide it.'

Fixing him with a cold stare, Gordon-Walker ignored his outburst and again requested a decision. Seretse reiterated that such a decision was not his to give. At this, the Minister got to his feet, terminating all discussion, and said he would now put the matter to Cabinet and that Seretse and his lawyer would be informed of their position shortly. Turning on his heel he left the room, leaving Liesching to see the visitors out.

That evening a note was delivered to the flat summoning them to another meeting in the Minister's office at 6 pm on 6 March 1950. Gordon-Walker had received the Prime Minister's go-ahead to proceed with Seretse's banishment.

At the Cabinet meeting on the morning of 6 March, he was authorised to tell Seretse the government would postpone a decision on whether or not he should be recognised as Chief for a period of not less than five years. Tshekedi would be similarly exiled, but only from the Bamangwato Reserve, not from the entire Protectorate. The chieftainship would be placed in suspension and the Resident Commissioner would take over the functions of 'Native Authority'. Seretse should be offered an allowance of £1 100 a year on condition he and his wife did not return to Bechuanaland without permission. Arrangements would be made for Mrs Khama to return to London and receive proper medical attention.

The polished tabletop between them glowed in the light of the chandelier above it. The wind howled outside the tall, sash windows. Fraenkel had persuaded Seretse to allow Rathcreedan to be present as a further witness to the government's underhand dealings. Gordon-Walker baldly stated the Cabinet's decision.

Seretse raised his eyes from the gleaming table. 'Am I to understand that I am being kicked out of my own country?' he demanded.

'We can't allow you to go back for at least five years,' the Minister replied. 'The decision has been taken with great care and it is thought, on the whole, to be the wisest and fairest solution.'

Fraenkel shook his head, amazed that the man could utter such nonsense with a straight face.

'Must I simply accept this injustice? Is there no appeal?' Seretse said, looking desperately from Fraenkel to Rathcreedan.

Hopeless though he knew it to be, Fraenkel leapt to Seretse's aid. 'The British authorities gave an assurance that if both Mr and Mrs Khama came to England they would be allowed to return to Bechuanaland,' he said.

Liesching spoke for the first time, pointing out that in fact the Resident Commissioner had clearly stated he could give no such assurance in writing.

Seretse stared at Gordon-Walker. This was the face of the enemy. Full of rage, he spoke low and fast: 'I am well aware that the government has the power to exclude me from my own country, but I feel strongly that I have been tricked into coming here and now I'm not allowed to return. Why did you invite me here? I am bitterly disappointed at the way I have been treated. It was too much, I suppose, for you to recognise me as Chief, since I had broken all the rules and married a white woman. The Protectorate is very small and weak compared with Southern Rhodesia and South Africa, but I didn't expect a British government to sacrifice me and my people to them. We have trusted the British since the days of my grandfather. This will destroy not only our faith, but the faith of all the colonial peoples in the integrity of the British. Why didn't you make it clear at the very beginning that you had no intention of recognising me?'

Gordon-Walker was unmoved. He had consciously put his head on the block over the Seretse affair, in exchange for his Cabinet seat. 'We gave you the chance to resign voluntarily,' he replied.

'What happens if I defy you?' asked Seretse.

'The moment you arrive you'll be removed.'

At this point, the venerable Viscount Addison could no longer remain silent. His vague distaste at the proceedings he had been asked to witness had increased with each meeting. 'We're not looking at permanent exclusion. This matter will be looked at again in five years,' he said kindly. From his vantage point of almost a lifetime, he failed to appreciate that five years to a 27-year-old was a very long time indeed.

Seretse replied bitterly that he was well aware that he was being excluded from his rightful inheritance because of a hidden agenda, and that he doubted very much if things would change in five years. 'You'll always find some good reason for keeping me out of my country,' he said.

Acutely sensitive to the South African issue, and aware that Seretse was alluding to this, Gordon-Walker made the mistake of protesting too much. 'We've done our best to look at the problem from the point of view of the best interests of the Tribe. I must emphasise that our decision was not reached through fear of any attitude that the Union of South Africa might take up,' he said. 'Let us move on. What about Mrs Khama?'

Seretse was silent for a moment. What about Ruth? What about the baby? Would she want to come over and be with him? Or would she be prepared to wait out her time in Serowe, without him? Would he be able to survive another long separation from her?

'I will let you know what we decide,' he said wearily.

'It is very important that you say nothing to the press about this until Monday 13 March,' the Minister continued peremptorily, 'as we wish to make the announcement simultaneously in the House of Commons and to the Tribe in *kgotla*.'

Fraenkel made another attempt to get hold of a copy of the Harragin Report, but the Minister dismissed him like a bothersome fly, saying the report had been of a purely advisory nature.

Seretse's personal dislike and resentment towards Gordon-Walker had now reached such a point that he was unable to bring himself to shake the Minister's outstretched hand. He remained seated as the other man turned and left the room. Fraenkel and Rathcreedan bade farewell to the other officials, solicitously escorted Seretse outside and summoned a taxi. The young prince walked silently between them.

On the way back to the flat, he sent a cable to Ruth: *Tribe and I tricked. British government to take over Territory. Am barred from whole of Bechuanaland Protectorate. Love Seretse.*

By the time the taxi drew up in front of Airways Mansions, Seretse had made a decision. Anxious not to break faith with the British throughout the tortuous period of the several *kgotlas*, the judicial inquiry and the long wait for recognition, he and Ruth had avoided the most determined, and lucrative, efforts of the international press to get them to spill the beans. The British had now broken faith with them, and Seretse no longer felt bound by the gentleman's agreement he had upheld for nearly two years. Within an hour, representatives of every major British newspaper jostled for standing room in the flat. Seretse had called an impromptu press conference.

Speaking steadily, he faced the bank of microphones. 'The British people deserve to know what sort of government they have elected,' he said, and went on to outline the deception and betrayal of himself and his Tribe. Without embellishment, he told them all that had happened. The journalists, many of them Tory supporters, could not believe their good fortune. Pressed for his own personal comments, Seretse said simply: 'I was stunned speechless. His calm unemotional manner was as unfeeling as if he were asking me to give up smoking,' and 'It hurts a lot, it hurts as much as being told your people don't matter. The fantastic thing is that the British government believes my white wife and I will be a disturbing influence in the Territory and the people who have asked us to rule them will revolt as soon as we accede to their request. I maintain this is because they wanted to appease Dr Malan and keep South Africa in the Commonwealth. We are just a small backward race and it is quite easy to deal with us. If any government can do anything lower than this, then I would like to know what it could be.'

Seretse then announced that he would fight the decision and challenged the government to publish the Harragin Report, which would show, he told the press, that the governments of South Africa and Southern Rhodesia had brought pressure to bear on the British.

The story received wide coverage in every major newspaper, with most of them castigating the government severely. *The Times* summarised the feeling of the day: '*If the Bamangwato do not object to a white consort and the prospect of a half-breed succession, it would not seem to be for the Imperial Government, pledged before all nations to respect the equal rights of all races, to overrule them in their own domestic concerns. There, if principle were to prevail over expediency, should be an end to the argument . . . No good can come of compromise involving injustice to individuals if its aim is to blur the outline of the truth.*'

The South African *Natal Mercury* commented: '*The whole episode was a sad and sorry chapter in the distinguished history of British colonial administration.*' Other papers in Africa, Asia and the Caribbean condemned it as '*a grievous thing*' and '*an awful example of bad statesmanship*' and warned of '*long loyalty to Britain being destroyed*'. The *New York Times* criticised the British for giving way to Malan '*when the wider problem of native feelings throughout Africa is infinitely more important. The whole continent of Africa is heaving under the same disturbing forces that have transformed Asia since the war.*' South Africa was portrayed as the villain, alongside Britain – a pariah state, out of step with the brave new world.

Back in Serowe, Ruth had been appalled to receive Seretse's cable. Together with Seretse's close relatives and friends, she listened constantly to the BBC and the South African radio stations, anxious for news of what was happening in London. They were not disappointed. The story was the lead item on almost every news bulletin. And once the papers started arriving, first from Johannesburg and then by airmail from London, they were fully in the picture.

At the same time, Ruth was bombarded by the press corps in Serowe for her comments. Following Seretse's lead, she welcomed their attention and spoke freely of her shock and dismay at the British duplicity and her own anguish at being separated from her husband. Six months pregnant, 25 years old, alone in the middle of Africa, her husband a virtual prisoner of the British – her plight moved all but the stoniest hearts throughout Britain and the rest of the world.

Seretse was amused to read Noel Monks' racy copy in the *Daily Mail*. Knowing his Ruth, he could be sure Monks had employed a great deal of poetic license in writing the story. But this was no time to carp about details like that.

Monks had written: '*It's like a bad dream. And to think they nearly got me there too. It makes one ashamed of being British. No colour bar and British democracy – my eye! Queen Victoria would turn in her grave. It was my husband's grandfather who sought Queen Victoria's protection. A precious lot of protection the Bamangwato are being given now. Those little nitwits*' (at this Seretse burst out laughing – visualising with glee Gordon-Walker's certain distress upon reading it) '*in the administration who have been hoping and praying that I would get fed up in a few weeks and scamper off back home to London are going to be disappointed. I'll stick here till they carry me out feet first.*' Slapping the paper with his hand, Seretse laughed again. 'That's my girl!'

When the *News Chronicle* called Gordon-Walker at home for a comment on Seretse's statement, he was livid. 'There's nothing I can say at the moment,' he replied curtly. When he read the papers the next day he was even more furious, and immediately dispatched a note summoning Seretse to his office at 11.30 am on 8 March 1950. Then he contacted the Prime Minister for an urgent meeting. There would have to be a statement made in Parliament. The main problem was the Harragin Report – Seretse had challenged them to show it to him, and the press was now baying for blood. Gordon-Walker contacted several senior Conservatives, alerting them to the highly sensitive nature of the report and persuading them not to object to the government's statement that it would not be published. It was agreed that the Opposition would restrict its criticism to the government's shilly-shallying. Then there were their fellow Labour MPs to consider. How could they restrain the potential critics within their own party?

At 11.30 am Seretse and his lawyers were shown in. Gordon-Walker was angry and made no attempt to disguise it. He did not shake Seretse's hand again and delivered a diatribe about the newspaper reports. 'I thought there had been a clear understanding and agreement between us that we would make no statements to the press,' he stated. 'I can no longer talk freely. I can no longer trust that our confidence will be respected.' Seretse stared at him without replying, enjoying the older man's discomfort, secure in the knowledge that right was on his side, and with it the fair-minded British public.

'Is Mrs Khama going to join you here?' the Minister asked.

'I don't want her moved,' Seretse replied curtly.

'Very well then.'

Once again the Minister prepared to curtail the meeting, but Rathcreedan stopped him. Seretse was involved in a legal dispute, he said, and his presence was required in the Protectorate in connection with this. Aware of his now considerably weakened position, Gordon-Walker grudgingly accepted this, but insisted that 'no interference in the affairs of the Protectorate will be tolerated'.

A few hours later the Minister was on his feet in the House of Commons. Seretse and Fraenkel watched from the shadows of the strangers' gallery. As the Minister informed the House that the government 'viewed with grave concern the danger which recognition would cause to the unity and well-being of the Tribe and the administration of the Protectorate' Seretse was sickened. However, the press had done its job well, and several members were shifting restlessly in their seats at the Minister's monologue.

As he told them of Seretse's prohibition from the Protectorate for at least five years, Reggie Sorensen, MP for Leyton, interrupted: 'Is the Minister aware that this matter is already having grave repercussions in many parts of the world, particularly the Commonwealth? Can he give an assurance that press reports of Seretse having been tricked have no foundation? May I ask whether in this matter the Minister has had any communication from the Union of South Africa?'

Gordon-Walker's reply horrified the CRO staff: 'We have had no communication from the government of the Union nor have we made any communication to them. There have been no representations and no consultation in this matter.' The South African press had twice reported that Malan had condemned the marriage and demanded the transfer of the territories.

At this point Winston Churchill, leader of the Opposition, arose. Aware that his party had agreed not to rock the boat on the question of the Harragin Report, he nevertheless felt he could not let the question of trickery pass. It was a point of honour. 'Have we not, as it were, enticed this man to come over here to have talks . . . and now that he wishes to go back . . . he is to be stopped by force?' he asked.

Under the great man's piercing gaze, the Minister replied: 'I have done my utmost throughout to preserve honour between man and man in this matter.'

The House became rowdy. Raucous cries arose from the back benches. More members stood to challenge the Minister. Labour MP Fenner Brockway asked him if he was aware of the 'very grave concern among all sections of our community at the fact that a colour bar has determined the government's decision on this matter'. The Minister denied this. The leader of the Liberal Party, Clem Davies, expressed his regret at the government's interference in relations between a man and his wife. Churchill suggested man and wife should be re-united before any further action was taken. Gordon-Walker reiterated the threat to peace and order in the Protectorate. It was all most unsatisfactory.

Churchill rose once again and pronounced: 'It is a very disreputable transaction.'

The debate was given wide coverage in the press, which served to further increase public sympathy for the young Englishwoman and her royal husband. Letters of tribute and sympathy began to appear in the newspapers and arrive at the post office in Serowe. It became clear to everyone that Seretse and Ruth had been sacrificed to save the British from having to defend the Territories against transfer to South Africa.

The Spectator stated unequivocally: '*In this matter, the government is wrong and public opinion right*.' A leading newspaper in Calcutta declared: '*for every white man placated in South Africa a hundred Indians and Pakistanis have been affronted. The Labour Party has created for itself a situation for which Moscow might have prayed.*'

Even the Americans, battling with their own 'negro problem' protested, although not as vociferously as some of the Commonwealth nations. The Americans for Democratic Action, whose chairman was Hubert Humphrey (later vice-president of the US), protested privately to Gordon-Walker. The Liberal Party offered Seretse the chance to fight Gordon-Walker in forthcoming elections, but he declined.

An avalanche of hostile public opinion ensued. Several public meetings were held at which the government was denounced. Antiracism groups around the world had welcomed Labour's election victory, believing the party to be firmly opposed to all forms of racial prejudice, particularly the apartheid policies of the new South African government. The Labour government's decision to ban Seretse stunned them and irrevocably damaged their positive opinions. Many African, Indian and Caribbean students in London at that time went on to become leaders in their own countries. Their witnessing of Seretse's treatment soured future relationships with Britain and made a mockery of the hitherto revered British sense of justice.

Even the previously supportive LMS now turned on the government. Orchard wrote eloquently to Gordon-Walker, urging him to make a 'clear, factual and comprehensive' statement in order to check the 'rising tide of passion and prejudice' which had convinced both Africans and Europeans that 'Seretse has been victimised and a small African people sacrificed to political expediency'. The Rev Haile of the LMS was furious at the government's shabby handling of the whole affair and urged Orchard to make a public statement, which he did: '*The London Missionary Society urges His Majesty's government to declare it to be their policy to oppose such racial discrimination in any of the territories for which it is responsible.*' The LMS urged the government to return Seretse to Serowe, warning of '*much more danger in his non-return*'.

The international outcry condemning the government's treachery had a demoralising effect on colonial officials in Africa and India. The Civil Service Club's newsletter was inundated with letters expressing distaste. Civil servants took the unprecedented action of publicly dissociating themselves from the government's position. Many threatened to resign. '*The confidence of people cannot be gained if they are given reason to think that their interests are liable to be sacrificed to our good relations with other countries . . . I do not think I exaggerate in saying that a number of us might feel inclined to look around for different work,*' wrote David Roberts from Nigeria's northern province. '*This sort of thing could make one's job in the Colonies quite distasteful,*' wrote Peter Radcliffe, an assistant District Officer.

A meeting of women celebrating International Women's Day held a mass protest in London, as did The League of Coloured Peoples. A few days later, thousands of Britons gathered in Trafalgar Square to hear Fenner Brockway declare that the majority of Labour MPs were now opposed to the ban. Seretse stood, to loud applause, and thanked the British people for their support. Meanwhile, his fellow African students in London rallied solidly behind him and started a barrage of written complaints to the Prime Minister. Several organizations protested vehemently, especially the West African Students' Club at Oxford, the Campaign Committee for South Africa and the High Commission Territories and a group of students at the London School of Economics.

The Seretse Khama Fighting Committee was formed and held a mass meeting in central London on 11 March. Reggie Sorenson told the 1 000-strong crowd that what the government had done would 'intensify suspicions about the white man's real intentions throughout Africa'.

Seretse, tired and depressed, made a short statement and then left to attend yet another protest meeting. The outpouring of public sympathy had been beyond his expectations and he was both excited and comforted by it. But the hectic round of public engagements was taking its toll. He still found time to write to Ruth regularly, and allowed himself a tired smile as he related how Learie Constantine, the famous West Indian cricketer who was the energetic force behind the fighting committee, had challenged Gordon-Walker's statement that there was no racial discrimination in Britain. The Minister had agreed to meet him and three other men representing black organisations in Africa and the West Indies. Constantine had given Gordon-Walker a concise encyclopaedia published in London and asked him to read out the definition of 'Negro'. It read: *Negro – breeds fast and is a growing menace.*

Succumbing to the pressure of public opinion, the Minister finally announced, on 15 March 1950, that Seretse would be allowed to return home temporarily to Lobatse to collect his wife and sort out his personal affairs. Seretse cabled Ruth that evening: *Awaiting government ok to go home. Expecting it soon.*

Gordon-Walker cabled Baring, asking urgently if he could find some way that Seretse could be allowed to stay in the Protectorate. Baring's response was unequivocal – he warned of 'serious repercussions' in South Africa and said it would be impossible to govern Bechuanaland if Seretse were there. On 16 March the Minister faced his hostile colleagues in Cabinet. The swell of antagonistic public opinion drowned both Baring's advice and his lone voice. Seretse should be allowed back to the Protectorate forthwith, Cabinet decreed. Furthermore, he should be brought to his wife's side as soon as she went into labour. The Minister was also asked to consider banning Seretse only from the Bamangwato Reserve, and not from the whole country.

When he relayed this instruction to Baring, the High Commissioner sought a meeting with Smuts, who told him baldly that any recognition of Seretse by the British would result in a general election and an overwhelming victory for the hardliners within the racist Nationalist Party. Baring cabled London that the threat of a military annexation of the Protectorate was more real than ever.

Whitehall and the Houses of Parliament hummed like a hornet's nest as the government tried desperately to avoid a debate on the issue. On buses and in trains, in pubs and teashops across the land, the talk was of little else but the raw deal meted out by the Labour government to the African Prince Charming and his faraway, pregnant, White Queen. Close to midnight on 28 March, Fenner Brockway at last succeeded in forcing a debate. 'Colour prejudice is the cause of some of the most dangerous divisions in the world,' he said. 'Seretse and Ruth's marriage was a symbol of how that division could be healed. I believe the government have started on a course of appeasement with the South African government which stands for the principle of refusing to recognise those who belong to the black race as members of the human family at all.'

The debate raged for an hour, with members from all parties denouncing the way in which the matter had been handled. But Gordon-Walker weathered the storm without giving an inch.

Seretse left London on 24 March 1950 , having waited for the White Paper to be released. It had not been worth waiting for. A paltry document, it cast no further light on the affair and was condemned as a 'highly disingenuous document'. His letter to *The Times* was published that morning and widely applauded: '*I have been banished from my people who have wanted me and also from the land to which I belong. For what? No crime, except that I have married an Englishwoman . . . the present law in South Africa forbids the marriage of a native to a European. There is no such prohibition anywhere in the colonial empire, yet it was the policy of racial discrimination which influenced the Imperial government in their decision regarding my succession to the chieftainship. The questions which the British people have to ask themselves are: Is our conscience clear over the whole event? Have we allowed expediency to prevail over political integrity? Upon these answers alone is greatly dependent, morally and politically, Britain's future status as the mother country of the Commonwealth.*'

13

Separation

RUTH CLIMBED WEARILY UP THE STEPS TO THE WELCOMING SHADOWS OF her verandah. The child was heavy within her and the heat of summer lingered, although it should have been autumn. She was almost accustomed, by now, to the sameness of the weather. Gone were the changing seasons every few months, the shortening and lengthening of the days, the changing of the clocks. The dividing line between winter and spring, summer and autumn was virtually non-existent here – where the sky remained blue for weeks, if not months, on end, and the temperatures soared into the 30s day after day from September until May.

She had just returned from a meeting with the Tribe's elders, where the High Commissioner's announcement that he was calling a *kgotla* meeting for 13 March had been discussed at length. Ruth had pointed out to the assembly that she had heard Sillery giving Seretse his word that no British official would address a *kgotla* while her husband was out of the country.

The Bamangwato had become increasingly belligerent as the British authorities continued to ride roughshod over their democratic decision to accept Seretse as their Chief, notwithstanding his marriage to a white woman. Normally courteous and law-abiding, they were in no mood now to be summoned to a *kgotla* by the same authorities who had removed their Chief by subterfuge. The absence of the Chief made a disintegration of law and order, previously inconceivable, a distinct possibility. They gladly agreed with the suggestion that they should not attend such a *kgotla*. Thus the boycott was conceived.

Alan Bradshaw had been extremely protective of Ruth during her husband's absence. Appalled at the couple's treatment by the British, he had made himself unpopular with the white community and the administrative officials by speaking out forcefully at every opportunity. He thoroughly supported the idea of a boycott and moved to Serowe from Palapye to keep an eye on things. On his advice, Ruth moved to Palapye to stay with Doris in order that she should not be implicated by the British in having caused any disturbances.

Phetu Sekgoma and the other senior tribesmen took care to ensure that their supporters were aware of the need for persuasion, as opposed to any form of intimidation. Small groups of people peacefully informed tribesmen coming into Serowe that the *kgotla* had not been called by their Chief and therefore should not be attended. To a man, they agreed.

Alan returned to Palapye and jubilantly informed Ruth and Doris that the boycott had been a success. The two young women laughed helplessly as he mimicked the High Commissioner.

'There he was, dressed up to the nines, His Majesty's grand proconsul and plenipotentiary supreme, strutting about like a turkey cock with nobody to gawp at him. The only people in the *kgotla* ground were a group of whites, all tarted up in their Sunday best and ready for a bit of entertainment, and the press. And they didn't half give His Excellency a rough ride. That obnoxious press secretary of his, Nicholas Monsarrat, was apoplectic.'

'Brilliant!' said Ruth. 'I can't wait to tell Seretse all about this.'

'Well, I can tell you the press chappies were not at all impressed,' said Alan. 'Monsarrat told them the people had been prevented from coming to the *kgotla* by bands of thugs. One of the journalists asked H E to confirm this and he turned to Langley (the Protectorate's police chief) who said smartly: "I have received no reports of violence or intimidation, sir." Monsarrat was so red-faced I thought he would have a fit on the spot.'

'Wonderful,' said Ruth, her eyes shining. 'Seretse is going to be so encouraged! I'll send him a cable first thing in the morning.'

When she arrived back in Serowe, Phetu and a delegation of tribesmen came to report formally to her the total success of the boycott. 'We distributed a statement to all the journalists telling them we would no longer pay the annual tax because the British have decided to break the agreement made between King Khama and their Queen when the Protectorate was first established,' he said proudly.

Ruth complimented them all warmly on the success of their endeavours, and a bond was forged between Tribe and queen that would stand firm for the next half century and beyond. She was later quoted by Monks as having said: 'Well, I am sorry if anyone was rude to Sir Evelyn, but I think it is about time we started being rude to someone.'

Baring had been shocked by this demonstration of the Tribe's bitterness and resentment. When groups of youths in Serowe attempted to burn down the house of one of Tshekedi's supporters a few days later, the much-touted myth of 'disturbances among the Tribe' became a reality – not because of Seretse's presence, but because of his absence. Baring immediately gave instructions for the police force to be beefed up through transfers of men from Basutoland, Swaziland and Southern Rhodesia. Armoured cars were driven to the border between the Protectorate and Southern Rhodesia, and High Commission officials arranged for British troops to be airlifted into Serowe. Forbes McKenzie, tougher and more experienced than Sullivan, was transferred from Swaziland to become District Commissioner in Serowe.

A few days later, Ruth looked up from the book she was reading, startled to hear a car driving up to the house. She was not expecting anyone. Rising to her feet, she recognised the Bradshaw's vehicle with Doris at the wheel. Her pleasure at the unexpected visit turned to alarm as Doris emerged from the car, a handkerchief to her mouth, her eyes red from crying.

'Doris, whatever is the matter?' cried Ruth.

'Oh Ruth,' sobbed Doris. 'We've been given a week to leave the Protectorate. Alan has been transferred.'

'What! Why?'

Leading Doris to a chair and calling for a tray of tea, Ruth tried to calm her friend.

'Apparently the Resident Commissioner or the High Commissioner or some-body up there complained to the Chamber of Mines about Alan,' said Doris, 'and so they've transferred him. Just like that.'

'Doris, I just can't bear the thought of losing you.'

'Me neither. The British have done the South Africans a favour, so now I suppose the South Africans are reciprocating.'

'Do you know where you are going?'

'No, we have to go back to Johannesburg, and they will reassign us from there,' replied Doris, blowing her nose.

When her friend had left, Ruth sat staring out across the little valley, glori-ously green after the short but abundant rainy season, towards the shimmer-ing, distant hills. So many precious things had been taken from her by her countrymen since she had fallen in love with Seretse – her job, her wedding day, her privacy, her husband (three times now), her best friend. How much more would have to be sacrificed at the altar of their prejudice? She sighed deeply, and laid her hands on her stomach as the baby moved. This was something else that Seretse was missing – watching her womb grow with his child and feeling the baby kick against his hand.

She resolutely shook off her black mood and went inside to prepare a batch of scones. Noel Monks was coming for tea at 3.30 pm – with some exciting news, he had said.

Upon hearing that the British were allowing Seretse to return to Lobatse, Monks and fellow journalist Redfern had made arrangements for the small plane that would bring Seretse from Victoria Falls to Lobatse to refuel en route at Mahalapye. Ruth would go by car to the airfield there, and meet Seretse while the plane was being refuelled. She spent the next few days in a state of agitated excitement, washing her hair, doing her nails, looking at her watch a hundred times a day in an effort to make the time go faster.

She left at 3 am, having hardly slept a wink, driving carefully through the darkness in Seretse's Chevrolet. Monks drove ahead of her with his photographer, composing headlines in his mind.

At the airfield, the journalists hung back, leaving Ruth some private space in which to wait for her husband. She scanned the sky anxiously. Finally, a distant droning made itself heard in the stillness. Shielding her eyes against the rising sun, she followed the speck as it grew larger. Seretse was inside. She longed for his arms. She hoped the baby would kick for him, although it seemed to have been rocked to sleep by the bumping and swaying of the journey.

As the plane began to descend, she ran towards the middle of the field, unable to stand still a moment longer. The roaring of the engines filled the air. She was laughing and waving. It rolled to a stop, the door opened, and passengers began to come down the steps. Redfern and some other journalists. Nobody else. She turned to Monks, her eyes wide with disbelief.

'Don't worry, this is just the advance party,' Monks told her quickly. 'The other plane should be just behind them.'

Redfern came up to them, with a grim face. 'I am so sorry,' he jerked out, 'some bastard leaked the plan.'

'What? What's happened?' asked Ruth.

'The Brits have refused him permission to land here. They've ordered the pilot to refuel at Francistown. I'm so sorry.'

With that, the sound of another plane reached them and they all looked up. A second plane was descending towards them.

'You'll be able to catch a glimpse of him at least,' Monks shouted over the noise of the engines. Again Ruth ran out into the centre of the airfield, waving, her eyes searching the approaching plane's windows for Seretse's face. The pilot flew as low as he dared and then turned to make another swoop. Ruth blinked tears away angrily lest they blind her. Dust swirled around her as the plane's thrust hit the earth, clouding her vision further.

From the plane, Seretse saw her lonely figure, hair glinting in the sunlight, her dress wrapped by the wind about her swollen belly.

As the plane disappeared from view, she stumbled towards the car, gesturing angrily for the journalists to leave her alone. Respecting her privacy for once, they followed her slowly back to Serowe.

The Church of England newspaper of 6 April 1950 summed up everyone's feelings: *'Who would have believed that any government would have been capable of such a mean, petty and utterly despicable trick as to deprive Seretse of the opportunity of meeting his wife who had travelled 250 miles through tropical country just to have a little time with her husband?'*

Upon arriving in Gaborone, Seretse was taken by road to the quarters prepared for him by the British in Lobatse. He smiled grimly when he saw the cramped little house, furnished with an iron bedstead, two unpainted chairs and a table, two tin mugs, two tin plates, two rough metal knives, forks and spoons. Wait till Ruth saw this!

He immediately made formal application to go and see her in Serowe. After several days' delay, it was denied. Fraenkel informed the press, who faithfully relayed the story to the British public. Allowing Seretse to return had done little to pacify public opinion, and emotions ran high.

Seretse decided to make a secret trip to Serowe in the middle of the night, but before he could put his plan into action, Ruth took matters into her own hands. She decided to make herself ill so that the authorities would be forced to allow him to come to her. But first she had to fool her doctor, a man of integrity whose professional ethics would not let him distort the truth about her condition.

She kept herself awake for three nights in a row, by means of an alarm clock and a thermos flask of tea. Then, in a state of exhaustion, she visited her doctor and begged to see Seretse.

Alarmed at her condition, Dr Moikangoa notified the British authorities. There was a flurry of cables – McKenzie to Ellenberger, Ellenberger to Baring, Baring to Gordon-Walker, who realised that with public opinion inflamed the way it was, the loss of the couple's baby could bring down the government. He issued instructions that Seretse was to be given permission to visit Serowe for five days, but forbidden to attend any public meetings or interfere with the government of the Tribe in any way.

Determined to make the most of the time allowed, Seretse planned to arrive just after midnight on the first day, April 16th.

Worn out by her self-imposed ordeal, Ruth spent the next few days in bed. The shrilling of a bicycle bell awoke her on the third afternoon and she looked out of the window to see one of the household staff accepting an envelope from a khaki-clad messenger. Her heart began to pound. Had the ruse worked?

She ripped the envelope open and her eyes devoured the message. He was coming! He was coming today! She laughed joyously. Energy coursed through her and she got up at once, anxious to prepare a celebratory meal for him. Hastening to the kitchen, she soon had the staff peeling vegetables, cutting fruit, whipping cream and stirring sauces.

Dinner-time came and went, but she was so keyed up she couldn't eat. Sitting on the verandah, she settled down to wait. The child in her womb kicked sturdily. Flicking through her playing cards she tried to concentrate on a game of patience. Members of the press corps arrived to keep her company. Straining her ears for the sound of a vehicle, she heard only the night sounds of Serowe.

At last, shortly after midnight, the growling of the Bedford grinding up the rutted, dusty track came to her on the night breeze. The crowd of pressmen and photographers gathered around to capture this poignant meeting. Flash bulbs flared, lighting up the dark night. She ran awkwardly down to the gate and clambered up the running board as Seretse drove up to the house. As he leapt from the truck and caught her in his arms, the hard-bitten lot found themselves retreating into the shadows, subtly awed by the moment.

The news that the Chief was home spread rapidly through the village and by sun-up there was a crowd waiting at the *kgotla* ground. Messengers came to request his presence, but Seretse replied that the British had ordered him not to address them and asked them to disperse peacefully.

As he and Ruth sat at the table in the bay window enjoying a leisurely breakfast, men and women began to arrive. Soon the yard was full of silent, squatting Bamangwato. It was impossible for them to relax with the crowd of people sitting staring at the house, and Ruth was terrified that this would give the British an excuse to send Seretse away again. Eventually he went out and explained that the British would not allow him to speak to his people. But still they kept coming, and waiting – a silent protest of loyalty to their king and disobedience to the British, whose role had changed from that of protector to oppressor.

Later that morning Ruth and Seretse drove to the District Commissioner's office to fulfil the terms and conditions of Seretse's visit. All along the way, their car was mobbed by cheering Bamangwato as it had been when they had arrived eight months previously. Taking Ruth's hand to help her out of the car, Seretse kept it firmly in his as they climbed the steps.

McKenzie rose from his desk to greet them formally, but the ignominy of the situation was too much for Ruth, and she snapped: 'Prisoner reporting.'

Seretse squeezed her fingers and greeted McKenzie cordially. After a brief, awkward exchange of small talk, they left.

During the next few days, Ruth and Seretse spent hours sitting together on their verandah greeting the hundreds of people who came to pay tribute to the presence of the Chief in their midst. At night they behaved like any other parents-in-waiting, whispering and laughing as the baby moved restlessly, teasing each other, imagining whether it was boy or girl and what names they would choose. Although the number of hours left of the visit was uppermost in both their minds, neither mentioned it to the other.

'I could come back to Lobatse with you, you know,' Ruth murmured once.

'I know. Do you want to?'

'Do you want me to?'

'You know I do,' he groaned.

She sighed, summoning all her strength to bolster their resolve. They had agreed months ago that the baby should be born in Serowe. She mustn't give in now. Although she wasn't exactly sure of the dates, she knew it couldn't be more than six or seven weeks before their child would arrive.

'Just a few more weeks,' she murmured. 'We can make it!'

Mysteriously, their love fed on itself, multiplied, renewed their strength, banished bitterness, poured courage into their hearts and brought a blessing of peace. At last they slept, the golden child in her womb encircled by their bodies.

On the last day of Seretse's visit, choirs of schoolchildren joined the throng in the garden, their sweet voices rising in the still air. Their presence conveyed their love and longing directly to Seretse's heart. Every now and then an elderly crone would stand and sway rhythmically to the sound of the singing. He stood on the verandah steps, his eyes surveying the tattered remnants of his kingdom. Directionless. Confused. Not understanding the white man's ways, feeling only his oppression. The singing died away. Still the people sat on, their number swelling with a stream of new arrivals until the yard was packed.

Seretse was anxious. The tension was mounting, even as the sun began to sink, still blazing, in the fathomless sky. Administration officials hovered nervously; the police force was summoned and waited – just out of sight.

Seretse turned and glanced at Ruth, seated just behind him. 'I'll have to speak to the people,' he muttered. 'I can't just say nothing.'

'Yes,' she said, 'yes, but don't say anything that will . . .'

'Don't worry, I'll just ask them to leave peacefully.' Squaring his shoulders, he turned to face the crowd.

A quiver of expectation rippled through the patient Bamangwato like wind on a pond.

'The British government did not want this to happen,' Seretse said, effortlessly projecting his voice to the outer-most edges of the gathering. 'They wanted me to sit at my house all alone. This crowd will show the British that the Bamangwato love me.' He told them that he had to leave at midnight that night and would not return for five years. 'But we must obey the law. I want you all to go back to your homes now and cause no trouble.'

And because he was their Chief, the people obeyed him, drifting off into the dusk. Ruth reached out to take his hand. They both sat anxiously for a while, waiting for a response from the British, but nothing happened. Night fell. Determinedly gay, each for the other's sake, they dined.

'I'll be back soon,' Seretse told her confidently. 'They have promised to send for me as soon as the baby is on the way.' Ruth nodded, but said nothing. She didn't believe them any more.

Life in Lobatse was intolerable for Seretse. The press highlighted the indignities he was forced to suffer – living in an ill-furnished house, watched all the time by officials, prevented from being with his pregnant wife, forbidden to speak to his subjects, enduring enforced idleness for weeks on end. Their sympathy for him was enhanced by the presence of the High Commission's press attaché, Monsarrat, whose unfortunate manner served only to further alienate the press from the administration. Public outrage in Britain continued to simmer, but the government stood firm.

Fenner Brockway wrote a personal note to Gordon-Walker: '*I do beg of you not only to recognise the immediate human problem of his domestic circumstances but to remove all impression of an absence of human approach.*' But the Minister had hardened his heart, and nothing was going to budge him now. In a curt reply he said that Seretse was lucky to be in the Protectorate at all. Given the potential for public disturbance, his movements had to be carefully monitored. Furthermore, he pointed out, Ruth could go to Lobatse if she wanted to. Only her stubbornness in remaining in Serowe kept the couple apart.

Seretse's one relief from the boredom of his days, mostly spent reading, smoking and playing cards, was the ongoing negotiation with his uncle concerning an out-of-court resolution of their dispute over the vast royal cattle holdings. Tshekedi had claimed certain herds as his own in terms of Khama's will, while he was happy to acknowledge as belonging to Seretse those of Sekgoma's will. Seretse had been prepared to sue his uncle in the High Court in Lobatse concerning his grandfather's will. They went on a couple of trips together to the cattle posts lying outside the Bamangwato Reserve and recovered something of their old camaraderie, though Seretse's marriage was never mentioned.

Early one morning Ruth awoke with a sharp pain in her abdomen. She cast her mind back to what she had eaten the night before, thinking the pain was due to indigestion. But there it was again. There were still three or four weeks to go before the baby was due. By 7 am the pain had reached a point where she was really alarmed. Climbing into the green Chevrolet, she headed off to the hospital to find her doctor.

Surprised to see her, he put her under observation, and soon announced that labour had indeed begun. As she was wheeled away to the ward, Ruth overheard him on the phone giving instructions that the District Commissioner should be informed.

'Tell them to send for Seretse right away,' she called after him. 'He must come now. Tell them quickly. He must come quickly!'

But Seretse was not informed until lunchtime, presumably to delay his arrival in Serowe until late at night when there would be less chance of public demonstrations and unrest. He was given a four-week pass to go home.

At 1.30 pm, Ruth gave birth to a little girl. Seretse was still desperately searching Lobatse for Uncle Phetu and his truck. By 2.30 they were on the road, careening dangerously along the narrow track until Phetu insisted he take the wheel in order to ensure they arrived safely in Serowe.

Holding the infant to her breast, and forcing herself to relax by sheer strength of will, Ruth gazed down at the child. Seretse would want her named Tebogo, after his mother. But would he agree also to Jacqueline – the name she wanted? When she had first suggested it, he had joked about it being too exotic. But she loved the name and as she looked into the little brown face, with its big dark eyes, she felt it suited their little princess perfectly. She stroked the tightly curled fist gently with her forefinger. Honey-coloured, that's what she was. Pure honey.

At 5 pm the doctor popped in to check on her and was amazed to see her sitting up, still waiting for Seretse.

'Is he here?' she pounced as soon as he entered the room.

'Ruth!' the doctor exclaimed. 'Are you still awake? You must be worn out.'

'I want to see Seretse.'

'Of course you'll see him, the minute he arrives. But you must get some sleep. You need your strength. I will wake you as soon as he arrives, I promise.'

But Ruth was determined she was not going to miss the look on his face when he first saw the baby. She stayed sitting propped against the pillows, her eyes wide open. A few hours later, the handle of the door moved and she shot upright, willing Seretse to enter. But it was the doctor again. He was distressed to find her still awake. 'If you are not asleep in an hour I will give you something to make you sleep,' he told her sternly. 'Seretse will not thank me for letting you get into a state of complete exhaustion yet again.'

'I want to see my husband,' Ruth said slowly, enunciating each word carefully as though she were drunk.

Moikangoa turned on his heel and went to fetch a sedative. What a woman – her strength of will was incredible! He administered the sedative and when, at 11 pm, Phetu's lorry roared into the hospital grounds, he escorted Seretse to her room, assuring him all had gone well but that Ruth was heavily sedated and would probably not wake until morning. As he opened the door and Ruth, still awake and sitting upright, joyfully cried out, the doctor could not believe his eyes. He shook his head in amazement and retreated.

Keeping one arm around Ruth, Seretse leaned awkwardly over the cot next to her and gazed at his firstborn.

'Her eyes are exactly like yours,' said Ruth.

'She's so beautiful,' he murmured, amazed at the emotion swelling in his chest at the sight of the tiny creature. He could hardly breathe with the pain and the wonder of it. Stretching out a forefinger, he caressed the soft head carefully. 'So beautiful.'

Ruth leaned her head back against his shoulder and in a few minutes was asleep. Seretse smoothed the matted hair back from her forehead and manoeuvred his large frame into a more comfortable position on the narrow hospital bed.

14
Golden Princess

THE BABY WAS NO TROUBLE AT ALL. SHE FED HUNGRILY AND SLEPT PEACE-fully. After a few days Ruth felt well enough to go home. Gifts for the baby flooded in. True to tradition, the Bamangwato brought chickens and goats, woven baskets and mats, decorative clay pots and carved wooden articles. From their friends among the white community there were baby clothes and fluffy toys from the department stores of Johannesburg. After about 10 days, gifts from family, friends and well-wishers in England began to arrive, weighing down the postman's delivery bicycle, until Seretse had to go and fetch the packages from the post office in his car.

For a month, the young couple went through the learning curve common to all new parents – short snatches of sleep, dirty nappies, worries about burp-ing, shouts of delight when the infant smiled for the first time, anxious mo-ments when she would not stop crying despite being clean, fed and rested, and so on. Dozens of royal aunties came to inspect the child, give advice, and profess their satisfaction that she was indeed a beautiful baby.

She was christened Jacqueline Tebogo. Seretse quickly mastered his fear of dropping this delicate creature and held her proudly at every available opportunity. Her skin-tone deepened within a few weeks to the shade of milk chocolate and her adoring daddy called her 'my golden princess'.

The four-week grace period in Serowe, allowed him by the British on ac-count of the baby, were soon up. The couple had hoped against hope that the British might relent and let them stay. Their presence had caused no disturbances. Even when the authorities insisted they leave the Bamangwa-to Reserve and return to Lobatse, they still hoped they might be allowed to stay there. Seretse sent messages to his people, entreating them not to come and see him off, in case that gave the British a reason to banish him. In the middle of June, they left, the car piled high with trunks.

If they had known what was going on in the corridors of power, their hopes would have been alternately raised then dashed. The mood in Cabinet, occasioned mainly by the public outrage against the 'inhuman' treatment of the couple, was to let them stay in Lobatse. Gordon-Walker sought Baring's advice on the matter. The High Commissioner was adamant – they must not be allowed to stay. The South Africans would not stand for it and he himself could not be held accountable for the repercussions that would undoubtedly result.

His already stiff backbone thus further reinforced, Gordon-Walker went back to his Cabinet colleagues – who reluctantly agreed with the Minister's recommendation, based on Baring's unyielding position, that Seretse and Ruth must be expelled from the entire Bechuanaland Protectorate. He managed to convince them it would be impossible to set up an alternative method of government for the Bamangwato if Seretse lived among them but was not acknowledged as Chief by the British. He also made disparaging remarks about Ruth, who he said was 'astute and ruthless and has made it clear that she intends to cause as much mischief as she can'.

In an effort to anticipate every possible objection from his colleagues, Gordon-Walker went on to advise against leaving Ruth in the Protectorate as that would only stir up public opinion again and lay the government open to charges of separating husband and wife. 'Besides, we would be under constant pressure to allow him to visit her and that would be intolerable,' he said firmly.

The minutes of the meeting recorded the real reasons for the young couple's banishment: '*We must do our utmost to keep the Union in the Commonwealth for strategic, economic and other reasons. If the Union got into a mood to defy us and the world there is very little we could do to hold the Territories. Quite apart from force, any form of economic boycott would render us helpless. Seretse's case repre-*

sents the one set of circumstances that could unite and inflame all white opinion in the Union against us. Mixed marriage arouses highly charged emotions and can drive the South Africans to completely irrational attitudes and actions. There is overwhelming evidence that if, as it would seem to the Union, the UK set its official seal upon mixed marriages in the midst of southern Africa by recognising Seretse, there would be an outburst of uncontrollable emotion and anger in the Union which would throw the whole of white opinion behind Dr Malan.'

Discussion then turned to the practical steps necessary to get them out as quietly as possible. Once again Gordon-Walker showed what stern stuff he was made of: 'I don't think there will be too much of a stir but if we have to use force we must count on a fierce, but perhaps not very long, outburst of criticism.'

The couple was mercifully unaware of these discussions. Seretse would never know the full details and Ruth would only discover them more than a decade after his death, when journalist Michael Dutfield began digging into mountains of newly-released government documents.

Ruth had been appalled, as Seretse had known she would be, by the accommodation provided for them in Lobatse. They had only the barest minimum of furniture and household goods, and no attempt whatsoever had been made to make the place comfortable or attractive. Ruth set about making the best of it, delighting in her baby and drawing comfort and strength from her husband.

One day they were shopping in one of Lobatse's few dark, cramped general dealer stores. Ruth became aware that all the customers and indeed the shopkeeper himself had frozen into stunned silence. She had grown used to people reacting to her presence in a variety of strange ways, but this was very strange indeed. She looked around in alarm and Seretse took her arm.

'Ruth, my dear, come and meet my uncle,' he said.

Another royal uncle, thought Ruth. Goodness, how many of them could there be? She had already met more than a score. She smiled and held out her hand as Seretse guided her towards a smart, stocky gentleman, who immediately doffed his hat and said 'How do you do?' in a most English manner.

Suddenly she realised this was not just another uncle – this was The Uncle – the man who had prevented their marriage in church, the man who had instigated the judicial enquiry, the man who had almost broken Seretse's heart, and hers with it.

'How do you do?' she said, through stiff lips.

Tshekedi was smiling at her, and as she glanced at Seretse for reassurance she was surprised to see him smiling too. Both men shook hands heartily and Ruth, in a daze, heard Tshekedi asking when it would be convenient to come around and see the baby.

'Come over this afternoon, Uncle,' Seretse answered jovially. 'Ruth makes very good cream scones, you know!'

'Cream scones? My word, that would be a treat. I haven't had a cream scone since my last visit to Margery in Oxford! I'll be there. 4 pm?' Ruth nodded wordlessly and managed a smile.

As soon as they were in the car she turned a questioning gaze on Seretse. 'I didn't realise you two were getting along together so well now,' she said.

'Well, I did tell you we'd had a couple of good trips together and that the relationship was on a better footing.'

'But after all he's done to us! How can you be so friendly – as if nothing had happened?' Her voice rose. 'He's the one who prevented us getting married in church! If it hadn't been for him I would have had been able to walk down the aisle with you and make my vows before God!'

'Look,' said Seretse, putting his hand over her clenched fists, 'without the connivance and cooperation of the British my uncle could have done nothing. They have used him like a pawn in a chess game. He has suffered as much as we have. And he has been banished too. I know he loves me and the Tribe. All he has done has been out of love. Misguided maybe, but love nonetheless. I can't remain angry with him and I can't ignore his overtures of reconciliation. I'll meet him halfway. More than halfway – and I expect you to do the same.'

'All right,' she muttered. 'But it's very difficult to pretend he was not our arch enemy at one stage. I can't be perfectly friendly and relaxed with him.'

'I know,' said Seretse, 'but you can do it if you try. You can do anything.'

After a moment she nodded, and he squeezed her hands. 'Good for you,' he said, and started up the engine.

The visit went brilliantly. Tshekedi waxed lyrical about Jacqueline's beauty and resemblance to her mother. Both men were relaxed. Tshekedi was surprised to find himself admiring Ruth's strong personality and her obvious devotion to Seretse. A few days later, uncle and nephew went off in a truck together to inspect a disputed cattle post.

When Seretse returned, he was ebullient. 'We sat by the camp fire each evening and reminisced about the good old days. It was almost as if the rift between us had never been. But I noticed he was careful not to mention our marriage at all. We only talked about the land, the cattle and some recent *kgotla* cases.' He told her he had reached a fair settlement with his uncle, who had also agreed to purchase a large number of cattle. 'That'll give us a comfortable nest egg for the future,' he said cheerfully, relieved that money worries would be over for now.

'I'm glad you had such a good time with him,' said Ruth. 'But do you think he's become reconciled to the thought of me as your wife?'

'I'm not sure about that,' Seretse replied. 'And I'm not going to open it up for discussion unless he does. Our relationship is too tentative still. I'll just take one step at a time. For the moment I'm simply glad that the animosity between us seems to have subsided.'

He went on to tell her that Tshekedi had some very interesting ideas about the future government of the Tribe, including a form of tribal council to replace the chieftainship. 'I think he's right. The chieftainship is outdated in this modern world. It can't survive in its present form. We're going to have to devise some method of moving towards a more modern system of government which, at the same time, doesn't totally destroy the positive aspects of our culture and heritage.'

Ruth nodded. She, too, had spent many of her lonely hours in Serowe thinking about how the Bamangwato could move forward into the modern world without sacrificing too much of their precious past.

A few days later, Nettleton, who was acting Resident Commissioner in Sillery's absence, was instructed to break the news of the Cabinet decision to the couple in Lobatse. The blatant deception in the White Paper had so disgusted Sillery that he had requested long leave in Britain. (When his leave was up, Baring asked him not to return.) It was an awkward meeting. Ruth, in particular, had been hoping against hope that they might be allowed to stay – even if it meant enduring the cramped house in Lobatse for several months. Seretse merely shrugged philosophically, although she saw a shadow of pain cloud his normally steady gaze. He was determined to betray no emotion in front of the Englishman.

'I'm sorry,' said Nettleton, his conscience pricking him severely. 'But Cabinet has decided you will have to leave – in the interests of the Tribe.'

'Don't insult my intelligence. It's in the interests of the Tribe for me to stay.'

'I'm afraid the decision is final,' replied Nettleton. 'When would it be convenient for you to leave?'

'No date would be convenient,' Seretse said coldly. 'We will have to be ordered out.'

Nettleton said he would make arrangements for 11 August or thereabouts. Ruth stared furiously at the floor as he and Seretse discussed matters such as the shipping of their household goods and the necessary inoculations. As soon as the official had left, she put her arms around Seretse and laid her cheek against his chest. Seretse stared over her head at the shimmering heat haze above the distant veld. He couldn't speak. Banished! It had happened. He had been expecting it, but now that it had actually happened he felt devastated. Never to see this dusty land again, never to smell the sweetness of the first rain, never to close his eyes against the acrid smoke from a cooking fire or run his fingers over the damp nose of a robust young steer. He closed his eyes in anguish and held Ruth tightly.

The Bamangwato reacted to the news by intensifying their policy of passive noncooperation. It became impossible for the authorities to collect taxes in Serowe, and McKenzie found himself unable to summon the people to a *kgotla*. They simply stayed away. He was beside himself, particularly when a bad outbreak of foot and mouth occurred just outside the Bamangwato Reserve. It was essential that information be given to the people about what to do to prevent the killer disease from decimating their herds. Eventually, in desperation, he resorted to sending his staff throughout the highways and byways of Serowe with a loud hailer, shouting out instructions at every corner. The juggernaut of British overseas administration ground onwards.

Tshekedi, when he heard the news, was appalled. He felt his own banishment bitterly, and that was just from the Reserve. His heart went out to Seretse at the thought of him being exiled to England, so far away from his land of sunshine and wide expanses. Uncharacteristically impulsive, he jumped into his truck and drove to Pretoria to beseech Baring not to enforce the banishment order. But the High Commissioner was like a stranger to him. Cold and unfeeling, he dismissed him with a curt refusal.

Discussing the meeting with Seretse when he returned with the bad news, Tshekedi became more and more convinced that Baring was at the root of the problem. He and Seretse both knew, from the reports of their many influential friends in England, that Parliament and, indeed, Cabinet were in favour of allowing Ruth and Seretse to stay in southern Africa. 'I think our former trust in him has been misplaced,' Tshekedi told his nephew.

Having been informed by Nettleton that Ruth and Seretse would under no circumstances agree to leave the country voluntarily, the British administration was forced to issue them with official banishment orders. This it did on 2 August.

The unpleasant task of serving the orders fell to Baring's deputy, W A W Clarke, who took Ellenberger along for moral support. Ruth and Seretse had resigned themselves to the inevitable and were determined to conduct themselves with dignity and fortitude. They offered the visitors tea and Ruth went into the kitchen to prepare it. Determined not to make small talk with the 'enemy', Seretse followed her. He found her setting a tray with the tin cups that had been the government issue in the house when he had first arrived. He grimaced at her and reached up to take from the shelf the china cups and saucers he had bought subsequently. She shook her head and mouthed 'No!'

Removing the tin cups, Seretse laid the tray with the china.

She removed the china and replaced the tin mugs.

Seretse gripped her wrists and removed the mugs again.

The kettle boiled. Ruth put out her tongue at Seretse and finally allowed him to take the tray through, set with the china.

The visitors drank their tea in awkward silence, bewildered by the suppressed merriment in their expressions whenever Ruth and Seretse happened to meet each other's glance. Finally, Clarke cleared his throat and, in evident embarrassment, handed his deportation order to Seretse, who accepted it calmly. He then took a step forward to give Ruth hers. She stared at him coldly, keeping her hands firmly down at her sides. Clarke, furious with her for making him stand there like a fool, glanced helplessly at Ellenberger and then appealingly at Seretse.

Ruth said: 'This is the first direct step that the government has taken towards me. I find it surprising and ridiculous that a woman could be regarded as a danger to peace.' Seretse moved to her side and put his arm around her waist, accepting the sheaf of paper from Clarke and nodding a curt dismissal to the two officials.

Clarke wrote later to Baring: '*I am compelled to some admiration for Ruth, whom I had not met before. She has been through a lot, including loneliness, and yet she is neat in appearance and composed in manner. She displays a quick intelligence and a ready wit. She undoubtedly has courage.*'

Baring read Clarke's letter with a feeling of alarm and made arrangements for two white policewomen to make the long journey down to Bechuanaland from Southern Rhodesia to be on hand there when the time came for the couple to leave – just in case Ruth had to be put on the plane by force.

During the next few weeks, the couple packed up their belongings and sent instructions to their household retainers in Serowe about what to pack, what to send and what to store. They received hundreds of visitors wanting to bid them farewell personally. Through it all the baby Jacqueline, now three months old, was their only source of joy in an unhappy time. Seretse's sister Naledi had been helping out with the baby and they had decided she should go with them to England. Seretse could not bear to leave his closest relative behind and, besides, Naledi was keen to study as a nurse.

The foreign press corps received the news of their banishment with dismay. They, too, had been hoping for a happy ending to what most of them now acknowledged as a fairytale love story. Their sincere expressions of support warmed the couple's hearts. John Redfern and a few others decided to ask Ruth to a farewell lunch at the Lobatse Hotel. The hotel was strictly for whites only and Ruth was reluctant to go without Seretse, but he urged her to go along and enjoy herself as a gesture of thanks towards the journalists who had become their friends during the long, lonely wait for the British to make up their minds. So, dressing with her usual elegance, Ruth went.

As she entered the hotel lounge for sherry before lunch the hum of conversation died, and a number of local whites and some British officials stood up and, with calculating rudeness, walked out.

At that moment a member of the hotel staff approached and informed the group that Mrs Khama was no longer a member of the European community, and therefore 'not entitled to enjoy the facilities of the hotel'.

Redfern began to argue heatedly with the man, but Ruth put her hand on his arm. 'John, it doesn't matter, let's just leave,' she said.

'No,' insisted Redfern. 'This is nonsense. I won't accept it.'

The staff member then suggested they should all take their drinks through to one of the bedrooms so that they would not 'upset' the regular customers.

Redfern snorted in disgust. He took Ruth's elbow and escorted her from the hotel with elaborate courtesy. 'You'll be better off away from here, my dear,' he told her. 'How can you and Seretse possibly live here, among people like this? It would drive you mad in a month.' Ruth simply nodded.

Seretse just laughed when she related the incident to him. 'Well, well,' he said. 'So you are no longer a member of the European community. What a pity!'

'It's not funny!'

'We'll have the last laugh, that I promise you. Now, put it out of your mind. You are a *Mongwato* now. Just a pity that you're so pale and sickly looking!'

At last the departure day dawned – 17 August 1950. A large crowd of about 350 members of the Tribe gathered at the airport to see them off, together with the leaders of the other main tribes. Seretse and Tshekedi had already issued a statement announcing their partial reconciliation.

His mood sombre, Seretse addressed his people for the last time: 'Had I at any time since June 1949 had the slightest indication that a substantial majority of my people wished me to leave, I would have resigned without any pressure whatsoever. Since my return from England, representatives of every subtribe of the Bamangwato have visited me at Lobatse, given expression of your loyalty, and convinced me that the Bamangwato nation is now more united than at any time in living memory. This has brought me solace at a moment when I have to leave you with deepest sorrow.

'I want you to know that I leave you unwillingly. I am going because my wife and I have been served with an order to leave the country. I had planned that, with God's help and your cooperation, I would have been able to introduce reforms for the advancement and happiness of my people. To be deprived of the opportunity to do so is a sad and bitter disappointment to me. While I am gone, I give you this advice: pay your taxes and obey all lawful orders given to you by the government. Above all, pay due homage and remain loyal to His Majesty King George VI. To each one of you, my wife and I with sorrowful hearts express our deep appreciation of your loyalty and unlimited kindness. Your welfare and happiness will be our constant concern wherever we may be. May God bless each one of you and protect you.'

Although everything within them cried out to protest at the enforced going of their Chief, the Bamangwato were still. Good behaviour might hasten his return. They wept silently, commoners, headmen and chieftains alike. The British officials looked on stony-faced, as Ruth and Seretse, moved beyond endurance by this heartfelt and dignified display of emotion, wept too.

They flew from Gaborone to Livingstone in a Royal Air Force plane allocated to the High Commissioner's office. From there they were to catch the flying boat to Southampton. Monsarrat provided the official escort. He had been strictly instructed by Baring not to allow anything to go wrong with the 'exit' – as Seretse's banishment was euphemistically termed in official circles – and not to permit any 'stunts' or 'demonstrations'. Accordingly, Monsarrat had theatrically ordered the plane to be surrounded until take-off by police and Royal Airforce guards, in order to foil any kidnap or rescue attempt.

However, as they flew over Serowe, he suggested to the pilot that it might be fun to buzz the place. The streets below erupted in a colourful chaos as thousands rushed, shouting and waving, into the dirt tracks and pathways that rabbit-warrened the village. To Ruth, Seretse and Naledi gazing down from the windows of the small plane, it looked like an ants' nest disturbed by a careless kick. But these were no ants. These were their loved ones, neighbours, friends – their people. As the plane pulled away, Serowe dwindled to a toy town, a child's playful scattering of people, animals and shaggy huts.

In Livingstone, the District Commissioner's house was made available to them. Monsarrat dealt effectively with the swarming pressmen and Ruth and Seretse were left in peace to enjoy their last night in Africa. They stayed awake late, unable to sleep for the sorrow that overwhelmed them at the price they had been forced to pay for their love. Gazing up at the stars, her head pillowed against Seretse's chest, Ruth sighed, worn out from the emotions of the previous few days.

'I never thought it would come to this. You've had to sacrifice everything for me – your birthright, your country, your people. If I hadn't married you, none of this would have happened.'

'Don't ever say that again,' said Seretse, his voice harsh. 'You mean more to me than anything else in the world. You know that. Besides, we'll be back. They aren't going to get away with this – you mark my words.'

Seretse knew the British would never allow the flying boat to depart without him. He was in no hurry to leave Africa and he took perverse delight the next morning in enjoying a leisurely breakfast on the verandah of the residence, overlooking the lush Zambezi Valley. Aware of Monsarrat's agitation, he continued to chew his toast and marmalade deliberately. Watching the young press attaché sweating, Ruth smiled to herself. Let Seretse have his fun, she thought. Heaven knew, he had enjoyed precious little during the past several months.

But at last Seretse could no longer postpone the moment. He nodded at Ruth and Naledi, picked up Jacqueline and strode towards the car. Minutes later they were walking the gangplank onto the high-winged Sunderland, bobbing in the current of the crocodile-infested Zambezi River. Seretse squared his shoulders, turned and waved courteously to the relieved Monsarrat and entered the plane.

The next day's Johannesburg *Star* complimented Seretse on '*a great deal of dignity*' in the manner of his leaving.

15

Banished

WITH DETERMINATION, DOROTHY ELBOWED HER WAY THROUGH THE CROWD waiting at the Southampton docks, closely followed by Muriel. The late afternoon sunshine danced on the wavelets of Southampton Water and the crowd rustled with anticipation as the lumbering Sunderland flying boat appeared on the horizon. The slap of water on wood, the creaking of timbers, the shrieks of the seagulls and the chatter of the waiting throng were drowned as the roar of engines grew steadily louder and the ungainly bird made its way towards the dock.

It hit the water, and Dorothy held her hands to her ears and grimaced at Muriel as the engines thrust into reverse with a roar. The boat came bobbing towards the quayside, the engines churning the dark water all around them to a foaming mass of white. Gripping the rail with her gloved fingers, Dorothy strained forward to see the passengers disembarking.

'There they are!' she cried suddenly, catching sight of Seretse, wearing his black trilby and holding the carrycot. As her daughter emerged at his side, Dorothy began to wave frantically, calling 'Ruth, Ruth – over here!'

The couple was exhausted from the trip. The baby was fractious and they were dreading the press ordeal while recognising that they had to woo this ally as never before if there was any hope of them ever getting home again.

Dorothy unashamedly put her sharp elbows to work once more and was soon embracing her beloved daughter. Giving Seretse a quick hug, she halted the flow of human traffic as she stooped to peep into the carrycot where Jackie, disturbed by the clamour, was fretting and waving her tiny fists. 'Oh, Ruth,' said Dorothy, tears springing to her eyes, 'she's beautiful! I believe she looks more like Seretse.'

'Don't be silly, Mother,' said Ruth, not sure if she was laughing or crying, 'you can't possibly tell yet.' Seretse put his free arm around her and shepherded the little party forwards.

At that moment, the ever-vigilant press corps thrust forward with a barrage of flash bulbs and began shouting questions: 'What are you going to do now, Seretse?' 'What do you think of the British government's behaviour?' 'Are you going to be meeting the Minister?'

Seretse held up his hand for quiet and said loudly: 'I have a lot to say. I will hold a press conference at the Grosvenor Court Hotel in Mayfair at 8 pm this evening. You will all be welcome there. I'm afraid I cannot answer questions here.'

Disappointed, the press parted reluctantly to allow them through, but one desperate photographer shouted boldly: 'At least show us the baby, Chief!'

Smiling broadly, Seretse reached into the carrycot and gently lifted out his golden daughter – holding her proudly before them in much the same way his grandfather had presented him to the assembled *kgotla* some thirty years before. Dorothy clucked disapprovingly as the baby blinked in the glare of the flashlights.

Several hours later, Jacqueline, content after a feed, a bath and a nap, was once again held aloft before a crowd of inquisitive, though largely sympathetic, journalists. The promised press conference was in full swing and Seretse, in the tradition of all proud new fathers, had provided free drinks all round. He delivered an eloquent statement in which he recounted the train of events that had led to his banishment. He told of his sore disappointment at the government's behaviour in tricking him into coming to London for talks and then banishing him for spurious reasons.

'I'm convinced it is all about South Africa,' he stated. 'The British government is obviously trying to appease the Malan government.'

Asked whether he was bitter about what had happened to him, Seretse replied : 'No, I'm not bitter – I'm just sad and extremely disappointed that it has come to this. I fear for my people. They are leaderless now. They want me to be their Chief. They want my wife to stay with me.'

He confirmed that he would receive an annual allowance of £1 100 from the government during his exile, which was to be for an initial period of five years.

The next day the papers were full of headlines about the 'Golden princess' and 'Honey-coloured Jacqueline', condemnations of British treachery and reports of widespread African, and international, outrage. They changed nothing. The family remained at the Grosvenor for a month – an extremely trying experience with a small baby, Ruth later admitted. She and Seretse hunted for alternative accommodation, leaving Jackie with Naledi while they searched the suburbs of London for a suitable flat. On October 4th, with profound relief, they left the hotel and moved into No 7 Fernshaw Mansions in Chelsea.

Ruth had been taken with this old but attractive block the first time they saw it. It was located in fashionable Chelsea and a recent coat of paint had given it a prosperous air. Now all they needed was for their consignment of household goods and their car, which had been shipped duty-free at British government expense, to arrive from Serowe.

Ruth and Naledi were busy scrubbing the old wooden floors, while Seretse dusted the ceilings from his precarious position atop a rickety step-ladder, when they received notification that their goods had arrived. Descending from his perch, Seretse rushed off to the docks to collect his precious Chevrolet and to arrange for the crates to be transported to Chelsea as soon as possible.

After completing numerous official documents in triplicate, he found himself with the keys to the car in his hand, along with an undertaking from a removals company to deliver the furniture and effects the following day. He followed a burly dock-worker to a warehouse where, at last, the Chev was located. Grimacing at the thick layer of dust and grime covering the car, he climbed behind the wheel, only to find himself suddenly surrounded by a surly-looking gang of dockers.

'Hey, you! What you doing with that car?' one of them yelled. Suppressing a quiver of alarm, Seretse waved and smiled nonchalantly, and pressed the starter, praying that the battery would not be dead. The engine stuttered into life.

One of the workers slammed his open palm on the bonnet, while another gestured angrily for Seretse to open the window. He opened it a crack and said politely: 'Excuse me gentlemen, I need to get my car out of here.'

'Your car!' shouted the man. 'Who says it's your car?'

'Yes,' replied Seretse quietly, 'this is my car.'

The men looked at each other. 'Where's a nigger get a car like that?' said one.

'I have the papers here,' said Seretse steadily, holding them up to the windscreen so that the onlookers could read them.

The man leaned closer and peered at the document. '. . . Property of one Seretse Khama,' he read out.

'Seretse Khama?' echoed another. 'Why, isn't that the Chief who's been in the papers? The one with the English wife?'

As they began to argue among themselves, Seretse saw his chance and gunned the engine. Waving his exit pass out of the window, he headed for the barrier and was soon beyond their reach.

They spent the next few days unpacking boxes and making themselves at home. Ruth arranged their leopard skin and buck karosses on the walls and floors, and they were comforted by these reminders of home. News from Serowe reached them regularly in letters – which Seretse awaited anxiously – and via occasional visitors.

Letters from his cousin Goareng had informed them that the Tribe was steadfastly resisting all attempts by the British to create an alternative form of administration. They wanted their Chief, and that was that. They refused either to form the new advisory council, which the British had proposed as an interim tribal authority, or to elect a new Chief. Seretse was their Chief. If he could not reign, nobody else would be permitted to do so. However, tension between Seretse's supporters and those of Tshekedi who had moved to Rametsana, ran high. There were constant minor outbreaks of violence and much cattle theft.

The British authorities wrongly interpreted these incidents as evidence that Tshekedi and Seretse were still hostile to each other. And of course it suited their purpose to perpetuate this idea, because it enabled them to continue hiding behind the lie that they had refused to acknowledge Seretse as Chief in deference to the wishes of the Bamangwato themselves.

The government's White Paper had referred vaguely to a dynastic feud – giving the impression that it was between Seretse and Tshekedi. In the vacuum created by the enforced absence of both these immediate descendents of King Khama, a plethora of influential headmen had begun jockeying for popular support. Dynastic intrigue, never far below the surface in traditional tribal society, but previously constrained by the presence of the rightful Chief or his regent, simmered to the fore. It disrupted the perennial rhythms of sowing, cultivating and harvesting and caused the delicately-balanced tribal loyalties to erupt in waves of anxiety, emotion and frustration. This raised anti-Tshekedi feelings to fever pitch – he was seen as being responsible for Seretse and Ruth's banishment.

They were shocked to learn of the October 17th arson attack on Tshekedi's lovely old house in Serowe. He wrote to tell them that the fire had destroyed all the Khama family memorabilia, including photographs and press clippings of King Khama's visit to Great Britain in 1895, as well as his precious bible with its personal engraving from Queen Victoria. Seretse was very upset by his uncle's letter, which indirectly accused him of being responsible for the blaze via Phetu Sekgoma, Seretse's agent in the Protectorate, who had been left in charge of all his property and, most importantly, his cattle.

'For heaven's sake,' Seretse raged to Ruth. 'How can he possibly think I would do such a thing? What the hell has Phetu been up to? I can't believe he would have had anything to do with this either! What is going on out there?'

Pacing like a caged lion up and down the living room, he shook the letter violently. 'I must find out exactly what happened,' he shouted and lunged towards his desk to draft a cable to Phetu.

'I'm sure Phetu had nothing to do with it,' said Ruth. 'He'll explain everything. Just wait for the next post – there's bound to be a letter from him.'

Grabbing his hat and jacket, Seretse stormed out to send his cable. As the door slammed behind him, the baby began to wail.

A reply from Phetu received a few days later assured Seretse he had had nothing to do with the arson attack. Seretse was mollified, but a few days later was cursing his luckless relative once again when he received a curt missive from Tshekedi informing him that Phetu had been discovered digging wells for Seretse's cattle on the Nata River in an area that Tshekedi and Seretse had agreed would be used for grazing by Tshekedi's herds.

Seretse threw his hands into the air in despair. 'What am I going to do?' he asked Ruth furiously. 'I need to go out there myself and sort out this mess. How can I ever get anything done while I'm imprisoned here, six thousand miles away?'

'Why don't you persuade your uncle to come over and discuss things with you face to face?'

Seretse seized on this idea immediately. 'Yes!' he exclaimed. 'I'll do that.' And once again he was at his desk, his pen flying over the paper, and then out of the door and down to the post office.

No sooner had one hurdle been cleared than another came into view. The Labour MP Fenner Brockway, whose sense of fair play and deep-seated hatred of discrimination in any form, particularly racial, had made him a formidable adversary of the establishment in the Seretse affair, was anxious to help. He stood up in Parliament and told the House that he had information that Tshekedi was now agreeable to Seretse being recognised as Chief of the Bamangwato, and the government should therefore allow Seretse to return forthwith.

Tshekedi had actually made no such public admission and wrongly assumed that Seretse had encouraged Brockway to make the statement. Another fiery cable arrived, plunging Seretse once more into rage, followed closely by despair. The mistrust and resentment between uncle and nephew that had been dissipated beside the campfires a few months previously, reared up once again.

Ruth and Seretse tried to be strong for each other. They constantly made the best of things, spoke positively and sought the silver linings in the depressing clouds that billowed around them. One small consolation was that the Anglican Church, which had so strongly opposed their marriage initially, had been vocal in its criticism of the government's handling of subsequent events. However, the formerly strong ties between state and church were already severely eroded, and the clerical outrage ran unheeded over government feathers like rain off a duck's back.

Another consolation was the regular visits they received from their old Nutford House friends. Muriel, too, was a frequent visitor, and it was almost like old times as they all sat around the lounge, drinking whiskey and discussing colonialism, discrimination and the rise of nationalism in India and Africa. They agreed unanimously that the racist government of South Africa was at the root of Britain's peculiar handling of their marriage. What none of them knew at the time, however, was the British self-interest that had been occasioned by Malan's threats to withdraw from the Commonwealth and the stalling of the uranium talks.

Young officers from the CRO were dispatched from time to time pay a 'friendly' visit to the couple – and to report back to those in command, who were forever anxious that Seretse would become 'a target for communist propaganda'. But they need not have lost any sleep over that.

Naledi soon began her nursing studies, Seretse returned to his law studies and Ruth enjoyed mothering her baby. The Khamas, it was reported, were sensibly preparing themselves for a long exile. The government allowance – on which he did not pay tax as he was, technically, still a student – combined with the capital realised from the sale of his cattle, enabled them to live in relative comfort. They could even afford domestic help, so that Ruth was not always cooking, cleaning and washing nappies.

'Lewis wants to take us to dinner next Friday,' said Seretse one morning as he opened the mail. 'Shall we go?'

'We might as well, I suppose,' replied Ruth. 'He's one of the nice ones from the CRO, don't you think?'

'Yes. In fact I rather like him. At least we'll be able to get some firsthand news about what's going on there – and a free dinner!'

Ruth laughed. 'Where shall we get him to take us?'

'How about that place in Soho Charles was telling us about? What's it called?'

'The Czada. That's a good idea. I fancy an evening in Soho. Perhaps we could even persuade him to go on to the Sugar Hill after dinner. We haven't been out dancing for ages. It would be fun.'

'Absolutely! Soho, here we come! Heaven knows we could do with a bit of fun.'

'Don't forget to ask Mrs J if she can come in and babysit Jackie. Until at least 2 am.'

'Wicked woman! Abandoning your baby to go gallivanting around London until the small hours! This wouldn't happen if you were in Serowe.'

'You're dead right, it wouldn't. One of the few compensations of being here, wouldn't you say?'

'Oh I see! Now we're getting it! You wanted to be here all along!'

'That's right,' she said. 'I just love the fog, the traffic, the rationing, the slush. Let's go out and enjoy it all!'

'What? No steak?' asked Seretse, as he studied the menu at the Hungarian restaurant they had chosen in Dean Street.

'Sorry, old man,' exclaimed Lewis, anxious to please. 'Shall we go somewhere else?'

'No, no. I'll have the beef stew – that'll be close enough,' said Seretse cheerfully. The conversation returned to the perennial subject of rationing, which was taking a long time after the war to sort itself out. Fresh beef, in particular, was still scarce and the lack thereof caused Seretse great hardship.

'I don't know what I'd do without our Mr Bones,' he said, savouring his stew.

'Who's Mr Bones?' asked Lewis.

'Our local butcher,' said Ruth. 'He and Seretse are good friends and he believes it's his life's task to keep the Chief supplied with beef. Although I keep telling him it's not good for him.'

'Of course it's good for me,' protested Seretse. 'I was raised on it . . . plenty of it. And look at me now!' He flexed his biceps.

After dinner, Lewis acceded readily to Ruth's suggestion that they go on to the Sugar Hill Club in St James. There was a large and congenial crowd of all races already there by the time they arrived.

'Hello, Chief,' cried a burly Jamaican as they squeezed their way towards a vacant corner table.

'Macdonald, my friend,' said Seretse, slapping the man on the shoulder. 'Lewis, meet Jamaica's greatest athlete, Macdonald Bailey.'

Before long they were at the centre of a group of Africans and West Indians, all talking loudly and enjoying the light jazz music for which the club was renowned. Eventually, Ruth managed to persuade Seretse to stop talking and take her onto the dance floor. The evening sped by.

Lewis was an earnest young man. He liked Ruth and Seretse and was impressed by Seretse's sense of humour and lack of bitterness towards the British who, in Lewis' opinion, had treated him shabbily. During his CRO assignments to check on the couple he went out of his way to ensure they both had a good time. He also made a point of inserting subtle, positive, comments into his reports in the hope that his seniors might be persuaded to relent towards Seretse. One report stated boldly: '*It would to my mind be a tragedy if his excellent qualities were to be frustrated by bitterness, inactivity, or neglect.'*

All too soon it was Christmas. Determined to stay cheerful, Ruth sent Seretse out to find a Christmas tree and busied herself decorating the flat with colourful streamers and baking mince pies and plum pudding. They had accepted an invitation from George and Dorothy to have Christmas dinner at Lewisham with other members of the family.

Early on Christmas morning they awoke to find that a light dusting of snow had transformed the world. Warm beneath a thick kaross, they sat together in an armchair and looked out of the window.

'It is beautiful, isn't it?' said Ruth.

Seretse nodded. His mind's eye was seeing a different Christmas scene – a shimmering expanse of shallow, reed-fringed water where thousands of antelope, buffalo, elephant, zebra, giraffe and wildebeest were gathered in the dawn to drink their fill. The Okavango. He and his uncle had made regular expeditions to this paradise at the edge of the desert in northern Bechuanaland, and the wonder of it had never ceased to thrill him. The cold, white scene before them was beautiful – but his heart longed for his homeland.

Later that morning they set off with Naledi and Jackie for Lewisham, where a traditional English Christmas dinner awaited them. Over sherry, they told George and Dorothy the whole story of their problems with the Commonwealth Relations Office, and George, although not effusive, at least made the effort to welcome his son-in-law with normal courtesy. They achieved a mutual bond of respect that would never ripen into friendship, but would last until George's untimely death in 1957.

The crowd shifted restlessly in the heat, like a field of corn in a dust-devil wind. Ten thousand of the Bamangwato had walked hundreds of miles to attend the first *kgotla* to be held in more than a year. Word had gone out weeks before to the cattle posts – a very important man was coming across the water from England to visit them. Perhaps he would bring the

Chief back with him? All they knew for sure was that he was coming – the Minister himself – a direct emissary from His Majesty the King.

Although it was the middle of the rainy season, with crops in the field, and the cows bearing young, they left everything and plodded through dust and heat to the *kgotla* ground in Serowe.

A great murmuring began. Here they came. A smart procession, flanked by the impeccably uniformed Bechuanaland Police Force, made its way towards the VIP seating at the head of the ground. The Resident Commissioner, resplendent in white with gold brocade, led the way. Behind him was the guest, in a dark suit and smart hat, with several district officials bringing up the rear. The Tribe looked anxiously for the figure of their Chief – but he was not there. They turned to each other in dismay and a rumbling began, but the Resident Commissioner held up his hand for silence and the courteous Bamangwato obeyed.

The visitor rose to address them: 'Doo-may-lang, Baman-gwato,' he said in tortured Setswana, causing a few of the younger men to snigger. Gordon-Walker went on to speak vaguely about the development of water resources and abattoirs, but never once did he touch on the subject they had all come to hear about. What had become of their Chief? What were the British doing to him and his wife and baby? What was to become of the Tribe – leaderless now for more than a year? When at last the people, represented by Monametse Chiepe (a rising young political star), were given the opportunity to reply, the message was simple: 'Give us back Seretse. Banish Tshekedi.' These were the wishes of the Bamangwato, about which the British government professed to be so concerned.

With a wave of his hand, Gordon-Walker bade farewell – to the people and to their wishes – and left Serowe as soon as possible.

He was already formulating a new strategy, a racial propaganda exercise to ensure the Bamangwato thought twice about the wisdom of demanding their Chief back: *We need to start a judicious campaign among the people about the dangers of a half-caste Chief,* he wrote to his officials. *The ideal outcome would be that the Bamangwato themselves should say to Seretse he must either abandon Ruth and become Chief or renounce the chieftainship. If we firmly exclude Tshekedi, I believe this may happen.*

His minute caused consternation in the CRO and was hastily suppressed by the officials, who were appalled at the mere suggestion of the British government embarking on such an overtly racist endeavour.

Jackie, her face smeared with cream and cake crumbs, was banging a teaspoon on the tray of her high chair. Delighted at being the centre of attraction, she crowed with joy at the doting adults who sat around the table enjoying a Victorian sponge which Ruth had baked, with carefully hoarded butter and eggs, for her daughter's first birthday. The couple had moved again – this time to a flat in Albany Street on the eastern side of Regent's Park.

Caressing her dark curls, Seretse sat beside his baby daughter and tried to distract her from the teaspoon banging. The doorbell rang.

'I'll get it,' said Dorothy, jumping up.

Ruth looked questioningly at Seretse. 'Are you expecting anyone?'

Seretse did not answer her. His eyes were riveted on the living room door, through which his mother-in-law had just ushered his uncle. Tshekedi had been in London since early spring, Seretse knew, battling with lawyers, friends, members of parliament and prominent acquaintances to get his banishment from the Bamangwato Reserve rescinded. His uncle had not contacted him once, and he had stubbornly refused to make the first move, despite Ruth's persistent suggestions that he should. And now here Tshekedi was.

Realising that Seretse was stunned, Ruth moved quickly towards Tshekedi. '*Dumela rra*,' she said, 'how good to see you, Uncle.'

Seretse stood up, forcing himself to smile. 'Uncle,' he said formally.

Tshekedi shook hands all round and bent over the baby, chucking her under the chin and holding out his forefinger for her to grasp. '*Dumela*, little one,' he said tenderly, and stroked her curly mop just as Seretse had done a few moments earlier. After he had downed two slices of cake and several cups of tea, Tshekedi adjourned with Seretse to the study, where they talked for half an hour.

The birthday party continued in the living room, but Ruth was wildly curious to know what was being discussed in the study. As soon as the visitors – and Tskekedi – left, she handed Jackie over to Mrs J to be bathed and sat Seretse down, demanding to be told everything.

'There's nothing to tell, really,' said Seretse, his voice flat. 'He's determined to get his banishment lifted and he's adamant that he will never seek the chieftainship for himself. He asked me to support his return publicly, but I said I could not do that unless he publicly accepted our marriage.'

'What did he say?'

'Nothing. Just shook his head.'

Ruth groaned. 'Now what are we going to do?'

'Just keep on pressing for our own return,' he replied.

But she could see that hope had died in him. He didn't even have the energy to get angry any more. He was just accepting it.

Reconciliation with his uncle seemed impossible, so Seretse poured his energies into drafting a fresh appeal to his archenemy, Gordon-Walker, proposing that he be allowed back to his homeland on probation. His argument centred on the need for a strong administrative hand to assist in bringing peace, democratic government and a progressive improvement in the standard of living for his people.

The issue of whether his children could or would or should inherit the chieftainship was a matter, he said, which could safely be left in abeyance for many years. Seretse believed this humble approach might persuade the authorities to open the door an inch. Once his foot was in, he could proceed. But, once again, the door was slammed in his face before he managed to get so much as a toe inside. Yet again the young couple faced this defeat squarely. Each setback seemed only to weld them more closely and more powerfully into a single unit – devoted to each other, loyal and committed to their marriage.

Seretse, however, grew increasingly alarmed at the news from home, which indicated that the fabric of Bamangwato society was suffering irreparable damage. There were outbursts of disturbances here and there. The young people, in particular, were becoming restive. The gentle Bamangwato way of life was under threat. He grew fearful for his people as never before. He tried to warn the authorities, but his appeals fell on deaf ears. The government was determined to perpetuate the myth that the presence of Seretse and Tshekedi in Bamangwatoland was a threat to peace. Nothing else. The truth was that Seretse's absence threatened the peace – as time would show.

At the end of June, they were invited to tea in the members' dining room of the Mother of Parliaments by Tom Driberg, a Labour MP, and to listen to the debate on Tshekedi's appeal against his banishment. Through dogged hard work and tenacity, that wily old politician had managed to convince a sufficient number of MPs from all three parties to raise the question of his banishment in both the House of Commons and the House of Lords. However, the dice was thoroughly stacked against him as the government was even more economically and militarily dependent upon South Africa than it had been a year previously. In addition, Cabinet was committed to placating the largely racist white community of Southern Rhodesia in order to get its proposed Central Africa Federation up and running.

Their conversation was interrupted by the ringing of the bells. Ruth and Seretse headed for the Strangers' Gallery while their host and his fellow MPs went into the chamber.

The debate began at 3.45 pm – and they were all still there at 10 pm. Attlee told the House sanctimoniously: 'I think it all to the good that in the midst of present world affairs the House should devote a day to the affairs of a small tribe in Africa and concern ourselves with the rights of individual citizens.'

Lord Salisbury supported the motion: 'The banishment raises fundamental questions of British justice. A British citizen should not be deprived or restricted in his rights or liberties except as a result of some offence of which he has been convicted under the law. No one should be condemned without a trial. That is the broad principle on which the British way of life has been founded and it applies to all British citizens of all religions, and races and colours. So far as I know, this man (Tshekedi) has not committed any offence or crime of any kind and the government's decision to exclude him appears to be entirely contrary to the principles of British justice.'

Ironically, when the Conservatives came to power later that year, Lord Salisbury, as Minister for Commonwealth Relations, would be the one to announce Seretse's permanent exclusion from the chieftainship.

Winston Churchill, leader of the Opposition, said: 'We have had a deeply interesting debate and I think I may say that I have rarely listened to a debate which has caused more heart-searching on both sides of the House than this. All of us want to give a right, honest, sincere, truthful opinion upon the issues that are before us.'

But honesty and sincerity were not evident in those hallowed precincts that day. History records that the parliamentary whips forced MPs to vote against their consciences. The vote was lost by 300 – 279, to keep Tshekedi banished. It is said that Churchill met one of the Labour members going to vote and remarked with a grimace: 'We are both going in the wrong direction.'

One of Seretse's friends, Michael Foot, recalled later that it had been 'the worst vote I ever cast in the House'.

Ruth and Seretse were very tired when it was all over, but they pressed forward with a throng of others to offer their condolences to Tshekedi. He shook their hands warmly and promised to come and see them before he left England. The evening had depressed them, revealing clearly as it did, the extent of the political machinations and deceptions they were up against in their struggle for justice and honour between African and European, between governors and those governed.

In July 1951, rioting erupted in Serowe. The disturbances, characterised by disorganised crowds armed with sticks and stones but without real targets, lasted 10 days and spread throughout the Territory. The police were helpless in the face of the huge numbers involved. Completely uncharacteristically, the women became violent and joined the mobs, inciting further hysteria with their high-pitched wailing and ululating. Drums were beaten. The protestors tore their clothes. The whites were terrified and cowered behind locked doors, but none were harmed. The Tribe's misery over the abduction of their Chief overflowed in a directionless flow of emotion. Lamentations for the young Chief throbbed incessantly. A contingent of eighty policemen was airlifted in from Southern Rhodesia to help restore order. Hundreds were arrested. The storm eventually blew itself out.

Seretse issued a press statement in London: '*I maintain that my position as Chief of the Bamangwato, with the overwhelming and devoted support of the Tribe, enables me alone to solve the present issues without the use of force – and events will prove that I am right.*' Once again his appeal was rejected.

Instead, the government prolonged everyone's agony by sending a delegation of three observers to hold another major *kgotla*, ostensibly to seek the people's views but in reality as a sop to those MPs of all parties whose consciences were still bothering them, and to the press, who continued to rally behind Seretse. The three stooges, as they became known – a retired trade unionist, an academic and a former independent MP – were tasked with obtaining an answer to the simple question: 'Was Tshekedi welcome back into the Bamangwato Reserve or not?'

Seretse and Ruth were highly amused when they read Goareng's letter describing this visit, during which the trio travelled more than 1 500 miles throughout the Protectorate, holding innumerable village *kgotla* meetings – but could get no agreement for a special *kgotla* to be held to discuss Tshekedi's return. '*As we have noted in the past, the extreme dryness, abundant sunlight and heat of our country is prone to produce nervous irritability in Europeans,*' wrote Goareng. '*These three were no exception.*'

Seretse was reading the letter aloud to Ruth as she fed Jackie her dinner. 'Oh my goodness, I can just imagine it,' he said. 'Apparently the trade union man told Goareng he believed the Bamangwato's strongest weapon was their tongue. They can talk an Englishman out of existence, he said.'

'Well, I hope that teaches them a lesson,' said Ruth.

The account of the historic women's *kgotla* held in Serowe and attended by about 2 000 women moved them profoundly. This was the first time the women had ever been considered or consulted formally in the history of the Tribe. Dressed in their best cotton frocks and freshly laundered *doeks*, they were fully aware of the importance of the occasion, but had no idea how they would communicate to these white men the depth of their sorrow or the extent of the anxiety and confusion brought about by the abduction of their Chief. Their lives had fallen apart with the collapse of their carefully ordered world. They sat silently, many with babies suckling, while the younger children cavorted on the fringes of the crowd. Having made their opening address the three Englishmen waited patiently for a response. But the women could not speak – they were unaccustomed to speaking in *kgotla*. That was for the men.

At last, one was persuaded. She knelt in the dust. 'Where is Chief Seretse? Where is the Chief's wife? Where is the child?' she choked, tears glistening in the sun as they rolled down her cheeks. And with that, the damn burst. The women wept. The storm of emotion swirled around the *kgotla* ground, threatening to engulf the three embarrassed white men, stunned by this display of mass sorrow. The women sobbed as though their hearts would break. And they told the visitors what they thought of Tshekedi: 'We hate him! Our fowls, our goats and the mice about our corn bins – all hate him! Give us Seretse.'

The report resulting from this comedy-turned-tragedy was, once again, contrary to what the government had wanted. The observers could not agree on their findings and submitted two versions – both emphasising the desire of the people for Seretse's return. The gist of both reports was that the Tribe's wishes were that Tshekedi should only be allowed back once Seretse was firmly on the throne and had given his permission. Publication was therefore strategically delayed for a few months, and the whole situation was overtaken, and subsequently buried, by the fall of the Labour government in October 1951.

Autumn became winter. Christmas came and went. Jackie was walking confidently and beginning to talk. It was 1952 already. The Khamas moved house again, this time to a rented house in the country – at Chipstead, near Epsom in Surrey.

'I think we have a better chance with the Conservatives in power,' said Ruth.

Muriel was over for tea and they were discussing the collapse of Labour. 'Don't be so naïve,' exclaimed Muriel.

'But just look at what we have suffered under Labour,' said Ruth. 'They're the ones who banished us, for goodness sake!'

'Calm down!' interjected Seretse.

'Well then, what do you think?' Muriel asked.

'I just don't know,' Seretse replied. 'It was Churchill who objected quite strongly to the way Labour handled our banishment in the first place.'

'But he still voted in favour of it, didn't he?' pressed Muriel.

Ruth's faith in the Conservatives was justified at last when an urgent review of the 'Seretse affair' was ordered.

'Told you so,' she crowed to Muriel over the telephone.

'I hope you're right,' replied Muriel seriously, 'But I have my doubts, I have to tell you.'

'Well, as a matter of fact, we have been invited to cocktails with the Secretary of State for the CRO.'

'What! When? Where?'

Unable to contain her excitement, Ruth regaled her sister with all the details. They were to go to Lord Ismay's private London residence on 13 March. 'Can't think what I'm going to wear!'

'Well, don't ask me,' said Muriel. 'You're the glamorous one in the family.'

Ruth laughed. 'Wouldn't it be wonderful if he says we can go back?'

On the other end of the line, Muriel shook her head at her younger sister's hopefulness. Her pragmatic self was certain Ruth was going to be hurt yet again. 'It would be wonderful,' she said quietly into the receiver. 'Just wonderful.' There was no way she would take away Ruth's hope – it was all she had.

Lord Ismay was a genial fellow, a personal friend of Churchill's and determined to get along with everyone if at all possible. He had already held several meetings with Tshekedi and had engineered considerable easing of the restrictions caused by the banning order. It would not be long before Ismay agreed to the former regent's return to the Bamangwato Reserve as a private citizen. However, his officials were not prepared to let this happen and the negotiations bogged down in a welter of confusion. Ismay then turned his attention to the other Khama – Seretse.

The couple had been greatly encouraged by his quoted comments in the papers to the effect that: '*It is one thing to prevent a man from becoming a ruler but it is another, and terrible, to banish him from his country.*' However, they were unaware that behind the scenes at the CRO the new Minister was regarded as something of a liability. His days were numbered and the officials connived to keep him in the dark on a number of issues – rendering him powerless to make any real decisions. Within a week he would be replaced by the ultra-right Lord Salisbury – a hard and unyielding man who got along famously with the CRO staff.

The evening was a success. Lord and Lady Ismay were charming and soon put Ruth and Seretse completely at ease. In turn, the young couple delighted the elderly aristocrats with their obvious devotion to each other, their cheerfulness and sense of humour. It was deemed impolite to mix business with pleasure, so an appointment at the Minister's office was fixed for 24 March, and the conversation turned to more pleasant matters.

Ruth and Seretse could hardly wait. They were convinced that this kindly peer would do the right thing and secure their return home to take care of the unhappy Bamangwato as soon as possible. Ismay greeted them genially. Lord Salisbury was less welcoming, and as his thin lips parted in a formal smile that never reached his eyes, Ruth felt a pang of dismay. She and Seretse were both dismayed when Ismay introduced Salisbury as the new Minister who would take office within a few days.

Ismay then proceeded to make it clear that Seretse could never go home as Chief, and appealed to him to renounce the chieftainship once and for all. Seretse explained, for the umpteenth time, that the chieftainship was not something he could take up or lay down. He was born to be Chief. The Chief was an intrinsic part of the Tribe and only the Tribe could refuse the Chief. His Tribe had made it abundantly clear that they wanted him as Chief and therefore, his hands were tied. He would be prepared to renounce the chieftainship, he said, if his people agreed. But he must be allowed to serve them in some political fashion. The vacuum left by the death of the tribal way of life would be very difficult for them and must be filled by some democratic form of government. It was his responsibility, by virtue of his birth as a Khama, to ensure that this was satisfactorily established. He could not, would not, abandon his people.

Nodding sympathetically, Ismay then tried another tack. He encouraged Seretse to consider a fresh start in life, using his talents to pursue an interesting career – perhaps in the diplomatic corps. He suggested that Seretse might like to join the Colonial Office and serve in Jamaica. Seretse and Ruth were stunned – but neither betrayed any emotion. They listened quietly to Ismay's remarkable proposals and fatherly advice, and when he suggested that they think about it and come back in two days, they rose meekly and left.

Seretse drafted a formal response to each of the points raised by Ismay, but his careful replies cut no ice with Salisbury, who was in the chair at the next meeting. He fixed Seretse with his piercing eyes and declared coldly that all his proposals were impracticable – even his willingness to give up the chieftainship but retain full political liberty in order to discharge his obligations to his people.

Questioned about his response to the Jamaican offer, Seretse replied: 'I would like to serve the Jamaican people, but I cannot take bread out of any Jamaican's mouth.'

When Seretse boldly said he believed the British government's behaviour over the previous three years could only be explained by 'the intervention by the Union of South Africa', the new Minister lost patience and snapped irritably: 'You leave us with no alternative but to make your exclusion from the chieftainship permanent and final.' He then adjourned the meeting, saying he would make an official statement to that effect the next day.

Not until they were safely home did Seretse allowed himself to show the extent of his disappointment. Sinking down onto the edge of a chair, he buried his face in his hands and muttered: 'To think that I can never go home again, never ever.'

Ruth grasped his hands and forced him to look at her. 'Never say never, Seretse,' she said fiercely. 'Never! Promise me!'

16
Exile

THE PRESS, AND INDEED THE COUNTRY, WERE SHOCKED. THE DAILY EXPRESS verbalised popular opinion: *The Marquis of Salisbury's first deed as Commonwealth Secretary is to confirm the expulsion of Seretse Khama from his own land and his own people. And his first deed is a bad, mean deed which should arouse shame and anger throughout the country. For the nation's good, Lord Salisbury's first deed as Commonwealth Relations Secretary should be his last.*

Immediate debates were demanded in both the Commons and the Lords. The decision was criticised as vindictive, unjust, hasty and in direct contravention of the desires of the Bamangwato. But the Labour Opposition was hobbled by its own past. The reasoning behind and phrasing of the White Paper were shrouded in mystery and confusion and, in effect, they didn't have a leg to stand on. So the new government was able to weather the storm without wavering.

Neither did it waver during the next several weeks when a delegation of six senior Bamangwato, led by Kgamane Keaboka, arrived by sea to protest against the return of Tshekedi and the continued exclusion of Seretse. They were accorded an interview with Salisbury, as a matter of courtesy.

They made impassioned pleas: 'It has become very clear to us that the government has not considered the welfare of the Tribe in coming to its decision. It has been influenced by the views of persons and bodies outside Bechuanaland. In effect, it appears to us the government is exercising a colour bar, for we can see no reason for not confirming Seretse as Chief except that he has married a white wife. The Tribe has lost all confidence in the government.'

They made eloquent speeches, painstakingly explaining to the white men the fundamental elements of Bamangwato culture which were at stake – that for Seretse to reject his birthright would bring dishonour to the House of Khama and to the people; he could not possibly be so disloyal. Eventually, in desperation, they said he could be relieved of the chieftainship if only he could be allowed to return – in any capacity. But even when they bowed so low, and offered to pay such a high price, they were simply ignored. And eventually, after visiting Seretse and Ruth on several occasions, they returned, empty-handed and downcast, to Serowe.

Seretse sent with them messages entreating his people to be law-abiding, to pay their taxes and to avoid disturbances, in the vain hope that their good behaviour would hasten his return.

True to his promise to Ruth, Seretse refused to admit defeat. The next round would become known as the campaign trail. The Seretse Khama Campaign Committee had been active for some time, but Seretse had been occupied lobbying the government directly. He now became more involved with the committee, and for several months he travelled throughout Britain address-ing meetings of all sorts of pressure groups. His first engagement was at a protest rally in London on 15 April 1952 held by Racial Unity.

With Ruth watching him from the front row, Seretse spoke without notes, and with his own brand of humour: 'I am not bitter, but I am frustrated be-cause I am compelled to live here and do absolutely nothing. I have not yet been able to find out what I have done wrong. I have been told that my marriage is contrary to native custom, but I can prove that it is not. I find it difficult, for all my Oxford training, to understand the people I have been dealing with – although some of them have been to Oxford too! Perhaps they went to a different college. We still in Bechuanaland regard ourselves as British and we still have a great deal of confidence in British justice, fair play and decency. Don't destroy it by allowing your government to carry out this unjust decision without a protest from you.'

On 2 May he spoke at another committee meeting and a week later he attended a protest gathering organised by the fiery Brockway, who described

Seretse's banishment as 'an intolerable crime against humanity and an outrage against democracy'. He was applauded when he stated that, by refusing to accept Seretse and his marriage, Britain had missed the chance to show South Africa an alternative future of racial equality.

Meanwhile, in St Paul's Cathedral, a Jamaican priest named Marcus James delivered a sermon on behalf of a new movement called Christian Action, in which he compared South African Prime Minister Malan ('the world's high priest of racial hate') with Hitler, and called on Christians to crusade against racial idolatry rather than against communism.

The campaign committee cleverly exploited the new spirit of public sentiment in Britain against racism at home and colonialism overseas, while the press obligingly put forward Seretse and Ruth as the tangible, human face that brought home to the British public the implications of apartheid in South Africa and the presence of increasing numbers of black people in Britain. Seretse spoke openly of the Bamangwato's loss of faith in the British government as a result of their contemptuous treatment. He referred often to the government's blunder in offering him the Jamaican post: 'I have been here for three years now and during that time I have been a very good boy. But where has it got me? If it is true, as has been said, that I am not fit to rule, that I am irresponsible, how can I hope to serve ably and properly the Jamaican people? If I am fit to be the assistant governor of Jamaica, I think I am more fit to be the ruler of my own people.'

The British Council of Churches added its voice to the outcry and sent a delegation, led by the Archbishop of Canterbury, to see Salisbury on 9 May. But the steely gaze never faltered and the clergy departed, suitably chastened and totally ineffectual.

On 23 May 1952 the British government issued an order-in-council barring both Seretse and Tshekedi Khama, together with their children, from ever succeeding to the chieftainship of the Bamangwato.

'The clever devils,' Seretse said to Ruth, as he read the statement in the newspaper. 'By making it an order-in-council they've made sure that I can't challenge it through the High Court. And it says they've empowered the High Commissioner to fill the vacant throne with someone designated by the Tribe.' He snorted derisively. 'How long is it going to take them to understand that the Tribe wants **me** to be Chief. They're never going to designate anybody else.' He slammed his fist onto the table. 'And listen to this: "The High Commissioner should take all action appropriate to ensuring tribal unity." That's a joke. They've destroyed the Tribe. Now they want to unify it. Hah!' He crumpled the newspaper and threw it into the wastepaper basket.

Aware of the tension in the room, Jackie, who had been quietly playing with her blocks on the carpet, started fretting and ran to Ruth. Her father was normally so gentle and smiling.

'Ssh, it's all right, sweetheart,' Ruth said, rocking the child on her lap. Would it ever end? Her nerves were frayed by Seretse's frequent impotent rages and her own helplessness in the face of his frustration.

There is a limit to the number of impassioned speeches a man can make. There is a limit too, to the attention span of the public, and to the possibility of maintaining a level of emotion and outrage for any length of time. People get bored. The wind blows. In the face of government obduracy and competing headlines, the campaign trail was unsustainable. The Council for the Defence of Seretse Khama reconstituted itself to enable it to campaign against the abandonment of the Protectorates to South Africa. However, despite having an illustrious membership of several members of parliament, peers of the realm, authors, painters, actors and playwrights as well as prominent Africans and Caribbeans, the council was little more than a lobby group. The tide went out in Britain.

But in Serowe, after a long low, it came in again – a stormy, destructive tide that swept all before it, causing mayhem. For the first time the peaceful Bamangwato countryside was witness to the instruments of modern peacekeeping: pistols, steel helmets, riot guns, tear gas and mesh-wired lorries. These had never been needed before. At the end of May a *kgotla* was called at which the delegation of six were to give a report back concerning their failed visit to Britain. A large crowd of women, their traditional status altered forever by the removal of the Chief and the *kgotla* of the three stooges, stormed the ground and tried to prevent the District Commissioner from speaking.

Once again, frustration and bewilderment at the abrupt termination of a centuries old way of life, spilled over into confusion and violence. Police reinforcements were brought in, but the people were uncontrollable. When finally the emotion was spent, three policemen were dead and 12 injured.

The authorities reacted with an iron fist, arresting 150 people and sentencing Phetu Sekgoma, Keaboka and several others to hard labour. They announced that forthwith Rasebolai Kgamane, third in the line of succession after Seretse and Tshekedi, would rule as the African Authority with 13 councillors.

For the next four years the Bamangwato resolutely and consistently refused to nominate another Chief or accept the imposition of Rasebolai as *kgosi*. Just as resolutely and consistently a succession of British administrators tried to insist that they do so. It was a stalemate. The *kgotla* ground fell into disrepair, the people became listless and sullen, the administration ground onwards, with little or no development in the key areas of health, agriculture or education. The British constantly refused to permit the development of a legislative council or to extend to the Bamangwato any political rights, using the empty excuse that they were 'not ready'. Seretse and Ruth watched from a distance in impotent agony of mind and heart.

In August Seretse received news that, despite the Tribe's desire to have him excluded having been firmly established by independent observers, his uncle had finally succeeded in having his banishment order lifted by the Conservatives.

As a young man, Seretse had never really wanted to be the Chief.

'And if I'm honest, I don't want to be Chief now,' he told Ruth. 'But I do want to serve my people. I was born to serve them and I can't get away from that. But I think what I'm saying is that I recognise intellectually that the era of chieftainship is past. This is the 20th century – democracy is the future. The chieftainship is an anachronism which cannot possibly survive in this modern world.'

She nodded, encouraging him to go on.

'But in my heart, deep down, I am a Khama – royalty is in my veins. I have to acknowledge that. And so there is some regret – at an emotional level.'

'Of course there is. It's only natural and you shouldn't feel ashamed of it,' she said.

'What I want to do,' he said, the thoughts that had been fermenting in his mind for many months coalescing into a clear statement, 'is oversee the peaceful, practical, successful, rational transformation of the Tribe into a nation. To hand over the chieftainship formally and properly to some democratic institution, with the people's full understanding and approval and cooperation. What has happened in Bechuanaland – this rough and thoughtless beheading of the chieftainship, with no decent burial and no mourning period to allow the people to adjust – this had been a tragedy. And I will strive with every breath in my body and every ounce of my energy to put it right one day.'

It was to be another four years before Seretse could begin to put his words into action. Four weary years of frustration and waiting which stretched his and Ruth's endurance almost to breaking point. Four years of hoping, and having hopes dashed. Years of lost opportunities and wasted time.

Sometimes the enforced inaction gave way to indolence and lethargy, of mind and body. Seretse's law studies had become a chore. He neglected them. He smoked and drank too much and everything lost its savour. It was life – but not life abundant. But there were also times of joy: watching their children grow; feeling their love deepen and ripen as they took solace in each other during the lonely times; experiencing rich friendships and good times of family togetherness. And so time passed.

Ian Khama Seretse Khama was born on 27 February 1953 – a healthy infant, golden skinned like his sister, with a mop of crinkly hair and a sweet, contented smile.

His parents' hopes were raised again when he was but a month old. A petition asking for the confirmation of Seretse as Chief had been signed by almost 11 000 people and was presented to Parliament by Fenner Brockway. But nothing came of it.

A month later, *The Times* published a passionate letter from Daniel Lipson, one of the three luckless observers. Again, hope flared. *'Will the government now not recognise the facts and withdraw its embargo on Seretse? Delay is dangerous. Is it wise to run the risk of barbarous practices of the Mau Mau spreading to the Protectorate? Are we not laying up trouble for the future by our refusal to allow the Bamangwato the only Chief it wants? I presided last year at a crowded meeting in the Birmingham Town Hall at which Seretse made a statesmanlike speech more in sorrow than in anger and gave me the impression that he is a friend of Britain. Will not the Prime Minister send for him and judge for himself, the kind of man he is? Before it is too late and with good grace let both government and the opposition admit that they have been wrong about Seretse's right to be Chief of the Bamangwato and allow the Tribe its choice. Such action would be in line with the best traditions of British policy.'*

But money and uranium, as always, spoke louder even than principled Englishmen.

Yet again, when the baby was six months old, sitting up on his own and delighting them with his toothless smile, Ruth and Seretse's hopes burned brightly. The Labour Party conference agreed that the banishment of Seretse was a blot on the party's record, a blot of which the whole movement was now ashamed.

The tenacious Brockway, who has been described as looking like a vicar on holiday, told the conference that Seretse's only crime was giving affront to Dr Malan in South Africa. 'There is now a dangerous situation in the colonies and Protectorates,' he said. 'Antagonism to white people is growing and Seretse has become, in many countries, the living symbol of unfair treatment.'

He asked for assurances that a new Labour government would put right in its early days the wrong done to Seretse. The assurance was given. But the Conservatives ruled strongly, and there was no general election in sight.

Seretse decided that his family needed to put down some roots. He was tired of moving constantly and paying rent. They could always sell, if and when they were allowed to go home. It would be a good investment. So he and Ruth went house-hunting – leaving the children in the care of a friendly and competent au pair. They found what they wanted in Addiscombe, Surrey – 'Aldwick', a five-bedroom, redbrick mansion, built in mock-Jacobean style in Mapledale Avenue on a 1936 suburban estate, with hilly countryside, green fields and long hedgerows just a few minutes' walk away.

Life at 'Aldwick' was pleasant enough. Ruth's family came for Christmas, and early in the new year they held a big house-warming party for all their friends. Jackie turned four years old and went to the neighbourhood nursery school. Ian delighted them with his antics, walking before he was a year old and running everywhere a few months after that.

Seretse made friends with the local butcher who was not at all averse to keeping 'the Chief' supplied with a few extra chops and a good joint for roasting from time to time. He joined the local cricket club, and on a Saturday afternoon could be spotted, the only black face, resplendent in starched white flannels and shirt, skilfully wielding his bat on the manicured village green. Come Wednesday and Friday evenings he could be found, in his comfortable tweed jacket, conversing amiably with the locals over a few pints in the village pub. Sometimes Ruth joined him and the couple was a popular addition to village life. Their story was well-known, and their cheerfulness in adversity and obvious devotion to each other won the hearts of many. They spent happy hours in the saddle, exploring the English countryside and galloping across the wide fields under the open sky. It was good to be out of London.

Both Seretse and Ruth devoured all the newspapers, becoming increasingly well-informed on world events and, in particular, developments in Africa. News came regularly from Bechuanaland, but no letters from Tshekedi. His relationship with Seretse seemed to have been deep-frozen and neither man was willing to make the first step towards thawing it out.

Their friends came regularly to visit. They discussed developments in Rhodesia, where the Federation of Rhodesia and Nyasaland had been formed the previous August in an attempt by the British government to create a middle way between the newly independent, socialist black states and the white-dominated governments of South Africa, Angola and Mozambique.

Their old friend Harry Nkumbula had returned to Northern Rhodesia, where, with Kenneth Kaunda, he led the Northern Rhodesian African National Congress, which was opposed to Federation. He, and many others, believed it to be nothing more than a clever attempt to keep power in the hands of the whites. The settler population had amply demonstrated that it was totally unsympathetic towards the wishes of African people. Godfrey Huggins (the Federal Prime Minister) stated publicly that he saw the Federation as a horse and rider partnership – with the white man as the rider. He also said it was not wise to entrust the vote to those who made decisions by studying the entrails of a goat.

The previous year, Malan had tried to persuade the British to implement his African Charter – a scheme to bolster white settlement in Africa and preserve indigenous peoples from outside contacts. 'He wants to create a great apartheid over the whole continent,' Seretse had said at the time. In a sense, he saw the creation of the Federation as a step in the same direction. In April 1953 Malan had won a landslide victory, virtually wiping out the opposition United Party and, with it, British hopes for a cosy, official relationship.

Other frequent visitors who became firm friends over the years were Tony and Caroline Benn. Tony had just been elected to the House as the youngest Member of Parliament in history and he soon became a firm supporter of Seretse's, campaigning tirelessly to right the injustice done to his friend.

'I don't know why I feel such a strong emotional kinship with you,' he said once, 'I suppose it is because we are both chiefs – only you want to be one and I don't!' The socialist Benn had renounced his heredity peerage as a practical demonstration of his firm belief in the equality of mankind and the iniquity of the British class system.

American-born Caroline Benn and Ruth became great friends. They both smoked cigarettes in long cigarette holders that matched the colour of their outfit. Looking at the overflowing ashtrays after one long, entertaining evening, Ruth said to Caroline: 'Honestly, I don't know why I smoke. It's a disgusting habit!'

'No, it's not,' said Seretse, lounging in his armchair and puffing at his cigar. 'It's one of life's few legal pleasures.'

'Nonsense,' said Caroline. 'Ruth's quite right. It is disgusting. Why do we do it?' She stubbed out her half-smoked cigarette.

'It's nothing but a social affectation with you two,' said Tony. 'Look at those holders you use – they're just fashion accessories!'

Ruth laughed. 'You're right, Tony,' she said. 'Come on Caroline, let's give it up. I will if you will.'

'You're on,' responded Caroline with alacrity. 'I know – let's make a pledge. If we're ever tempted to smoke again we have to ask the other's permission. Okay?'

'Agreed,' said Ruth, passing her holder and box of cigarettes to Caroline. 'And permission is only to be granted in the direst of circumstances.'

'Absolutely. Tony and Seretse, you are witnesses.'

'Right-oh,' agreed the two men, regarding their wives indulgently.

'Let's take a bet on how long it lasts,' suggested Tony.

'Two weeks,' responded Seretse with a grin.

'Go ahead, bet,' said Ruth, 'but be warned, you're going to lose money.'

Recognising the glint in Ruth's eye, Seretse put both hands in the air. 'I know that look,' he told the others. 'No bets.'

And sure enough, neither woman ever took so much as another puff.

In his diaries, Benn describes Ruth as a 'compassionate conservative' and Seretse as 'a true royal but a socialist at heart'. Later in life Seretse liked to tell the story of when young Hilary Benn, of whom he was very fond, climbed up on his knee and said artlessly: 'I don't believe you're black all over.' Seretse had responded: 'And I don't believe you're white all over!' He had then proceeded to draw up his trouser leg to show his black leg and undo a few shirt buttons to display his black chest. The child was enchanted.

1954 sped by. People in Serowe never gave up hope of Seretse's eventual return. Their letters of support, which arrived sporadically across the years, warmed his heart. In September 1954 the papers gave coverage to a petition sent by the Tribe to the new Queen, Elizabeth II. Perhaps they believed she carried some of her great-great-grandmother's spirit and that she, too, would look kindly upon a King of the Khamas. She cannot fail to have been touched by their heartfelt cry: '*Great White Queen, we are desperate. The Bamangwato are sad. Over our land there is a great shadow blotting out the sun. Please put an end to our troubles. Send us our real Chief – the man born to be our Chief – Seretse.*' But she could do nothing. The all-powerful CRO officials were still firmly of the opinion that: 'The reinstatement in a position of authority on the Union's doorstep of an African with a white wife and half-breed family would unite and inflame against us all the white population of the Union.' In order to cover its tracks, the government continued to peddle their main argument – that the split between Tshekedi and Seretse was irreconcilable.

Soon it was time for the Labour Party's annual conference again. The five-year mark of Seretse's exile was approaching – the period originally decreed by the Labour government in March 1950 for review of sentence. The indefatigable Brockway yet again ensured that Seretse's case was high on the agenda and spoke passionately about the 'gross denial of human rights' involved in his continuing banishment. The party dispatched its Colonial and Imperial liaison officer, John Hatch, to interview the CRO and thereafter to Bechuanaland – where he found Tshekedi by no means irreconcilable to his nephew's return. The ex-regent told Hatch that neither he nor his followers had ever opposed Seretse's return home as an ordinary citizen. The only problem was his nephew's own obduracy in hanging on to his claim to *bogosi*. Amazed to find Tshekedi personally so amenable towards Seretse, Hatch duly reported back. But nothing happened.

In July 1955 the couple was invited to attend the launch of John Redfern's book entitled *Ruth and Seretse, a very disreputable transaction*. Redfern, a journalist for Lord Beaverbrook's Express group of newspapers, had met them both in Serowe in 1949 while covering the 'Seretse Story' for his employers. His respect for them had deepened into friendship over the years, and when they moved to 'Aldwick' they discovered he was a close neighbour, with young children similar in age to their own.

It was a glittering evening. Redfern made an excellent speech, concluding with a quotation from the last paragraph of his book: '*I believe that there are sufficient people in this country, in all parties in Parliament and outside, to see to it yet that wrongs done are righted and Seretse goes home to the Bamangwato, who are waiting for their Chief.*' Even the hardened critics applauded. The book received widespread publicity and several good reviews. Commonwealth Relations officials admitted that it was well informed, but took Redfern to task for questioning their careful illusion that the British government's appeasement of South Africa had been motivated purely by humanitarian concerns for the welfare of the Territories.

The racist South African press raged against the book. '*This book is undoubtedly part of a bitter, prejudiced conspiracy to set the world against South Africa . . . Afrikaners in general, Dr Malan, the Dutch Reformed Church,*' said *Die Burger*. '*Nothing would give some socialistic longhairs and negrophilist clerics more pleasure than a year-long crusade for the reinstatement of Seretse.*' But all in all Redfern's book went a long way towards bringing the case back to the attention of the international public. The tide was getting ready to turn again.

Suddenly, out of the blue, Tshekedi reestablished contact – firstly via his friend and ally David Astor, whose *Sunday Observer* newspaper published a call for Seretse's return home as a private citizen, then through mutual friends, Noni Jabavu and her English husband, who visited Ruth and Seretse after staying with Tshekedi and Ella. The message was clear – ask my nephew to tell me how he feels we might cooperate and assist each other. This was what Seretse had been waiting for. He quickly cabled his uncle indicating that he was in favour of a round-table conference.

Ruth was delighted to see a new light in his eyes and a new spring in his step. Even the timbre of his voice changed subtly – it became stronger somehow, more assured, vibrant with energy after a long time of being flat with acceptance, weariness and patience.

The tide pressed on. Despite the continued opposition of CRO officials, the Secretary of State, Lord Home, boldly exercised his authority and ordered yet another review of Seretse's case.

In Serowe a *kgotla* was held at which the Tribe was presented with the possibility of mining development. The Anglo-American Corporation of South Africa had expressed an interest in prospecting for copper, coal, diamonds, nickel and asbestos. The Bamangwato steadfastly refused to enter into any negotiations without the return of Seretse. At last, after being powerless for so long, they had found a weapon. The local administration was desperate to find some alternative source of income for the Cinderella territory that was a constant drain on its coffers. This issue also gave the Tribe the upper hand as far as Tshekedi was concerned. He was concerned that if he was not allowed to be involved in the negotiations the wily multinationals might succeed, robbing the Bamangwato of most of the profits. But in order for the Tribe to allow him to take part, Seretse had to come home.

Hope burned brightly. Early in 1956, Seretse began to give interviews again: 'I have no doubt that if it rested with the ordinary British people I should be back home any time. But it is the British Cabinet that must give the decision. I feel restless – an urge to get back to where I rightly belong.'

He talked eagerly about impending government plans for development in his country. 'The plans will not work if there is no life, no enthusiasm among the people there. I believe I could help in bringing those plans to a good end and it would be my aim and joy to do so.'

The tide pressed on. The excesses of the South African government's apartheid policies were at last exposed for all the world to see. There was a barrage of unfavourable publicity in the world press. At Easter Trevor Huddleston published *Naught for your Comfort*, a devastating critique of South Africa's race policies. Huddleston received widespread publicity and succeeded in bringing into the spotlight the sheer immorality of apartheid. Anti-apartheid demonstrations outside South Africa House in Trafalgar Square began to take place regularly. At the same time, the Tomlinson Report was published, clearly outlining the South African government's plans for utilising the High Commission Territories as heartlands for 'Bantu homelands' in its pursuit of total racial separation.

This was the last straw. At last the camel's back of British appeasement of its powerful, wealthy, Commonwealth member was broken. The time for a parting of the ways had come. A few weeks later, in June, the abrasive Strydom arrived in Britain for a Commonwealth prime ministers' conference. Prime Minister Eden found the surly Strydom particularly difficult to stomach. The British delegation to the conference winced visibly when Strydom appealed to the British people to 'be proud of your race and heritage . . . which like ours is white and European.'

'Uncle, how good to see you!' Seretse pumped his visitor's hand vigorously and then laughed as Tshekedi pulled him into a rough embrace and slapped him on the back. The pain and bitterness of the past eight years telescoped backwards into a distant pinprick. After a brief, but warm, greeting to Ruth and the children, the two men secluded themselves in the study for several hours.

'We must strike now,' Tshekedi said, leaning forward across the desk. 'There is a breach between the British and the South Africans, but it could be closed again soon. We must act immediately.'

Seretse nodded his agreement. His restless spirit was like a wild animal thrusting itself against prison bars. He could not keep it caged much longer. 'What do you suggest?' he asked, as the old respect and trust for the wise, solid man who had always meant so much to him came flooding back.

'The chieftainship is dead,' Tshekedi stated baldly. 'It belongs to yesterday, and we must prepare for tomorrow. Our people need progress and development. We need democratic institutions.'

'You are right. I have been thinking much about that.'

'We must prepare a joint statement and seek a personal audience with Lord Home,' continued his uncle. Seretse nodded and drew towards him the lined legal pad he used for making notes. He scribbled as Tshekedi dictated: 'One. We must both renounce the chieftainship for ourselves and our heirs. Two. There is no longer any dispute between ourselves. We both wish to live freely in the Bamangwato Reserve with our families. Three. We will do everything in our power to help develop representative institutions, such as a Tribal Council. Four. We will not dispute the right of Rasebolai Kgamane to be the 'African Authority'. Five. We humbly request permission to return home as free citizens with full political rights, and to be allowed to serve our people in any capacity to which they may wish to elect us.'

They spent some time polishing the phraseology and finally both men were satisfied.

'Now, we must keep everything secret. The press and the parliamentarians are our friends. But one false move, one untimely revelation could destroy everything,' declared Tshekedi.

'Yes absolutely.'

A few days later Tshekedi arrived to spend a few days at 'Aldwick' with Ella and his two older boys, who had been brought over to attend school in the UK. It was a happy time. The two boys were keen riders and accompanied Ruth on several early morning canters. The house resounded with Seretse's infectious laughter. Ella and Ruth went on walks through the village, while the men closeted themselves in the study to make up for eight lost years of communication and camaraderie. The evenings were spent in animated discussion about the future and the steps they all would take to restore peace and prosperity to the people they loved.

Lord Home responded with alacrity to the Khamas' request for an appointment and on 25 August 1956 the two men appeared before him with their signed statement. He was keen to solve once and for all this awkward issue which had so dogged successive British governments for the best part of a decade. And, one of a new breed of politician, he was well aware that the Imperial era was over. He immediately set in motion a number of enquiries into various aspects of the case, notably a political assessment of the likely impact on South Africa's claims to the Territories.

Within a few weeks he had the answers at his fingertips. The South African government was suffering from the impact of the world's disapproval and had decided not to risk further opprobrium by pursuing its demands for incorporation. Home dashed off a memo to Cabinet and presented it on 11 September. Cabinet was delighted to be able to endorse such a neat conclusion to what had been an exceedingly messy business.

The official announcement was made on 26 September 1956. The British government was pleased to announce that Seretse and his family would return forthwith to Bechuanaland as private persons, and that he and Tshekedi would henceforth be permitted to play their parts in the affairs of the Tribe through a Tribal Council headed by Rasebolai Kgamane.

With one final surge, the tide thrust itself joyously at the shoreline.

John Keith won the toss against his colleagues in the CRO for the pleasure of giving Seretse the news. Unfortunately it had to be over the telephone. He would have given anything to see the look on the face of the man whom he had come so much to respect and admire as a true 'officer and a gentleman' when he received the word that his weary exile was over.

Seretse's intent expression told Ruth that this was not just a casual phone call. She shushed the children and watched her husband with rapt attention. He replaced the receiver carefully, but she saw that his hand was shaking. Rising from her knees where she had been playing with Ian, she held out her hands to him. Seretse walked deliberately towards her and caught her into an embrace so tight she could hardly breathe.

'We're going home,' he whispered. 'We're going home at last.'

At that moment, Tshekedi, Ella and the boys returned from a ramble in the countryside. Seretse strode towards his uncle and clasped his hand, beaming and pumping it so vigorously that Tshekedi, after a glance at Ruth's beaming face, immediately understood.

'They've agreed?' he asked quickly. Seretse and Ruth both nodded. And then pandemonium broke loose. There were hugs all round, exuberant shouts from the boys, laughter and congratulations. Seretse hurried to his liquor cabinet and took out a bottle of champagne he had bought years earlier in a moment of high hope and anticipation of victory. He had never dreamed it would take so long. But at last, they were going home. Ruth produced an ice bucket and glasses, but before he had a chance to pop the cork, the phone began to ring. The press had been tipped off somehow.

'Yes,' Seretse said into the receiver, making the same comments he was to repeat a hundred times over the next few days. 'Yes, we are delighted. This is a great day. Of course we shall miss our friends. I shall be leaving as soon as possible.'

A comment in *The Observer* four days later encapsulated the moment when it remarked that the enthusiasm of the Khamas was '*quite infectious – you would think there was no place in the world so wonderful to live as in Serowe!*'

'How soon can you be ready to leave?' Seretse asked, as they prepared for bed much later that evening. The champagne had been consumed, together with several more bottles brought by well-wishers as the news spread through the chilly autumn like a wildfire across the bone-dry winter plains around Serowe. The Redferns had been first to arrive, followed shortly by other press members, then the Benns, and Charles and Braim. Telegrams had already begun to pour in.

'You go,' said Ruth generously, aware of the energy coursing through him. 'I'll pack up and follow you as soon as I can.'

'Are you sure?' he asked, well aware of the value of the gift she was offering him. 'I can't leave you to do all that on your own.'

'Yes, you can. Your heart is there already – your body should follow.'

'No,' he said seriously, 'my heart is here.' And he touched his hand to her breast. 'It will always be here. You are my heart.'

For the second time that day, Ruth's eyes filled with tears. 'And you are mine. But go to Serowe. Go quickly before they change their minds.'

'What if we are separated again?' he asked, unable to believe that this was the end of it all, or rather, the beginning. What if something went wrong? What if the British changed their minds? What if the South Africans did something appalling – as they were well capable of doing, something that would ruin it all again?

'They'll never separate us again,' declared Ruth, her voice full of prophetic assurance. 'You go – soon. The children and I will follow within a month. I promise you.' And he believed her.

17

Home At Last

SERETSE ENVELOPED RUTH IN ONE LAST EMBRACE.

'This is our last separation,' he said.

She stood holding Ian and Jackie tightly by the hand on either side of her. Not even the joy of going home at last, not even the knowledge that his family would join him within a matter of weeks, could eclipse the wrench of leaving her. There had been too many partings.

'See you soon,' she said, smiling bravely.

'Bye bye, daddy,' shouted Ian, clutching the toy aeroplane which was his pride and joy. He had been given it by his nursery school teacher when she announced to the class that Ian would be leaving them, going far away in a big aeroplane to live among lions and elephants. Jackie waved shyly. She was not at all sure that she wanted to go to the land of lions in a big, noisy, machine like the one her daddy was now heading towards.

As he neared the steps of the plane, Seretse turned and raised his hat in farewell to the crowd of well-wishers and press who had gathered to see him off at Heathrow Airport. It was 9 October 1956. Earlier, Ruth and the children had watched as he had faced a crowd of reporters and photographers.

'I want to help my people develop a democratic system, raise the standard of living and establish a happy, healthy nationhood. I have renounced the chieftainship as I have always been prepared to do. I will be taking part in local politics if I so wish,' he had declared.

An editorial in *The Times* that morning had praised his and Ruth's 'integrity and dignity' while commenting caustically on the ineptness of the British administration throughout the affair: '*The fundamental mistake was committed when, this decision having been taken for deeply based imperial reasons,*

the attempt was made to disguise it as a concession to the wishes of the Tribe . . .
All the subsequent embarrassments have flowed from the intellectual dishonesty
of this unhappy procedure.'

'Well, I'm glad they've admitted at last that it was dishonest,' Ruth had
commented brusquely when Seretse read the article to her. Britain's duplicity
in vigorously condemning apartheid in public while remaining South Africa's
most powerful diplomatic ally for reasons of national interest had always
disgusted her. She was not surprised, decades later, when the secrecy and
deceit surrounding the uranium deal were finally revealed.

The South African press took a different line altogether, with the *Rand Daily
Mail* deploring '*the British tendency to see Seretse as a sort of African Duke of
Windsor*'. But Seretse simply shrugged his shoulders in dismissal when the
racist contents of *Die Transvaler* were translated for him a few days later,
saying the decision to allow them back was 'an offensive condoning of mixed
marriage'.

These sour comments could in no way diminish the delight of the Bamangwato at the return of their Chief, nor Seretse's joy in coming home at
last. A few days later, the *Rand Daily Mail* reported: '*The crowd surged and
swayed around Seretse, stretching out their hands to touch him, pat him, caress
him. It was sheer joy*'.

He arrived in Francistown by plane and journeyed on to Serowe by road,
via Palapye. Everywhere there were wild scenes of jubilation, characterised
by much throwing of hats into the air – Seretse's included – as well as shouting, ululating and singing. For the first several hours, Seretse was unable to
address the crowds – there was too much noise. His progress was slow as
people threw themselves into the path of the car to kiss the bonnet. It was
just as well Ruth and the children had not accompanied him. They would
have been overwhelmed by this mass display of emotion.

Tshekedi and Ella welcomed him warmly – a far cry from that dismal homecoming in 1948 when his uncle had behaved like an ogre. Eight long years,
almost to the day, had passed since then. As he gazed out of the window

at the fathomless sky above, bright with stars he had not seen for so long, a gentle breeze reached him, wafting the wood smoke from a thousand cooking fires. Serowe might lack the comforts of Addiscombe. The Bamangwato might be less educated than his neighbours in Croydon. The bioscope in Palapye might be a far cry from the West End – but he was home. And it felt sweet. He pushed aside the thoughts of how much precious time had been wasted, and how much work needed to be done, and slept. His last thought was of Ruth, resolutely preparing to leave her homeland once again to follow him.

Ruth put the children to bed and sat down at Seretse's desk. It was a heavy task that faced her. Selling up the house, packing and shipping all their possessions, disposing of the animals, leaving her family and friends, transplanting her children. But Seretse was in Serowe. Seretse wanted, needed, to be in Serowe. And where he was, she wanted to be also. Eight years of marriage, two children, the emotional torment of exile, the battle against depression and despair – all these had done nothing to diminish her love for him. Their exile had revealed depths to his character she had not imagined existed. And of course parenthood had added another dimension to their relationship.

She smiled at the photograph of him that stood on the desk. He was crouched down in the garden, Ian at his side, playing with a wooden train engine, laughing. Ruth squared her shoulders. First, she would get a good night's sleep, and tomorrow she would start to pack. She had promised him that she and the children would join him within a month. And she always kept her promises.

Seretse plunged headlong into action. The lethargy he had become accustomed to feeling evaporated in the brilliant Serowe sunshine. For the next several weeks he travelled around the country, visiting remote cattle posts and villages, greeting his people and explaining his renunciation of the chieftainship. But this made no difference to the Bamangwato. Seretse was born to be their Chief. He would always be their Chief. Terminology, so agonised over by the British, meant little to them. Here he was, at last. The waiting and confusion was over. In their thousands they knelt before him and praised God for his safe return. In vain Seretse tried to persuade them that 'any man who thinks he will make me Chief is wasting his time'. The greybeards just shouted back at him: 'What we were fighting for is here before us'. A new atmosphere of peace and harmony spread across the land, so tangible that even the British administrators remarked on it. Gone were the sullen resentment, the listless noncooperation, the angry stares and muttered curses. The Bamangwato were happy once more.

The former loving father-and-son relationship between Seretse and his uncle was reestablished and together they commenced the awesome task of restoring the life of the Tribe on three fronts – economic, political and administrative. However, much damage had been done to the previously harmonious relationship between the Bamangwato and the British. Suspicion on both sides ran deep. The colonial administrators were still uncooperative, making the whole business vexing. For example, it took them seven months to agree that Tshekedi should be secretary of the Tribe, as proposed by Seretse, and an eight-month dispute followed Tshekedi's proposal of Seretse for the post of vice-chair.

True to her word, Ruth and the children arrived in early November 1956. Her parents and Muriel had been a wonderful help with the packing up and moving, and she had found an eager buyer for their house. The only sadness had been bidding farewell to her parents – but at least this time she was leaving with her father's blessing.

Seretse had prepared a bungalow for them in the centre of Serowe, and managed to get them safely ensconced without the huge uproar that had accompanied his return. However, it was not long before people realised they had arrived. Then they came in their hundreds to welcome the Chief's family. The visitors squatted for hours in the small yard, gazing at the golden children, talking to them in Setswana, fussing over them, uncertain just how to demonstrate their love and delight at this fruit of their Chief's loins. It was all so different and difficult – and yet, somehow, they had to let him know they were happy to have him home and that they were fully prepared to love and accept his pale wife and children too. Ruth's evident devotion to her husband and family, together with her disarming lack of airs and graces, had quickly won the respect and admiration of the Bamangwato. She was friendly without being familiar, dignified without being distant – a perfect Chief's wife, in fact.

But despite the euphoria of being home, and their deep sense of victory and achievement at having won the mammoth battle with the mighty British government, Ruth found things difficult at first.

'I don't think all this attention is good for the children,' she complained to Seretse one evening after yet another entire day of visitors. 'And I'm really sick of feeling like an animal in a zoo, being stared at all day long!' she added.

'Don't worry, the novelty will soon wear off. And it's not doing them any harm, you know. Just try to stick it out for a few more days. It's a small price to pay, don't you think?' As always, his common sense and loving support melted away her irritation and frustration.

He was so alive here. She had noticed the difference in him the minute she had arrived. He had merely been existing in England. Now he moved differently, his voice was vibrant, his eyes were constantly alert, his laughter boomed more often. Yes, indeed, it was a very small price to pay.

Seeing the children playing in the dust, always dirty, being embraced by unwashed old women and shaking hundreds of sweaty hands had given her considerable anxiety. She didn't want them to get sick. But it was all right. As long as Seretse was there it would always be all right.

'Now what's for dinner?' he said.

Ruth gave a yelp and rushed into the kitchen where the Mongwato cook she was training stood patiently beside a pan of burning potatoes – waiting to be shown how to mash them into a creamy mound to go with the sausages.

After an early supper the children were put to bed and Ruth and Seretse settled down to enjoy their favourite time of the day. Putting one of his huge collection of records on to the radiogram, Seretse drew Ruth down beside him on the comfortable settee they had placed on the verandah. She leaned against him, gazing into the huge, black sky with its adornment of jewels that never ceased to thrill them both. This was the time they reserved just to be together – nothing was allowed to interfere with it. As they made the transition from living in limbo in England to real life in Bechuanaland, they found they treasured it more and more. There was so much to talk about, so many ideas to share and, especially for Ruth, so many questions to ask and adjustments to be made.

Seretse had taken up the threads of his old relationships once more, especially with his childhood companions and cousins, Goareng, Lenyeletse and others. Having not spoken his native tongue much for the past 10 years, he delighted in having long discussions in Setswana from which Ruth was naturally excluded. So they found they needed this evening time to stay in tune with each other.

Visitors frequently remarked on how completely Ruth, the English lady, managed to blend into the African environment which was her husband's heritage. She grew to know the minds and feelings of Africa and its people in a way few white people can ever hope to do. Although she sometimes came across as controlled and distant, there could be no doubt she was Seretse's sustaining support, and her deep love for him was a powerful force. Equally, his love for her was unwavering in its steadfastness and carried her through many difficult times.

In the early days, their main topic of conversation was the District Commissioner, Bruce Rutherford, and his wife Jessie. Seretse had been aware since shortly after his arrival that he was under strict surveillance 24 hours a day. The spies made no effort to disguise their interest in his every word, every move – and Seretse was beginning to find this extremely irksome. In addition, the Rutherfords were notably cool in their attitude towards the royal couple, and had obviously set the pace for the rest of the white community. With the exception of Tommie Shaw and his wife Barbara, in Palapye, white Bechuanaland society made it patently clear that they were not overjoyed at having a mixed-race couple in their midst.

Seretse began to flex his muscles in a variety of ways. He was the Chief of the Bamangwato in all but the administration's eyes – and the sooner they realised it, the smoother life would be for all concerned. Rutherford fumed impotently, but there was nothing he could do. His days were numbered.

Before they knew it, Christmas was upon them. Cards began to pour into the Serowe post office, assuring them that they had not been forgotten by their many friends and well-wishers around the world.

'Oh, my goodness, I haven't done the cards yet,' exclaimed Ruth in December. 'How long will it take for them to get to England, do you think?'

'Only a week or so,' replied Seretse. 'Don't panic – you can send them airmail.'

She improvised a Christmas tree with a leafy marula sapling and soon she and the children were hard at work making decorations for it.

'What's going on here?' asked Seretse cheerily one afternoon, coming into the kitchen where Ian and Jackie stood on stools, their mouths bearing the evidence of much licking of spoons and bowls. The smell of spices wafted through the house.

'We're making the Christmas cake,' Ian shouted. 'I stirred it.'

'So did I,' said Jackie quickly, beaming when her father lovingly mussed her tight mop of curls. They persuaded him to give the pudding a stir. Anxious as she was to embrace her husband's culture, Ruth also wanted her children to know something of the traditions with which she had grown up, and still treasured.

On Christmas morning, the children woke when it was still dark to open their stockings. Awakened by the shouts of excitement, Seretse grunted and rolled over.

'Who invented Christmas?' he groaned. Before Ruth could reply, they were hit by a small whirlwind as the two children leapt onto their bed, both talking at once, brandishing their stockings and exclaiming over the contents.

'That'll teach you to loll in bed on Christmas morning,' Ruth teased, as he warded off blows from Ian, who had received a pair of toy boxing gloves.

'Daddy, daddy, my doll wants you to brush her hair,' squealed Jackie, bouncing up and down on his chest. Leaving Seretse to cope with the children, Ruth wrapped a bright sarong over her nightgown and went out on to the verandah to sip her early morning tea in peace.

Gazing out at the brightening day – so unlike her childhood Christmases – she felt a stab of homesickness for her family and the crisp, cold winter's weather. The heat was so oppressive. But she quickly suppressed the pang and hurried inside to dress the children for church.

As they walked to their seats in the front of the huge, dim, building the choir started singing 'Oh come all ye faithful', which had been translated into Setswana by one of the early LMS missionaries. Ruth swallowed as a lump came to her throat. Sensing her feelings, Seretse took her hand and squeezed it hard.

Sitting through the service, with his wife and children beside him, Seretse was overwhelmed by memories of his grandfather. Closing his eyes, he could almost see the noble figure of King Khama sitting in his throne-like chair.

'I wonder what you think of us all now, grandfather,' he asked inwardly, and almost started as he experienced a distinct sensation of approval. Smiling faintly, he gave himself up to his reverie while the preacher droned on. 'I am well pleased, my boy. Black and white are all the same – except for the skin. We are all the children of God. You've done well,' he imagined his grandfather saying to him, the old eyes bright with affection. Opening his own eyes, he caught Ruth looking at him. Had he nodded off? But she just winked at him, and he was reassured.

Seretse was determined that his family should live as comfortably as possible in Serowe. He had plans drawn up for a spacious bungalow with several bedrooms, two bathrooms and a lovely broad verandah to be built on the ridge above Serowe – where they would catch every passing breeze and be far enough away from the village not to be disturbed by the noise and the smells, yet close enough to be part of the community. Ruth was thrilled. She had battled uncomplainingly with the dust and the flies and the noise and the stuffiness of Seretse's father's old house in which they lived in the centre of the village.

During the following months, Ruth became even more involved with the women of Serowe, who genuinely loved her and increasingly looked to her for upliftment from their abject poverty and lack of schooling. She started giving first-aid classes for the local Red Cross and introduced a child welfare scheme where mothers, along with their babies, could come for lessons in nutrition and hygiene.

Both she and Seretse spent every spare minute up at the building site. With everything having to be imported from South Africa through the local traders, and the unreliability of volunteer labour, the construction was full of frustrations. But slowly and surely the project progressed. Seretse chivvied the builders mercilessly and by mid-September the house was habitable, although construction work would continue for another year, during which time the constant presence of builders, dust and noise nearly drove Ruth mad. But she had a happy time choosing the furnishings for their new home. Because of the great heat she chose soft, light fabrics in pale cream and shades of beige, tan and rust. She decided to leave the wooden floors bare, with just a few colourful rugs here and there, and of course their karosses and animal skins which had been such precious reminders of home during their exile.

The move gave the Bamangwato an opportunity to demonstrate the community spirit which is the essence of African culture. By first light a huge group of willing helpers had assembled. At first Ruth was dismayed, but Seretse assured her big tasks like this were always a community affair. She stood helplessly by and stared in amazement as he directed the helpers. Before long, Tshekedi arrived with one of his Bedford trucks, which was rapidly loaded and sent trundling along the new road to the house on the ridge.

A stream of women carrying an assortment of household goods set off on foot in its dusty wake. 'But how am I going to find anything the other end?' Ruth moaned.

While Seretse stayed behind to oversee the next load for the truck, Ruth bundled the children into the car and went up to the house. Again she was greeted by hundreds of willing hands which swiftly emptied the car and took the children off to play. She was amazed to see a cooking fire already burning in the back garden with huge cast-iron pots of maize porridge and stew bubbling away.

The Bedford had already been unloaded, its contents neatly arrayed on the verandah, and was setting off on its second trip. A line of men stood beside the items on the veranda and indicated smilingly to Ruth that she should direct them where to place them. Aware that she was experiencing a vital new dimension of her husband's culture, Ruth bowed her head in acknowledgement of their willing service and began to direct them. When the sun reached its zenith, Seretse called a halt and the people gathered in two distinct groups – male and female – under the shade of a large tree beside the cooking fire, washing their hands in a communal bowl preparatory to eating.

Seretse took Ruth's hand. 'Come on, darling, we must join them.'

'But I've made sandwiches and a flask of tea. Can't we just eat inside by ourselves? It's so hot out there.'

'I think they would be offended,' said Seretse, with the gentleness that always characterised his dealings with her difficulties in accepting certain aspects of his culture, particularly those relating to hygiene.

At this point she glimpsed Ian and Jackie squatting in the dust with their new-found playmates, delightedly gobbling porridge and stew with their fingers from a communal tin plate on the ground. 'Oh, no!' she gasped, and surged forward, but Seretse restrained her, holding her hand tightly.

'Ruth,' he said firmly. 'Let them be. They will come to no harm.' He led her outside and immediately two chairs were produced and set in the shadiest spot. A young woman knelt before them with an earthen bowl of water while others produced individual plates of food, beaming at the honour of serving the Chief and his wife in their midst.

In November 1957, they held a housewarming party. Seretse had been tempted to dispense with the old, though still strictly enforced, tribal ruling that forbade blacks to drink alcohol and required whites to secure a liquor permit. But he was reluctant to rock the boat too hard at this early stage, so Ruth had obtained the permit. She spent hours in the kitchen teaching her staff how to make an attractive variety of canapés. The guests, most of them the more junior colonial officers and white traders with whom Seretse was in daily contact through his efforts to improve the management and marketing of livestock, were most impressed with their new home which was, by Serowe standards, palatial. They had also invited Seretse's colleagues on the council, a number of cousins and, of course, Tshekedi and Ella.

'Now remember, no blacks are allowed to drink alcohol,' Seretse said loudly as he welcomed his guests. 'The bar is self-service – but I am not going to be held responsible if anyone leaves here on unsteady legs!' Everyone laughed, and proceeded to enjoy themselves. Ruth was a born hostess, moving among all her guests with charm and ease. Glancing across the room as her laughter captivated group after group, Seretse caught her eye and smiled. She constantly amazed him with her indomitable spirit and her willingness to adapt to new situations. Despite the difficult road that his love for her had caused them to travel, he shuddered at the thought of what his life would have been without her. Glancing out of the window he saw his brown children playing happily with the black and white children of the visitors, all oblivious to the significance of their different skin colours. If only adults could behave like that, he thought. Well, at least he could ensure that in Bechuanaland they did.

Before they knew it, Christmastime had come round again. The house was bedecked with hundreds of cards. But this time, Ruth had been better prepared. The house had taken a giant bite out of their savings and money was tight. In addition, the South Africans had imposed punitive tariffs on the importation of Bechuanaland beef, rendering Seretse's massive herds unsaleable. Sometimes Ruth thought she would scream with frustration when she accompanied Seretse on his trips to the cattle posts, where the magnificent beasts grazed in their hundreds, glossy and healthy, but worthless unless markets could be found.

1957 had been a difficult year. The first major hurdle they had faced was finding a school for Jackie. Eventually, Gwen Blackbeard, who ran a small primary school for white children in Serowe, had agreed to take her. Neither Ruth nor Seretse was happy with her being in an all-white environment during her formative years, but they had no option – other than sending her far away to boarding school in Southern Rhodesia, which they were both extremely loath to do. She was a bright little thing and had adapted well to her new life. Despite her continued aversion to the invasion of their personal lives by the press, Ruth had permitted their old friend, John Redfern, to interview Jackie on her 7th birthday. She smiled as she recalled the little girl's comments: 'I like London better. I do miss the telly. But, well, it is fun here.'

Ruth and Seretse were anxious the children should, from an early age, be aware that their colour was not an issue. Ruth, in particular, was determined they should be equipped to deal with the racism they would undoubtedly encounter growing up in southern Africa. Already Jackie had asked her why she and Ian were a different colour from both Ruth and Seretse as well as from the other children in the village. At that time there were very few people of mixed race in the Protectorate – only some light-skinned Bamangwato. She and Seretse had discussed the matter on numerous occasions and had decided the best way to handle it would be to build the children's confidence by telling them repeatedly they were very special, golden children, no matter what anybody else might say, and mummy and daddy loved them very much. God made people of all different colours, Ruth would tell them often, showing them picture books of children from different parts of the world. God did not prefer the black or the white or even the golden children. He loved them all just the same. Both Jackie and Ian appeared quite content with this explanation and Ruth prayed it would stand them in good stead for the rest of their lives.

The couple had decided to have a break from the oppressive social ostracism to which they were subjected in Serowe and sample the nightlife of Francistown. It was common parlance that this railway town boasted two hotels – the Grand Hotel, which was not grand, and the Tati Hotel, which was tatty. As they walked through the swing doors of the latter one evening, the hubbub of the saloon bar hushed. The unspoken law was that it was reserved for whites, and, in accordance with South African custom, white males only.

'It was lucky old Millard happened to be there that night, or I don't know what would have happened,' said Seretse, chuckling. He and Ruth had been spirited into a corner by the friendly senior district officer, John Millard. They were the subject of a few pointed stares, but after a while the boys at the bar turned back to their beers and propping up the bar. Seretse did not push his luck by ordering an alcoholic drink, but he surreptitiously swapped Ruth's gin for his lemonade.

'I couldn't believe it when Millard told me a few days later that white South Africans do not take nice girls into public bars,' he told Ruth now. 'Sorry, love. That must have really convinced them that you are a wicked woman.'

'I'm just grateful Jessie Rutherford never heard about it,' said Ruth. 'I would never have lived it down!'

'I'm going to have to do something about this racial discrimination though,' said Seretse thoughtfully. 'There's nothing on the statute books, but in practice it's almost as bad in Bechuanaland as it is in South Africa. And yet, it's strange, I haven't come across a single government official in the Territory who has personally advocated racial discrimination – yet they do nothing practical to ensure that it's eradicated. The hoity-toity British officials and their wives continue to look down their noses at everybody else, and the Afrikaners persist in their mistaken belief that God has created them to keep the natives in their place.'

Ruth nodded in agreement. 'They seem to be particularly paranoid about women,' she commented. 'Do you remember those outrageous rumours that went around about Bamangwato men all looking for white wives?'

Seretse laughed. 'Yes, that was after the cricketer's wife asked you to find her a decent African husband, wasn't it?'

'Yes – on the verandah of the Tati Hotel of all places!'

'You've got to laugh sometimes. But you, my darling, have been wonderful this year. I can't believe how hard you've worked with the women. I hear glowing reports all the time about how well the adult education classes are doing.'

'It's been tough going,' Ruth admitted. 'But I do believe it's starting to make a difference – and that's so encouraging. I think the Girl Guides is taking off, too. We have had so many new members in the past few months I can hardly believe it.'

'And the concerts?'

'Yes, they've raised more than £500 towards the community centre. And the vegetable garden project is flourishing, despite these wretched sandy soils and lack of water.'

'You're a real *mohumaghadi*,' he told her. Her face fell. 'Hey, what's the matter?'

'Well, I feel I've failed in one regard, no matter how hard I've worked.'

'What are you talking about?'

'Setswana,' she said. 'The children are chattering away fluently – I can't even understand what they say. I just can't seem to get my tongue around it. It's so, so . . . foreign!'

'Oh, my Ruth,' Seretse said, squeezing her shoulders. 'It doesn't matter. Really it doesn't.'

But she knew that it did matter, very much. She determined to master it.

Ruth, far more than Seretse, had been wounded by the hurtful comments that had found their way back to them from various sources within the community. People were saying Seretse was not a proper Mongwato because he failed to control his wife – she had far too much freedom, she wore trousers and she couldn't even speak the language. Vicious gossip from the white tea parties warned it would surely be just a matter of time before Seretse 'turned native' once again and warmed his bed with a concubine or two. In addition, there had been unpleasant criticism among the blacks of her fund-raising activities at the weekend soccer games where she ran refreshment stalls. This had been particularly hurtful because she had put hours and hours of work into this project, often sacrificing her whole weekend to organise supplies, supervise staff rosters and even serve behind the counters herself.

Seretse loved his soccer. He always had. And when he started to organise regular soccer matches in the village it had seemed an ideal opportunity to support him, to be with him at weekends and to raise money for the building of a much-needed Serowe community centre. Instead of appreciating her dedication, the Bamangwato had derided her efforts and criticised Seretse for allowing her to demean herself in this way. He had merely shrugged the comments off, declaring them to be petty and beneath contempt, and gone on to demonstrate his enthusiasm for sports by adding athletics, boxing and tennis tournaments to his weekend programmes.

To support Ruth's fund-raising efforts, he organised for a hedge to be planted around the soccer pitch and charged people a small fee to watch the big matches – which made them complain all the more! Whenever the opprobrium became too much for Ruth, she would closet herself in her bedroom and take out the shoeboxes full of cards and letters that she constantly received from around the world. This was her fan mail, and rereading the positive and encouraging comments from men and women she had never met, but who approved of her courage in sticking by Seretse, never failed to lift her spirits.

But all these problems paled into insignificance compared to the shock that had hit them in July 1957. Seretse was admitted to hospital in Serowe for several weeks with a kidney complaint. It had sapped his energy and good cheer, and Ruth was desperately worried about him.

He railed against his illness, shouting to Ruth: 'Why now? When I've so much do? Why has my body let me down like this?'

She tried her best to calm him, but he was an impossible patient and sometimes, as she drove home after visiting time, she despaired of being able to cope if it went on much longer.

However, after a long convalescence, he seemed to recover completely – although she found herself watching him constantly for signs of a relapse – and went on to become a key figure in the new Tribal Council. This was the administration's response to pressure from Seretse, Tshekedi and Rasebolai for a new deal for the Tribe.

In its infancy, it was hardly more than an advisory body – but it was a start and Seretse was well pleased. In effect, it brought to an end the ancient system of tribal rule by a hereditary Chief with absolute power, which both Seretse and his uncle had planned during their discussions in Britain in 1956. Democracy had been subtly introduced. The *kgotla* was held in the normal way and every man had his say. But then those present were encouraged to vote by show of hands for the election of 25 men to sit on the local council.

The challenge facing them now was to extend this principle throughout all the tribes of the Bechuanaland Protectorate – and ultimately to put an end to tribalism altogether, forming one nation.

Christmas passed quietly. Ruth's parents had been planning to come out and spend it with them in Serowe, but her father had fallen ill and had died in early December. Ruth tried to put on a cheerful front for the children's sake, and they decorated the tree and made the Christmas cake and pudding as they had the previous year. She was comforted only by the memories of happy times she and her father had shared after their reconciliation, and the fact that he had at last come to accept Seretse as a son-in-law.

1958 began with their discovery that Ruth was pregnant with twins. Before King Khama's time, the birth of twins had been regarded as an evil omen, and one had always been killed immediately. But now the new life in Ruth's womb appeared to be a positive sign.

The dawn had come at last in Bamangwato politics, and with it new hope and vigour. The ant-ravaged stockade in the *kgotla* ground was replaced and the old camelthorn tree, charred and twisted by a lightning strike years ago, was removed. The people offered voluntary labour to clean up Serowe and fill in the gullies caused by erosion. Britain at last seemed to be accepting responsibility for the Territories and Joint Advisory Councils were established, which, in time, would lead to the formation of a Legislative Council – the first step on the long road to self-government. Although progress would be slow, painfully so at times, the journey had begun and the Bamangwato knew it. There was a palpable air of confidence and self-esteem among the Tribe once again. Something precious that had ebbed away under British rule since the reign of King Khama was coming back – dignity.

There was a changing of the guard among the British administrators which, more than anything, changed things for the better for Ruth and Seretse – and indeed for the whole of southern Africa. Seretse's nemesis, Percivale Liesching, had ended his tour of duty in South Africa and been replaced by the liberal Sir John Maud as High Commissioner. The new Resident Commissioner was Peter Fawcus, who had been a junior official at Serowe a decade earlier, and had protested at Seretse's banishment.

The Rutherfords had been replaced by David Robinson, whom Seretse called Robbie. He was a fellow Oxonian, and the two men, both intelligent and alert to the sensibilities of others, struck up a special friendship. This fortuitous placing of the pawns by the grand chess master in the CRO in London marked a turning point for Bechuanaland.

It started in Serowe – where the atmosphere became even more relaxed and more detached from the growing tensions of the subcontinent. Robinson was amazed at Seretse's evident lack of bitterness at his treatment by the British, and encouraged the rest of the white community to give him due credit for this. He was to come to rely increasingly upon Seretse's pragmatic solutions to the numerous problems that surfaced along the tortuous path to self-rule, particularly his middle-road position in the ongoing battle between traditionalists and modernists.

Interestingly, at a time when international debate was raging about whether or not to engage South African sporting teams at home or abroad, sport played a significant role in breaking down the barriers in Bechuanaland. Seretse's beloved soccer was the ice-breaker. He had ironically christened his team 'The Miscellaneous' – a subtle dig at the notorious 'Miscellaneous Offences Act' under which blacks in South Africa and Rhodesia who showed any tendency towards nationalist leanings were being locked up for the most trivial misdemeanours.

With Robbie's help, there were regular fixtures between this motley group and a team of black and white government officers. These events, much enjoyed by an enthusiastic crowd of all races, were unthinkable in South Africa, where the government had outlawed all mixed-race sporting teams and events.

In June 1958, with Ian and Jackie bouncing excitedly on the back seat of the car, Seretse drove through Serowe to the hospital to collect Ruth and the new babies.

'How does it feel to have your progeny doubled overnight?' Moikangoa greeted Seretse, who laughed and slapped him exuberantly on the shoulder.

'Wonderful! Just wonderful! Thanks for taking such good care of them, Don,' he replied.

At that moment, 34-year-old Ruth appeared on the hospital porch, with two nurses carrying the twin boys, and he leapt forward to embrace her.

'I hope you're still so happy at 2 am tomorrow morning,' she teased.

Ian and Jackie were fascinated at the sight of these minute replicas, both with a mop of black curls just like their own. Ruth and Seretse had spent happy hours discussing names for the twins. They had finally decided on Anthony, for Tony Benn who had been, and remained, such a staunch ally and friend, and Tshekedi, to cement the reconciliation between Seretse and his uncle.

'I can't wait for Mother to arrive,' Ruth said that evening as she flopped into her favourite armchair on the verandah. 'It's hectic, having two babies at once.'

'Neither can I,' agreed Seretse. 'I've hardly seen you all day.' Settling himself beside her he reached for her hand. 'Thank you, darling,' he said tenderly, 'for giving me all these beautiful children!'

'Say that again,' she challenged him, as a wail from the nursery indicated that her brief respite was over already.

'I'll get it,' said Seretse, leaping to his feet.

Dorothy arrived a few weeks later, in time for the twins' christening – a jubilant affair attended by the whole community.

'Oh, Mother,' said Ruth, hugging her tightly, 'I've never been so pleased to see you in all my life.'

Dorothy was shocked at how wan and drawn her daughter looked. 'Off to rest with you, right now,' she ordered.

'I can't, I've still got to ice the Christmas cake. And I've got to make sure there's enough food for all the visitors. It seems as if Seretse has invited the whole village.'

'I'll take care of all that,' said Dorothy firmly and bundled her off to the bedroom. Peeping in later, she saw Ruth fast asleep and smiled contentedly. Later that evening she gave Seretse the job of putting the children to bed and took Ruth a tray of soup and toast.

Tip-toeing past an hour later, Seretse glimpsed his wife and mother-in-law deep in conversation. Ruth was pouring her heart out to her mother. Good, he thought. That's just what she needs.

'Mother,' she was saying, 'it was awful. Soon after we moved in, these carloads of South Africans arrived. They were so rude. I couldn't believe it! They just drove right up to the door and stared at us as if we were animals in the zoo.'

Dorothy clucked sympathetically and stroked her daughter's hair back from her troubled brow. 'It's all right, my darling. That's all over now. If any of them come now they will have me to deal with.'

Ruth laughed weakly at her mother's fierce expression. 'And then Seretse was so ill,' she continued, 'it was terrible. He was angry and depressed, not like himself at all.'

'Well, he's fine now,' said Dorothy practically, 'and you just need a good rest.'

Ruth lay back on her pillows with a sigh. Her eyes closed and Dorothy tucked the bedclothes around her as if she were a child again. 'Good night, darling,' she said, and tip-toed out with the tray.

Dorothy stayed for several months and, in true grandmotherly fashion, took much of the burden of childcare off Ruth and Seretse. Ruth quickly regained her former vitality and she and Seretse resumed their active engagement in all aspects of village life.

The Bamangwato were abuzz with hope and excitement. Sizeable deposits of copper had been found in the Territory and the administration had managed to sidestep the regional mining giant based in South Africa, Anglo-American. Long and tortuous negotiations initiated by Tshekedi and his international network of influential contacts had been under way for some time now. These culminated in a deal with the Roan Selection Trust, which seemed committed to negotiating a Bamangwato concession that would really benefit the people. Seretse was particularly pleased that he and Tshekedi had managed to avoid doing business with the South Africans. They were determined that any mineral development would create local employment and lessen dependence on their unfriendly neighbour. Funds from the project were also desperately needed to develop the cattle industry, provide a modern abattoir, more boreholes and some decent roads to truck the stock to the railheads.

From this joyous highpoint, however, life began to get difficult again. Seretse's financial position was extremely precarious and he became embroiled in a controversy with his agent over corruption and mismanagement. The South African embargo on Bechuanaland beef continued and he battled to find alternative markets for his cattle. Improvements and finishing touches to the house continued to drain his resources and he became extremely depressed.

18
Black Knight

'SERETSE, YOU KNOW YOU SHOULDN'T EAT BEEF – AND NEITHER SHOULD you be drinking alcohol.' Ruth was very angry. 'If you can't stand the peer pressure from Lenyeletse and others I'll simply have to stop them coming to the house. You can't go on like this. What about me and the children?'

'I'm sorry,' Seretse muttered, 'but it's so frustrating.'

'I do understand, of course I understand,' she said, sitting on the edge of the hospital bed and taking his hand in hers, 'but you have to listen to the doctor, for my sake. With mother back in England, it's so hard for me to keep running back and forth to the hospital. The whole family is suffering. We know now that red meat and alcohol seem to trigger these attacks. So you've simply got to stay away from them.'

Clutching his hand she tried to infuse her own strength of will into him.

Seretse closed his eyes against the intensity of her expression. She did try to understand, but he knew she couldn't. How could she? Raised on that mush the British called beef, how could she possibly comprehend his passion for the good red beef of his country? And as for the periodic darknesses that descended to imprison his soul and cloud his vision, he had never dared tell her about those. Sometimes it seemed her bright presence was all that kept him going.

He had suffered a serious relapse, and Ruth was having to shuttle between home and the hospital, worried about leaving the babies for long stretches with household staff, despite the fact that her mother had drilled them meticulously in all aspects of childcare and hygiene. She sat silently beside him, still holding his hand, unable to think of anything to say that would cheer him up. All she could do was maintain that physical connection and pray that her touch would sustain him somehow. '*In sickness and in health . . .*' the words of the marriage ceremony came back to her. They had both been so young and healthy when they made those vows. She realised now that she had spoken the words without the slightest idea of what she was promising. So this was what it meant – this anxiety, this helplessness, this anger, as the beloved was transformed before one's very eyes from a vibrant mate to a pathetic figure beneath a hospital blanket. Eventually she stirred.

'Don't go,' he said immediately, opening his eyes and tightening his grip on her hand.

'I have to, I must fetch Jackie from school.'

'Why can't you arrange for somebody else to do that?'

'Seretse . . .' she said wearily, 'you know I can't. The children need me too.'

'Sorry . . .' He stirred restlessly in the narrow hospital bed.

Ruth hesitated, then bent and kissed his brow quickly and left. His hand lay empty on the spotless but threadbare coverlet. He could not summon the strength to clench it closed.

It was March 1959. Seretse was ill again. After a few weeks Ruth managed to persuade the doctor to let her nurse him at home. At least she would be spared the draining division of her time between home and hospital, and the children would be able to see more of their father. He spent hours of his convalescence watching the lively 10-month-old twins playing with their blocks and wooden train engines on a kaross at his feet. Dorothy was making arrangements to come out and live with them permanently in July. Muriel had settled in Zambia, working for the LMS, and there was nothing to keep her in England. Their old friend John Redfern came to visit. He spent hours chatting to Seretse and was a great help in taking his mind off himself, releasing Ruth to get on with other things.

Seretse had only been fully recovered for a couple of months when news arrived that Ella had rushed Tshekedi to hospital in Bulawayo where renal failure had been diagnosed. He was very upset and immediately began to make plans to go to his uncle. However, his trip was delayed by the signing of the Roan Selection Trust mineral deal, and Tshekedi was transferred to a hospital in London. Seretse followed him as soon as possible, taking with him a copy of the Bamangwato Concession for his uncle to sign as a witness.

Within a week he was back with Tshekedi's body to organise the biggest funeral Bechuanaland had seen since the death of King Khama half a century previously. His uncle had died a few days after his arrival in London. Seretse had been at his bedside with Ella and his two older sons.

'I can't believe it,' he said to Ruth as they sat together beneath the stars on the night he arrived home. 'One minute he was alive, full of energy and ideas. And a week later he is in his coffin. How can that be? He was never sick in his life. I never knew him take a day off. He was always bursting with vigour. Most people couldn't keep up with him.' He wiped his eyes with his handkerchief. He had been weeping unashamedly for the best part of an hour. Ruth tried desperately to comfort him.

'At least you have the satisfaction of knowing that you parted friends,' she said.

'Yes. Yes. I'm really grateful for that,' he agreed. 'These past few years have been wonderful. It's as if all the harsh words and hurts never happened. Do you know what he said to me at the end? He said: "There's no such thing as race, you know". To me, it was like a blessing on our marriage at last, a sort of confession that he had been wrong about opposing it. I just started weeping. Ella had to comfort me – and yet I was supposed to be a tower of strength for her!'

'I always felt deep down that he disapproved of me,' said Ruth.

'Well, now we know he didn't. And then he said: "It is finished. Let there be peace".'

'He really was a remarkable man.'

'And I'm determined to give him a stupendous send-off,' said Seretse, squaring his shoulders.

The funeral was attended by more than 20 000 people from all over the world. Tshekedi was laid to rest beside the impressive tomb of his father King Khama in the family burial ground amid the rocks high above Serowe. The graveside orations rang with praises of this extraordinary man who, despite his rough edges, had dedicated his life unselfishly to his people in true and noble Khama tradition.

Shortly after the funeral, news reached them that Harold MacMillan, the British Prime Minister, was coming to visit. In retrospect they would often look back on this moment, the significance of which they could not possibly have fathomed at the time.

The British Prime Minister's visit in 1960 ushered in the Year of Africa. He went on from Bechuanaland to deliver his famous 'Winds of Change' speech in Cape Town – assuring the world that the end of white supremacy was in sight. Robbie loved to tell the story, which had infuriated his superiors, of Seretse impudently pointing out to MacMillan that the line-up of Joint Advisory Council members resembled a draughts board – carefully alternating white and black faces. The Prime Minister had roared with laughter while Fawcus had frowned at this irreverence for what he regarded as a rather satisfactory demonstration of his scrupulous racial sensitivity. Seretse, his antennae always highly tuned for any evidence of racial bigotry, delighted in poking fun at officialdom's clumsy and superficial efforts to right the racial injustices of decades. But at the same time, he was generous in giving credit where credit was due and always applauded the efforts of those who were sincerely trying to throw off the habits and prejudices of a lifetime in order to adjust to a new reality.

1960 continued to be a momentous year. Seretse was listening to the BBC news on the radio one evening in March, when he called urgently to Ruth, who was putting the children to bed. Leaving Jackie to read a story to the two-year old twins, she rushed through to the living room. Seretse's expression was grim and she herself went numb with shock as they listened to the impersonal tones of the newsreader relating the events of that morning –

21 March 1960. Sixty-seven people, including children, had been shot by the South African police in Sharpeville, south of Johannesburg – most of them in the back.

'And they're our neighbours,' said Seretse. 'Heaven help us.'

A few weeks later, an English-speaking farmer attempted to assassinate Prime Minister Hendrik Verwoerd, but he survived. These two events did much to hasten the distancing of the British from the regime in South Africa. British prestige was further enhanced by the release of Nyasaland's Dr Hastings Banda from jail in April, and by the Bechuanaland administration's sympathetic treatment of the South African political refugees who began to flood into the Territory. One of the first of these was Oliver Tambo, an old friend of Seretse's from Fort Hare, for whom he arranged a safe house in Serowe. An effective refugee pipeline was organised, with active assistance from the British, through Bechuanaland north to Zambia and Tanzania via the Caprivi Strip.

But the Year of Africa was, sadly, a year of illness for Seretse. The demon struck again and again until, distraught by his frequent relapses, Ruth took him to Bulawayo for a series of tests and X-rays. A blockage in the duodenum was revealed. Surgery in Britain was advised.

When they received the news, Ruth thought she would faint. It was not yet a year since Tshekedi's death. What if . . . she could not allow her brain to finish the thought. Seretse put his arm round her.

'Ruth, darling,' he said insistently. 'It's all right. It's just a blockage. We'll go to London. I'll have the operation and everything will be fine.'

Oh God, she prayed silently, clinging to him. Please don't let him die. Please. I can't live without him. Please God.

Walking them back to their car after the farewell *kgotla*, at which the elder Bamangwato had once again demonstrated their mistrust of the British by demanding that Seretse should not leave with Ruth, Robbie too tried to allay Ruth's fears.

'Try not to worry,' he said, putting a friendly arm around her shoulders.

'Oh, Robbie,' she said. 'How can I not?'

'I know, I know,' he said. 'But he'll be all right, you know. Now, is there anything I can do to help?'

She hesitated and then said cautiously: 'Well, we're in an awful bind financially as you know. What do you think this is going to cost us?'

'Don't you worry about that. I've already taken the liberty of chatting to H E about it. He's been making noises at the CRO and I'm pretty sure they will foot the whole bill for you. Good gracious, it's the least they can do after all they've put you through in the past.'

'Robbie!' exclaimed Ruth, amazed at this uncharacteristic display of generosity on the part of the administration. 'How absolutely wonderful! Thank you so much.'

'Don't mention it,' he replied gruffly. 'You just take good care of our man!'

'You know I will,' she replied, climbing into the car where Seretse was waiting patiently.

'What was all that about?' he asked as they drove off.

'Wonderful news! The CRO are going to cover all your medical expenses in London.'

'Are they now? That's fantastic. Guilt money, I suppose!'

'Absolutely, but at least that's one less thing to worry about.'

Leaving the children was the next ordeal. Despite the presence of their beloved grandmother, they were very upset at their parents' departure. Ian, in particular, was distraught. He clung to Ruth, sobbing and begging: 'Please can I come with you, Mummy? I promise I'll be good, all the time.'

Ruth, her heart sore, gently prized the little fingers from her neck. 'Darling, we'll be home soon. Grandma will take good care of you, and I'll send you lots of lovely picture postcards from London. I promise.'

Seretse opened his eyes groggily. Ruth, who had been sitting at his side waiting for the effects of the anaesthetic to wear off, leaned forward anxiously.

'Hello, darling,' she said softly. 'How do you feel?'

'Awful,' he groaned, '. . . as though I've been kicked by a horse.' Ruth attempted a smile.

The hours of waiting, first while Seretse was in surgery and then as he lay motionless in the recovery room, had seemed interminable. Try as she might to take them captive, thoughts of him dying continued to intrude. He drifted off to sleep again and she found herself praying incoherently over and over again. Please God, don't take him. Please let him live. I love him so much . . .

A few hours later Seretse was much brighter, sitting up in bed as Ruth read him the evening papers. There was a tap on the door and the doctor entered.

'Well Mr Khama, how are we doing?'

'What have you done to me, doc?' responded Seretse. 'Which vital parts of my anatomy am I missing?' The doctor chuckled.

Ruth, white-faced and tense, had had enough of this male bonhomie. 'Please,' she begged, 'just tell us what you found.'

Sensitive to her distress, the doctor perched on the edge of the bed and said seriously: 'His pancreas was very inflamed, and in my experience that means just one thing – diabetes.'

'Diabetes!' exclaimed Ruth, her eyes widening in shock.

'I am afraid so,' nodded the doctor. 'We'll have to do several more tests, of course . . .'

The couple spent the rest of Seretse's life – the next two decades – fighting their enemy, diabetes. Their task was to maintain Seretse's blood sugar levels by diet as far as possible, and through intravenous injections whenever necessary. One of the medical definitions Ruth had found stated: '*Diabetes gives rise to depressions of spirit, which often lead to an overwhelming temptation to eat and drink too much. This, of course, exacerbates the diabetes.*'

In addition to being his wife, best friend, secretary, business associate, confidante and mother of his children, Ruth became Seretse's doctor, nurse and bodyguard. This last role was the most difficult, and sometimes put almost

344

unbearable pressure on their relationship. Seretse often rebelled against her strict diet regimen, while she railed at him for his lack of self-control when faced with the temptation to eat and drink to excess. But through it all, their enduring love – forged from the start in the fires of adversity – overcame these incredible odds, to triumph again and again. To this day, Batswana from all walks of life credit Ruth with having kept Seretse alive for another 20 years.

Ill health caused Seretse to miss out on a number of vital meetings during that momentous year, but under the able guidance of Robbie, progress continued. By this time Seretse had been appointed to the post of Tribal Secretary, a post equivalent to that of Secretary of State. The JAC had formally proposed the establishment of a Legislative Council with a four-man executive committee – trainee cabinet ministers, in effect – of whom Seretse would obviously be one. He also sat on the JAC's constitutional committee, tasked with coming up with an appropriate constitution for the Territory. Under the terms of this, approved in December that year, Her Majesty's Commissioner, Sir Peter Fawcus, became Governor, directly responsible to the Secretary of State for the Colonies in London.

Seretse did manage to attend a *kgotla* addressed by the new High Commissioner, Sir John Maud, in August 1960, where important issues of drought relief and colour discrimination were raised. Seretse told Maud in no uncertain terms: 'Moderate leaders of African opinion would find it difficult to convince their fellows (to remain moderate) if sources of racial friction were not removed.'

On that occasion he met the young journalist, Quett Masire, who would later become his Vice President. As he told Ruth later: 'He is a remarkable young man. I enjoyed his audacity. He'll go far, you mark my words.'

There was also progress on the livestock front. Seretse became a board member of BP Abattoirs Ltd, which led to the formation of ECCO Canners – thus providing a vital export market for beef which had formerly been restricted to on-the-hoof sales to South Africa.

In December 1960 a group of young radicals formed the country's first political party – the Bechuanaland People's Party. They tried ineffectually to boycott elections for the Legislative Council, which eventually became a reality in early 1961. Seretse ignored them, as did all but their fellow young radicals. The inaugural session of the Council took place in Lobatse on June 20th with due pomp and ceremony. A smart line of black policemen, the pennants of their lances fluttering in the breeze, marched across the carefully manicured lawns to the sounds of martial music. Uniforms were the order of the day, with the British civil servants adorned in white, high-collared uniforms and solar topees, clanking with medals, and Chiefs Bathoen and Khali gloriously attired in the uniforms, helmets and plumes presented to their forebears by Queen Victoria in 1895. Not to be outshone, Sir John Maud graced the occasion in a splendid gold encrusted black uniform with a white ostrich-feather cockade hat.

Ruth, seated in the visitors' gallery, had eyes for only one man. Her husband was simply dressed in a charcoal grey suit. As he entered the white-walled chamber and bowed to the Speaker, he smiled up at her.

He rose to take the oath of office, holding a blue Bible in his right hand: 'I, Seretse Khama, do swear I will be faithful and bear true allegiance to Her Majesty Queen Elizabeth the second, her heirs and successors in accordance with the law. So help me God.'

The speeches were eloquent: 'Respect of man for man is the foundation of all human happiness. We have it here, thank God, in Bechuanaland. It is the characteristic of the Protectorate way of life and it is our great achievement. Because of it, we in this Territory can look our older, richer more developed nations in the face with pride,' said Maud. 'Africans, Europeans and Asians in this country are going to be brought, by a joint purpose and determination, to even fuller recognition of their common humanity and mutual dependence. We share this ideal – mutual respect for one another, and a determination that no man's place in society shall be determined by the colour of his skin.'

Chief Bathoen continued this theme: 'Neither Africans nor Europeans want to dominate each other, nor do they want to be dominated. We want to live and let live and work together in this country, which we all regard as our home.'

As Seretse said later: 'It is a meaningful step on the road to democracy. I think we've made a very sound start. It may seem too slow to some people but it's been very natural and we've carried the people with us. There has been no great fuss and bother. As we gain experience, we will move forward. I must say I'm quite satisfied with this pace. Rushing ahead would be disastrous. Look at the mess all around us!'

His approach to politics was so eminently pragmatic. It might make him unpopular in certain quarters, but he was convinced it was the only way. He believed it was ridiculous to talk about Africa for the Africans if they had no training or experience and were not ready to run the show.

'If they ask you to stand for Prime Minister, will you agree?' asked Ruth.

'I don't know,' he mused, considering her question carefully. 'When the time comes I want the best-trained, most qualified man to have the job, and I don't care what his colour is. Heaven knows we have precious little talent, and we must make full use of it. But before we can even think about that, we've got to concentrate on breaking down tribalism. That's my main aim for the immediate future. Just look at the harm it's done in the Congo and Kenya. It must be eradicated here. But, as with everything else, it's going to be a long, slow process and there's no rushing it. But what do you think? Do you think I should become Prime Minister?'

'Well . . .' she said slowly. 'I suppose it's what you were born to do.'

Seretse had become increasingly involved in politics since the beginning of the year and more and more of the administrative work running their three large cattle ranches had fallen to her, in addition to all her welfare and charity work and, of course, the children. But she knew that he was the best man for the job.

'Yes,' she said, after a pause. 'I think you should. There's no-one else who

could do it more effectively.' She was committing herself to sharing him forever with the entire nation.

He smiled and gripped her hand. 'We'll see,' he said. 'It's a long way off.'

By the end of 1961 things had progressed to such a point that Seretse felt
the time was right to consider the idea of forming a national democratic
party. This move had been prompted by the activities of the BPP, whose
empty and hot-headed rhetoric Seretse firmly believed could never secure
stability, independence and prosperity for the new nation. He and Masire
drafted a constitution for the new party, while Ruth willingly acted as secretary. The Botswana Democratic Party (BDP) was launched, in February
1962, in the south of the Territory near Gaborone, outside the Bamangwato
Reserve, so there could be no accusations of tribalism levelled against it.
Seretse was President, with Masire as Secretary and a white trader, Benjamin
Steinberg, as Treasurer. The party operated on a shoestring and, thanks to
the disruptive activities of the BPP, had difficulties accessing funds that were
available to emerging African nationalist political parties.

Phillip Matante, leader of the BPP, attacked Seretse constantly: 'The BPP
is leading Bechuanaland out of darkness and into freedom. I have no evidence that Seretse Khama will do anything to further this aim. Much to the
contrary. He is a European, eating with them, schooling his children with
them. He is selling the BP to Rhodesia. They are trying to federate the BP
with Rhodesia.'

Seretse devoted much of his energies towards the establishment of the beef
processing and export industry and fought hard for profits to go to small-
scale cattle producers. As the majority of his people were cattle owners, he
regarded livestock exports as the only feasible, and most democratic, basis
for economic development. The country was one of the poorest in Africa,
possibly in the world, with an annual per capita income of just $50.

With constant vigilance, he and Ruth were managing to keep his diabetes under control, and he suffered no serious attacks of ill health. By sheer

strength of will, Ruth managed to take the onerous task of monitoring his daily intake of food and drink in her stride, while he diligently battled the constant temptations to indulge his love of fatty, red beef and tall, thirst-slaking beers. But they were both under considerable strain and working hard.

Early in December, Rhodesia Railways announced the desegregation of its dining car on the train between Bulawayo and the border with South Africa.

Seretse decreed a holiday. 'Put on your glad rags,' he told Ruth gaily. 'We're going for a ride.'

'Where to?'

'It's a surprise – just be ready in half an hour.'

They motored into Palapye and parked at the railway station.

'What's going on?' she wanted to know.

'I'm taking you out to lunch,' he said, grinning.

'In Palapye? Well, that's just great.'

There was a loud toot and the train puffed majestically into the station. Seretse bowed elaborately and handed her on to the train. Holding her elbow, he steered her through the corridors to the dining car, where a steward seated them at a table for two, laid with fresh flowers, silver cutlery, crystal glassware and monogrammed crockery.

Without asking for their order, he disappeared, only to be back within moments bearing an ice bucket and a bottle of champagne. Handing her a fizzing glass, Seretse raised his own.

'To you, my darling. The most amazing woman in the world.'

Ruth leaned back in her seat and laughed. 'This is crazy,' she said. 'You're crazy! Why are we doing this?'

'Don't you think it appropriate that we, the region's most prominent, perhaps the region's only, mixed-race couple, should celebrate the desegregation of this remarkable moving restaurant?'

As the champagne bubbles tickled her nose, the cares and concerns of the children, the ranches, the accounts, the sick babies in Serowe, all fell away.

'Yes,' she told him. 'When you put it like that. Yes, I do think it is most appropriate.'

They enjoyed a leisurely four-course luncheon before leaving the train in Lobatse late that afternoon, whence Seretse had arranged for them to be driven back to Palapye.

From then on, the pace of change began to speed up considerably, and their lives became hectic. The Federal government, dominated by the white minority, had banned several African parties and jailed many of their leaders, including Kaunda and Banda for a short period. The British tried vainly to keep the Federation intact, but the elections of 1962 were boycotted by all African parties plus the Dominion Party, resulting in an overwhelming, though hollow, victory for Roy Welensky and his United Federal Party.

Britain finally realised that the Federation was causing more problems than it was solving, and in December agreed to grant Nyasaland internal self-government from 1 February 1963. On 3 July the decision was reached to dissolve the Federation officially as of 31 December 1963.

In January 1963, recognising the inevitability of independence, South Africa announced that from July 31st the existing roadblocks at the borders of the three Protectorates would become official border posts, requiring passports for all other travellers and passbooks for Africans. A month later Rhodesia followed suit. In April Seretse was given the portfolio of constitutional and racial affairs in the Executive Council. The BDP started opening local branches all over the country, taking the party to a wider public than the middle class which had been its initial constituency. In July, leaders of the three political parties (the BPP had now split into two) were invited to attend constitutional talks in Lobatse. One-man, one-vote was agreed. Bechuanaland was well on the way to nationhood and, in recognition of this fact, Rasebolai retired at the end of the year as titular head of the Bamangwato.

Through all these momentous developments, Ruth and Seretse worked as a team. Seretse's lieutenants all had a high regard for her opinions, for she was well-read, practical and efficient. In addition, she was a tireless and cheerful worker – organizing the sewing of election campaign rosettes, helping to raise funds and entertain members of the party executive.

Ironically, now when the peoples of Bechuanaland had been persuaded to forego their tribal divisions and move forward to democratic party politics, the British chose to declare that 'in deference to the wishes of a Tribe that had come to set aside African racialism and to take to their hearts the foreign white woman Ruth and her half-African children as full members of their community', young Ian Khama had been given the right by decree to rule the Bamangwato when he came of age at 21.

'I don't believe it,' exclaimed Ruth. 'After all this time!'

'You know our motto. Don't look back! At least they're making an effort to undo the harm they've done. Let's give them credit for that,' said Seretse.

'I suppose so. But will the Bamangwato even want a Chief when he is 21? And what will they need a Chief for then anyway?'

'The traditional ways are going to take a very long time to die out. I'm sure they will still want a Chief then. And if Ian wants to, he can be their Chief. The spirit of Khama lives on. There has been a Khama on the throne for nearly 200 years, after all.'

Ruth looked across the verandah to where her lithe young son, with the deep wide-set eyes so like Seretse's, was engaged in an energetic game of table tennis with his sister. He was a cheerful and affectionate child, a source of great delight in her life. 'Let's not tell him now,' she said. 'He's too young to be thinking of things like that.' Seretse agreed, and no more was said about it.

Muriel had been urging them for some time to pay a visit to Zambia, where she particularly wanted them to meet Kenneth Kaunda, the new Prime Minister of Northern Rhodesia. In May, Ruth put her foot down. They both needed a break and she felt it was important that Seretse should establish contact with a neighbouring black leader.

They went. The two men liked each other immediately. They were both vehemently against racism of any form, and both had a great sense of humour. Their friendship was to stand firm throughout their lifetime.

The following month, a new constitution designed to lead to Independence was announced. The Johannesburg *Star* of 4 June summed it up: '*Bechuanaland's new constitution is a model of racial cooperation. While we and the world critically watch the often turbulent transition to self-rule of other states in Africa, Bechuanaland has been quietly busy very swiftly preparing for the same step right next door. It is an object lesson to those who dogmatically assert that moderation and stable political progress are unattainable by a backward, impoverished African nation.*' Elections would be held within months.

Seretse's pleasure at this latest development was short-lived, however, as he heard the same day of the death of his beloved Robbie in a car crash while on holiday in Britain.

'He was indispensable,' he grieved to Ruth. 'A friend in a million. And he was the perfect person to head up the new civil service. What on earth shall I do without him?' They buried their grief in hard work, setting themselves a punishing schedule to tour the country and campaign for the coming elections.

The press was most anxious to learn of the BDP's attitude towards South Africa, and Seretse forcefully enunciated his party's policies: The country would be a safe haven for refugees in the region, but would not be used as a springboard for attacks on neighbouring countries; the economic situation dictated a policy of neutrality towards white-controlled South Africa and, consequently, Bechuanaland could not implement sanctions against that country.

Seretse was also most insistent on the use of the term 'nonracialism', distinguishing it from the inequitable, quota-based power-sharing systems of 'multiracialism'. He totally rejected any form of racism as a political policy. Evidence of his capacity for solid statesmanship was soon apparent to all.

A few months later, Seretse and Ruth decided to spread their wings a little in order to give Seretse an opportunity to further hone his statesman skills at international level. Their first port of call was Salisbury were they visited Jackie, now an attractive teenager who attended an exclusive multiracial boarding school for girls in the leafy suburb of Arundel. From there they flew to New York to visit the United Nations headquarters, where Seretse introduced himself and the BDP's policies to Secretary-General, U Thant.

Ruth's heart swelled with pride as she watched him address the UN special committee on colonialism with debonair confidence, despite the fact that his country was amongst the poorest in the world with a population of barely half a million. His country might be tiny and insignificant in the scheme of things, but he himself was outstanding. He took his place on the world stage with dignity. His most important message to the UN was that they should disregard the baseless propaganda being fed to them by the hot-headed Matante. Vital contacts were made with the Ford and Rockefeller Foundations in New York.

They also visited Washington, where Seretse, on behalf of the Bechuanaland government, signed documents for a loan of six million dollars from the World Bank's International Development Agency. The funds were to be utilised for construction of a road between Francistown and Maun – vital for the trucking of cattle.

On their way home they passed through London, Nairobi and Dar-es-Salaam, renewing contacts with old friends such as Tony Benn and Charles Njonjo. Seretse also had brief meetings with Kenya's Jomo Kenyatta and Tanzania's Julius Nyerere, which were to develop later into firm friendships.

The next few months were spent in campaigning, interspersed with a number of regional trips. Seretse was rapidly becoming a figure to be reckoned with in southern African politics and they were invited to visit Basutoland, for the inaugural ceremony of Roma University, and to Zambia and Kenya to attend the Independence celebrations in October and December respectively. Meanwhile, the colonial secretariat made cumbersome but steady progress towards elections.

Ruth was convinced Seretse would become Prime Minister, while he refused to look further than the next step. He diligently fostered a close relationship with the British administrators and boldly spoke of his conviction of the need to preserve a nonpoliticised, nonracial civil service. He somehow distanced himself from the details and reserved his energies for strategic decision-making. His national stature grew by the day as the Khama charisma worked its old magic on people from every tribe.

The move of the Territory's administrative capital from Mafeking to Gaborone, just inside the Bechuanaland border, was a significant development. This anomaly had existed for more than 60 years with the British constantly vacillating, deterred primarily by the enormous costs involved. Even as late as 1961 Fawcus had been battling with his superiors for approval for the move. Permission had grudgingly been given for construction work on the new capital to begin in October 1963. In early 1965, 150 families of pioneering British civil servants uprooted themselves, their domestic workers, their pets and belongings to undertake the 100-mile trek through the barren veld to the struggling settlement where the noise, dust and confusion of construction work would make their lives miserable for the next five years. The end result, however, was a well-planned city with a modest, but attractive, legislative building, well-laid out government buildings, a power station, a luxury hotel and a modern hospital.

Election day was set for 1 March 1965 and Ruth and Seretse made one last swing around the country by private plane, train and car. People by now were accustomed to seeing them together everywhere – a formidable team, united by their devotion to each other and their commitment to the Khama legacy which the passage of time could do nothing to dispel.

'You really are a campaign trail veteran now,' said Seretse, as she slumped exhaustedly against him after yet another gruelling trip. 'I am so thankful for your support. Don't know what I'd have done without you.'

'I wouldn't have missed it for anything,' she said.

Seretse chuckled. 'And you did enjoy Operation Snowflake, didn't you?'

'That was inspired!'

This exercise had involved the dropping from the air of tens of thousands of leaflets on bushman settlements all over the Kalahari, telling the people not to be afraid to vote.

Seretse polled a crushing 5 904 votes in his own constituency, while his opponents had totalled less than 100 votes between them. The BDP had won 28 seats and the BPP only three. Contrary to all expectations, the shy and elusive bushmen had turned out in their thousands to vote, electing the only white candidate, cattleman and trader Ben Steinberg.

'Looks as though Operation Snowflake really worked,' said Ruth to Seretse when it was all over. They had just returned home from a victory celebration at the Serowe community centre. Seretse was elated by his party's victory.

'I knew we would win, but I didn't expect quite such a landslide,' he said. 'The thing that thrills me most is the way people responded to being given the vote. Thousands must have travelled as much as 150 miles to get to the polling booths.'

'Incredible,' said Ruth.

'And the press is saying that never before have people travelled by such a variety of means to cast their votes. Donkeys, bicycles, horses, ox-wagons, mules, camels and dug-out canoes.' He ticked them off on his fingers.

'What a wonderful experience it's been,' Ruth said.

Finally admitting to himself what had been obvious to everyone else for more than a year, he said: 'Gaborone, here we come! You'd better start packing.'

'I already have,' Ruth replied.

At the swearing-in ceremony in Gaborone a few days later, Seretse laid the foundation stone for his country's future peaceful and harmonious success: 'This will be a country where black and white can exist and work together in peace and harmony. It will be a living example of the creed of true racial partnership, one which may help to sway the policies of the countries around us.'

It would be more than a decade before other countries in the region began to achieve their freedom from minority domination – Mozambique and Angola in 1975, Zimbabwe in 1980, Namibia in 1990. And in none of these countries did the change come without bloodshed and destruction. As for South Africa, whose Prime Minister sent a message of congratulations to Seretse and lifted the ban on his entering that country, it would be four weary, bloody decades before universal adult suffrage would be extended to all her peoples.

Guiding Ruth around the floor in a skilful foxtrot, Seretse whispered into her ear: 'You are the most beautiful woman in this room.'

'You'll have to do better than that, it's a very small room!'

They were at the celebratory ball in the Serowe centre.

'You are the most beautiful woman in this whole country.'

'A bit better. But it's quite a small country.'

'We've come a long way since Nutford House, haven't we?'

'In fact, the lounge at Nutford House was about this size,' Ruth said, re-membering. 'So maybe we haven't come very far after all!'

'Oh yes, we have,' he replied sternly, holding her closer to his starched shirtfront.

'Stop it,' she hissed. 'Everybody is looking at us!'

'But there's no Jessie Rutherford to disapprove,' said Seretse. Smiling con-tentedly, they adjusted their steps as the band moved on to a waltz, and continued to glide around the room, oblivious to everything except their joy in the dance.

'So, we have come a long way, haven't we?' he insisted.

'Yes, Prime Minister,' Ruth murmured, while he grinned serenely over the top of her head at all and sundry.

Soon the family was settled in the Prime Minister's official residence, close to the government offices complex in central Gaborone. Seretse, who never lost his sense of the ridiculous, named it 'The Woodpile', and delighted in disconcerting the most pompous visitors by telling them: '. . . and I'm the nigger in it'.

Ruth battled to establish her garden, hampered by the lack of water and the poor soils. Seretse telephoned her two or three times a day from his office a few hundred metres down the road.

The infant government was working smoothly – but nothing dies as slow a death as prejudice. One day the twins, Anthony and Tshekedi, came home from their nearby multiracial primary school and solemnly announced: 'Someone at school said our father is a kaffir.' True to their policy of treating all racial discrimination as beneath contempt, Ruth and Seretse burst out laughing. The twins joined in and the whole thing was over and forgotten by teatime.

The euphoria of victory was short-lived. A terrible drought hit – the worst in nearly half a century. The earth became like concrete. There was total crop failure. A sizeable portion of the nation's wealth – 250 000 cattle – died. Crippling famine followed. Seretse and Ruth worked night and day devising relief schemes and coordinating thousands of officials and volunteers of all races, working long hours in the scorched bush at food distribution depots. Wealthy international hunters on safari gave the carcasses of animals they shot to starving villagers.

Once again Seretse and Ruth took to the road, this time to mourn with their people. Cattle died before their eyes. They saw vultures too gorged to fly, hopping from one carcass to another. Emaciated children clung to their hungry mothers. In a desperate attempt to harness international assistance to carry their fledgling nation through this tragedy, they again travelled to Britain and the United States. The battle to feed people and save lives continued into early 1966.

Then, at last, the towering cumulus clouds built up once again over the desert. The precious *pula* returned. Torrential rains flooded the country, church bells pealed joyfully and Ruth and her people knelt in their thousands to give thanks to a merciful God. The flooded rivers almost caused Seretse to miss his plane to London for the Independence conference with Harold Wilson's Labour government. They were returning to the capital after a visit to Serowe when their headlights revealed a sheet of floodwater barring the road. The twins yelled with delight at the prospect of such an adventure. They abandoned their vehicle and waded hand-in-hand through the torrent to a ganger's trolley over the adjacent railway bridge. Once safely on the other side, Seretse arranged for the police to take them home.

In the meantime, an order-in-council in September 1965 had transferred the powers to summon and preside over Cabinet meetings from the office of the Queen's representative to that of the Prime Minister. Seretse announced this news to Ruth with great satisfaction. The journey was nearly over. The only dark cloud was the failure of the mining prospectors to discover any mineral deposits of worthwhile significance. For six years, the wiry geologists had been combing the desert wastelands in search of the precious minerals – mainly copper – which their initial investigations had encouraged them to believe were there.

'If only they could find something of value,' Ruth said one day, returning from a weary and depressing visit to Serowe, where children continued to waste away from hunger, diarrhoea and other diseases directly attributable to the poverty in which most Bamangwato still spent their lives. 'I thought they'd found kimberlite rock somewhere?'

'Yes, they did. That was what encouraged them to start negotiating the commission in the first place,' Seretse confirmed. 'But it looks as though it was a red herring.'

Ruth massaged her aching temples with her fingertips. 'If only we were sitting on a pile of diamonds. Even a few diamonds would help. Why should those beastly South Africans have them all?'

'Don't waste your time on wishful thinking,' said Seretse. 'We just have to get on and make the best of the little we have.'

'I know. But sometimes I just wish . . .' Although she didn't know it at the time, her wish was soon to be granted.

The first gemstones were discovered in the desert scrub 310 miles north-west of Gaborone only a year after independence. Botswana now produces

26 million carats of diamonds a year with reserves for at least three decades. From then onwards, the country experienced one of the fastest-growing economies in the world, with a real growth rate of 9-10% annually and a GDP of US $4.6 million. Under Seretse's watchful eye, wise and careful financial administration by the new government built up some US $6.5 billion in foreign reserves, while his personal integrity and insistence on transparent and responsible accounting earned the country an international reputation as one of the least corrupt countries in sub-Saharan Africa, rating above Japan and Italy in an international assessment of corruption.

Bechuanaland was now a self-governing colony en route to independence. But the pragmatic policies of the BDP were scorned by other African nationalists. Quett Masire, Seretse's deputy, returned from a meeting in Ghana cut to the quick by the hostility he had experienced.

'Damn Matante!' he swore. 'He told them our elections were phoney. It was terrible. They wouldn't even let me speak.' He went on to relate how their country had been denounced as a puppet and a stooge of imperialists and South African racists.

'Don't worry, Quett,' said Seretse grimly to the earnest young man before him. 'We'll show them.'

On 13 October 1966 Seretse made the national radio broadcast announcing that independence had been agreed to and would take place in 12 months' time. 'I am very proud that I was chosen to lead you through these last stages towards independence. I have never made wild promises to you in the past and I do not intend to start doing so now. When Bechuanaland achieves independence it will not mean we will all be able to sit back and take things easy. It will mean everyone will have to work hard because it is not a naturally rich country which can march along the road to prosperity as a matter of course. Nevertheless, Bechuanaland has one great natural resource – her people, and I am sure they will not fail her. God bless Bechuanaland.'

The year 1966 had been tumultuous. They had been to America again, where Seretse had received an honorary doctorate from Fordham University. The white minority government in Rhodesia had unilaterally declared independence and Britain had declared sanctions against it. Racial tension in South Africa had reached new heights and Verwoerd had been slain by an assassin's knife.

Muriel had got married in Zambia. Seretse had sat beneath the blazing crystal chandeliers of the baronial conference room at London's historic Marlborough House to sign the Independence Charter. Cattle continued to perish, although the drought had lifted. The 4 500 square mile Chobe game reserve had been mapped out. The first local government elections had been held, with the BDP winning 135 seats and its opponents 29. Ruth and Seretse had toured Israel and come home to implement their successful *Ipelegeng* Food for Work programme, which dignified labour and discouraged begging. Seretse had won world approval by refusing to spend money on an army when so many developmental issues cried out for funding.

Preparations for independence had speeded up in the second half of the year. A design for a flag had been decided upon – predominantly blue to represent the nation's dependence upon water, with a wide black band flanked by narrow white strips signifying its nonracial nature, as well as a national coat of arms and a special independence stamp issue. Tens of thousands of copies of the new national anthem, democratically chosen by public voting with the help of the radio station, were distributed throughout the villages, where proud Bamangwato learnt the words by heart.

The conferring on Seretse of a knighthood a few days before independence, and the formal investiture by Sir Hugh Norman Walker in his white ceremonial uniform and plumed hat, had thrilled them both to bits. It was the crowning triumph to 18 years of devotion, commitment, anguish and sheer hard work. Ruth hid her delight behind the much-publicised, biting comment: 'Well, after the way they treated us, it was the least they could do.'

The weather seemed determined to bedevil the Independence celebrations as it had those of the first elections. A vicious dust storm had blown in from the desert, together with several tons of Kalahari sand. The 5 000-strong crowd gathered at the stadium huddled together under blankets, their eyes slitted against the swirling dust. The multiracial gathering included leathery white hunters and traders, modern-suited diplomats from the four corners of the earth, ragged herders in leopard-skin hats, UN field workers in khaki bush-shirts and baggy shorts, and wiry bow-legged policemen of the Kalahari Desert camel patrols.

Princess Marina, the Queen's cousin who had been sent from London to represent Her Majesty, gamely wrapped a scarf over her head and tied it under her chin. Ruth sent an aide scurrying off to fetch her extra fur coat and several warm karosses.

A diverse cultural programme featuring the Royal Scottish Fusiliers on bagpipes and a couple of traditional dance groups provided entertainment. Ten seconds before midnight the lights snapped out. The Union Jack was lowered to the stately opening bars of God Save The Queen. A spotlight drew all eyes to a pristine white flagpole and slowly the flag of the new nation was unfurled. Botswana was born, its new name reflecting the national reality of the diverse tribes who for centuries had inhabited this barren spot on the planet. Seretse stood to attention in the centre of the stadium as the band played the new national anthem. Then, smiling at Ruth, he walked regally back to the grandstand and took his place at her side. The crowd erupted with applause and ululating. As fireworks boomed and flashed amid the sand clouds and a victory beacon blazed into light on top of Khali Hill, the thrilled spectators yelled 'pula' and 'tau tooma' (big lion - Seretse) until they were hoarse.

The fact that quite a few African and Commonwealth nations had shunned the invitation to attend the independence celebration of this impoverished, insignificant little nation could do nothing to dampen the ecstatic jubilation of the crowd nor the quiet satisfaction enjoyed by Ruth and Seretse at the road travelled thus far.

In a statement issued after the ceremony Seretse encapsulated with humility and dignity the modest ambition of the world's newest nation: 'We will in no way attempt to interfere in the affairs of others. While we do, and will continue to, deplore any policies in any other states which appear to us to be inhuman – and we will strive by force of persuasion and example, and not by force itself, for an amelioration of conditions as we deem unacceptable elsewhere – we will strive to live on terms of good neighbourliness with all states. My government and I have one main object – the creation and preservation of a peaceful corner on the surface of the earth in which, in every possible field, the standard of living of the people will steadily rise and as Batswana we can take our place, proudly and properly, amongst the peoples of this world.'

On the morning of 30 September 1966 he was sworn in as President of Botswana at a simple ceremony in front of the new national assembly building, After addressing the gathering, he walked purposefully to Ruth's side, squeezed her hand and bent to kiss her, oblivious to the sidelong glances of the assembled dignitaries. He couldn't have made it without her, and he didn't care if all the world knew it.

Then, donning his black homburg, with a radiant Ruth on his arm and a shooting stick in his hand, Sir Seretse led the assembled guests across to the yellowing, still drought-stricken, lawn of State House, to celebrate with a garden party.

Meanwhile, Britain's last colonial proconsul and his deputy left the country unceremoniously by steam train from Palapye. The Khama dynasty had been restored to its rightful throne and it was time for the 'protectors' – whom King Khama had requested to save his country from the invasion of white settlers almost a century before – to depart.

Postscript

SERETSE KHAMA WENT ON TO RULE BOTSWANA, WITH RUTH BESIDE HIM, until his death at the age of 59 on 13 July 1980.

During this time Botswana became a model non-racial, multiparty democracy in Africa – and an effective and serious challenge to the credibility of South Africa's racist policies.

The period of his rule was among the most turbulent experienced in southern Africa. His little country was surrounded by war – in Angola, Rhodesia (now Zimbabwe) and South West Africa (now Namibia) – and the bitter struggle against apartheid in South Africa. Botswana was an oasis of racial tolerance and peace, as well as a transit route for people fleeing these war-torn nations – both refugees and would-be ANC, ZIPRA and SWAPO cadres on their way to training camps in the north. Botswana was attacked several times by South African and Rhodesian commandos searching for guerrillas.

Despite all this, Seretse resisted having a national army for many years, because of the poverty of his country. When an army was eventually formed, the couple's eldest son, Ian, became its deputy commander, and later commander.

So firmly rooted were the institutions that Seretse Khama built that they survived his death from diabetes-related complications and cancer in 1980. He was praised as a pragmatic politician, who skilfully nursed his impoverished country towards prosperity, always putting the welfare of the people before ideology and yet never compromising their independence in the face of South African threats.

As one of the front-line presidents, he made a major contribution to the progress towards self-determination throughout southern Africa, and lived to see Zimbabwe gain its independence in April 1980.

At Seretse's funeral, Julius Nyerere, then President of Tanzania, described his and Ruth's marriage as: 'One of the greatest love stories the world has known. More than any academic book or political pamphlet it touched the surface of the pain caused by colonialism and racial discrimination.'

He lived to see one of his greatest dreams become reality – a southern African economic community, which would counter South Africa's dominance in the region. The SADCC came into being a few months before his death, with its headquarters in Gaborone.

Seretse saw only one of his children wed before his death, his daughter Jacqueline. Ruth lived another 22 years, a revered sort of queen mother. She remained active in social welfare and caring service of her adopted nation, principally through the Red Cross. She died on 23 May 2002 in Gaberone at the age of 78.

One of her proudest moments must have been the inauguration of Ian as Vice-President – a position he still holds at the time of writing. She remained dedicated to her family and was survived by all four of her children, as well as several grandchildren. Jackie works for the University of Botswana, while the twins Tshekedi (known as TK) and Tony are well-established businessmen in Botswana. Ruth's sister Muriel moved there from Zambia many years ago and at the time of writing still lives in Gaborone.

Between 1966 and 1980 Botswana had the fastest growing economy in the world. State mineral revenues were invested in infrastructural development, education, health and cattle production. Seretse's wise policies increased prosperity throughout the country, while his personal integrity and style of leadership kept the country free from the corruption which embroiled most other independent African nations shortly after independence.

He was succeeded by his most able deputy and lifelong friend, Quett Masire, whose 20-year reign cemented many of the positive aspects of Seretse's inaugural presidency.

Both Seretse and Ruth are buried in the royal burial ground high on the hill above Serowe, together with King Khama the Great, Seretse's father Sekgoma and his uncle Tshekedi. His epitaph reads: 'The most courageous and deliberate of men.'

Sources

Personal interviews
Muriel Sanderson (Ruth's sister)
Ian, Tshekedi and Tony Khama (Ruth and Seretse's three sons)
Naledi Khama (Seretse Khama's sister)
Phil Steenkamp (close advisor and permanent secretary to Seretse Khama)
Archie Mogwe (permanent secretary and Foreign Minister)
Sir Quett Masire (Deputy President who took over from Seretse as President)
Gausitwe Chiepe (Education and later Foreign Minister)
Mrs Gasennelwe (Red Cross)
Prof. Thomas Tlou (Historian)
Richard Lyons (Ruth Khama's lawyer)
Tony Benn, MP (close family friend)
Bill Woodford (close family friend)
Emmanuel Ontumetse (Seretse Khama's childhood friend)

Newspapers and periodicals
BOTSWANA
Mmegi
Daily News

UK
The Times
Manchester Guardian
Daily Mail
Daily Express

Daily Mirror
Evening News
Sunday Express
News of the World

USA
Time Magazine

SOUTH AFRICA
The Argus
Die Beeld
Die Burger
The Natal Witness
Rand Daily Mail
The Star
Sunday Times
Die Transvaler

Other documents

British government and protectorate of Bechuanaland records, official documents, minutes, memos, telegrams, speeches of Seretse Khama, etc.
British Library
British Newspaper Library
Library of the Netherlands Institute of Southern Africa
National Archives of Botswana, Gaborone
National Archives of Zimbabwe, Harare
Personal collection of South African newspaper clippings, courtesy of Wilf Nussey, former editor Argus Africa News Service
School of Oriental and African Studies library, London University
Tilburg Library

Books

A Marriage of Inconvenience, Michael Dutfield, Unwin Hyman, London 1990

Bechuanaland: Pan-African outpost or Bantu Homeland? London Institute of Race Relations, Oxford University Press, London 1965

Desert doctor remembers, Alfred Merriweather, Pula Press, Gaborone 1999

Evelyn Baring: the Last Proconsul, Charles Douglas-Home, Collins, London 1978

From the Frontline: Speeches of Sir Seretse Khama, Gwendolyn M Carter & E Philip Morgan, Rex Collings, London 1980

Khama: The Great African Chief, J C Harris, London 1923

King Khama of Bechuanaland, author unknown, London 1910

Naught for your comfort, Trevor Huddleston, Collins, London 1956

Ruth & Seretse: A very Disreputable Transaction, John Redfern, Victor Gollancz, London 1955

Seretse Khama 1921-1980, Neil Parsons, Willie Henderson & Thomas Tlou, Macmillan Boleswa, South Africa 1995

Seretse Khama and the Bamangwato, Julian Mockford, Staples, London 1950

Serowe: Village of the Rainwind, Bessie Head, Heinemann, London 1981

Tshekedi Khama, Mary Benson, Faber & Faber, London 1960

When rain clouds gather, Bessie Head, Victor Gollancz, London 1969

White Queen in Africa, Eric Robins, Robert Hale, London 1967

Index

Wilf Mbanga was the founding Managing Director of Associated Newspapers of Zimbabwe, publishers of the now banned *Daily News*, before going into exile. He was guest of the Stichting Tilburg Vrijplaats (City of Refuge) in the Netherlands, before moving to London, where he started *The Zimbabwean*, an independent print and electronic newspaper which he edits. He is married to Trish Mbanga, an author and journalist. Trish was founding Chief Executive of the Zimbabwe International Book Fair and ran the fair from 1991 to 2000. Their experience as a black-white couple in southern Africa during the past three decades inspired them to write the story of Ruth and Seretse, who had courageously walked the same path a generation before.